W9-BWE-680

The Twilight
Struggle

The Twilight Struggle

The Soviet Union v. the United States Today

Constantine C. Menges

The AEI Press

Publisher for the American Enterprise Institute
WASHINGTON, D.C.

1990

Distributed by arrangement with

National Book Network
4720 Boston Way   3 Henrietta Street
Lanham, MD 20706   London WC2E 8LU England

Library of Congress Cataloging-in-Publication Data

Menges, Constantine Christopher.
   The twilight struggle: the United States V. the Soviet Union
today / Constantine C. Menges.
      p. cm.
   Includes bibliographical references.
   ISBN 0-8447-3701-1 (alk. paper)
   1. United States—Foreign relations—Soviet Union.   2. Soviet
Union—Foreign relations—United States.   3. Soviet Union—Foreign
relations—1975–1985.   4. Soviet Union—Foreign relations—1985–
I. Title.
E183.8.S65M46   1990
327.73047—dc20   90-274
                                                                    CIP

AEI Studies 497

The AEI Press
Publisher for the American Enterprise Institute
1150 17th Street, N.W., Washington, D.C. 20036

Printed in the United States of America

In memory and appreciation of three creative scholars and gifted teachers who enriched my studies at Columbia University: Professor Lawrence H. Chamberlain, Professor William T. R. Fox, and Professor Otto Kirchheimer.

Contents

LIST OF TABLES

LIST OF FIGURES

Now the trumpet summons us again—not as a call to bear arms, though arms we need; not as a call to battle, though embattled we are; but a call to bear the burden of a long twilight struggle, year in and year out.

PRESIDENT JOHN FITZGERALD KENNEDY
Inaugural Address
January 20, 1961

Foreword

Constantine Menges provides significant insights into one of the most misunderstood and controversial issues of contemporary international politics—the struggle fought on three continents between two coalitions: on the one hand, the Soviet Union, the Socialist world network, and the governments of Afghanistan, Cambodia, Angola, Mozambique, and Nicaragua; and on the other, the armed indigenous resistance forces seeking to liberate their countries with help from the United States and others.

These conflicts have already had importance for the countries themselves, the regions, and the geopolitical balance.

The U.S. role in these struggles can be best understood through what came to be called the Reagan Doctrine—the set of ideas and beliefs that guided and (participants in this policy believe) justified U.S. help to indigenous resistance forces.

The Reagan Doctrine emerged from the interaction of the idea of freedom and the circumstances that existed when Ronald Reagan assumed the presidency in January 1981. Communist governments had been imposed by force and with foreign support in Afghanistan, Cambodia, Angola, and Nicaragua in the wake of civil wars. In each, anti-Communist resistance forces developed to oppose the new governments. Ronald Reagan and his associates believed it would be good neither for the countries involved nor for the United States if Communist governments were consolidated.

President Reagan and his administration thought aid to indigenous resistance movements was appropriate and consistent with U.S. international obligations. Specifically, we believed it in accord with the United Nations Charter, which is not designed to protect repressive, expansionist dictatorships or empires. Article 2.4 enjoins all member states to "refrain in their international relations from the threat or use of force against the territorial integrity or political independence of any state." But this prohibition of force was never intended to stand on its own but to be read in the context of the entire charter and as complementary to Article 51 (which affirms the inherent right to individual or collective self-defense) and to all the provisions of the charter concerning guarantees of human rights. The peoples who organized resistance were manifestly engaged in self-defense against foreign force.

In fact, the presence and roles of thousands of Soviet and Soviet bloc troops in these countries had already internationalized the internal struggle for power. Furthermore, it seemed clear that if client rulers had the right to ask for external assistance to maintain their rule, citizens deprived of rights had the right to ask for external aid in reclaiming them.

We further believed that a government that takes power by force and retains power by force has no legitimate grounds for complaint against those who would wrest power from it by force. And a government whose power depends on external support has no legitimate grounds for complaining that externally supported force is used against it. The Reagan Doctrine affirms the legitimacy of U.S. support for an insurgency against a dictatorial government that depends on external support. It does not *require* U.S. intervention. A U.S. role must also be consistent with U.S. national interests. The costs must not be too burdensome. The risks must not be too great. The long-range costs of not providing support must be greater than the costs of doing so.

The Reagan administration believed it prudent, and appropriate, to offer limited support to these insurgencies seeking to reestablish the independence of their nations and to prevent their full incorporation in the Soviet empire. The more strategically important the country, the more important it was to do so.

Constantine Menges brings to this new book knowledge gleaned in years of work on the Soviet Union, U.S. foreign policy, and developing regions. He was a participant as well as an observer in these events and knows them well. His analysis illuminates the complex struggles and is illuminated by his sophisticated understanding of these problems.

In his conclusion, Menges suggests that while the balance within the five countries is tilting against the resistance movements (except in Nicaragua), they can still succeed with reasonable political and material support by the United States and other countries that honor freedom. He also believes—and I agree—that the hopeful and dramatic movement of Eastern Europe toward democracy was encouraged by the resistance movements. They stemmed the powerful tide of Soviet success in establishing new pro-Soviet regimes. (No new Communist regimes were established after 1981.) They demonstrated that Communist victory was not inevitable—anywhere—and that even Soviet troops could be held to a stalemate, as in Afghanistan.

I do not doubt that the increased cost of continuing the war against Afghanistan helped Mikhail Gorbachev decide to withdraw Soviet troops and that the cumulative cost of continuing these wars helped him decide to reexamine the desirability of a policy of global expansion and conquest.

Constantine Menges's analysis is a welcome addition to the serious literature on these serious events.

JEANE J. KIRKPATRICK
Former United States Representative
to the United Nations

Preface

From 1975 to 1979 Moscow helped eleven new pro-Soviet dictatorships take power in nations on three continents. In five of these countries—Afghanistan, Cambodia, Angola, Mozambique, and Nicaragua—armed resistance movements arose against the Communist regimes. Beginning with Afghanistan, the United States and other countries provided military and other help to these anti-Communist resistance movements. This book describes and analyzes these wars and the policies pursued by the United States and Soviet Union in these conflicts.

The Twilight Struggle first describes the historical evolution of the Soviet strategy of indirect aggression and the origins of the Reagan Doctrine. For each of these five countries, the book then discusses the actions of the Communist regimes and the resistance movements, the political responses of the United States, the Soviet Union, and the regional powers, and the impact of these events on the balance between the opposing forces.

The concluding analysis interprets and compares the five Communist regimes and the resistance movements and discusses the effectiveness of the Soviet Union and the United States in accomplishing their respective foreign policy objectives. Since these dramatic and poignant struggles still continue, this book also examines the possible future implications of success or defeat for the anti-Communist movements for the five countries, the regions, and the geopolitical balance between the United States and the Soviet Union.

Placing these five conflicts in the broader perspective of U.S.-Soviet relations, *The Twilight Struggle* concludes that the hopeful and dramatic movement of Eastern Europe toward democracy in 1989 may have been helped by the anti-Communist resistance in three ways: it contributed to stemming Soviet success in the 1970s in establishing new pro-Soviet regimes; it stalemated more than 300,000 foreign Communist forces, finally compelling most to withdraw and giving the Soviet leadership a reason to avoid repeating Afghanistan in Eastern Europe; and it demonstrated that Communist regimes could be prevented from fully consolidating their power and possibly even defeated through fair elections or military means.

This book has its intellectual origins in my long concentration as a scholar and federal official on the issues of transitions from dictatorship to democracy, Soviet foreign policy, and U.S.-Soviet relations. In mid-1987 I was fortunate that Ambassador Jeane Kirkpatrick, as the counselor for foreign policy at the American Enterprise Institute, and Christopher DeMuth, AEI's new president, agreed that this subject warranted a serious research effort. At the same time, the Lynde and Harry Bradley Foundation of Milwaukee, Wisconsin, led by its president, Michael Joyce, with the able support of his vice president, Hillel Fradkin, provided the funds that made this book possible. At AEI, David Gerson, executive vice president, also played a major role in ensuring support for this project. And Gabriele Hills, director of personnel at AEI, facilitated this work through her effective management. I am grateful to all these individuals for their interest in and support for this project.

For two years I had the benefit of skilled, conscientious research assistance by Timothy Goodman, currently a Ph.D. candidate at Georgetown University. He compiled and synthesized the often elusive and fragmentary statistical data on each of the five countries and resistance movements, kept a careful chronological record of the five complex and fast-moving international negotiations, and provided important bibliographic suggestions.

A number of interns who worked part time at AEI on a voluntary basis in conjunction with a semester or summer in Washington programs sponsored by their colleges and universities also contributed to this project. I want to mention particularly William Joys of Amherst College, Thomas Baker of Cornell, William Smith IV of James Madison College at Michigan State University, John Brown of Wheaton College, and Robert Egge of Rockford College.

I am also grateful to Phillip Nicolaides, a friend and former White House colleague who was willing to read and offer a critique of most of the draft and who provided me with enormously useful suggestions for improvement.

In June 1988, Sandra Mulligan came to work for me and other scholars at AEI. In addition to all the other responsibilities of a secretary in an active office, she had virtually sole responsibility for typing this book in its first and revised drafts. Throughout these many months, she has been a thoughtful, skilled, and effective colleague, and I am deeply grateful for her superb work always done with grace and good cheer. I also appreciate the willingness of Meg Molyneaux to help at various times of great urgency.

My wife, Nancy Goldsmith Menges, has shared my sense that this book needed to be written and my hope that the peoples in these five countries may yet move from the shadow of oppression and war into the sunlight of freedom, independence, and genuine peace. Her encouragement, ideas, and understanding have always been important to me and have contributed to the completion of this book.

Although these and other friends and colleagues have all been important in the writing of this book, the contents and analysis reflect my judgments and are my sole responsibility.

CONSTANTINE C. MENGES
Washington, D.C.

The Twilight Struggle

1
Introduction

During the years of détente in the 1970s, as Moscow proclaimed that it was aiding "wars of national liberation" and would continue to do so, eleven new pro-Soviet dictatorships took power around the world.[1] The vast human suffering caused by the repression and economic failures of these new regimes sparked armed anti-Communist resistance movements in five of these countries: Afghanistan, Angola, Cambodia, Mozambique, and Nicaragua.

Soviet regimes had encountered resistance before. In the 1920s in Central Asia the Soviet government used guile, deceptive political settlements, and military force to defeat Moslems who rebelled after realizing they had been tricked by Lenin's false promises of autonomy. In 1940, Finland's armed resistance stalemated the Red Army, preventing the attempted conquest initiated after the Soviets' 1939 treaty with Nazi Germany. After World War II armed anti-Communist resistance in Poland, in newly annexed Lithuania, and in the once independent Ukraine was contained and then suppressed.[2]

In the late 1970s, however, new pro-Soviet regimes and their patron, Moscow, began to face armed resistance capable of threatening the newly established Communist power. During the 1980s, the resistance movements in these five countries posed a new challenge to the Soviet Union and gave the United States and the rest of the free world an opportunity to help liberation movements win. By establishing independent, non-Communist governments, they could reverse the momentum of decades of Communist victories. By the start of President Reagan's second term in 1985, the armed resistance movements had grown far stronger, although the five pro-Soviet dictatorships made massive efforts to defeat them.

The United States had other reasons for optimism about international political trends. Its strategic and conventional deterrent forces were improved and modernized; no new pro-Soviet regimes had taken power since 1979; Grenada had been liberated; President Reagan had advocated the extension of free, democratic institutions through peaceful means (such as the National Endowment for Democracy); and twelve countries, with a combined population of nearly

1

500 million people, were in the process of peaceful transition from right-wing dictatorship to democratic government.[3] It was in this context that President Reagan made a major announcement.

In his 1985 State of the Union address to a joint session of Congress—traditionally used to highlight major presidential initiatives—President Reagan committed his administration to the extension of freedom and praised the anti-Communist armed resistance movements:

> We declare anew to our fellow citizens of the world: Freedom is not the sole prerogative of a chosen few; it is the universal right of all God's children. . . . Our mission is to nourish and defend freedom and democracy and to communicate these ideals everywhere we can. . . . We must not break faith with those who are risking their lives—on every continent, from Afghanistan to Nicaragua—to defy Soviet supported aggression and secure rights which have been ours from birth.[4]

The recent Communist dictatorships opposed by resistance movements had been established through invasions, violations of international agreements, or armed subversion; therefore they all held power illegitimately. President Reagan went on to defend the international legitimacy of helping the anti-Communist resistance movements win: "Support for freedom fighters is self defense and is totally consistent with the OAS and UN charters. . . . [We should] support the democratic forces whose struggle is tied to our own security."[5]

This dramatic public statement followed five years of reported U.S. military support for the armed resistance in Afghanistan (initiated during the Carter administration), four years of nonmilitary aid to the anti-Communist resistance movements in Cambodia, and nearly three years of public debate about reported U.S. military support to anti-Communist insurgents in Nicaragua. Only days later, in February 1985, Secretary of State George Shultz followed up Reagan's statement with an eloquent, wide-ranging foreign policy speech, "America and the Struggle for Freedom." Shultz explained U.S. assistance to the forces of freedom in the world, with special emphasis on the armed anti-Communist resistance movements, and outlined a strategy for the Reagan administration. Among his key points were the following:

> A revolution is sweeping the world today—a democratic revolution. . . . Time and again in the last 200 years, we have lent our support—moral and otherwise—to those around the world struggling for freedom and independence. . . . Where once the Soviets may have thought that all discontent

was ripe for turning into Communist insurgencies, today we see a new and different kind of struggle: people around the world risking their lives against Communist despotism. We see brave men and women fighting to challenge the Brezhnev doctrine.[6]

After describing and endorsing the struggles of the anti-Communist resistance movements in Afghanistan, Angola, Cambodia, and Nicaragua, Shultz went on to proclaim:

This new phenomenon we are witnessing around the world—popular insurgencies against Communist domination—is not an American creation. In every region, the people have made their own decision to stand and fight rather than see their cultures and freedoms "quietly erased." They have made clear their readiness to fight with or without outside support, using every available means and enduring severe hardships, alone if need be. But America also has a moral responsibility. The lesson of the postwar era is that America must be the leader of the free world; there is no one else to take our place.[7]

At the same time, Shultz was explicit that U.S. support for anti-Communist resistance movements derived not only from "our historical sympathy for democracy and freedom but also, in many cases, . . . the interests of national security."[8] He then described the threats to U.S. security that the anti-Communist resistance movements were helping to counter:

For many years we saw our adversaries act without restraint to back insurgencies around the world to spread Communist dictatorships. The Soviet Union and its proxies, like Cuba and Vietnam, have consistently supplied money, arms and training in efforts to destabilize or overthrow non-Communist governments. "Wars of national liberation" became the pretext for subverting any non-Communist country in the name of so-called "socialist internationalism." At the same time, any victory of communism was held to be irreversible. This was the infamous Brezhnev doctrine. . . . Promoting insurgencies against non-Communist governments in important strategic areas has become a low-cost way for the Soviets to extend the reach of their power and to weaken their adversaries, whether they be China or the democracies of the West and Japan. This is true in Southeast Asia, Southwest Asia, Africa, and Central America.[9]

Senior Reagan administration officials shared this perspective on the Soviet threat at the beginning of the second Reagan administration. In January 1985, William J. Casey, director of the Central

3

Intelligence Agency, had warned against the global threat to U.S. security from what he called "subversive aggression" or "creeping imperialism":

> Nikita Khrushchev . . . proclaimed that communism would win not by nuclear war which might destroy the world, nor by conventional war which might lead to nuclear war, but by wars of liberation. In . . . twenty years, the Soviet Union was transformed from a continental power to a global power, acquiring bases and surrogates in Cuba, Vietnam, Ethiopia, Angola, South Yemen, Mozambique, Nicaragua, and Afghanistan.[10]

This speech—given weeks before President Reagan's State of the Union address—previewed the public declaration of a new U.S. strategy. It indicted the Soviet Union for "the horror of the wars and brutal repression inflicted by Marxist-Leninist regimes . . . compounded by the failure and devastation wrought by the bankruptcy of the Marxist-Leninist regimes' economic and political policies."[11] Casey summarized the forces arrayed on both sides and the new historical opportunity that beckoned:

> There are over 100,000 Soviet troops in Afghanistan, 170,000 Vietnamese troops in Cambodia, and 40,000 Cuban troops in Africa. This is worldwide military aggression directly and by proxy. That and the horror of it is the bad news. The good news is that the tide has changed. Today in Afghanistan, Angola, Cambodia, Ethiopia, and Nicaragua, to mention only the most prominent arenas, hundreds of thousands of ordinary people are volunteers in irregular wars against the Soviet army or Soviet-supported regimes. Whereas in the 1960s and 1970s anti-Western causes attracted recruits throughout the Third World, the 1980s have emerged as the decade of freedom fighters resisting Communist regimes. In many places, freedom has become as exciting and revolutionary as it was here in America over 200 years ago.[12]

In the first weeks of 1985 Casey—and then Reagan, followed by Shultz—made it clear to the world that the second Reagan administration would adopt new means to pursue the goal enunciated in 1947 as the Truman Doctrine: "It must be the policy of the United States to support free peoples who are resisting attempted subjugation by armed minorities or by outside pressures." Four decades later that task remained to be accomplished—the newly established pro-Soviet dictatorships that had seized power during the 1970s were in fact "armed minorities." Armed resistance movements were determined to end the subjugation of Afghanistan, Cambodia, Angola, Mozambique, and Nicaragua. Charles Krauthammer, an influential writer on public issues, in April 1985 called the newly declared policy the "Reagan Doctrine," saying it has "turned geopolitics on its head."[13]

A new approach was needed because, as one scholar put it, "The legacy of the Vietnam War effectively rules out the direct use of U.S. forces to combat the accession to power of Soviet-supported Communist regimes."[14] Krauthammer pointed to the Reagan Doctrine as the third post-Vietnam attempt by the United States to find a way to "defend its ideals and interests":

> The first was the Nixon Doctrine: relying on friendly regimes to police their regions. Unfortunately, the jewel in the crown of this theory was the Shah of Iran. Like him, it was retired in 1979 to a small Panamanian island. Next came the Carter Doctrine, declaring a return to unilateral American action, if necessary in defense of Western interests. That doctrine rested on the emergence of a rapid deployment force. Unfortunately, the force turned out neither rapid nor deployable. It enjoys a vigorous theoretical existence in southern Florida, whence it is poorly situated to repel the Red Army.[15]

As with all major initiatives in national policy, diverse sources coalesce to produce large changes. The necessity for innovation derived clearly from historical facts: During the détente of the 1970s, Soviet indirect aggression continued and then increased after gaining eleven significant victories. In the 1980s it posed serious threats to fourteen additional countries.[16] Except in unusual circumstances like Grenada's, U.S. combat forces could not be committed for long periods to help friendly countries defend themselves. Speaking to the United Nations in October 1985, President Reagan pointed out that the new Communist regimes are "almost from the day they take power at war with their people." "Marxism-Leninism's war with the people," he said, "becomes war with their neighbors. These wars are exacting a staggering human toll and threaten to spill across national boundaries and trigger dangerous confrontations."[17] Therefore, a way had to be found to counter the indirect aggression of the new Communist regimes, which were themselves the products of earlier Soviet indirect aggression.

In 1968 I observed the enormous political obstacles faced by President Lyndon Johnson's administration in giving South Vietnam sustained military support against a Communist movement aided by the Soviet Union, China, and North Vietnam. Alternative strategies were needed, I suggested, not only because of Vietnam but also because of "repeated experiences of the post World War II period,"

5

as in Guatemala, the Philippines, Iran, and Afghanistan.[18] Even when past Communist takeover attempts failed, the original conditions remained "to fuel a new outburst after a decade or so passes."[19] This analysis went on to formulate "democratic insurgency against a new Communist regime" as an alternative that rested on "a simple and again unproven premise: Communist regimes are very vulnerable to a democratic national revolution that is conducted with skill and the determination to succeed."[20]

The timing and tactics of such an anti-Communist insurgency were described by me in 1968 as follows:

> After the Communist government had been in power long enough to win that massive unpopularity and bewildered disdain which usually follows after more than six months to a year's experience with the garish consequences of Communist economic policy and the unremitting political control, repression, and direction, [a] resistance organization might make its move. The tactics used would [include] selective recruitment of cadre elements; efficient use of limited external material assistance; incessantly "political" warfare meaning establishment of model governments in areas free of Communist government control; attacks on Communist military units known to be demoralized and the like.[21]

Twelve years later, after serving as a foreign policy adviser to Ronald Reagan in the 1980 presidential campaign, I wrote a proposed "strategy to counter Soviet-supported subversive aggression and terrorism." Among its major action components were "sustained efforts to help moderates replace *newly established* Communist or pro-Soviet regimes in important regions," including Nicaragua, Cambodia, Afghanistan, Grenada, and Angola.[22] In December 1980 this strategic proposal was given to four cabinet-level foreign policy appointees of the president-elect—Richard Allen at the National Security Council, Alexander Haig at the State Department, Caspar Weinberger at the Department of Defense, and William Casey at the Central Intelligence Agency—during the planning for the first Reagan term.[23]

Subsequently, I accepted Casey's offer to serve as the National Intelligence Officer for Latin America with responsibility for CIA analytical work on that region, including Central America, and for representing the CIA in the policy planning process. At the CIA I suggested to Casey that the Reagan administration should adopt a global strategy of helping the anti-Communist armed resistance movements defeat the illegitimate and aggressive pro-Soviet dictatorships established during the previous decade.

INTRODUCTION

Casey was receptive to this idea, for two reasons: he was deeply concerned by the continuing threat from Soviet-aided indirect aggression; and he himself had been responsible for help to antitotalitarian resistance forces during World War II. Casey knew from personal experience how effective they could be, even against regimes as brutal as that of Nazi Germany. Casey felt deeply that the free world once again had a moral obligation to help those resisting Communist regimes that committed acts such as those he quoted from a Helsinki Watch report: "Civilians burned alive, dynamited, beheaded; crushed by Soviet tanks; grenades thrown into rooms where women and children have been told to wait."[24] He also knew the United States had a national interest in helping to defeat the continuing indirect aggression of a powerful totalitarian opponent.

From 1981 to 1984 Casey observed how effective the anti-Communist resistance movements were becoming at stalemating the Soviet Union and its allies on four continents. In one of his last public speeches, in late 1986, Casey drew lessons from earlier profreedom resistance movements for the contemporary anti-Communist insurgencies. What do they need to win? His answer:

The truth, as revealed in our World War II experiences and numerous struggles in the Third World since then, is that far fewer people and weapons are needed to put a government on the defensive than are needed to protect it. A resistance movement does not seek a classic, definitive military victory. External support is almost always a key factor in resistance success. A progressive withdrawal of domestic support for a government accompanied by nagging military pressure . . . is what helps bring down or alter a repressive government. The small and weak countries that are combatting Soviet inspired subversion, and the resistance movements that are combatting Marxist-Leninist repression do not need and cannot handle a lot of sophisticated military hardware. What they need is what always has been needed in these kinds of situations: small arms and training in their use in small unit actions, good intelligence, and good communications. We helped provide this with effect to the resistance against Nazi Germany and if we can muster our resolve and act before resistance assets are allowed to wither away, we can put these tactics to good use today.[25]

And Casey used history to answer the view that the anti-Communist resistance movements could not win:

We hear it said that these contras, *mujahideen,* and tribesmen led by Dr. Jonas Savimbi can't win. Who would have thought that George Washington's rag tag army, down to 3,000 men

7

at some points, could have, with covert assistance from France, thrown out of North America the British with the largest and most powerful army in the world? Who would have thought that the Vietcong, with Soviet covert aid, could have forced out of Indo-China an American army of half a million?[26]

In 1983 I joined the NSC staff at the White House. There, after the reelection of President Reagan in November 1984, I met privately with four members of the foreign policy cabinet, including Casey, who had continued to discuss geopolitical trends with me regularly. Again I urged a more systematic global strategy to counter Soviet indirect aggression, including a plan for helping all the anti-Communist resistance movements achieve the liberation of their countries before the end of Reagan's second term.[27] Casey seemed receptive, as did two others of the four cabinet-level officials.

At the same time, three of President Reagan's senior speechwriters had become interested in the anti-Communist resistance. They understood the moral and strategic imperative for the free world, and after working closely with President Reagan for many years they believed he would support a strategy for helping the freedom fighters—as he often called them—win, during his presidency if possible. On the NSC staff, I had worked closely with all three of these presidential speechwriters. One of them was in close touch with Casey, and another had a friend who as a private citizen had spent time in the field with the resistance movements and was convinced they could win if given help.[28]

As a result of these shared perspectives, William Casey in his January 1985 speech announced the "good news" that "the tide has changed" and that the anti-Communist resistance movements could win. Four weeks later President Reagan made his commitment to help the anti-Communist resistance forces to—as he put it in a later speech—"not just fight and die for freedom but fight and win freedom."[29] Although the author of the Reagan Doctrine was clearly President Reagan, William J. Casey brought the needed geopolitical and historical insight together. He proposed to President Reagan that helping the resistance movements win become a major focus of the second Reagan term.

In the fall of 1985, after the Congress—no doubt in part because of the declaration of the Reagan Doctrine—removed its prohibition on aid to the Angolan resistance, Casey brought President Reagan the proposal to initiate U.S. military aid to UNITA.[30] Although Secretary Shultz and the State Department had publicly opposed such military aid,[31] in November 1985 President Reagan informed the public that he had approved it.

In October 1985 the State Department prepared a draft for President Reagan's annual speech to the United Nations. Its major initiative was a three-step process for resolving "regional conflicts," as State was now calling these struggles for freedom. The State Department's proposed plan in effect assumed that the Communist regimes in Afghanistan, Cambodia, Angola, and Nicaragua would stay in power, although foreign Communist troops would be withdrawn. It was a significant departure from Secretary of State Shultz's ringing endorsement of the Reagan Doctrine only seven months earlier, as was Shultz's opposition to providing military aid to the anti-Communist UNITA movement in Angola.

Casey called to Reagan's attention ambiguous phrasing in the State Department draft that partially masked the contradiction between the State Department's "three-phase regional peace process" and the authentic goals of the Reagan Doctrine, and the president changed State's formula. The State Department had proposed that after all foreign troops withdrew from these Communist-dominated countries, each be welcomed "back into the world economy," with no reference to the reestablishment of independent non-Communist regimes. Reagan, however, said that "the United States would respond generously to their *democratic reconciliation* with their own people, their respect for human rights, and *their return to the family of free nations*. Of course, until such time as these negotiations result in definitive progress, America's support for struggling democratic resistance forces must not and shall not cease."[32] The objectives of "democratic reconciliation with their own people" and "their return to the family of free nations" were consistent with the Reagan Doctrine. They spelled the difference between merely seeking an end to a foreign Communist military presence in these countries and seeking an end to the Communist regimes themselves.

By the end of 1985 some commentary for and against the Reagan Doctrine was voiced, and a serious book, *Combat on Communist Territory*, concluded that the anti-Communist resistance movements could succeed with sustained support from free world countries.[33] But many Democratic members of Congress opposed military aid to the Nicaraguan resistance and in 1986 threatened to cut off U.S. military aid to UNITA in Angola. Meanwhile, other events indicated that Secretary Shultz was drawing back from making the Reagan Doctrine a major element of U.S. foreign policy.

Casey had always been realistic about what the Soviet Union and its allies would do to defeat the resistance movements. In his January 1985 speech he stated:

> Despite [the] reversal of momentum, the communists continue to come on strong to consolidate the positions they

have established. They are spending close to $8 billion a year to snuff out freedom in these countries. It is not necessary to match this in money, manpower or military weapons. Oppressed people want freedom and are fighting for it. They need only modest support and strength of purpose from nations that want to see freedom prevail and which will find their own security impaired if it doesn't. The communists have this strength of purpose but not the means to consolidate the far off positions they have established if the local resistance can count on durable support.[34]

Although the Communists could defeat the resistance forces, Casey said, they would not succeed *if* the free world and the United States met three conditions: "strength of purpose," "modest [but adequate levels of] support," and "durable support."

In the spring of 1986, Casey spoke again of the anti-Communist resistance movements as a "new phenomenon," a "reversal of roles," and "a historical turning point in the last half of this century."[35] Thinking perhaps of Shultz and others at the State Department, which dominated Reagan's foreign policy ever more as the United States moved toward a new phase of détente with Moscow, Casey added that the significance of this turning point that had resulted from the Reagan Doctrine "has not yet been fully appreciated and assessed by informed public opinion or, perhaps, even by historians."[36]

There was, however, one very significant political leader, besides Reagan, who, Casey believed, understood the importance of the anti-Communist resistance movements: the new Soviet leader, Mikhail Gorbachev. In April 1986 Casey said about Gorbachev:

A hallmark of his regime is an intensified effort to nail down and cement these bridgeheads [the new pro-Soviet regimes of the 1970s] and make them permanent. Having piled close to two billion dollars' worth of arms into Angola, Soviet advisors and Cuban troops are feverishly preparing a campaign, likely to be launched this month, designed to wipe out the forces resisting the Marxist government of Angola. Starting two months ago with half-a-billion dollars' worth of sophisticated weapons recently acquired, the Sandinista army, with Cuban helicopter pilots and combat direction, has been going all out to destroy the Contras down there before the Congress acts to renew assistance to them. Last week, some 1,500 Sandinista troops crossed the Honduran border for this purpose.[37]

Subsequent events have indeed shown that Casey was correct: Soviet leaders and their allies have used all means—military aid, covert operations (including assassinations), propaganda, political action, and diplomacy—to maintain the new Communist regimes in power and to isolate, neutralize, and ultimately defeat the anti-Communist resistance forces.

While international attention was focused on the four Reagan-Gorbachev summit meetings and on the continuing arms control and bilateral U.S.-Soviet negotiations, five major struggles were continuing in the shadows, in Afghanistan, Angola, Cambodia, Mozambique, and Nicaragua. These wars have commanded little interest except at the conclusion of diplomatic agreements promising peace. But these political-military conflicts have pitted the foreign policy objectives of the Soviet Union against the declared objectives of President Reagan. Would the Brezhnev Doctrine or the Reagan Doctrine ultimately win?

The military battles of this Soviet-U.S. conflict have been fought inside each of these five countries, but the political and diplomatic contests have matched the skills of Moscow directly against those of Washington. History has shown again and again that the Communists view diplomacy as the continuation of efforts to win, not to settle, a conflict, and that is how Gorbachev's Soviet Union has approached its duels with the United States.

In the nineteenth century the astute French observer of a young United States, Alexis de Tocqueville, wrote that in "foreign affairs democratic governments do appear decidedly inferior to others."[38] He said this was the case because "a democracy finds it difficult to coordinate the details of a great undertaking and to fix on some plan and carry it through with determination in spite of obstacles."[39]

A former president of the United States responded to this by observing hopefully that "America's inherent economic and political strength is so great that it overcomes our weakness in executing foreign policy."[40] But have these struggles in Afghanistan, Angola, Cambodia, Mozambique, and Nicaragua received the benefits of America's "economic and political strength"? Has the United States demonstrated the competence required to match the cunning and determination of Moscow and its allies? Will the leaders of the free world demonstrate the "strength of purpose" and provide the "durable support" that Casey saw were necessary to help these five countries regain their freedom?

Since the 1980s five poignant and fateful wars for freedom have been fought on three continents. Their outcomes will directly affect tens of millions of lives, shape the future of hundreds of millions living in adjacent countries, and affect the national interests of the United States. The outcomes will depend in part on the people in

11

each country, but perhaps in larger part on the comparative ability of the Soviet Union and the United States to attain their international objectives.

This study will first describe the historical evolution of the Soviet strategy of indirect aggression, which the Reagan Doctrine was intended to help defeat. Then, for each country, it will discuss the actions of the Communist regimes, the resistance movements, and the international political maneuvering and its impact on the balance between the opposing forces. It will conclude with an assessment of the likely implications for each country, the five regions, and the geopolitical balance between the United States and the Soviet Union of two outcomes: independent, free governments in Afghanistan, Angola, Cambodia, Mozambique, and Nicaragua, or a continuation of pro-Soviet dictatorships there.

2
The Soviet Strategy
of Indirect Aggression

A major change in modern international politics took place in 1917 when the Bolsheviks seized power in the Soviet Union. The Communist regime claimed the authority to transform Russian society completely and to control and dominate all institutions. The regime proclaimed itself the beginning of an inevitable worldwide transformation propelled by the "scientific laws of history."

The consequences of this first totalitarian regime included tens of millions of inhabitants of the Russian empire executed, starved, and imprisoned by successive Soviet regimes.[1] The central government gained absolute control by eliminating or dominating all other institutions and by setting up a vast network of secret police and informers to control dissent.

From the beginning, the Soviet government viewed foreign policy as an instrument to defend its internal control and extend Soviet power into other countries. Pursuing a dualistic foreign policy, it maintains normal diplomatic relations with virtually all governments. Its diplomats and embassies appear to function like those of other countries, and its commercial organizations buy and sell products and pay their bills. All Soviet leaders, including Stalin, have been active in international diplomacy, including summit meetings with Western leaders. Many of those who deal with the Soviet Union through traditional diplomatic means, as well as many media figures and some experts who follow international events, believe that these activities represent the most important dimension of Soviet foreign policy.

Yet an understanding of contemporary history and the profound changes in the modern era requires close attention to the second level of Soviet international action: its efforts to help pro-Soviet groups take power in foreign countries by pursuing a strategy of indirect aggression. Lenin, Stalin, Khrushchev, and others clearly expressed this aim. The Soviet Union would help to "liberate" foreign peoples from their non-Communist—hence "reactionary"—governments, thus increasing the number of pro-Soviet regimes and reducing the number of actual and potential enemies.

Soviet methods of indirect aggression have evolved over the decades, becoming more complex and sophisticated. As early as 1915 Lenin spoke of "national liberation movements," since he believed that the colonial world was "capitalism's weakest link."[2] He established the Comintern (Communist International) under the direction of the Soviet Communist party to provide inspiration, resources, agent networks, solidarity, and strategic guidance for foreign Communist parties seeking to emulate the Bolshevik seizure of power. The full resources of the Soviet state, including its intelligence and military apparatus, were available to the Comintern but never officially acknowledged, nor was assistance usually provided through governmental channels in ways that might implicate the Soviet state.

At the core of Marx's historical determinism was the belief that inherent conflicts among social classes in industrializing societies would make the owners of capital richer and the dispossessed proletariat poorer until the workers finally took power through revolution. According to this theory of history, Czarist Russia, far less industrialized than Western Europe, should have been among the last countries to experience Communist revolution. But, in the words of Jeane Kirkpatrick, Lenin, as a practical revolutionary, "emancipated Communists from the encumbrance of Marx's error . . . [and] decided that Russia could 'bypass' the capitalist stage of development. . . . Determinism was tacitly abandoned in favor of human intelligence, will, and power."[3]

Lenin redefined the concept of class struggle to mean the conflict between Communists and all others, as well as between the Soviet Union and all non-Communist states. Further, Lenin encouraged the formation of Communist parties in the preindustrial and colonial areas of the world.

Jeane Kirkpatrick describes the consequences of Lenin's transition from historical determinism to willed activism: "Once the transition from historical determinism to political voluntarism was made *on the operational level*, the capture of state power everywhere became the actual goal of the Communist movement."[4]

This insight leads to a realistic understanding of the techniques that Lenin and his successors used. In Kirkpatrick's words:

> Communist leaders are *both* pragmatic and dogmatic. Adaptation to historical experience has been named "tactics," and a substantial literature on tactics has been developed to guide the actual operations of Communist parties. This literature . . . is eminently realistic, pragmatic, and cynical.

Its analyses and prescriptions are ideologically neutral: the tactics they recommend could be utilized with equal success by any minority engaged in the uninhibited pursuit of state power. . . . All the while, classical Marxism is invoked to surround the quest for power with an aura of morality and science.[5]

Lenin's redefinition of historical determinism and his pragmatism meant that "Communists were free to look for support in any quarter, and to declare enemies all those who opposed their accession to power. . . . Their efforts are concentrated on whichever group is most alienated from existing authority, or least integrated into the existing structure of authority." Kirkpatrick also observed the enduring paradox that "the officially voluntaristic Western nations attach greater importance to economic and social factors than do the officially deterministic Communists."[6]

Through more than seven decades of Soviet indirect aggression, three continuing types of Western self-deception have inhibited a clear understanding of these activities. First, there has been "the tendency to project habits and values [which] has repeatedly led the non-Communist world to mistake a Communist party's temporary tactical position for its identifying characteristics, and temporary lulls in the Cold War for peace. . . . When the Communists negotiate agreements to gain time or a respite we feel that we have achieved peace." Therefore, we must ask whether the widely acclaimed political settlements negotiated with the Communists in Afghanistan, Angola, and Nicaragua are a genuine breakthrough or just another example of the Communists taking advantage of the wishful thinking of Western leaders weary of what President Kennedy once called "the long twilight struggle"?

A second source of Western self-deception derives from "semantic subversion," which is

fostered by the Communists themselves through their systematically perverse use of language. By calling "autonomous" that which is powerless, "federated" that which is unitary, "democratic" that which is autocratic . . . "popular" that which is imposed by terror, "peaceful" that which incites war . . . the Communists have made inroads into our sense of political reality.[7]

A third source of self-deception is related to this misuse of positive symbols and words, and to the moral authority which was claimed by Communists to derive from the ultimately beneficial consequences of their success. Among some in the West there has been a deep misperception, an almost subliminal feeling, that the

15

intentions of Communists are good even if their methods are often objectionable:

> The notion that Communists are somehow engaged in the struggle between rich and poor, haves and have nots, workers and employers, oppressed and oppressors leads to the persistent notion that Communism is *somehow* more democratic and progressive than its undemocratic rivals. And this notion in turn leads to a lingering, half-conscious inhibition among many democrats to judge the Communist party by the same criteria it judges competing undemocratic elites. The notion persists that Communists are somehow morally superior to other elites which use amoral means to gain power and impose repressive, minority dictatorships.[8]

After the 1917 Communist coup against the Social Democratic Kerensky government, an intense civil war was fought by those resisting the minority Bolshevik takeover. During the years of "War Communism," Lenin tried to diminish the size of the potential opposition coalition by granting to numerous "Soviet socialist republics" inhabited by non-Russian ethnic groups the rights of independence and even secession. Once the Bolsheviks won the civil war, they forcibly reincorporated the nations that had declared their independence. This nearly decade-long period of maneuvers and strategems—including deception, propaganda, political fronts, defective political settlements, broken treaties, terrorism, and the threat and use of military force—was a useful proving ground for techniques and tactics the Soviets would later use in their indirect aggression on a global scale. For Soviet leaders it provided valuable lessons. For the non-Communist world it should have provided fair warning.

Among the peoples reincorporated into the Soviet empire were Ukrainians, Byelorussians, Armenians, Georgians, and the Moslem peoples of Central Asia. At the same time, the Soviets made their first international conquest—using indirect aggression—with the establishment of effective control over Outer Mongolia in 1921. As a sign of Soviet prudence, Outer Mongolia was allowed to keep its nominal independence. A second Soviet conquest of the 1920s, Tannu Tuva, was officially annexed in 1944.[9]

Eight attempts at Communist revolution failed during the first decade of Bolshevik rule, in China, Iran, Bulgaria, Estonia, Germany (in 1919 and 1923), and elsewhere. Although several were largely spontaneous actions by local Communists, the Comintern was deeply and systematically involved in China and Germany. This indirect aggression abroad coincided with Lenin's New Economic Policy, which included steps toward a return to a market economy, the right of peasants to own land, the opening of emigration, and offers of amnesty to exiles abroad, along with *glasnost*-like openings, including the activation of numerous "opposition" newspapers—all of which were pointed to as the sign of a trend toward full democracy.[10]

The Comintern was, in Richard Shultz's phrase, "the general staff of the world revolution."[11] But after Lenin became incapacitated in 1924 and Stalin moved toward absolute power, the Kremlin professed to be concerned more with "building socialism in one country" than with fomenting revolution on a global scale. During the 1930s Stalin emphasized state-to-state relations and became increasingly fearful of the growing power of fascism, specifically in Hitler's Germany. Nevertheless, from 1936 to 1939 the Soviet Union conducted a multifaceted campaign—political, military, and covert—to bring Communists to power in Spain. This intervention involved not only Comintern-supported agents in Spain but also Soviet secret police, military personnel, and weapons. Spain also marked a new stage of sophistication in the Soviet propaganda directed at the leading democratic countries. It was so effective that thousands of volunteers from the democracies—non-Communists as well as Communists—fought for the Spanish Republic, even though the small Communist minority, using Soviet methods of penetration and organization, took control of the coalition supporting the Spanish Republic.

The Hitler-Stalin pact of 1939 assured the Kremlin that Nazi Germany would direct its aggression against the West. A secret protocol of the treaty gave Stalin a free hand to annex the independent Baltic republics of Estonia, Latvia, and Lithuania. For invading Poland from the east on September 15, 1939, sixteen days after Nazi forces invaded it from the west, he was given a sizable part of Poland. Although Western historians have known these facts for decades, the Soviet Union denied them until May 25, 1989, when "The Genesis and Beginning of World War II" was published in *Pravda*, the official publication of the Soviet Communist party. The result of a joint Polish-Soviet historical commission, this report acknowledged that the secret protocol of the Hitler-Stalin pact was the basis for the Soviet seizure of eastern Poland, which the *Pravda* article called "a serious violation of international reforms." The report makes no reference, however, to the part of the secret protocol that gave the Soviet Union a free hand in forcibly annexing the three Baltic republics.[12]

In October 1939 the Red Army invaded Finland. After a three-month war in which the hopelessly outnumbered Finns inflicted tremendous casualties on the invader, Moscow allowed Finland to keep its independence but forced it to cede an area roughly the size of Switzerland.

In 1941, after Germany invaded the Soviet Union and Japan had attacked the United States, the Grand Alliance was established by the United States, the United Kingdom, and the USSR. In 1943, as a gesture of good will toward the West, Stalin abolished the Comintern. Three summit meetings (Tehran in 1943 and Yalta and Potsdam in 1945) reached agreements on a postwar system intended to prevent war through great power cooperation in the newly established United Nations.

The Soviet leadership clearly renewed its campaign of indirect aggression against the West as soon as it was sure of the defeat of the Nazis, in 1944. Moscow helped nine pro-Soviet regimes come to power in the 1940s. At the same time, Soviet efforts were set back in nine other countries, including Italy, Greece, Iran, and Indonesia (see table 2–1), as well as in Turkey, which resisted Soviet coercive demands with U.S. help.

The Communist movements that took over Eastern Europe and China during the late 1940s made great use of propaganda and deception. At the Yalta summit, the Soviet Union had subscribed to the Allies' promise that "the peoples liberated from the domination of Nazi Germany would solve by democratic means their pressing political and economic problems." Moscow never repudiated this signed agreement. Instead, it set in motion an elaborate, deceptive, and gradual process in which Communist parties changed their names and formed "coalition governments" with non-Communist parties. In these Eastern European countries, Communists used democratic rhetoric, controlled elections, and parliamentary institutions to mask their drive for power.

In the post–World War II era the Soviets refined their methods of indirect aggression and multiplied their successes. They added new instruments and techniques, without putting aside any of the old ones, in the following sequence:

1917–1930s
1. The Soviet state and the Communist party of the Soviet Union (CPSU)
2. The Comintern and foreign Communist parties
3. Soviet-controlled front groups
4. Soviet intelligence services, civilian and military

1940s
5. Foreign Communist regimes (Eastern Europe and China— until the rift)
6. Penetration of the United Nations Secretariat and other mul-

tilateral organizations, for example, the UN Refugee and Rehabilitation Administration

1950s

7. Coalition with and incitement of anti-Western blocs within the United Nations and other multilateral organizations, for example, the Non-aligned Movement and regional organizations such as the Bandung Conference and the Organization of African Unity (OAU)

1960s

8. Stateless anti-Western terrorist organizations, for example, Palestine Liberation Organization (PLO), Popular Front for the Liberation of Palestine (PFLP), Black September, Red Brigades

1970s

9. Soviet diplomatic, propaganda, and logistical support for regular combat units of a Soviet ally (for example, North Vietnam, followed by Cuba in the 1970s) sent into combat to ensure the victory of pro-Soviet movements

10. Anti-Western, pro-Soviet regimes, for example, Libya, Syria

11. Systematic penetration and political action within UN institutions to bring about ostensibly neutral legitimation, political support, and funding for pro-Soviet movements such as the PLO, South West Africa People's Organization (SWAPO), African National Congress (ANC), Popular Movement for the Liberation of Angola (MPLA), and Front for the Liberation of Mozambique (Frelimo)

12. Soviet and allied personnel, techniques, and material aid to ensure the irreversibility of new Communist and pro-Soviet regimes

Since 1944 the Soviet Union has carried out its normal diplomatic relations in a wide variety of political tones, ranging from aggressive to peaceful, to neutral, and sometimes even cooperative. Through it all, the Soviets have steadily expanded their means of indirect aggression, as well as their ability to manage many of them simultaneously to bring pro-Soviet groups to power and keep them in power.

Ironically, this process has been so stealthy and so pervasive that few analysts or political leaders have fully understood the qualitative changes in Soviet revolutionary warfare. Moreover, reliable new allies—such as Cuba, North Korea, and Angola—have permitted Moscow to seem even more removed from regions of conflict. The more than 70,000 Cuban military, secret police, and other personnel that have helped keep the Communist regimes of Angola, Ethiopia, Mozambique, and Nicaragua in place have allowed Moscow a more hidden role. Cuba had its own "Cuba" in Central America—the

TABLE 2–1
Soviet Aggression through Subversion, 1920–1989

Successful Attempts	Unsuccessful Attempts
1920s Outer Mongolia (1921) Tannu Tuva (1921; annexed 1944)	Iran (1920) China (1924–1927, and continuing) Germany (1919, 1923) Hungary (1919) Austria (1919) Slovakia (1919) Bulgaria (1923) Estonia (1924)
1930s	Spain (1936–1939)
1940s Baltic states (1940) Yugoslavia Albania Hungary Poland Romania E. Germany N. Korea Czechoslovakia (1948) China (1949)	Iran (1944–1946) Greece (1944–1950) Finland (1948) Burma (1947–1950s) Malaysia (1948–1960) Indonesia (1948) Italy (1945–1948) France (1945–1947) Philippines (1946–1953)
1950s N. Vietnam (1954) Cuba (1959)	S. Korea (1950–1953) (open attack) Iran (1953) Guatemala (1954)
1960s	Congo (1960–1962) Venezuela (1962–1967) Colombia Guatemala Peru Brazil Indonesia (1965) Algeria Mali Ghana Bolivia (1967)
1970s Cambodia, Laos, S. Vietnam (1975) Mozambique (1975)	Colombia Guatemala Chile (1970–1973)

TABLE 2-1   (continued)

Successful Attempts	Unsuccessful Attempts
Guinea-Bissau (1975)	Egypt (1972)
Angola (1976)	Philippines (1972–)
Ethiopia (1977)	Portugal (1974–1976)
S. Yemen (1978)	Italy
Afghanistan (1978)	Saudi Arabia (1979)
Grenada (1979)	Iran
Nicaragua (1979)	Turkey (1978–1980)
	Uruguay
	Argentina
	Brazil
	Namibia (1975–)
1980s	El Salvador (1979–)
	Guatemala
	Honduras (1981–)
	Peru (1980)
	Colombia
	Bahrain (1981)
	Kuwait (1983)
	Tunisia (1981)
	Sudan (1986–)
	Philippines

SOURCE: Author.

Sandinista regime in Nicaragua—which in 1979 became a new spring-board for indirect aggression, permitting both Moscow and Havana to mask their involvement.

A brief review of Soviet indirect aggression in the postwar era provides perspective on contemporary events, including the ways in which Moscow helps Communist regimes under attack from resistance movements stay in power. The Comintern was reestablished officially in 1947 (operationally it may never have actually been disbanded). As new pro-Soviet regimes took power, Moscow not only worked with foreign Communist parties but assigned new Communist governments visible and politically risky tasks. Czechoslovakia, for example, took the role of weapons provider to many groups the Soviets wanted to arm, such as the radical Guatemalan regime of Jacobo Arbenz in 1954. Shultz defines revolutionary warfare as

the use of an illegal political organization and, until its final stages, irregular military forces. It is a protracted political-military activity. The instruments of revolutionary warfare include propaganda, psychological operations, political mobilization, establishment of a shadow government or infrastructure organization, guerrilla tactics, terrorism, and mobile conventional combat.

He also makes clear that "in the regional and international arenas, this shadow government seeks to become recognized as the legitimate alternative to the existing regime."[13]

The skill and cunning of the Soviet Union in the late 1940s brought nine countries into its orbit, an all the more remarkable accomplishment in years when the United States had a nuclear monopoly, a prosperous and undamaged homeland, and security from any possible military retaliation by Moscow. By contrast, Stalin presided over a war-ravaged country. His policies had led to the deaths of more than 18 million people in the 1930s, and World War II had taken an estimated 10 million lives. Almost all major Soviet cities and industrial facilities in the more developed eastern regions had been destroyed. Those who believe that Soviet economic difficulties now require Moscow to pursue a conciliatory foreign policy need only look at Stalin's determined indirect aggression in the 1940s. The calculus of a power-maximizing elite differs totally from that of elected democratic leadership.

Stalin was probably surprised at the extent and ease of his success. Would anyone in 1945 have imagined that the Western democracies, and the United States in particular, would stand by as China, their wartime ally against imperial Japan, was defeated by a Soviet-aided Communist movement that had avoided combat with Japan? The Chinese Communist victory owed much to Soviet-directed propaganda, which confused the U.S. leaders and public about the struggle. Using techniques developed during the Spanish Civil War, a variety of organizations and media commentators focused on the real, exaggerated, and imagined shortcomings of the Chinese Nationalist government and ignored the true political identity and purposes of the Chinese Communists. This propaganda led to termination of U.S. military aid to the Chinese Nationalists as well as to pressure from Washington for an unworkable coalition government with the Communists. All this demoralized the anti-Communist side, which had been in continuous combat against the Japanese invaders since 1931.

The Chinese Communist victory may have led Stalin to use direct rather than indirect aggression to bring all of Korea under Communist control. He may also have been emboldened by Secretary of State Dean Acheson's statement that South Korea was outside the U.S. defense perimeter. Korea—which had been subjugated by Japan at the turn of the century and annexed in 1910—came under the authority of the United Nations after its liberation from Japan in 1945. The Soviet Union immediately moved to establish a puppet Communist government in the north and resisted any moves toward free elections and reunification. When North Korea attacked South Korea on June 25, 1950, the Soviet Union was absent from the UN Security Council because it expected the attack to succeed too quickly for any counteraction. In the absence of the Soviet Union, the Security Council voted to condemn the invasion of South Korea and called upon UN members to assist in its defense. A three-year-long war— involving hundreds of thousands of American troops and casualties but no Soviet troops—ended in a truce that restored the *status quo ante*. This truce, which the Communist side reportedly accepted only because President Eisenhower threatened to use tactical nuclear weapons, has been repeatedly violated by the North Korean regime.

The Communist takeovers in Eastern Europe and China followed by the Korean war showed how weakness and ineffectuality against Soviet indirect aggression could lead to Soviet contempt and direct military attack. Following is a description of how the Soviet foreign minister viewed the weakness of the United States before the Korean attack:

> The United States had withdrawn its forces from Korea without leaving in their stead so much as a detachment with a flag. It had created only minimal military strength among the South Koreans. It had no pledge of defense. It had conveyed responsibility to the United Nations—something scarcely compatible with serious intentions. . . . The United States had suffered its forces within reach to go slack on household duties. It had dawdled on economic aid to South Korea.[14]

In other words, the actions of the United States suggested it had abandoned its interest in South Korea. The establishment of NATO in 1949 and the successful defense of South Korea helped to galvanize Western resolve. As in the case of Finland in 1939, the Soviet Union saw that direct aggression was more costly and less likely to succeed than indirect aggression.

After Stalin's death in 1953, Nikita Khrushchev "reinitiated the Leninist view of the Third World to advance Soviet interests in these regions."[15] With new Communist regimes established in Eastern Europe, China, and North Vietnam (1954), Khrushchev "believed that some of the newly independent states and their leaders, having strong nationalistic and anti-Western perspectives, presented opportunities for Soviet inroads. Examples included Egypt, Iraq, Ghana,

Guinea, Mali, and Indonesia."[16] In Lenin's view, a two-stage process would sometimes be necessary to achieve a Communist victory: first, through state-to-state relations and other means, the Soviet Union would work with the "national bourgeoisie," meaning non-Communist indigenous leaders like Nasser of Egypt and Sukarno of Indonesia, to encourage them in anti-Western directions; second, there would be a transition to full-scale Communist rule, again with help from the Soviet bloc to indigenous Communist groups.

This approach was publicly proclaimed at the Twentieth Congress of the Soviet Communist party in 1956, the meeting at which Khrushchev exposed and denounced Stalin's crimes against fellow Communist leaders and the people of the Soviet Union. Soon after, the approach was successfully tested in Cuba. Fidel Castro took power there in 1959 as the leader of a coalition of guerrillas and genuine democrats opposed to a rightist dictator. Within months, Castro began arming and training foreign guerrillas, who then launched guerrilla movements in their home countries—Panama, Nicaragua, the Dominican Republic, and Venezuela. Moscow immediately established close relations with the Castro regime, which moved rapidly toward tight repression at home and indirect aggression against a number of Latin American nations.

But Moscow also experienced significant failures during the immediate postwar period: the Communist insurgencies in the Philippines (1946–1953) and Greece (1944–1950) were defeated, and efforts to keep pro-Soviet coalitions in power in Iran (1953) and Guatemala (1954) failed.

In 1961 the Twenty-second Congress of the Soviet Communist party openly declared that the Soviet Union would help armed "national liberation movements." It stated that "Socialist [Communist] countries are sincere and true friends of peoples fighting for their liberation and . . . render them all-around support."[17] Soviet military and political support were given to the Viet Cong and North Vietnamese, who in 1959 initiated the war to conquer South Vietnam in violation of the 1954 Geneva accords—which were forgotten once they had served to remove the French and give the Communists control of half of the country.

During the 1960s, Moscow began expanding its military aid to some non-Communist governments to increase "friendly relations" and to penetrate sectors of their governments, including their military institutions. Shultz notes that from 1961 to 1964 Soviet military aid to developing countries amounted to about $2.5 billion.[18] By the 1980s this amount had grown to an annual average of nearly $16 billion.[19]

Starting in the 1960s the Soviet Union provided money, weapons, training, and intelligence to the PLO and to other armed movements, such as the various Palestinian terrorist organizations (including the Popular Front for the Liberation of Palestine and the PFLP–General Command). Moscow also provided political, financial, and paramilitary aid to anti-Western radicals such as the Popular Front for the Liberation of Oman and the Sahara Liberation Movement.[20] In 1966, with North Vietnam and North Korea, Castro organized the Tri-Continental Conference to coordinate armed subversion by anti-Western groups from Latin America, the Middle East, and Africa.[21] During the 1960s the Castro regime armed and trained terrorists and guerrillas mainly under the *"foco* theory" of revolution. According to this theory, a small group or *foco* of armed revolutionaries could start a spiral of violence and counterrepression, leading ever larger numbers of people to join the revolution until the target governments are ultimately overthrown.

From 1960, the Soviet Union provided Castro with increasing quantities of weapons and economic support. Castro's behavior was fully consistent with the announced Soviet intention of supporting armed anti-Western movements. At his news conference on November 20, 1962, President Kennedy described his agreement with Khrushchev ending the Cuban missile crisis:

> Chairman Khrushchev . . . agreed to remove from Cuba all weapons systems capable of offensive use, to halt the further introduction of such weapons into Cuba, and to permit appropriate United Nations observation and supervision to insure the carrying out and continuation of these commitments. We on our part agreed that once these adequate arrangements for verification had been established we would remove our naval quarantine and give assurances against an invasion of Cuba. . . . As for our part, if all offensive weapons systems are removed from Cuba and kept out of the hemisphere in the future, under adequate verification and safeguards, and if Cuba is not used for the export of aggressive Communist purposes, there will be peace in the Caribbean.[22]

This could be taken to mean that in return for a U.S. pledge not to remove the Castro regime through armed force, two conditions would have to be met: (1) the Soviet Union would remove the strategic missiles and any nuclear warheads it had placed in Cuba and would never again use the island as a base for such weapons; and (2) Cuba would cease its armed subversion in the Western Hemisphere. Obviously disappointed by these Soviet concessions, Castro simply ignored the prohibition against further armed subversion and increased his indirect aggression. During most of the 1960s, Castro's tactics and methods differed from those of Moscow and the Soviet-line Communist parties in Latin America. Nevertheless, Soviet military and economic aid continued.

In 1968 Moscow demonstrated what it does in a strong dispute with an ally. When the Soviet Union invaded Czechoslovakia to depose an independent-minded and liberalizing Communist regime, Castro initially refused to endorse the action. Moscow terminated its delivery of oil to Cuba, which had supplied about 90 percent of the island's needs, and cut other economic support. Within weeks, Castro had capitulated, approved the invasion of Czechoslovakia, and accepted Soviet guidance of the Cuban intelligence and other organizations involved in subversion abroad.[23]

As a result, in the late 1960s and the early 1970s, in the words of a State Department report: "Within the [Western] hemisphere, Cuba generally conformed to the Soviet approach of fostering state to state relations."[24] At the same time, Castro provided training, weapons, and clandestine support for a new wave of urban terrorist warfare against Brazil, Uruguay, Argentina, and Chile. This terrorism brought about severe counterrepression from the military, a breakdown of existing political institutions, and a cycle of violence that cost thousands of lives.[25] Castro was now imitating the dualism of Soviet foreign policy—restoring normal diplomatic relations with many Latin American countries while secretly aiding the violent left. Meanwhile the Soviet Union provided Cuba with an increased supply of weapons and an economic subsidy that in the 1970s reached 25 percent of its gross national product, roughly $4 billion per year. Moscow also built major intelligence collection facilities in Cuba, sent its navy and air force there on military exercises and reconnaissance missions, and maintained a military presence that grew to some 7,500 troops.

In 1971, despite the movement toward détente in Europe with the four-power agreement on Berlin, the Twenty-fourth Congress of the Soviet Communist party endorsed and extended the Soviet program of indirect warfare. Brezhnev pledged the Soviet Union to "give undeviating support to the people's struggle for democracy, national liberation and socialism" and "further to invigorate the worldwide anti-imperialist struggle."[26] According to Shultz, the Soviets increased their assistance to pro-Soviet armed groups such as the PLO and other Palestinian factions in the Middle East, both armed groups in Zimbabwe (ZANU and ZAPU), the MPLA of Angola, Frelimo in Mozambique, SWAPO operating in Namibia, and the ANC targeted against South Africa.[27]

At the 1971 Communist Party Congress, the Soviet leadership

was explicit in its view that the movement toward détente and peaceful coexistence with the United States was fully compatible with intensified ideological warfare and higher levels of assistance for "national liberation" struggles. Shultz concludes that in the view of the Soviet leadership, "the conditions of détente created an atmosphere in which these struggles could flourish."[28]

Soon after, the Soviet foreign minister expressed the Kremlin's sense of power by stating bluntly that in world politics "there is no question of any significance that can be decided without the Soviet Union or in opposition to it."[29] And the Soviet ruler was reported to have confided in 1973 to a then friendly foreign head of state that "our aim is to gain control of the two great treasure houses on which the West depends—the energy treasure house of the Persian Gulf and the mineral treasure house of central and southern Africa."[30]

The May 1972 summit meeting in Moscow (the first since 1967) formally opened a new era of détente between the United States and the Soviet Union. Brezhnev even signed a declaration on principles of international conduct that the United States viewed as a Soviet pledge to halt its indirect aggression.

In November 1972, Nixon won reelection in a landslide and decided to break the stalemate in the negotiations with North Vietnam by launching a sustained bombing campaign in December 1972. The Paris peace accords on Vietnam were signed in January 1973. President Nixon said they would "end the war and bring peace with honor to Vietnam and Southeast Asia." Democratic Senator Edward Kennedy of Massachusetts proclaimed: "The negotiators who achieved this agreement deserve our highest gratitude." And Democratic Congresswoman Bella Abzug of New York, an outspoken opponent of the war, expressed great satisfaction: "I cannot adequately express the depth of my relief that the bloodshed in Indochina is really coming to an end."[31]

Unfortunately, the agreement had two serious defects: against the protests of South Vietnam it permitted North Vietnam to maintain 120,000 of its regular troops inside South Vietnam; and its provisions for monitoring were inadequate. Within months, according to a U.S. government analysis published in 1986, the Communist side was violating the accord by refusing to withdraw all of its combat forces from Laos and Cambodia and by infiltrating tons of military supplies and 30,000 additional troops into South Vietnam.[32] The United States made virtually no response.

Believing that "peace had arrived," Congress sharply reduced military aid to South Vietnam. In the spring of 1975 North Vietnamese troops, with the help of indigenous Communist forces, conquered South Vietnam, Cambodia, and Laos. Early in 1975 President Gerald Ford had appealed to Congress to supply some $200 million in military aid to the Cambodian government of Lon Nol fighting a last-ditch struggle against the Khmer Rouge. "This is a moral question that must be faced squarely," Ford pleaded. "Are we to deliberately abandon a small country in the midst of a life-and-death struggle? Is the United States . . . now to condemn . . . a small Asian nation totally dependent on us?" On March 25, the House Democratic Caucus voted down the president's request, 189 to 49. Less than a month later the Khmer Rouge overran Phnom Penh and initiated a reign of brutality.

In June 1973, Nixon and Brezhnev had held a summit meeting, in Washington, with an emphasis on increased trade and improved economic relations. Some euphoric commentators hailed the summit as ending the cold war and opening a new and more positive relationship between the two superpowers. Yet in October 1973, on Yom Kippur, the most sacred and solemn day in the Jewish year, Egypt, with the full support of Moscow, launched an all-out surprise attack on Israel. As Israel recovered from the initial shock and, with massive American military aid, drove back the invaders, Moscow prepared to send in thousands of its troops to help Egypt. Only a worldwide alert of U.S. strategic forces and blunt threats from Washington deterred Moscow from taking this action.

The following month, the first overseas deployment of Cuban combat units took place. They were sent to replace depleted Syrian army units on the Israeli border.[33]

America's failure to enforce the Paris accords and to meet its commitments to South Vietnam probably emboldened the Soviet Union to step up its indirect aggression. In 1974, when the long-established authoritarian regime suddenly fell in Portugal, a large-scale covert effort by the Soviet Union nearly brought the Communist party of Portugal to power. Only belatedly did the Western democracies respond to prevent a NATO ally from becoming part of the Soviet bloc through subversion.

But, the Soviets used Communists inside the Portuguese government and in its colonial administration to help pro-Soviet armed groups take power in Mozambique in June 1975, and in Angola five months later. In Angola they employed a new technique: huge supplies of weapons were sent in along with some 20,000 regular Cuban troops to ensure the military victory of the Communist MPLA over non-Communist groups also fighting against Portuguese colonial rule. These victories were aided by propaganda successes:

> In the battle for world opinion, the Soviets and their witting and unwitting allies proved supremely successful in inter-

nationally delegitimating the regimes they meant to destroy. The Soviets showed themselves equally successful at camouflaging the Marxist-Leninist objectives pursued by organizations such as the MPLA, the Frelimo and the ANC.[34]

In the year before the Twenty-fifth Congress of the Soviet Communist party in early 1976, six additional Communist regimes had been established—in Cambodia, Laos, South Vietnam, Mozambique, Angola, and Guinea-Bissau. Leonid Brezhnev was "confident and assertive," viewing these victories as a sure sign that the "worldwide revolutionary process" was "gaining strength."[35] The new Soviet constitution of 1977 included an article committing the regime to support "the struggle of peoples for national liberation." CIA Director William J. Casey noted in 1983: "The Soviets advised [these] new radical regimes to mute their revolutionary rhetoric and to try to keep their links to Western commercial resources, foreign assistance and international financial institutions. Moscow's ambitions did not cloud recognition that it could not afford more economic dependents such as Cuba and Vietnam."[36]

In 1974 Ethiopia had entered a period of transition after the overthrow of its aging monarch, Haile Selassie. After several years of clandestine work, a pro-Soviet military faction, the Dergue, led by Haile Mariam Mengistu, seized power. Again, the Soviet Union supplied weapons and logistic support as about 15,000 Cuban troops moved into Ethiopia to prop up the new Communist regime. Barely reacting to this event, the Carter administration continued its discussions with Castro on normalizing relations. Nixon had begun these negotiations in 1974, and Ford continued them, despite Castro's military interventions in Africa.

In April 1978, the Soviet Union fomented a Communist military coup in neutral Afghanistan. In June 1978, in strategically located South Yemen, Cuban forces and Soviet and East German personnel helped consolidate the power of a pro-Soviet faction. In March 1979, Castro helped the New Jewel Movement install a Communist regime in the tiny Caribbean island of Grenada. And in July 1979, the Sandinistas, with extensive Cuban and Soviet support, took power in Nicaragua. This brought to eleven the new pro-Soviet dictatorships established during the 1970s. They then cooperated with the Soviet Union and its allies in all respects, including use of their territory for armed subversion against the next targets.

During the 1970s, the Soviet Union also directly and indirectly helped pro-Communist terrorist organizations stage attacks inside key NATO countries, such as Italy, West Germany, and Turkey.[37] The Red Brigades staged more than 2,100 terrorist attacks a year in Italy.[38]

29

In Turkey, an anchor of the NATO alliance, the Soviets used Bulgarian and various Palestinian terrorist groups to arm and train thousands of terrorists from both the extreme left and the extreme right. By September 1979, after violence claimed more than 2,000 lives in Turkey, martial law had been declared in nineteen provinces. A year later, the violence had reached the scale of civil war, with as many as forty deaths a day and ended only when a military coup imposed order and prevented both violent extremes from functioning.[39]

By the 1970s the Soviet Union had developed the full range of its means of indirect aggression. The essence remained what it had been since the 1920s: to use propaganda and political action to isolate and weaken the target governments, while legitimating pro-Soviet movements; and help pro-Soviet groups topple target governments by violence and all other means except regular formations of Soviet combat forces (Afghanistan in 1979 proving the rule).

The structure of collaboration that had evolved during the 1970s had three principal components:

1. The Soviet Union or its Warsaw Pact allies provided strategic guidance, intelligence support, military training, weapons, money, propaganda, and disinformation. Frequently Soviet allies were used as the contact with armed foreign groups. Czechoslovakia served this purpose with the Red Brigades, and Cuba with the New Jewel Movement.

2. Accomplice governments, including Cuba, Nicaragua, North Korea, Libya, Syria, and Angola, provided operational bases in addition to all the forms of support mentioned above. From these bases, anti-Western guerrilla and terrorist groups launched their attacks.

3. Stateless anti-Western guerrilla and terrorist groups used external aid to recruit members and obtain international legitimacy in the non-Communist world. They use both political and violent means in their efforts to attack and, if possible, replace target governments.

Three Soviet innovations of the 1970s were continued into the 1980s. First, Cuban combat forces with full Soviet intelligence and logistics backing were used to shift the balance of forces on the ground. Because the West did not protest the first use of Cuban forces to help Syria against Israel in 1974, these tactics involved few risks for Moscow—even when tens of thousands of Cuban troops were used to help Communist groups take and keep power. Other surrogate military forces—such as Vietnamese troops in Cambodia— were also sent to areas where they might be useful.

Second, non-Communist international groups and organizations were used to legitimate pro-Soviet armed groups. The Soviet Union succeeded in using the United Nations and the Organization of African Unity to provide legitimacy, as well as propaganda and economic support, for all the major pro-Soviet organizations in southern Africa: MPLA, Frelimo, SWAPO, and the ANC. After the first two of these armed insurgencies took power, they in turn contributed to the further legitimation of the others.

Third, Soviet propaganda and political action contributed to the misperceptions that led important elements of the non-Communist and democratic Left in Western Europe to endorse and provide aid for the PLO in the Middle East and Communist guerrillas in Central America. The Socialist International, for example, is a confederation of democratic Socialist parties that was founded in direct opposition to the Communist international and its totalitarian objectives and methods. In 1978, however, it began endorsing coalitions led by armed Communist guerrillas, first in Nicaragua, then in El Salvador, Guatemala, and Honduras.[40] Soviet political action has also been a factor in persuading some West European Socialist governments and political groups and the European Economic Community to provide tens of millions of dollars in aid to Sandinista Nicaragua and other newly established Communist regimes. This was a new development in postwar international politics and suggested a new division of responsibilities: Communists would hold power and impoverish their countries through central mismanagement, while free world countries would provide financial aid.

During the 1970s indirect aggression abetted by the Soviet Union failed in many countries but succeeded in eleven. Table 2–2 summarizes the targets and the hostile elements cooperating to bring pro-Soviet groups to power.

Given the momentum of Soviet success during the détente of the 1970s, further victories might have been expected during the 1980s. Sustained and sometimes dramatic attempts continued in at least ten countries. Yet no additional pro-Soviet regimes had been established anywhere in the world. How was the trend of the late 1970s reversed?

Like the Korean attack of 1950, the Soviet invasion of Afghanistan in December 1979 increased the determination of the United States and its allies to contain Moscow and its allies. Perhaps history had repeated itself: just as Stalin's astonishing success during the late 1940s led him to miscalculate the risks of open aggression in Korea, so it seemed that Brezhnev's success in the 1970s might have led to the decision to invade Afghanistan. This direct intervention by Soviet troops put an end to the so-called détente of the 1970s, which had indeed helped the Soviet Union attain many of its objectives.[41]

Second, the destabilization of the pro-Western government in

31

TABLE 2–2
POLITICAL-PARAMILITARY WAR AGAINST U.S. INTERESTS IN THREE STRATEGIC ARENAS, 1980

Target Countries	Destabilization Coalition
Latin America	
Colombia	Cuba
Venezuela	Regional Communist/guerrilla groups
Central America	USSR
Panama	Palestinian terrorists/Libya
Belize	
Mexico[a]	
Middle East	
Israel	USSR
Egypt	Pro-Soviet regimes (South Yemen, Syria)
Iran (post-Khomeini)	Cuba
Oman	Palestinian guerrillas
North Yemen	Libya
Persian Gulf regimes	
Saudi Arabia[a]	
Africa	
Zaire	USSR
Morocco	Cuba
Sudan	Libya
Namibia	Pro-Soviet regimes (Ethiopia, Angola, Mozambique)
South Africa[a]	Regional guerrillas/Communist groups (SWAPO)

a. Main strategic target.
SOURCE: Author, November 1980.

Iran in 1979 did not turn out the way the Soviet Union hoped. Although "the Soviets, Libya, and the PLO were all heavily involved in the campaign to overthrow the Shah,"[42] the successor regime was not *Tudeh*, the Iranian Communist party, but rather a Shiite Islamic fundamentalist theocracy. This created a danger to the southern border regions of the Soviet Union. Millions of Moslems live there, many from the same ethnic groups as those in Iran.

Third, in 1980, Ronald Reagan was elected president, in part because of the foreign policy setbacks in the Carter years. Affirming a vision of a strong, effective America, the new president conveyed an unambiguous determination to help friendly countries defeat

Soviet-aided indirect aggression. A new consensus arose for the expansion and upgrading of America's military forces, which was recognized in the major increases in President Carter's last budget, as well as in those of the first four Reagan years.

The new and vigorous American leadership contrasted sharply with the declining figure of Brezhnev, who was very ill in his last two years. His two successors also expired not long after coming to power, Yuri Andropov in 1982 and Konstantin Chernenko in 1985.

The new pro-Soviet regimes established in the 1970s demonstrated again that Communist victory brings to a country a predictable cluster of calamities: internal terror, mass executions, economic failure, and deprivation of every kind. Young people were conscripted into an expanding military, with some serving in indirect aggression against neighboring countries. Cumulatively, millions of innocent people died as a direct result of those eleven Communist victories in the 1970s. As William Casey wrote:

> This [subversive aggression] is not a bloodless war. Marxist-Leninist policies and tactics have unleashed the four horses of the Apocalypse—Famine, Pestilence, War, and Death. . . . In the occupied countries—Afghanistan, Cambodia, Ethiopia, Angola, Nicaragua . . . there has occurred a holocaust comparable to that which Nazi Germany inflicted in Europe.[43]

Those tragic consequences of Communist rule gave rise to armed anti-Communist resistance movements in five of these eleven countries: Afghanistan, Cambodia, Angola, Mozambique, and Nicaragua. During the 1980s these armed resistance movements received increasing popular support within their countries and increased external aid from free-world countries.

These movements represented a new historical phenomenon. Their continuing existence and their potential for victory would challenge faith in the inevitable Soviet domination of the planet. The tide of revolution had begun to turn against the edges of the Soviet empire. Victory for any resistance movement would be a sharp setback to the Soviet Communist leadership's sense of historical validation. It would undermine "the only tangible means of success the Soviet system could produce, the only proof that Communist ideology is still correct and the world revolution is still in the making."[44]

The Soviet regime behaved as though it knew that the example of a victory of an anti-Communist resistance movement over an established Communist regime might encourage challenges to its allies and even to the Soviet "dictatorship of the proletariat." Moreover, the preoccupation of these new pro-Soviet dictatorships with their own survival reduced their capacity to work with the Soviet Union against the next target countries and thereby reduced the momentum of indirect aggression in the 1980s.

With Gorbachev's accession to power in early 1985, the Soviet Union regained vigorous leadership. Four Reagan-Gorbachev summits since November 1985 opened a new U.S.–Soviet détente. As with the détente of the 1970s, the Soviet Union and its allies have conducted wide-ranging diplomacy on regional as well as bilateral issues. As in the 1970s, while normalizing relations with the world's major military and economic powers in the spotlight of international attention, in the "twilight" the Soviet Union continues its indirect aggression in the developing regions. And as in the 1970s, a significant proportion—perhaps a majority—of the Democratic members of Congress seem not to understand the facts of this indirect aggression. They continue to oppose military aid to friendly governments opposing Communist indirect aggression and movements resisting the Communist dictatorships that came to power in the 1970s.

The classic definition of power in international politics is "the capacity to achieve intended effects." For the past decade or longer, these wars between the Soviet-aided Communist regimes and the anti-Communist armed resistance movements have been a major test of the commitment, competence, and power of the two superpowers.

3
Afghanistan

During the 1970s a Soviet diplomat told a NATO defense minister from Norway that his country would be better off as a neutral, pointing to a prime example of contented neutrality on the Soviet border: "Look at how well we have gotten along with Afghanistan during many decades."[1]

Obviously Soviet diplomats no longer use this example. The bloody events following the April 1978 Communist military coup have revealed to all the world a panorama of suffering, wholesale destruction, massive human displacement, and indiscriminate slaughter. Those events have also highlighted the exceptional courage and dedication of the Afghan people as they fought against the imposition of communism by Soviet armed might and cunning.

Among the areas in the world where the people have risen to oppose Communist regimes, Afghanistan embodies a number of features that set its story apart from the others. Not some distant beachhead of the Soviet empire like Angola or Nicaragua, Afghanistan borders directly on the Soviet Union itself. The regime facing the Afghan resistance has not been only a satrap of Moscow, aided by surrogate forces like the Cubans. It has also included the Soviets' own armed forces. Over Afghanistan there has been a greater unanimity of outrage, as evidenced in the bipartisan reaction in the United States and as manifested in UN resolutions. Afghanistan is also the first salient of the Soviet empire from which Moscow has withdrawn significant numbers of combat forces.

Background

Visited by Alexander the Great on his way to India and later invaded by Genghis Khan and his Mongols, Afghanistan has long been a crossroads of the world.

Slightly larger than France, it is a landlocked country of high mountains and plateaus with an estimated population in 1978 of 15 million. Virtually all Afghanis are Moslem, 80 percent Sunni and 20 percent Shiite. The overwhelming majority of Afghans live in rural areas raising crops and sheep. Afghanistan also has enormous, mostly undeveloped, mineral resources. In 1978 its per capita income was about $240, the adult literacy rate was about 12 percent, and life expectancy at birth was about forty-two.[2]

The Pushtuns are the principal ethnic group, constituting about half the population. Many Pushtuns also live in Pakistan, which helps to explain that country's willingness to support the Afghan armed resistance and to assist the millions of Afghan refugees. Other groups include, in the south, a small number of the Baluch (the vast majority of whom are found in both Pakistan and Iran) and large numbers of the Tajiks and Uzbeks in the north, who also live in the Soviet Union just across the border (see table 3–1).

The long-established traditional culture has been centered in the family, ethnic group, village, and clan. As described by a longtime observer of Afghanistan, Rosanne Klass, this had produced a rough-hewn local democracy through the village-level council (jirga) in which all adult males participate in making decisions. In this secular community meeting Moslem clergymen are welcome to participate but by no means exercise a dominant role.[3] Always more important than the actions of the distant central government, this village self-governance may also have prepared the Afghan people for resistance at home and in exile.

The modern period can be traced to 1747, with the establishment

TABLE 3–1
CROSS-BORDER ETHNIC GROUPS IN AFGHANISTAN, PAKISTAN, IRAN, AND THE USSR
(in millions)

	Afghanistan	Pakistan	Iran	USSR
Total population	14.8	107.5	51.9	286.4
Pushtuns	7.0	3.5–7.0	—	—
Uzbeks and Turkomans	1.0	—	—	11.4
Tajiks	2.0	—	.025	2.9
Baluch	0.1	2.6	.85	—

NOTE: Dashes indicate no members of the given ethnic group in the country. SOURCES: *The World Fact Book 1988*, CIA, CPAS WF88-001; Rosanne Klass, ed., *Afghanistan: The Great Game Revisited* (New York: Freedom House, 1988); Henry Bradsher, *Afghanistan and the Soviet Union* (Durham, N.C.: Duke University Press, 1985); *Iran: A Country Study*, Area Handbook Series (Washington, D.C.: American University, 1978); and *Pakistan: A Country Study*, Area Handbook Series (Washington, D.C.: American University, 1984).

of the Afghan monarchy, which held sway until 1973. During the nineteenth century Great Britain, seeking to contain the expansion of the Russian empire, fought two brief and unsuccessful wars in Afghanistan (1839–1842 and 1878–1880).

Modern History. The Amir Abdur Rahman took the Afghan throne in 1880, after living in exile in Russia for twelve years. Well aware of Russia's imperial ambitions and British anxieties over Russian expansion, he sought to keep his country free of foreign intervention by establishing a policy of neutrality toward both Russia and Great Britain. In 1919, his son and successor was assassinated and succeeded by Amanullah, another of his sons. Amanullah entered into cordial relations with the new Bolshevik regime in Moscow, signing a formal friendship treaty in 1921.

In 1929 Amanullah was overthrown, when he attempted to replicate Kemal Ataturk's transformation of Turkey before generating support from any component of Afghan society. Soon thereafter, "Soviet forces in Afghan uniforms entered northern Afghanistan in a brief effort to reinstate Amanullah and set up a pro-Soviet government."[4] This early and often clandestine Soviet involvement in Afghanistan previewed future events.

Another member of the royal family became king but he was assassinated in 1933 by a member of a family active in left-wing movements and in Soviet efforts to maintain Amanullah on the throne. His son, then nineteen, succeeded him and ruled as Zahir Shah until 1973, when he was overthrown in a Soviet-aided coup engineered by his cousin and brother-in-law, former Prime Minister Mohammed Daoud, who then declared a republic and ruled as president.

Although never establishing close links, the United States recognized Afghanistan diplomatically in 1934 and sent its first representatives there in 1942. Afghanistan was neutral during World War II but it tilted strongly toward the Allies.

From 1946 to 1952, the monarchy liberalized its policies, holding parliamentary elections and permitting an independent press. Left-wing opposition groups emerged for the first time. As a result of their political agitation, however, which was believed to have been Soviet connected, this liberalization phase ended.[5]

In 1947, Great Britain ended its rule over India. Communal rioting and other factors led to the division of the former British colony into two new countries: Moslem Pakistan on the western border of Afghanistan (and what subsequently became Bangladesh in the east) and predominately Hindu India. When some Afghan leaders then raised the question of autonomy or even independence for the Pushtuns of Pakistan, Afghan relations with Pakistan immediately became strained. According to Rosanne Klass, "The Soviets supported the Pushtunistan issue. . . . The leader of the Pushtunistan movement in Pakistan . . . was and is openly Marxist; he was believed by British sources to have had Soviet ties as early as the 1920s."[6] Moscow thus appears to have viewed the Pushtunistan issue as a useful instrument against both Afghanistan and Pakistan for many decades.

Soviet Activities in Afghanistan. The year 1954 marked a key turning point. Prince Daoud had become prime minister the year before and, like his predecessor, sought—but failed to obtain—military assistance from the United States. His (and the Afghan) strategic purpose was to have a counterweight to Moscow to replace the former British presence in India. According to Leon B. Poullada, a former American diplomat in Afghanistan who has studied contemporary Afghanistan closely, the Soviet Union revived its efforts to dominate Afghanistan in 1953. Poullada describes this as a "calculated process," which, in his analysis, moved through five stages:

> Stage 1: (1953–1963) The establishment of a subversive infrastructure inside Afghanistan, especially during Daoud's first period of power.
> Stage 2: (1963–1973) The formation of a secret Communist party and the subversion and destruction of nascent Afghan democratic institutions.
> Stage 3: (1973–1978) The return of Daoud to power with Communist support in order to destroy the Afghan monarchy and as a figurehead for behind-the-scenes Soviet control via his Afghan Communist supporters.
> (*The activation of the next well-planned stages was probably optional, as needed.*)
> Stage 4: (1978–1979) The overthrow of Daoud when he was no longer useful and the installation of an openly Communist government completely subservient to Moscow.
> Stage 5: (1979 to the present)—When Stage Four proved inadequate, the physical invasion, installation of totally controlled puppets and absorption of Afghanistan into the Soviet bloc.[7]

In essence, Poullada describes what might ironically be called the "surprise of 1978," when Daoud was killed in a Communist military coup, as part of a twenty-five-year-long, clearly traceable Soviet effort to subvert its neighbor. He notes, for example, that each Soviet economic aid project during these years accomplished a political or strategic objective. According to Poullada, many hundreds of Afghan army officers were sent to the Soviet Union for training, especially after 1956. Some of these were recruited as Soviet agents and later played key roles in turning their country into a Soviet vassal state.

In 1961, the Pushtunistan issue nearly led to a war between Afghanistan and Pakistan. Since Pakistan was a U.S. ally, the Soviet Union seemed to try to foment a conflict between Pakistan and neutral Afghanistan that would weaken both. In 1963 the king demanded Daoud's resignation, both because of the prime minister's aggressiveness on Pushtunistan and because of alarm at the greatly increasing influence of the Soviets.[8]

This marked the beginning of another attempt at liberalization. A new constitution in 1964, which barred Daoud from returning to power, included provisions for freedom of speech, press, and religion. Parliamentary elections were also scheduled for 1965. On January 1 of that year the Afghan Communist party (named the People's Democratic party of Afghanistan, or PDPA) was secretly formed to exploit the electoral process provided by the new constitution. In the September 1965 vote, by secret ballot and with universal franchise, only four Communists won seats in parliament. The next month, the Communists provoked riots that overthrew the newly elected government. Over the next dozen years the PDPA instigated riots, strikes, and student unrest.

According to Poullada, the ten-year period of political liberalization from 1963 to 1973 was the last chance to save Afghanistan from communism. This failed partly because the king, angered and apprehensive as a result of the Communist-inspired agitation, refused to approve the creation of legal political parties. Moreover, the minuscule Communist party "worked underground and was secretly advised and subsidized by the Soviets. The Russians instructed the Afghan Communists to sabotage the democratic experiment because they rightly feared that the success of democracy in Afghanistan would spell the end of their hard-bought influence."[9] Poullada quotes a former Afghan minister of the interior of that period as stating unequivocally that "Afghan Communist leaders were controlled, paid, and ordered directly by KGB officers in the Soviet embassy in Kabul."[10]

During this critical time, the United States failed to support Afghanistan's experiment in political liberalization. Economic aid declined during these years, and the United States made no special efforts to encourage or support the prime ministers or their constitutional governments. The U.S. government also seemed to know little about Communist activities because "the CIA . . . both in Afghanistan and Washington, had for years concentrated all its effort and interest on Soviet bloc activities *and deliberately ignored internal Afghan matters.*[11]

In the early 1970s, central Afghanistan suffered severe droughts, causing widespread famine. The government's incompetent response provoked popular indignation and disenchantment with democracy. Although the United States sent food, belatedly, clearly the democratic government was endangered. The Communists now urged Prince Daoud to depose the king and proclaim a republic. Their purpose was to destroy the single most important political institution of national unity, the monarchy, and at the same time enter the government with Daoud. In July 1973, while the king was out of the country, a small group of military officers, including some trained in the Soviet Union, staged an almost bloodless coup, and Daoud returned to power as the president of a newly proclaimed Afghan Republic.

Daoud, however, proved to be more independent than the Soviets had expected. By 1976 he had removed many of his Communist and leftist supporters and had attempted to loosen the grip of the Soviet Union:

> He tried to diversify his sources of aid by turning to the wealthy Islamic oil states. His preferred instrument for regaining Afghan independence was the Shah of Iran, who responded with generous offers of economic aid and political support and tried, with some success, to improve relations between Pakistan and Afghanistan.[12]

The Soviets, therefore, moved to replace Daoud (and were part of the coalition that brought down the shah of Iran in 1979).

The Overt Communist Coup

From its first days, the Communist party of Afghanistan was divided into two pro-Soviet but mutually hostile factions. The faction known as Parcham ("Banner"), which worked closely with Daoud, drew its strength mainly from successful, educated, urban families, mostly from Kabul. It was led by Babrak Karmal. The Khalq ("Masses") faction, led by Noor Mohammad Taraki and Hafizullah Amin, was dominated by educated Pushtuns, especially in the army, who came from village backgrounds. According to Anthony Arnold and Rosanne Klass:

> They tended to be significantly less well-off economically than the Parchami. The doctrinal differences between the two factions were only tactical: Parcham was ready to pursue

a "common front" approach, i.e., outward and temporary
collaboration with non-Marxists, pending seizure of power.
Khalq on the other hand rejected such collaboration and
demanded loyalty to "pure," uncompromising revolutionary socialism.[13]

The Power Struggle. The tug of war between these two factions has
marked the entire period of Communist control in Afghanistan. After
the party was founded in 1965, they stayed together for little more
than a year. In 1967 Khalq expelled the Parcham faction (including
two later leaders of the Afghan Communist regime, Babrak Karmal
and Najibullah) from the party. The upshot was that the Parcham
faction set up its own parallel Communist party with the same name,
the People's Democratic party of Afghanistan. Arnold and Klass note
that both groups then

> began a frantic recruitment campaign, focusing especially on
> teachers and students. The first target was teachers, partic-
> ularly those specializing in teacher training: the long-range
> goal was to establish an infrastructure in the schools that
> would first influence and then recruit the youth who would
> form the power elite in the next generation.[14]

Other targets for recruitment, as is customary with Communist
groups, were journalists, other members of the media, government
officials, and military officers, especially those trained by Moscow.
But both groups refrained from openly recruiting those employees of
the state holding sensitive positions to keep from frightening the
authorities, although both factions developed small groups of secret
followers.

In the summer of 1977 both factions agreed to form a coalition
once again. They began cooperating and planning to seize power:

> Over the next several months, preparations for the coup
> proceeded apace, including (according to subsequent official
> accounts) ten rehearsals involving key military officers. Few
> knew the purpose of these exercises: even the participants
> believed in the carefully crafted cover story, i.e., that they
> were designed as defensive moves to protect the Republic
> from any coup attempts by royalists or rightists.[15]

In April 1978 the murder of one Communist activist (by PDPA
agents) led to massive demonstrations against Prime Minister Daoud.
Although Daoud ordered the arrest of the Communist leaders organizing the demonstrations, security agents who sympathized with the
PDPA let Hafizullah Amin, the Communist party contact with the
military subversives, have time to send messages triggering the

41

preplanned coup. Then on April 27, 1978, in a country that had experienced hardly any internal violence between 1929 and 1965, the Communists launched their very bloody coup. The prime minister and his family—including his grandchildren—were immediately killed along with several thousand others. A Revolutionary Council of military officers was declared during the fighting.

Only on May 1, 1978, with the coup having clearly succeeded, did the Communists step forward and name Taraki as president with Babrak Karmal becoming first deputy prime minister and Amin deputy prime minister and foreign minister. The new regime publicly denied any Communist leanings, announcing itself to be nonaligned and committed to "positive" neutrality. As Arnold and Klass put it:

> Despite the PDPA's well-known political positions—and the fact that, in its first month of existence, the DRA [Democratic Republic of Afghanistan] signed more than twenty new agreements with Moscow while Soviet advisers began pouring into Afghanistan—he [Taraki] seems to have been believed by a good many people who should have known better.[16]

Immediately after the coup a reign of terror began: mass arrests, torture, and secret executions, with the Soviet and East German secret police providing the immediate means to build a new and deadly Afghan secret police. The small Communist coalition, then estimated at only 5,000 members in a population of about 15 million, decided "to eliminate any potential non-Communist opposition. . . . First went the experienced political figures, religious leaders, and important civil servants, judges, army officers. Eventually the net spread to include lesser figures—teachers, writers, artists, students, bureaucrats, lawyers, merchants."[17]

Islam and all religions were persecuted and ridiculed. The Communist regime replaced the Afghan tricolor flag with an all-red banner. Estimates of those killed during the first eighteen months ran as high as 50,000; in September 1979 the Communist regime itself published an avowedly incomplete list of 12,000 persons executed.[18]

In the summer of 1978 the factional conflict in the Communist party split open in the regime. When Khalq emerged as the dominant faction in June and July, it ousted Babrak Karmal and other Parcham leaders and sent them abroad as ambassadors. In July 1978 the Khalq regime of Taraki and Amin detected a Parcham plot—perhaps including the Soviets—and moved immediately to arrest, torture, and execute a number of Parcham party members. The Parcham leaders abroad fled to Moscow, while several of those in Kabul found refuge in the Soviet embassy. In December of 1978, Taraki signed a friendship treaty with Soviet leader Leonid Brezhnev.

In September 1978 popular resistance to the regime began to spread nationwide, with massive desertions from the Afghan armed forces and an estimated 250,000 or more refugees fleeing to Pakistan. By this time thousands of Soviet military personnel had already entered the country. In fact, according to a French Communist source, 20,000 were in Afghanistan *before* the invasion.[19] These Soviet forces engaged in combat with mutinous Afghan troops and civilian armed resistance. After fifty or more Soviet military personnel were killed in Herat in March 1979, Soviet aircraft bombed and strafed the city, causing an estimated 20,000–30,000 civilian deaths.[20]

On February 14, 1979, just as the pro-Western government of the shah was being replaced by the Khomeini regime in Iran, the U.S. ambassador to Afghanistan was kidnapped. He was subsequently killed by Afghan police under Soviet supervision while they were ostensibly attempting to rescue him. By the summer of 1979, according to Klass, "military preparations in Central Asia were detected by western intelligence" for a Soviet military intervention in Afghanistan.[21] In September 1979 Taraki met with Karmal in Moscow as the Soviets sought to end the rift between the two factions. Taraki was reportedly ordered to eliminate Amin and agreed to do so. Amin, however, escaped the assassination plot and eliminated Taraki, taking sole control of the presidency, the foreign ministry, and the defense ministry.

Invasion. In December 1979 the Soviet Union invaded in force and placed Babrak Karmal, the leader of the Parcham faction, in power. Amin and his entire family were killed by Soviet commandos. The initial Soviet troop presence of about 85,000 grew rapidly to about 120,000, according to the U.S. State Department.[22]

Since then the Khalq and Parcham factions have maintained an uneasy coalition. The dominant Parcham faction controls the key government ministries, some of the military, and the ever-larger and more powerful secret police, KhAD, set up and controlled by the Soviet KGB. The Khalq faction, which controls the regular police force, has more influence with the armed forces, in which most of the officers and noncommissioned personnel come from the same small-town Pushtun background as the Khalq leaders. (See table 3–2.)

Western Reactions. These convulsive and bloody developments in 1978 and 1979 seemed to provoke very little Western reaction or lead

43

TABLE 3–2
AFGHAN COMMUNIST FACTIONS, 1965–PRESENT

	Parcham	Khalq
1965: both establish the PDPA	Includes Babrak and Najibullah	Includes Taraki and Amin
1967: split	Establishes a new, competing PDPA	Expels Parcham from PDPA
1977: coalition	Attempts by Soviet Union and Indian Communist party to unify the factions	
1978 April: coup	Babrak made first deputy prime minister	Taraki made president; Amin, deputy prime minister and foreign minister
July: split	Parcham ejected from power; Babrak and Najibullah among those sent abroad as ambassadors	Khalq under Taraki and Amin dominant
August:	Flight of Babrak, Najibullah, other ambassadors to Moscow; many arrested, tortured, some killed. Soviet embassy gives refuge to several key figures.	Discover Parchami plot (Soviets are also suspected)
December: treaty		Friendship treaty signed by Taraki and Brezhnev
1979 September:		Taraki visits Havana, meets Babrak in Moscow; told to remove Amin. Soviet ambassador sets trap for Amin, who escapes and kills Taraki.
December: Soviet invasion	Babrak brought to power by Soviet invasion	Amin killed by Soviets

TABLE 3–2 (continued)

	Parcham	Khalq
Coalition	Babrak becomes prime minister, president, party chief.	Gulabzoi is pro-Soviet Khalq.
1986	Najibullah replaces Babrak in all positions.	
1988		Gulabzoi opposes Soviet/Najibullah policy and is sent to Moscow.

SOURCES: Anthony Arnold and Rosanne Klass, "Afghanistan's Divided Communist Party," in Klass, ed., *Afghanistan: The Great Game Revisited;* U.S. Department of State, *Afghanistan: Eight Years of Soviet Occupation,* Special Report no. 173, December 1987.

to little real understanding of occurrences inside Afghanistan. According to the *New York Times* of May 2, 1978: "The coup that installed what appears to be a pro-Soviet party in power in Afghanistan came as a surprise to the United States Government, officials said today." On May 5, 1978, the *Times* reported, "The Carter Administration is so far rightly unruffled by last week's coup in Afghanistan. . . . A decade ago, a Communist gain anywhere would have been felt as a distinct loss for Washington. Most Americans now recognize that the world is more complicated." State Department officials in testimony to Congress seemed to have had no forewarning of the impending events. On March 16, 1978, only weeks before the Communist coup, Adolph Dubs, deputy assistant secretary of state for Near Eastern and South Asian Affairs (and the U.S. ambassador killed in February 1979), told Congress: "Internally the political situation is stable. President Daoud remains very much in control and faces no significant opposition. The process of political institution-building is moving ahead at a measured pace."[23]

Even months after the dramatic Communist seizure of power and repression had occurred, the Carter administration and most of the Western media paid remarkably little attention. In August 1979 the official post report of the U.S. embassy in Kabul blandly described the new regime as "leftist-oriented" and went on to say that "many economic and social reform programs had been announced by the new regime, but implementation of these potentially far-reaching changes in Afghan society will be formidable."[24] This report described the Communist party, the PDPA, as "Marxist-oriented" but immediately pointed out that the Taraki regime "retained many

45

elements of the Daoudist civil and criminal judicial systems, although it had stated that certain anti-revolutionary aspects [had] been discarded."[25]

Soviet-Afghan Human Rights and Economic Policies

Before the December 1979 Soviet invasion, the new Communist regime had already killed and imprisoned tens of thousands of people. The U.S. State Department estimates that 1–1.5 million Afghans (of a total pre-1978 population of 15 million) have died as a direct result of the Communist çoup, the Soviet invasion, and subsequent internal repression and combat. Beyond that, more than half the population of Afghanistan has become refugees: almost 4 million fled to Pakistan and about 2 million to Iran. Some 2 million more abandoned their rural villages, settling in the major towns to avoid Soviet and Afghan aerial bombardment and military operations.[26] Many of the civilian casualties were victims of systematic Soviet-Afghan massacres over the years. Figure 3–1 shows a number of these massacre sites as of 1985. Attacks on civilian targets intensified in 1986–1987, when under Gorbachev they were the worst ever.

Human Rights Abuses. In 1984 the United Nations named a rapporteur to report on human rights in Afghanistan twice a year: once to the General Assembly and once to a commission in Geneva. Those reports describe a continuing pattern of serious human rights abuses.

The main prison in Kabul, designed to hold only a few thousand common criminals, has held more than 20,000–25,000 political prisoners from the start of the regime. According to the U.S. State Department, prisoners are held in cells of 300 to 400 persons with no room to sit or lie down. Another report tells of single cells in which more than 800 Afghan children aged eight to fifteen were being held; and the regime promised to release them if their parents "let them be used as spies in Kabul and Pakistan."[27]

> Torture and mistreatment of prisoners continue to be widespread and systematic. . . . During incommunicado detention, physical and psychological torture is used. . . . Prisoners are beaten; subjected to electric shocks; burned with cigarettes; immersed in cold water or snow; forced to watch other people being tortured; placed in cells with the corpses of other torture victims; and deprived of water, food, and sleep.[28]

In 1987 the UN rapporteur concluded that there were over 50,000 political prisoners being held by the Afghan regime.[29] The fate of an Afghan high school teacher arrested in 1981 on suspicion of involve-

FIGURE 3-1
Known Massacres and Aerial Attacks on Afghan Villages by Soviet and Soviet-backed Afghan Forces, Late 1985

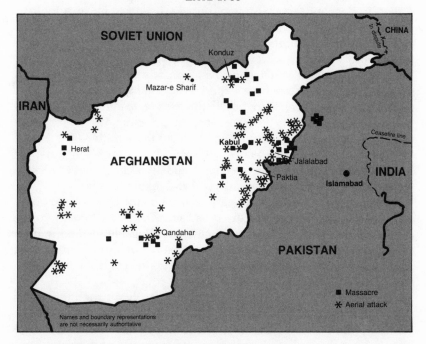

NOTE: Map also shows cross-border attacks in Pakistan.
SOURCE: Adapted from U.S. Department of State, *Afghanistan: Six Years of Soviet Occupation*, Special Report no. 135, December 1985, p. 12.

ment with the resistance provides a clear sense of the horrors visited on these prisoners:

> After Nasery endured 13 nights of torture and 13 days without sleep, . . . three agents came to the cell and said they were taking her to another place. As they led her into the new room, she started to gag. The room smelled of rotten meat. It was dim. Her eyes adjusted slowly to the light. Her head was bowed and the first thing she saw was a severed finger. She jerked her head away. And then she saw a severed foot, a leg, clumps of hair, what looked like eyes, a woman's breast, every imaginable part of the human body. "Go see your boyfriend," one of the agents said, laughing, as he pushed her across the room. She slipped in fresh blood and tried to pull back from the dead body of a young man

47

half-covered by a bloody sheet at the end of the wall. "You can sleep with him tonight. This is the room where your fate will be decided."[30]

Evidence suggests that from the fall of 1978 until at least 1984, Soviet troops and their Afghan proxies used chemical and toxic weapons.[31] With the same type of weapons the Soviet Union and its allies killed tens of thousands of civilians in Laos after the consolidation of the Communist regime there in the late 1970s. The State Department reports that when toxic weapons were used, "guerrilla fighters in Afghanistan have experienced fatality rates of up to 70 percent, and large civilian populations have experienced rates of nearly 100 percent."[32] The State Department estimates "47 separate chemical attacks with a claimed death toll of more than 3,000."[33]

Although the United States led a worldwide protest against the Soviet use of toxins, reports as late as mid-1989 claim that the Kabul regime has returned to using chemical and toxin weapons.

Among the most vicious weapons used by the Soviet Union have been booby trap bombs disguised as toys intended to maim young children who pick them up out of curiosity. Reliable testimony from refugee sources, neutral relief agencies, and numerous foreign and Afghan physicians indicates that thousands of children have been killed or maimed by these bombs.[34]

The infant mortality rate has jumped sharply during these years of war and repression, as high as 50 percent in some areas. In addition, more than 80 percent of the country's schools (about 2,000) have been destroyed, as have a hundred hospitals and several hundred mosques. One report says that almost all indigenous doctors and health personnel have been either killed, imprisoned, or driven into exile, resulting in a resurgence of diseases like malaria and diphtheria that had long been under control. Barnett Rubin concludes that these diseases explain why infant mortality has reached 300 to 400 per 1,000 (compared with a rate of about 18 per 1,000 in the United States and an average of about 115 per 1,000 in other developing countries at Afghanistan's prewar per capita income of about $200).[35]

Between 1980 and 1985 more than 50,000 Afghans were sent to the Soviet Union for training, of whom almost 24,000 were young people, 20,000 of them children between four and eight. Up to 400,000 Afghans may have been sent to the Soviet Union for education and indoctrination.[36] Among these children sent to the Soviet Union about 10,000 at any one time were there for long-term civil and military training. According to the State Department, credible reports indicate that the regime kidnaps Afghan children for use as spies.

Economic Disruption. The Afghan economy has declined but less than might be expected. Cumulative inflation through 1987 has been about 300 percent. Food production has decreased, with overall damage since the invasion amounting to about 5 to 10 percent of the cultivated areas.[37] Some contend in 1989 that the economy is in serious crisis, however, citing prefamine conditions in certain regions.[38]

According to one careful analysis, Afghanistan, which is extremely rich in minerals and natural gas resources, has been forced to "pay" the Soviets for the invasion and occupation. This analysis concludes that between 1979 and 1987 from 70 billion to as much as 500 billion cubic feet of natural gas has been "sold" to the Soviet Union at only about a fifth the comparable world price. The Soviets have thus received a direct royalty from Afghan gas of up to $600 million per year.[39]

Another source claims that the massive increase in the import of "industrial products" from the Soviet Union after 1979—products for which Afghanistan has to pay—was substantially the very Soviet military equipment used to invade and occupy the country. A member of a Gorbachev delegation visiting India in 1986 said in an interview that the war in Afghanistan was costing Moscow nothing:

> We are paid for everything we are sending to Afghanistan. . . . All our expenses—I state all twice—are paid by Afghanistan. . . . There is a giant gas field in the northern part of Afghanistan, and by supplying the gas, Afghanistan is paying us for everything. . . . Afghanistan is supplying us not only with gas . . . but also with fruit, with skins and agriculture, cotton.[40]

The Soviet Union has been siphoning off over these years many of the natural resources and much of the hydroelectric power from the northern region of Afghanistan along the Soviet border. In addition, according to Elie Krakowski, a seasoned observer of Soviet activity in Afghanistan, the Soviets have followed a markedly different strategy in the north. There, in the Oxus River basin on the other side of the towering Hindu Kush mountains, the land is flatter, and the people for the most part have the same ethnic background as those immediately bordering them in Soviet Central Asia—Tajiks, Turkomans, and Uzbeks.

According to Krakowski, the Soviets have embarked on a strategy intended to absorb the northern region—formally or informally—into the Soviet Union. As he puts it, "Moscow has sought both to exploit and to build up the northern region while at the same time wreaking havoc, destruction, and desolation on the rest of the country."[41]

Moreover, while the Soviets have tried to depopulate other regions of Afghanistan, they have sought to keep and co-opt the population in the north. The Soviets, he says, have undertaken economic development efforts, including the construction of two dams. They have also apparently revived a long-dormant separatist movement in the north. Further, the Soviet Union has established a separate administration for the north, and a number of the northern villages when occupied by the Soviets enacted town-to-town agreements with their counterparts in Soviet Central Asia.

In sum, most of Afghanistan's richest natural resources are in the northern part of the country, the peoples of which are ethnically akin to those in the adjacent Soviet border areas, and the topography makes it much easier to control the population.

Soviet-Afghan Military and Political Actions

Virtually all observers agree that the Soviet leadership expected its massive invasion and the violently installed new Communist leadership to suppress the rebellion quickly and quash all serious resistance to the puppet regime. By the spring of 1980, however, the Kremlin decided it would need a strategy for a much longer-term occupation.

With about 20,000 troops in Afghanistan before the invasion, the Soviets had added another 20,000 by the end of 1979. By the summer of 1980, their expeditionary force had swelled to about 85,000, backed by another 30,000 Soviet combat forces on the Soviet side of the Afghan border participating directly in combat inside Afghanistan as needed. As indicated in table 3–3, total Soviet combat forces inside Afghanistan grew to about 120,000 by 1987, supplemented by another 30,000 in contiguous Soviet areas, for a total of about 150,000.

The Afghan Army. During this same time, the Afghan army decreased from a precoup strength of about 110,000 to only about 89,000 in 1980. Afghan armed forces remained much smaller than they had been before the Communist coup; by 1987 they had dwindled to 50,000 in the army, 30,000 in the militarized police (under the Khalqi Interior Minister Gulabzoi), and 20,000 in the secret police for a total of about 100,000. The Afghan army was decimated by desertions, and what was left was distinguished by ineffectiveness and low morale. By the end of 1988 it had shrunk to a mere 43,000.

Estimates of the resistance forces—the mujahedin—are more difficult to arrive at, since they are mostly guerrilla volunteers. But by 1987 the number of resistance fighters in combat at any one time had grown to about 120,000—with an estimated 120,000 more available from their home villages and from bases outside of Afghanistan,

TABLE 3–3
SOVIET-AFGHAN REGIME FORCES, 1978–1988
(in thousands)

	1978	1979	1980	1981	1982	1983	1984	1985	1986	1987	1988
Soviet Union											
In Afghanistan	20	40	85	85	85	105	115	115	115	120	60
Used against Afghanistan		30	30	30	30	30	30	30	30	30	30
Subtotal	20	70	115	115	115	135	145	145	145	150	90
Afghan Regime											
Armed forces	110	89	43	45	55	75	60	55	55	50	40
Armed police										30	30
Secret police										20	20
Tribal militias											25
Subtotal	110+	89+	43+	45+	55+	75+	60+	55+	55+	100+	105+
Total	130	159	158	160	170	210	205	200	200	250	195

NOTE: Soviet forces for 1981 and 1982 were assumed to be the same as in 1980; for 1985 and 1986, the same as in 1984. No estimates for Afghan armed police, secret police, or tribal militias were available except for 1987 and 1988, as indicated. Therefore the Afghan subtotals are minimal estimates. Numbers in italics are author's estimates based on the data.

SOURCES: U.S. Department of State, *Afghanistan: Six Years of Soviet Occupation*, Special Report no. 135, December 1985, p. 8; State Department, *Afghanistan: Five Years of Soviet Occupation*, December 1984, p. 2; State Department, *Afghanistan: Eight Years*, p. 16; and State Department, *Afghanistan: Soviet Occupation and Withdrawal*, Special Report no. 179, December 1988.

principally in Pakistan. As of 1989 there were roughly 350,000 Afghan resistance fighers, roughly half of them actively fighting at a given time.

Soviet Military Tactics. After he came to power in 1985, Mikhail Gorbachev escalated the Afghan war. He appointed a new commander and ordered changes in the Kabul government to broaden its support. In 1986 he invited the world press to witness what the State Department called a "Soviet withdrawal deception." In the summer of 1986, Gorbachev announced: "Before the end of 1986, six regiments will be returned from Afghanistan to the homeland. . . . These units will return to their areas of permanent deployment in the Soviet Union and in such a way that all those who are interested can easily verify this."[42]

A U.S. government analysis noted that the air defense units withdrawn were insignificant, since the mujahedin lacked an air force, and that the tanks being removed had probably been deployed just shortly before, to fill out the withdrawal parade. Gorbachev also introduced new and improved motorized rifle regiments to replace the ones withdrawn. Two previous "withdrawals" had occurred: one in 1980, several weeks before the Moscow Olympics, and another in early 1986, shortly before the UN vote on Afghanistan.

In nine years of constant warfare, the Soviets changed their tactics. Initially, "they concentrated on major cities and on areas along the road between Kabul and the Soviet Union. They launched large attacks, with up to 20,000 troops in their frequent drives into the Panjsher Valley and their high-altitude carpet bombing." In 1984 they announced that they would seal the Pakistan border. From then on they put great effort into stopping the flow of supplies to the resistance, increasingly relying on helicopters and small unit tactics. Elite Soviet commando units were now used more and more frequently in these small raids, night ambushes, and fast attacks on resistance supply lines and bases. These tactics were successful for a time in the mid-1980s, but the resistance learned how to counter them. Then in 1986 the United States began supplying the resistance with Stinger shoulder-fired anti-aircraft missiles. These missiles began to take an increasingly heavy toll on helicopter gunships.[43]

A third tactical phase for the Soviets began in 1987. By then they were stalemated, no longer completely controlling the air. They conducted fewer operations in the border areas, reduced their efforts at supply interdiction, and shifted their emphasis to operations intended to keep the resistance off balance while the Soviets built up the defenses of the major cities. In the summer of 1987, Soviet forces pulled entirely out of some isolated bases.

The Soviets gave out no casualty figures until mid-1988, but by 1984 cumulative Soviet casualties (killed and wounded) were estimated by U.S. analysts at about 20,000 to 25,000; 1985, 30,000; and by 1987, 33,000 to 38,000.[44]

Soviet Political Tactics. On the political front, the Soviets faced two challenges: to resolve or reduce the struggle between the two factions of the Afghan Communist party and to create some semblance of popular support for the Communist Afghan regime. The Kremlin clearly preferred to work with the Parcham faction, which was willing to use popular front coalitions if they seemed likely to serve its purposes. Getting rid of Amin and installing the Parcham leadership had been a major reason for the Soviet invasion.

In December 1980, the regime established the National Fatherland Front (NFF) through which it hoped to co-opt non-Communist tribal, religious, and other communal leaders in addition to the Communist-established unions and social organizations. Few non-Communist Afghans, however, were willing to take part.

Although the Kabul regime continued its repression, it made significant efforts to moderate its symbolic tone, blaming the dead Amin for the actions that had aroused opposition. Religion was no longer criticized and, for even greater effect, Communist leaders now made a show of their devotion to Islam. In 1981, to create the appearance of a broader government, Sultan Ali Keshtmand, who comes from the minority Shiite rather than the predominant Sunni community, was made prime minister, serving until 1988. He was reappointed in mid-1989 as Soviet agreements were being reached with Shiite Iran.

In the effort to stabilize PDPA power and win public support, the regime shuffled the cabinet and party constantly over the next several years, most of these changes reinforcing Parcham's dominance. By mid-1983, Parcham had achieved almost total control of the Communist central committee, while Khalq clung to its grip on the Ministry of Interior and the militarized police and retained significant influence over a number of military officers.

In late 1985, prodded by Gorbachev, Kabul again launched a major campaign for "national reconciliation" designed to undercut support for the resistance, win public support, and project an international image of legitimacy. In April 1985 the regime convened a Grand Assembly (called a *Loya Jirga*) made up of hand-picked tribal leaders and local assembly party delegates from a number of areas. The regime promulgated a new constitution and made major efforts to win the support of Pushtun border tribes by offering concessions if they would oppose the resistance. For the most part this effort failed.

Succeeding in neither pacifying the country nor pulling the Party together, Babrak Karmal was replaced in 1986 both as president and as secretary general of the Communist party by the KGB-trained Najibullah, who had headed the KhAD (Afghan secret police) since January 1980. Stepping up the pace of this "national reconciliation" strategy in January 1987, Najibullah offered to include non-Communists in the government if they were willing to "accept the irreversibility of the Afghan revolution." This proposal had three main elements: (1) a unilateral cease-fire (never observed); (2) participation in the regime by opposition representatives, creating a "national unity government"; and (3) the 5–6 million refugees would be encouraged to return. As the State Department put it, the purpose of the national reconciliation campaign was to convince the Afghan people to " 'reconcile' themselves to continued PDPA [Communist] domination."[45]

With the Stinger-armed resistance gaining effectiveness, and confronted by the failure of its cosmetic political moves, the Kabul regime convened another Grand Assembly in 1987, announced yet another new constitution, and changed the name of the country from the Democratic Republic of Afghanistan to the Republic of Afghanistan to make it sound less like a Soviet satrapy. Kabul also announced that it was not "Socialist."

Through all of these political maneuvers and posturings, the Kabul regime never did manage to win any noticeable increase in popular support. The people recognized the cosmetic nature of its overtures, as the regime continued to pursue brutally repressive policies and had to rely on forced conscription. Draftees were thrown into battle with little or no training, with predictable results: high casualties and desertions. In early 1988 the momentum both politically and militarily was clearly with the Afghan resistance movements.

Afghan Resistance Movements

Nasir Shansab, an Afghan analyst, describes how, slowly and gradually, the anti-Communist armed resistance began to build after the people's initial submission following the April 1978 coup: "During its first days in office," he wrote, "the new government launched a campaign to portray itself as benevolent, forgiving, and intent upon serving the people. . . . Since the Communists had such a firm grip on power, the hostility the population felt toward them dissipated into feelings of hopelessness and resignation."[46]

He tells how the Communist leaders "sent out thousands of inexperienced cadres . . . high school and university students who had interrupted their studies on party orders to serve the rural communization campaign."[47] Their lack of respect for traditional Afghan values—especially in the countryside—and the simultaneous repression led to the emergence of the resistance.

The first reported rebellion, according to this account, occurred in October 1978 and was harshly extinguished by government tanks and bombing. The Herat rebellion of March 5, 1979, led to the killing of some twenty-five thousand civilians in government and Soviet reprisals. By the summer of 1979 the first known mutiny of army units had occurred; in crushing it, the regime reportedly killed more than four hundred officers and men. The initial insurrections were isolated. In each case government forces were able to stamp them out quickly, going from house to house in the insurgent area and immediately executing any young men they found. By 1979, with hundreds of thousands of refugees in Pakistan and Iran, resistance organizations began to emerge and to seek recruits among the refugees for combat inside Afghanistan.

By 1981 the regular Afghan army, diminished by thousands of desertions to the resistance, was incapable of military effectiveness. Soviet and Afghan government forces had relinquished efforts to keep a presence in all provinces by the middle of 1981.[48] Although by 1982 Soviet "massive sweep" operations had some temporary success, as soon as Soviet forces withdrew, the resistance, armed largely with captured Soviet weapons, would reclaim dominance in the countryside. Shansab writes:

> By 1983 the resistance was better armed than ever before, had gained valuable battlefield experience, had strengthened its organizational structure, and was confident that it could continue the struggle indefinitely. . . . Most units had heavier weapons . . . [and] had come to see that mobility and surprise were their best weapons, and that they should avoid frontal and prolonged contact with the enemy's superior firepower.[49]

The First Resistance Coalition. In 1985 the resistance took its first steps toward establishing a loose coalition of the seven major political parties leading the struggle; that coalition continues to the present. By this time the resistance encompassed most of the population inside Afghanistan, refugees in Iran and Pakistan, and others in exile. On the military side, the resistance included hundreds of groups all over the country. By 1987 a Soviet army correspondent gave the following description of a resistance supply train: "Caravans sometimes number up to 300 or 400 pack animals. They travel not only on camels but they use trucks and tractors. Their guards are mobile—on horseback or motorcycles."[50]

Western sources estimated that by the beginning of 1987 the resistance or mujahedin had inflicted more than 25,000 casualties on the Soviets, destroyed 800 aircraft, and destroyed or captured more than 3,000 vehicles. By this time Western sources believed Moscow's intervention consumed the equivalent of $3–12 billion annually.[51] In its support of the resistance effort, the United States reportedly provided 150 Stinger anti-aircraft launchers to the resistance in 1986 and shipped at least 600 more the following year.[52] A U.S. government analysis assessed the strength of the mujahedin in 1987:

> Improving resistance strength also comes from more training and combat experience (which leads to better tactics), expanded cooperation (inter-group fighting has steadily declined), and the rapid development of a communications and supply network. . . . The resistance's cumulative military and political successes have greatly boosted their morale, which, in 1987, rose to its highest level since the invasion.[53]

In January 1987 the resistance responded to Najibullah's call for national reconciliation. The seven leaders of the resistance alliance appeared together before a demonstration of hundreds of thousands of Afghan refugees and mujahedin to publicly denounce the Communist regime in Kabul. The program they announced was an uncompromising demand: "A total and unconditional withdrawal of Soviet forces; an interim Mujahideen government, which would hold free and fair elections; and, resistance unity and arbitration of inter-party disputes."[54]

In July 1987 the resistance again rejected the regime's proposals, renewing its earlier assurances that after the Soviets left, the resistance would not wreak indiscriminate vengeance on personnel of the Kabul regime. The resistance coalition promised to pursue a non-aligned foreign policy and maintain "correct relations" with all Afghanistan's neighbors.

The Resistance Alliance. The resistance alliance that emerged from this political and military cooperation against Moscow and Kabul consists of seven major organizations, all Sunni led. Three have programs calling for the restoration of secular institutions with a loose central government essentially based on the Afghan concept of the *jirga*, or assembly. Grounded in revivalist Islamic movements, the other four groups want religion to have the dominant role in the new government of Afghanistan. They would prefer to see the new government rest on an assembly called a *shura*, which emphasizes membership by clergy and deference to Islamic law.

Abdul Rashid explains the difference between these two institutional bases for possible future government:

> The *jirga* . . . (assembly) is a uniquely Afghan political institution which may be on the village level or on a larger scale—regional, tribal or communal. The jirga is called to deal with specific issues, and all adult male members of the concerned community participate in decision-making in accordance with conventional codes. While of course Islamic law is always implicit in societal decisions, and religious figures may participate in a jirga, it is . . . essentially communal and secular.

On the other hand, as Rashid explains:

> The *shura* is a distinctively Islamic governmental institution found throughout the Muslim world—a consultative and advisory body whose members are drawn from the religious community, particularly those well-versed in Islam. Their role as advisors to a government or ruler has distinctly religious overtones.[55]

Compromise between the two views of a future Afghan government, however, may be possible. Both elements of the resistance coalition agree on the importance of Islam as the guiding religious principle of the society, and both accept the idea of consensual decision making through an assembly in which elected representatives of the society participate. The rejection by the four groups proposing Islamic government of any possible restoration of the monarchy and their demand for a dominant formal role in government for Islam are major disputed issues.

Table 3–4 names the seven Sunni-led resistance organizations, which are based in Pakistan, and the Shiite resistance groups based in Iran.[56]

Among the three "secular" parties, the National Islamic Front for Afghanistan or NIFA (also known as Mahaz) is led by Pir Sayed Ahmad Gailani, a hereditary Sufi Moslem leader; the NIFA program calls for secular government founded on Islamic law and Afghan traditions with a parliament based on free elections. A second group, the Movement for the Islamic Revolution of Afghanistan, is headed by Maulawi Mohammad Nabi Mohammadi, a former professor of religion and Afghan parliament member; it follows a centrist program calling for popularly elected government based on Islamic law and

---

TABLE 3–4
ORGANIZED RESISTANCE TO THE COMMUNIST REGIME IN AFGHANISTAN

PAKISTAN-BASED "UNITY OF SEVEN"[a]

Proposing secular governance

National Islamic Front for Afghanistan/NIFA (Mahaz-i-Milli Islami Afghanistan). Led by Pir Sayed Ahmad Gailani.

Movement for the Islamic Revolution of Afghanistan (Harakat-i-Inqilab-i-Islami Afghanistan). Led by Maulawi Mohammad Nabi Mohammadi.

National Front for the Rescue of Afghanistan (Jabba-i-Milli Najat-i-Afghanistan). Led by Professor Sibgatullah Mojadidi.

Proposing Islamic governance

Islamic Party/Khalis (Hezb-i-Islami/Khalis). Led by Maulawi Mohammad Younis Khalis.

Islamic Society of Afghanistan (Jamiat-i-Islami Afghanistan). Led by Professor Burhanuddin Rabbani (a Tajik, Rabbani is the only non-Pushtun party leader).

Islamic Union to Free Afghanistan (Ittihad-i-Islami B'rai Azad-i-Afghanistan). Led by Abdul Rasul Sayyaf (a Sunni, but with close times to Saudi Wahabi Islam).

Islamic Party/Hekmatyar (Hezb-i-Islami/Hekmatyar). Led by Engineer Gulbuddin Hekmatyar.

IRAN-BASED ORGANIZATIONS

Organization for Victory (Sazman al-Nasr).

Islamic Movement (Harakat-i-Islami). Led by Sheikh Asaf Mohseni.

Party of God (Hezb-i-Illahi).

Combined Friends of the Islamic Revolution (Jabba Mutehid-i-Inqilab-i-Islami).

NOTE: Sunni are 80 percent of the population, and Shiite are 20 percent.

a. The Pakistan-based organizations are predominantly mainstream Sunni; all but one leader is Pushtun. The Iran-based organizations are predominantly Shiite.

SOURCE: Author.

the traditional *Loya Jirga*. Mohammadi, who is vociferously anti-Communist, reportedly receives considerable support from tribal leaders and mullahs as well as the urban middle class.

The third secular party, led by Sibgatullah Mojadidi, a member of one of the most respected religious families in the country, is the National Front for the Rescue of Afghanistan, which calls for a return to the traditional institutions of pre-Communist Afghanistan, including a constitutional monarchy. Mojadidi took his M.A. from al-Azhar University in Cairo and taught Islamic theology at Kabul University in the 1950s; King Zahir imprisoned him in the 1960s on suspicion of plotting to assassinate Khrushchev. Mojadidi was chosen to head the resistance interim government formed in 1989.

Of the four main religious or "Islamist" parties, the Islamic party (Hezb-i-Islami) of Younis Khalis split from the original Islamic party, formed after the 1973 Daoud coup to advocate the Islamic revival. The Khalis group is comparatively less radical and has at times moved closer to the three secular groups. Khalis, an author, editor, and teacher of Islamic studies in the 1950s, became politically active in 1965 and went into hiding after the Daoud coup. In 1985 he was chosen to be the first spokesman for the resistance alliance, and in October 1987 the field commanders chose him as the resistance leader for the following eighteen months.

A second Islamist group, the Islamic Society or Jamiat-i-Islami led by Burhanuddin Rabbani, the only major leader who is not Pushtun, also split from the original Islamic party in 1978 to establish the Jamiat. Since 1984 it has reportedly moderated its original support for the radical Islamic revival program and gained the allegiance of many non-Pushtun groups in northern and western Afghanistan. Two of the best-known mujahedin commanders, Ahmad Shah Massoud of Panjsher and Ismail Khan of Herat, are affiliated with this party. Rabbani took his doctorate in Islamic philosophy from al-Azhar University in 1968 and later became dean of the faculty of Islamic law at Kabul University. He joined the Islamic movement there in 1968, was elected its leader in 1972, escaped arrest in 1974, and moved to Pakistan.

A third group, the Islamic Union to Free Afghanistan, or Ittihad-i-Islami, was originally the first attempt at an alliance of resistance groups and, when that collapsed, survived as a party. Gradually it lost support and followers because of its overemphasis on political, diplomatic, and propaganda efforts, its paucity of field operations, and its involvement with Arab supporters of the Wahabi sect eager to convert Afghans. It continues to receive significant financial support from Saudi Arabians and often sides with the Hekmatyar faction.

Ittihad's leader, Abdul Rasul Sayyaf, earned his M.A. at al-Azhar University, taught at Kabul University, and was active in the prewar Islamist movement. Imprisoned during the mid-1970s, he was released in a post-Soviet invasion amnesty in 1979, fled to Pakistan, and in 1982 became chairman of the first effort to form a seven-party alliance.

Finally, the Islamic Party (Hezb-i-Islami) of Gulbuddin Hekmatyar was formed in Pakistan after the 1973 Daoud coup by Afghans associated with the Islamic revivalist movement and the militant international Muslim Brotherhood. In the 1970s both Khalis and Rabbani broke with Hekmatyar to form their own parties. According to widespread reports, its "members have declined significantly. . . . [It] remains important, in part because of ties to Pakistan's influential Jamaat Islami political party . . . and to the Muslim Brotherhood."[57] Hekmatyar, a Pushtun born in 1947, was an engineering student at Kabul University and reportedly spent four years in the Afghan Communist party. Said to have been arrested in 1972 for killing a Maoist student, he fled to Pakistan where he joined other exiles in founding the Islamic party and instigating an anti-Daoud insurrection attempt in 1975.

Some observers believe that effective unity within the resistance is impossible because of the differences between the three groups calling for secular government and the four demanding an Islamic type of government in postliberation Afghanistan. An analysis of the historical development, leadership, and current situation of the resistance alliance, however, suggests that at least among the first five of the seven Pakistan-based groups listed in table 3–4 a basis for consensus can be found. Each of the three organizations calling for secular government includes many religious leaders, and leaders of all three have long-established relationships with important Islamic religious communities: Gailani, the leader of a Sufi religious order; Mohammadi, the former leader of an influential Islamic school; and Mojadidi, a leader of one of the most respected Afghan religious families.

At the same time, the Islamic party under Khalis, as well as Rabbani's Islamic Society (Jamiat), may perhaps have become more willing to consider a governmental form that is far less a radical theocracy than that demanded by Hekmatyar.

The most disruptive element in the seven-party alliance is Hekmatyar's group, widely described as calling for the "most radical-revivalist Islamic theocracy," as "pro-Khomeini," "pro-PLO," and "violently anti-American and anti-Western as well as anti-Soviet."[58] There are many questions about Hekmatyar; some in the resistance believe that he conspired with the Kabul regime and that his group killed a number of effective commanders of the other parties.[59] In July 1989 Hekmatyar's group reportedly ambushed and either killed immediately or executed soon thereafter perhaps thirty Afghan rebel leaders, including over half a dozen senior field commanders, all from Jamiat.[60] The fact that Hekmatyar's Hezb also probably operates out of Iran, where it is called *Jundullah* and is managed jointly with the leftist Iranian Revolutionary Guards, raises further questions.

Little is known about the resistance organizations that operate from Iranian territory with the support of the Iranian government. One analysis concluded that these would almost inevitably be Shiite Moslem groups, and that since Shiites are only about 20 percent (or less) of the population in Afghanistan and since these groups did not receive a great deal of support while Iran was fighting against Iraq, these groups had not been, and were unlikely to be, a major factor in comparison with the alliance of seven Sunni groups. Further, this analysis reports that up to 1987 the government of Iran "has made strenuous efforts to impose unity among them [the Iranian-based groups]" but failed.[61]

The fighting between the two major Iran-based groups has probably cost thousands of lives. Moreover, "Iranian favoritism toward Shiite groups and leaders drove away the Sunni leaders, reducing Iranian influence with the main Afghan Resistance organizations and the Sunni majority of the Afghan population."[62] These Iran-backed groups are much smaller than the mainstream organizations based in Pakistan. Neither their military role nor their political role is very significant in the resistance or in Afghanistan.

Nevertheless, as events evolve, the Islamic party under Hekmatyar, the Islamic Union under Sayyaf (which tends to side with Hekmatyar), and the Shiite groups supported by Iran could coalesce into an opposition to the postliberation governance plans of the five major parties in the Pakistan-based alliance. The Soviet Union will likely use its June 1989 rapprochement with the post-Khomeini regime in Iran to mount a two-level strategy to split the Afghan resistance. Immediately after this Soviet-Iranian agreement, the Kabul regime replaced its Sunni prime minister (a non-PDPA member) with the Shiite Sultan Ali Keshtmand, a leading Parchami. This choice probably indicated that for Kabul, playing the Iran-Shiite card took precedence over the posture of a "broad-based" government—at least for the time being.

The greater unity of the Pakistan-based resistance alliance was illustrated in 1987 by its decision to hold a *shura* in which each of the seven parties had equal representation. In November 1987 Khalis, then chairman, led a leadership delegation to New York during the UN General Assembly's annual debate on the Afghanistan issue and subsequently met with President Reagan in Washington.

International Support. External aid for the Pakistan-based resistance alliance has come not only from the United States but also from Egypt (before Sadat's death), from China, and from Saudi Arabia. According to the *Economist*, U.S. assistance to the Afghanistan resistance had increased from $75 million in 1983 to $470 million annually in 1986, and totaled about $947 million in those four years.[63] The *Washington Post* estimated that Saudi Arabia was contributing about $250 million annually.[64] President Zia reportedly told an American journalist in January 1988 that Chinese support is as important as U.S. support.[65] If one extrapolates from the admittedly sketchy published accounts, by 1988 resistance organizations might have been receiving more than $1 billion worth of external support annually.

The United States and other countries have also contributed to humanitarian assistance for Afghan refugees in Pakistan. Through April 1989 this aid totaled more than $900 million.[66] The Department of State reported in 1987 that its humanitarian aid program sought "to develop the capabilities of the Afghan resistance Alliance to provide education, health, and agricultural services to the people inside Afghanistan."[67] This support included the provision of textbooks and instructional aids for 660 schools inside Afghanistan, a literacy program for adults, and a health training program that graduated 240 basic health workers every three months. The United States has also helped to establish and supply hospitals inside Afghanistan.

In early 1988, a U.S. government assessment summarized the effectiveness and success of the resistance:

By early 1988, the *mujahidin* had seized the tactical initiative. Soviet troops reacted to situations created by the resistance while attempting to breathe life into the moribund Afghan army. . . . First, the level of cooperation among groups fighting inside the country [Afghanistan] reached unprecedented levels. Mujahidin commanders, aware of the value of such cooperation, set aside previous differences and suspicions. . . . Operational coordination among commanders representing different resistance parties in different localities has increased markedly. Moreover, they have shared captured supplies as well as intelligence, and some groups have shared fighters for given operations. Second, in mid-year, mujahidin commanders decided to avoid costly frontal assaults, opting instead to retain the classic guerrilla strategy of surrounding, isolating, and harassing garrisons and then waiting for them to fall.[68]

Without question, 1987 marked a major positive turning point in the war for the future of Afghanistan. Would the intensified international diplomacy of 1988 sustain or undercut that momentum?

International Alliances, Diplomacy, and Proposals

The international political dimension of this conflict has always been extremely important and complex. The coalition of countries supporting the Kabul Communist regime included the Soviet Union and all of its allies, along with India. While expressing the hope that Soviet troops would leave Afghanistan, India nevertheless refused to condemn the invasion and has maintained diplomatic and economic relations with the Communist regime in Kabul since its inception (some observers also allege clandestine military support). On the other side, Afghanistan's three neighbors—China, Pakistan, and Iran—all opposed the Communist coup and the Soviet intervention and provided help for the anti-Communist resistance forces. Additional support for the resistance has also come from the United States, Saudi Arabia, and other pro-Western Islamic countries.

Balance of Power. Table 3–5 provides an overview of regional balance-of-power politics, which has directly affected the positions taken by Afghanistan's neighbors with regard to the civil war.

The complex balance-of-power relationship that has evolved in the South Asian region is based on a dual system of implicit alliances.[69] The starting point was the withdrawal of Britain from its Indian empire in 1947 and the resulting partition of the Indian subcontinent into two new countries, Moslem Pakistan (East and West) and predominantly Hindu India. The first of three brief wars fought between these two new nations in 1948–1949 resulted in the de facto partition of the still-disputed Kashmir region. In 1965 a second brief war was fought over Kashmir, and this time the Soviet Union mediated a peace agreement. In 1971 Pakistan lost a third war and was forced to allow East Pakistan to become independent as the new state of Bangladesh.

Meanwhile, when the Communist movement took power in China in 1949, it signed a friendship treaty with the Soviet Union. For the first ten years the two countries had cooperative relations, but by 1959 there were visible signs of strain. In the 1960s the Communist regime in China became highly aggressive, seeking to outdo Moscow in providing political and military support to armed anti-Western "liberation" movements. In 1962 Chinese forces seized and occupied

63

TABLE 3–5
Regional Balance-of-Power Politics, 1947–1990

Pakistan vs. India	China vs. India	China vs. USSR
1947: Partition 1948–49: Brief war over Kashmir 1965: Brief war over Kashmir 1971: War; secession of Bangladesh from Pakistan 1972: Agreement on lines of control in Kashmir 1976: Diplomatic relations resumed 1989: Combat on Siachon glacier: summit meeting 1990: Mobilization of border	1954: Nonaggression pact 1962: China attacks and occupies part of India's North-East Frontier Agency; territorial issues unresolved	1949: Friendship treaty 1959: Beginning of serious disputes 1960: Serious border skirmishes 1969: Rumors of possible Soviet preemptive nuclear strike. China's opening to the U.S. begins 1978: Soviet-backed Vietnam invasion of Cambodia, Chinese attacks into Vietnam 1979: Soviet invasion of Afghanistan 1989: Summit

Source: Author.

a part of India's North-East Frontier Agency, which it still claims. Since then India has looked to the Soviet Union for military supplies as well as for political-military support to balance the perceived threat from China. For its part, Pakistan has looked to China to bolster it against the very real threat from its powerful neighbor India. Pakistan has also sought and received political support as well as military and economic aid from the United States since the 1950s.

The Soviet-backed coup in Afghanistan took place in the context of these balance-of-power arrangements, some of them informal and tacit. India was partially aligned with the Soviet Union to balance off what it felt was a dangerously aggressive Communist China. At the same time Pakistan, an anti-Communist Moslem state aligned with the free world, was effectively allied with Communist China.

Since it normalized relations with Beijing in 1978, the United States has sought to maintain friendly relations with all four of these countries and has directed its diplomacy to forestall military confrontations—especially between Pakistan and India, two countries whose historical, cultural, and territorial rivalries have made them a regional powder keg.

From Pakistan's perspective, the Communist coup in Afghanistan and the subsequent Soviet invasion posed a clear and present danger. Islamabad also knew that the Communist regime in Kabul was permitting the al-Zulfiqar terrorist group—established by the sons of the late Prime Minister Zulfiqar Ali Bhutto—to operate from its territory against Pakistan. In addition, the government of Pakistan knew that the Soviet puppet regime in Afghanistan openly threatened to revive the decades-old secessionist movements among Pakistani Pushtuns and Baluchis, which could shatter and destroy Pakistan. In 1985 when Kabul sponsored a national assembly of Pushtuns from both sides of the border and began to proclaim the need for their "reunification," Pakistan's concern became even more acute.[70]

From 1978 on, Kabul also threatened to support a separatist movement in Pakistan's vast Baluchistan province, citing its own (tiny) Baluch population and a supposed Pushtun-Baluch relationship. In 1985 Kabul openly called for Pushtun and Baluchi ethnic groups to secede from both Iran and Pakistan and unite under Afghan sovereignty. Babrak Karmal minced no words: "Pushtun and Baluchi brothers, unite. . . . Wherever you live, defend the honor and dignity of the borders of your sacred land, the free, independent, and new revolutionary Afghanistan."[71] Beginning in the 1980s, the Afghan Communist regime was also training an army of (Pakistani) Baluch and Pushtun tribesmen for armed actions in Pakistan. Such armed insurgency, aimed at the dismemberment of Pakistan, would have suited India's interest in further weakening a neighbor with which it had fought three wars. For its part India allegedly supported a separatist movement in Pakistan's southeastern Sind province.

From the Soviet point of view, a consolidated Communist Afghanistan, taking the military risks and paying the political costs for ethnic-based armed subversion, might well accomplish Moscow's geopolitical purpose of neutralizing Pakistan, a strong U.S. ally and a perceived obstacle to further Soviet ambitions in the Persian Gulf, the Indian Ocean, and south Asia. At the same time it would weaken Iran, a radical, fanatically Islamic regime whose influence on tens of millions of Moslems in the Soviet Union could be a source of trouble in the years ahead.

From China's perspective, the Soviet Union, with which it shares a border of more than 4,000 miles, was an ever-present danger. Beijing, convinced that the 1978 Vietnamese invasion of Cambodia could not have taken place without Soviet encouragement and support, was well aware that Moscow backed the 1978 coup in Afghanistan. China, therefore, had a keen interest in stemming the tide of Soviet aggression in its immediate region, fearing that failure to do so would encourage further Soviet expansion at its expense, notwithstanding the deterrent factor of the Chinese thermonuclear arsenal.[72]

For its part, Tehran undoubtedly knew that Kabul had invited two pro-Soviet Iranian groups—the Communist Tudeh party and the armed Fedayeen-e-Khalq guerrillas—to set up operations on Afghan territory. As of 1983, these groups continued to operate from Afghanistan.[73]

Strategy to End Aid to the Resistance. Just as they used the theme of national reconciliation to try to reduce popular resistance internally, the Soviet Union and its Afghan ally also attempted to use international negotiations as a means of cutting off support for the resistance. In both cases these political and diplomatic maneuvers began in 1980. Two months after the Soviet invasion, Armand Hammer—a U.S. industrialist with close business, family, and political ties to the Soviet Union dating back to the 1920s—was saying that Leonid Brezhnev had told him Moscow wanted to withdraw its troops but needed assistance from other countries to do so.[74]

In 1982 the secretary general of the United Nations began "proximity talks" between the regime in Kabul and the government of Pakistan, which refused to legitimize Kabul by dealing with it directly. Although the United States and the Soviet Union did not participate directly, they were consulted; the Afghan resistance was excluded. Clearly, the Soviet Union and its Afghan client were using these talks and various proposals they put forth over the years to create the perception that they were flexible and interested in a reasonable settlement. These moves, along with various unilateral cease-fire announcements, reconciliation proposals, and troop rotations deceptively announced as troop reductions, were all part of a calculated strategy to reduce international opposition to Soviet intervention in behalf of the puppet regime in Kabul.

After Mikhail Gorbachev took power in the Kremlin in 1985, the pace of the Soviet political and diplomatic offensive quickened, and Soviet and Afghan coercive operations against Pakistan were sharply escalated.

The first Reagan-Gorbachev summit meeting took place in Geneva in November 1985. The following month the Department of State embarked on a major initiative regarding Afghanistan. According to one author:

> The U.S., which had previously declined to provide an advance written guarantee of a UN-negotiated settlement,

sent a letter stating that it was indeed prepared to guarantee such an agreement. . . . Issuance of the letter was justified as being a goodwill gesture intended to encourage Gorbachev's stated desire to find a political solution. Soon after, however, the talks in Geneva reached a dead end. . . . It turned out the Soviets, through their Afghan surrogates, were offering to withdraw only four years *after all aid to the resistance was cut off.*

This former U.S. diplomat concluded that "once again, the Soviets had achieved a significant change in U.S. policy [the decision to provide an advance guarantee of a UN settlement] with nothing but words."[75]

By the spring of 1986 the Soviet Union had changed the Afghan leadership, replacing Karmal with Najibullah. In early 1987 the regime launched another major drive for "national reconciliation," proposing a coalition government. Later that year it suggested that a multiparty government could be restored, led by King Zahir. (Despite the fact that Moscow and Kabul have reportedly floated this proposal in various formulas, the king has said repeatedly he will not participate in any government with Communists.) The Soviet Union also softened its position, saying that it would be willing to withdraw all its troops in eighteen months instead of four years—after all aid to the Afghan resistance had been cut off. Diplomatic activity intensified as both Soviet Foreign Minister Shevardnadze and Under Secretary of State Michael Armacost visited President Zia of Pakistan in January 1987.

In September 1987 the eleventh round of UN-sponsored proximity talks took place. Moscow offered to speed up its withdrawal timetable by two to sixteen months after a cutoff of all outside aid to the resistance. The talks then became deadlocked, and there was no further movement. The following month a delegation of the resistance alliance met with President Reagan, who promised them that U.S. aid would continue until an independent non-Communist government existed in Afghanistan and further stated that he would make no agreement on Afghanistan unless the Afghan resistance also accepted the terms of the negotiated settlement.

Following the stalemate of the UN proximity talks, Pakistan proposed the creation of a UN peace-keeping force as a way to expedite the withdrawal of Soviet troops. This force would monitor the complete cutoff of all outside military aid into Afghanistan in the event of a settlement. Soon thereafter the Soviet Union proposed that Arab countries create a multinational Islamic force to oversee a transitional period in Afghanistan. Soviet envoys reportedly told Arab leaders that Moscow was ready for a phased pullout of troops from Afghanistan in exchange for guarantees of a neutral regime there.

At the same time Armand Hammer announced that since February and March 1987 he had been shuttling between the Soviet Union, Pakistan, and Afghanistan in pursuit of a political settlement. He urged all parties to accept a coalition government with the participation of the former king, an idea fully in accord with the Soviet position. All proposals for restoring the king practically guaranteed a massive split in the resistance. In mid-November 1987 the Soviet foreign ministry spokesman said that "Soviet troops would withdraw from Afghanistan in seven to twelve months, provided an international agreement is signed" and "no other state interferes."[76] The meaning was clear: aid to the resistance would have to be terminated at the *beginning* of the withdrawal.

On November 30, 1987, Armacost apparently linked the cutoff of U.S. aid to the resistance to Soviet willingness to specify a withdrawal date, saying this had been the "sticking point" for many months in U.S.–Soviet talks on this issue.[77] At the same time Najibullah stated that Soviet troops would leave Afghanistan within twelve months after the United States and Pakistan cut off aid to the resistance. These statements were all made on the eve of the December 1987 Reagan-Gorbachev summit in Washington, D.C.

Final Negotiations and the Geneva Agreements

This Washington summit provided the occasion for another round of discussions about Afghanistan. On December 4 in a presummit briefing a senior Gorbachev adviser hinted (as did Najibullah) that the Soviets would withdraw within twelve months if the United States would agree to halt all aid to the resistance *as the withdrawal began*. At the same time the UN mediator held a secret meeting in Geneva with Afghan and Pakistani diplomats in an effort to break the deadlock.

At the U.S.–Soviet summit Gorbachev offered to withdraw Soviet troops in twelve months or less but refused to set a starting date. Although a working group of U.S. and Soviet officials had apparently discussed a cutoff of U.S. aid to the resistance, at the summit President Reagan was reported to hold to his position that the date and duration of a Soviet withdrawal must be set with no link to any preconditions.[78]

At the conclusion of the U.S.–Soviet summit on December 10, 1987, Gorbachev stated that "from the first day" the Soviet timetable for withdrawal is announced, the United States must agree to a "beginning of the end to arms and financial supplies" to the resistance. If the United States did this, the Soviets would cease military operations on the day the timetable was announced.[79] President Reagan, though, explicitly rejected even a temporary cutoff of aid to the resistance before a complete Soviet military withdrawal.

Armacost then "clarified" President Reagan's statement by contradicting it. Reportedly, Armacost reaffirmed the State Department's commitment to stop supplying weapons to the resistance once a timetable for Soviet withdrawal was agreed upon.[80] This sharp difference in views set the stage for a serious political battle within the Reagan administration as the final negotiations on Afghanistan began.

Congressional Support. Since the Soviet invasion, bipartisan congressional support for aid to the Afghan resistance and for its eventual victory had always been broad. A small bipartisan group of senators and congressmen, though, decided to give special attention to the Afghan issue. Foremost among these was Republican Senator Gordon Humphrey of New Hampshire, who was extremely concerned when the State Department contradicted President Reagan's explicit statement that aid to the resistance must continue until all Soviet troops were out and an independent, non-Communist government was in place. From hearings on State Department diplomacy regarding the Afghan issue, Humphrey had concluded that the State Department's 1985 offer to guarantee a UN-negotiated settlement— before its content was known—had been undertaken without the knowledge or consent of President Reagan.[81] The senator was concerned that the State Department, in its rush to reach some settlement with the Soviet Union on this issue, might without the president's knowledge make further compromises that would ultimately prevent the resistance from winning and perpetuate a pro-Soviet regime in Afghanistan.

Senator Humphrey and the bipartisan group of senators and congressmen believed that if the Soviet Union promised to withdraw its troops by a certain date but had a year or so during which aid to the resistance had been cut off, they could undertake such intensive military and covert operations, as well as political destabilization, that the resistance would be too physically weakened and psychologically demoralized to challenge the Communist regime effectively, even if most Soviet troops were withdrawn. These congressmen recognized the difficulty of verification along the thousand-mile Soviet-Afghan border and that the ethnic similarity of populations along the border would make it relatively easy for the Kremlin to bolster the Kabul regime with Soviet troops in Afghan army uniforms or otherwise disguised. They also feared that the Soviets might continue

69

to support the Kabul regime with military operations mounted from bases on Soviet soil, operations that would not be subject to any effective international response.

These congressmen saw an intensification of Soviet efforts to intimidate Pakistan into cutting off aid to the resistance by destabilization, terror, and subversion as likely. All these dangers convinced the legislators that a badly negotiated agreement would be worse than no agreement at all and could deal the resistance a severe—even fatal—blow. President Reagan and a bipartisan coalition in Congress had always defined success in Afghanistan as both the removal of all Soviet troops *and* the establishment of an independent, non-Communist government in place of the Kabul Communist regime.

In December 1987 Senator Humphrey accused the State Department of effectively selling out the Afghan resistance by excluding it from the international negotiations over Afghanistan's fate, just as Allied negotiators at Yalta had decided the fate of Eastern Europe forty years earlier.[82] The deep misgivings among many of President Reagan's supporters about this possibility prompted efforts to reach him directly with this information. Senator Humphrey's analysis was sent along with other material that was to be given to the president in California over the New Year's weekend. Meanwhile, former Defense Secretary Caspar Weinberger was in Washington and asked to speak to the president about this important turning point.[83] Those efforts may have had some effect. On January 4, 1988, the White House reportedly instructed the State Department that U.S. policy would be as follows: no aid cutoff until all Soviet troops had left.[84] A few days later Secretary of State George Shultz, perhaps in response to pressure from the bipartisan coalition in Congress, stressed that the Soviet troop withdrawal must be "front-end loaded" and acquire a "certain inevitability" before the United States would end aid to the resistance—which in any case would be ended gradually, not all at once.

Momentum to Settle. In early January 1988, however, Under Secretary Armacost was in Pakistan meeting with President Zia, and Soviet Foreign Minister Shevardnadze was in Kabul on a working visit. Soon after, Lally Weymouth of the *Washington Post* visited Pakistan, met with President Zia and other senior officials, and reported:

> There is pressure on Pakistan to agree to a settlement at the upcoming Geneva meeting with the Afghan government, scheduled for March 2. . . . Pakistan's President Zia . . . told me in an interview last month that he would not sign the Geneva Accords with the Soviet-backed president of Af-

ghanistan, Najibullah. Zia said he would sign the accords with a coalition government formed of and by Afghans and controlled by the *mujaheddin* and Afghan exiles.[85]

There were essentially four key issues during the final months of negotiation in early 1988. The positions of the main participants and the final outcome are summarized in table 3–6.

The conclusion of this analysis is inescapable: in three out of the four issues the Soviet position prevailed in the final agreements. Only the action of the U.S. Senate blocked the Soviet position on aid to the resistance.

Momentum toward the final negotiations began to build dramatically on February 8, 1988, when Gorbachev offered to withdraw Soviet troops beginning on May 15, 1988, and ending ten months

TABLE 3–6

POSITIONS ON KEY ISSUES IN THE FINAL NEGOTIATIONS ON AFGHANISTAN

	Pakistan, Reagan, U.S. Congress	U.S. State Dept.	USSR/Kabul	Result
Resistance should be included in the negotiations.	Yes	No	No	No
Aid to resistance must continue until all Soviets are out.	Yes	Halt at signing	Halt at signing	Ambiguous; significant U.S. slowdown after signing; cutoff of Stingers for many months
Non-Communist government must replace Najibullah during withdrawal.	Yes	Not needed	Najibullah to stay	Najibullah stayed
Effective verification is required.	Yes	UN symbolic effort	UN minimal team	UN minimal team

SOURCE: Author.

71

later, provided a settlement was reached by March 15, 1988. The Soviets reportedly suggested that half their troops would be removed within the first three months after the pullout began, adding that all Soviet military advisers as well as combat troops would be withdrawn.

During the complex and fast-paced final negotiations to meet the Soviet deadline, the major issues of resistance participation and effective verification received little attention. Not represented at the negotiations and opposed to its content, the resistance refused to accept the final settlement. Moreover, the verification provisions agreed upon were totally inadequate to provide any effective and objective assessment of what would really happen. In the event, although both sides have claimed many hundreds of violations since the final agreement was concluded (as of mid-1989 Kabul alone claimed well over a thousand), the small, fifty-man UN Good Offices Mission divided between Afghanistan and Pakistan has been unable to confirm a single violation by either side.

Determined to see a non-Communist government replace the Najibullah regime during the withdrawal of Soviet troops, Pakistan also wanted the resistance to receive assistance until all Soviet troops had left. On January 24, 1988, President Zia had asserted that he would never sign a settlement with Najibullah or any other Kabul government dominated by the Communists. Yet within weeks his position changed. How did that happen?

For years the Soviet Union had pressured Pakistan with air, artillery, and terrorist assaults—most though not all carried out through its Afghan clients and the agents of KhAD. These increased sharply after Gorbachev took power in 1985. As indicated in table 3-7, the number of Soviet-Afghan attacks jumped from 196 in 1984 to 495 in 1985, 1,761 in 1986, and an estimated 1,843 in 1987. During these years total Pakistani casualties were estimated at about 5,000 by a U.S. government report.[86]

After Gorbachev took office, the terrorist attacks inside Pakistan became more ferocious and more frequent and were clearly coordinated with Communist international negotiations and political operations. That same government report goes on to say,

> Kabul's agents target public facilities like shopping centers and schools. A single bomb blast in Karachi in July [1987] killed more than seventy people. More than 1,000 saboteurs have been arrested in Pakistan in connection with the terror campaign. . . . Many have confessed that they were paid, trained and given targets by Afghan intelligence officials.[87]

TABLE 3-7
CASUALTIES IN PAKISTAN DUE TO BORDER VIOLATIONS BY SOVIET-AFGHAN REGIME FORCES AND TERRORIST BLASTS, 1980–1987

	Air Attacks		Artillery Attacks		Terrorist Explosions		Total	
	Violations	Killed/injured	Violations	Killed/injured	Violations	Killed/injured	Violations	Killed/injured
1980	174	6	25	—	—	—	199	6
1981	94	8	17	—	—	—	111	8
1982	59	—	22	4	2	4	83	8
1983	93	2	41	8	47	31	181	41
1984	119	394	49	62	28	56	196	512
1985	256	57	121	44	118	269	495	370
1986	779	106	495	176	487	1,014	1,761	1,296
1987a	684	742	619	216	540	1,381	1,843	2,339
Total							4,869	4,580

NOTE: Dashes indicate data not available.
a. Data extrapolated from source. The source had data up to and including October 1987; I took the monthly rate and added two more months.
SOURCE: State Department, *Afghanistan: Eight Years*.

73

In March 1988 Lally Weymouth, the *Washington Post* reporter, wrote from Pakistan,

Last July 14 [1987], a remote-control device triggered three car-bomb explosions in Karachi, killing 72 Pakistanis and injuring 260. Then, on Sept. 19, a bomb exploded at a bus stop in Rawalpindi, killing five and injuring 19. These brutal bombings provide just two examples of Moscow's secret war of terror against Pakistan. The Soviet-directed campaign began in the early 1980s, in an effort to pressure Pakistan to stop providing a base of operations for the *mujaheddin* in Afghanistan, and it has escalated sharply during the last two years. . . . The Soviet campaign shifted in 1985 to what [a] Pakistani intelligence report calls "a high-intensity terrorist campaign" aimed at high-impact targets such as urban population centers, transport and communications facilities . . . selected to cause maximum loss of life and property, to generate fear and create widespread panic. . . . One Pakistani expert attributes the change in Soviet terror tactics to Mikhail Gorbachev. When Gorbachev took office in 1985, he argues, the Soviets turned to "real hard-core terrorism. . . . [Under] Gorbachev, it [the bombing] really became a killing operation."[88]

In addition to these and other pressures from Moscow and Kabul, the Zia government was also pressed by the U.S. State Department to agree with its views. The State Department had an important source of leverage that some in Congress believe it may have used. In late September 1987 Congress had failed to renew a legislative waiver permitting continued economic aid to Pakistan despite that country's refusal to allow inspection of its nuclear facilities.[89] Therefore, to obtain the $700 million in military and economic aid, Pakistan was dependent on the State Department to persuade Congress to renew the waiver.

The Pressler amendment, another lever for exerting pressure on Pakistan, required the termination of all U.S. aid to Pakistan unless the president could certify annually to Congress that Pakistan did not possess nuclear weapons and that continuation of U.S. aid would reduce the risk that Pakistan would acquire such weapons.

The State Department, some believed, might have told President Zia that only if he were "reasonable" in the final negotiations on Afghanistan would Pakistan be granted a renewal of the waiver and receive the certification required by the Pressler amendment. Not long after the January 1988 Armacost visit, Pakistan took the first step away from its earlier insistence on the establishment of an independent non-Communist government as an integral part of any negotiated agreement. On January 12, 1988, President Zia and his prime minister declared their acceptance of some Communist involvement in a future Afghan government. Zia went on to say that the resistance leadership would have to be persuaded to compromise on this. Alliance spokesman Younis Khalis, however, reportedly said, "We will never accept any Communist element in a future government of Afghanistan."[90] Pakistan's first public concession was followed a few days later by a new demand from Najibullah: all resistance training camps in Pakistan must be dismantled before any Soviet withdrawal began. He claimed that negotiators in Geneva had already agreed to this.

Timing the Aid Cutoff. Meanwhile, the bipartisan congressional majority led by Senator Humphrey and Democratic Congressman Charles Wilson of Texas was determined to persuade the Reagan administration to maintain military aid to the resistance at least until all Soviet troops were out. As they worked to put this in a formal statement, Secretary Shultz provided them with their only success when he agreed to positive symmetry, whereby each side could aid its ally if the other did. Shultz affirmed that the United States would "insist that at any time we stop any military assistance to the freedom fighters, the Soviet government must stop any assistance to the government in Afghanistan it is supporting."[91] Nevertheless, when a senior State Department official contradicted Shultz's new position a few days later, proresistance senators pressed for a resolution to buttress President Reagan and the bipartisan congressional majority against the perceived preference of the State Department for an early cutoff of aid.[92] On February 29, 1988, the Senate voted unanimously (74–0) to urge the administration to maintain military aid to the Afghan resistance until all Soviet troops had been withdrawn.

In March 1988, Pakistan dropped its insistence that a new transition government be established in Afghanistan before it would sign a Geneva agreement. The issue was resolved when the Soviet Union and Kabul agreed to a "private" negotiating role for the UN mediator who would begin talks with the Afghan parties in trying to form an interim government.

Thus by the end of March President Zia no longer insisted on a new non-Communist Afghan government, and the State Department had agreed to positive symmetry. President Reagan and Secretary Shultz spoke by telephone with President Zia and Prime Minister Mohammed Khan Junejo, reportedly to cement their understanding that, notwithstanding the UN-proposed agreement, both countries would continue aiding the resistance unless the Soviet Union terminated its military aid to the Kabul regime.[93] The Soviet foreign minister immediately rejected this declaration as unacceptable and illegitimate.

In early April 1988, Gorbachev met with Najibullah and announced that the Soviet Union and the Kabul regime had come to an agreement on the timetable of the Soviet withdrawal: the Soviet pullout would begin on May 15, 1988. The United States, they said, had agreed to guarantee the settlement, leaving only the final signing in Geneva. President Zia then declared that the United States and the Soviets had agreed on positive symmetry. The impending agreement, although widely praised in the Western media, was again rejected by the resistance alliance.

Later in April a massive explosion in an ammunition storage facility outside the capital of Pakistan destroyed thousands of tons of weapons intended for the Afghan resistance, an estimated 1,100 people were wounded, and 93 were killed. Most observers suspected the Soviet-directed Afghan KhAD.[94] Nevertheless, the next day President Reagan announced that the United States would serve as coguarantor of the Afghan accords with the Soviet Union and that Shultz would sign the agreements with Shevardnadze and the representatives of Pakistan and the Kabul regime in Geneva on April 14. Hailing the agreements as "a major contribution to the improvement of East-West relations" Reagan reaffirmed that the United States would continue to support the resistance as long as necessary.[95] A. M. Rosenthal, however, raised a number of questions in the New York Times, including the most important one for the future:

> President Reagan still owes the "valiant" Afghan resistance fighters he loves to praise—and the American public—specific answers to specific questions. . . . Precisely what are American plans to help the Afghan resistance win the one political goal for which they have been fighting for 10 years— the establishment of a non-Communist government? Or are we just going to wish them well?[96]

Debate within the U.S. Government. Throughout the last months of debate within the U.S. government about the final terms of the Geneva accords, the key issue had been the timing of the aid cutoff to the Afghan resistance.

In December 1987, in response to the State Department's announcement that it would stop aid as soon as Soviet troops began withdrawing, Senator Humphrey stated, "This contradicted President Reagan's repeated assurances that aid would continue until all Soviet troops were out of Afghanistan." He went on to say, "Our diplomats not only acted contrary to what the president would have wanted but kept him in the dark. . . . [This is a] betrayal. . . . We have no right to endanger the gains the Afghans have made at a terrible price."[97] A number of analysts and commentators, including A. M. Rosenthal, echoed this concern. In late February 1988, Rosenthal wrote that before the end of February Reagan would get a letter "from at least 29 senators of almost every political shading urging him to step in and clear things up. They want him to make sure himself that aid to the resistance is not cut off until all Soviet troops leave Afghanistan and Moscow ceases aid to Kabul."[98]

About the same time, former UN Ambassador Jeane J. Kirkpatrick criticized those in the Reagan administration who were too eager for any agreement. She concluded: "It is inconceivable that the administration of Ronald Reagan would accept a deal that leaves a residual Soviet presence in Afghanistan, a Communist government in Kabul aided by Moscow, while cutting off the flow of assistance to the Afghan resistance. It could not be."[99]

On April 12, 1988, six Republican foreign policy experts and conservative leaders met with President Reagan and his senior advisers, urging him not to sign accords until they provided for the immediate installation of an independent, non-Communist government in place of the Kabul regime. In return, the Afghan resistance would offer safe conduct to all Soviet troops and members of the Kabul regime who wished to leave and amnesty to those staying. Although President Reagan engaged in a spirited discussion with his visitors, he took the advice of the Department of State.[100]

On the night of April 13, 1988, with Secretary Shultz already en route to Geneva, the accords were shown to U.S. senators for the first time. Then on the morning of April 14, 1988, the Geneva accords were signed by representatives of Afghanistan and Pakistan with the Soviet Union and the United States signing as guarantors. There are four separate instruments:

• The first is a bilateral agreement between Afghanistan and Pakistan by which each pledges not to interfere in the internal affairs of the other, including a promise not to threaten or use force in any form in violation of national boundaries.[101]

• In the second instrument, a statement signed by the United States and the Soviet Union, both countries agree to refrain from interfering and intervening in the internal affairs of Afghanistan and Pakistan and to respect the commitments contained in the bilateral agreement between them. This is essentially the guarantee by both the United States and the Soviet Union of the agreement between Pakistan and Afghanistan.

• The third instrument is a bilateral agreement between Afghanistan and Pakistan on the return of refugees from Pakistan to Afghanistan.

- The fourth instrument is an agreement on "the interrelationships for the settlement of the situation relating to Afghanistan." Here the Soviet Union agrees to a phased withdrawal of its troops starting on May 15, 1988. Half the troops were to be withdrawn by August 15, 1988, and the withdrawal completed by February 15, 1989.

The accords also include a memorandum of understanding on the role of the UN secretary general in verifying compliance with all these undertakings. This memorandum provides that the secretary general will designate an "inspection team" of five to fifty military officers, divided between Afghanistan and Pakistan (a maximum of twenty-five in each country), who would monitor compliance with the agreement.

Finally, in a unilateral statement the United States reserved the right to act on the principle of positive symmetry: "It retain[ed] the right to provide military assistance to parties in Afghanistan. Should the Soviet Union exercise restraint in providing military assistance . . . the U.S. . . . [would] similarly exercise restraint."[102] The State Department said that Moscow agreed to this formula in an unpublished exchange of letters April 9–10, 1988. Selig Harrison, in an article in *Foreign Policy*, says that "authoritative Pakistani and American sources state that the Soviet response only took note of the U.S. stand while recapitulating the mutual non-interference pledges made by Afghanistan and Pakistan."[103] The unilateral U.S. statement concludes that "by acting as a guarantor of the settlement, the United States does not intend to imply in any respect recognition of the present regime in Kabul as the lawful government of Afghanistan."[104]

Response to the Accords. The signing of the Geneva accords on April 14, 1988, produced a near-universal international consensus—at least publicly and in the media—that the war in Afghanistan was now "over" and that the Afghan resistance had "won." Some of these optimists assumed that as soon as the Soviet Union began pulling its troops out, the Communist regime would begin to crumble. In fact, a senior State Department official predicted that the Kabul regime would "splinter and fall of its own weight even before the final Soviet pullout . . . and that its early demise would be inevitable."[105]

Others were far more doubtful, pointing out that the Soviet Union clearly wanted a pro-Soviet Communist regime to remain in power in Afghanistan.[106] Critics of the accords, including the author, warned that the Kremlin would set in motion a combination of conciliatory and coercive stratagems designed to end international support for the resistance and weaken the political and military cohesion of the resistance groups. At the same time the Soviets would strengthen the forces of its client in Kabul.

The critics of the accords were also concerned that the State Department, now dominant in shaping Reagan administration foreign policy, would seek to reduce the flow of aid to the Afghan resistance before all Soviet troops were out—taking at face value assurances that the Soviets were reducing their military aid to the Communist regime. These critics pointed out that Moscow, invoking the doctrine of symmetry, could claim to have ceased supplying the Afghan army and could call on the United States to quit aiding the mujahedin.

Lally Weymouth quotes a senior Western diplomat in Kabul as saying: "The Soviet Union doesn't want to abandon Afghanistan. The Soviets want you, by diplomatic means, to help them stay in Afghanistan. . . . They want to deceive your country. . . . Afghanistan isn't Vietnam. Afghanistan is at the border of the Soviet Union. They want to stay and they want the guarantee of the United States that they can stay."[107]

Supporters of the accords, though, emphasized that the withdrawal of Soviet troops by February 15, 1989, would create a major political setback for the Soviet Union. They were convinced all Soviet troops would be withdrawn in the framework of the timetable and that the Communist regime would inevitably be replaced by a new government in Kabul.

After the Geneva Agreements

Far from ushering in an era of peace for beleaguered Afghanistan, the beginning of the implementation of the Geneva accords on May 15, 1988, ignited a new and even more intense period in the Afghan war. Both sides pursued their ultimate objectives with renewed vigor. By their actions the Soviets showed that they intended to use the accords and their own political and military resources to ensure that a strong Communist regime would still be in power in Kabul after all (or most) Soviet troops had been withdrawn. Pakistan and its allies (the United States and China) intended to continue providing aid to the Afghan resistance to aid in the establishment of a new, independent, non-Communist government.

Soviet Goals. During the following months, the Soviets took a series of diplomatic, political, and military steps, both conciliatory and coercive, using carrots and sticks more or less simultaneously.

One major goal of the Soviet Union and its Kabul ally was to persuade the resistance to accept a role in the government of Afghanistan and, of course, to stop its armed opposition. After the national reconciliation approach of 1986 and 1987 failed, a new constitution in 1987 arranged for the formation of political parties other than the PDPA, including an Islamic party, to join the Communists in a "broad-based," that is, coalition, government. Relying on a Soviet script, Najibullah created the facade of a parliamentary democracy in which the Communist party would apparently have only a small role, at the same time stressing the "Islamic" character of the new government.

As provided for in the new constitution, "elections" were held from April 5 to 15, 1988, for the new national parliament. Participation was minimal, and the resistance opposed the elections. As described in a State Department report, there were "no secret ballots; candidate lists were not published until after the polls opened; polling booths were unmanned; and 13-year-old children voted (the legal age is 18)."[108] As a result of this complicated "reverse rigging" maneuver, overt Communist party candidates technically won only about 22 percent of the seats in parliament.

The purpose of the political manipulations, according to the State Department, was to create a legislature in which the Communists would appear to be a minority, thus lending credibility to the policy of national reconciliation. The new prime minister, Mohammed Hassan Sharq, was not a member of the Communist party; his appointment was initially touted as an indication of a new "broad-based" approach. Subsequently, however, published reports that he was and continues to be a longtime clandestine Soviet agent reduced his usefulness in this respect.[109]

A few months later the regime created two more ostensibly independent parties from older party organizations. In the following months both Kabul and Moscow repeatedly strove to portray this new "broadened" regime as a genuine coalition holding legitimate power that the resistance should join.

Reorganization in Kabul. As in the past, Kabul had to pay a price for its efforts to neutralize and divide the mujahedin. Conflicts within the two PDPA factions, Parcham and Khalq, intensified. In October 1988, the Soviet deputy foreign minister, Yuli Vorontsov, who had supervised and coordinated the Communist side of the negotiations while retaining his post as deputy foreign minister, was appointed ambassador to Afghanistan to enhance Soviet influence throughout the crucial period during and after the troop withdrawal.

The October 19, 1988, meeting of the PDPA leadership initiated two sets of changes within the regime. First, within Parcham, some of Babrak's supporters who had never reconciled themselves to his dismissal were purged and replaced by Najibullah's loyalists. At the same time, the leading Khalqi in the regime, Interior Minister Gulab-zoi, who had commanded the special 3,000-man armed police militia, was removed from his post at the Kremlin's behest and bundled off as ambassador to Moscow. These purges opened the way for further political maneuvering by Moscow and Najibullah in the direction of ostensible concessions toward a broad-based government.

This reorganization was followed in November 1988 by the first talks between the Soviet Union and a resistance delegation in Pakistan. In December Soviet representatives met with resistance representatives in Saudi Arabia to discuss the composition of a possible new government, a meeting held against the background of massive Soviet military escalation in Afghanistan.

During 1988 the resistance had become better organized politically. On January 31, 1988, the resistance alliance had called for a government in Afghanistan composed of the resistance, refugees, and Afghan Muslims living in the country. As the State Department reported, "This . . . was as far as the resistance was prepared to go in response to Najibullah's call for a coalition government. As no member of the PDPA would be considered a good Muslim by the resistance, it constituted a rejection of any future role for dedicated PDPA members."[110]

On February 23, 1988, the alliance proposed a more detailed transitional government structure: a supreme council comprising the leaders of the seven resistance parties, a head of state, and a twenty-eight-member cabinet made up of fourteen resistance members, seven refugees, and seven Moslems living inside Afghanistan.

Later in the year, the alliance adopted a constitution based on Koranic law, and in late October 1988 announced a plan for a broad-based *shura* to be elected by Afghans living inside Afghanistan as well as by the millions of Afghan refugees outside. The goal was to have an interim government ready by February 10, 1989.

Moscow's Machinations. Meanwhile, Moscow continued seeking to use the Geneva accords to its own advantage. In early May 1988, Najibullah had made an official visit to India where he was warmly received. Reports suggested that India publicly endorsed him. One Indian official picked up the Soviet propaganda line about the resistance leaders, accusing them of "seeking to install a fundamentalist Islamic regime in Kabul."[111] The timing of this visit conveyed a clear message to Pakistan, ever sensitive to the foreign policy views of its huge and unfriendly neighbor.

On May 14, 1988, the day before the Soviet troop withdrawal was scheduled to begin, Moscow's military commander in Afghanistan announced that his country would leave behind some $2 billion worth of military equipment for the Afghan army. He further promised that 25 percent of the Soviet troops would be out by the time the Reagan-Gorbachev summit in Moscow began on May 30.

As the Soviet troop pullout began, Moscow made certain that it received plenty of international media coverage, then and later, setting a pattern that would be repeated in the coming months. Despite the televised hoopla and well-staged farewell ceremonies for Soviet troops at Afghan airports, in fact no independent way existed to verify exactly how many Soviet troops had been in Afghanistan or how many had left or where they went, and no way to know when and if some were redeployed or later returned in Afghan uniforms to certain major towns and bases.

As the Soviet withdrawals began on May 15, the press repeatedly quoted unnamed U.S. government officials—presumably from the State Department—who said they expected to see the resistance move quickly to take over key towns and provincial capitals. One diplomat cheerfully predicted, "The streets of Kabul will be littered with uniforms as these guys [the Communist forces] go back to their villages."[112] Others believed that only the secret police would stay loyal to Najibullah, that the Soviet pullout would leave him in control only of Kabul and its environs, and even there only briefly before a total collapse.[113]

On May 20 the Afghan regime sent the United Nations Verification Group in Kabul a diplomatic note accusing Pakistan of continuing to allow weapons shipments to the resistance. This was the opening round of an escalating series of Afghan and Soviet protests against continued military aid to the resistance through Pakistan. A week later the Soviet Foreign Ministry sent Pakistan a note threatening that if it did not cease aiding the resistance, the Soviet Union would slow the troop withdrawal and take other, unspecified, steps."[114]

The Reagan administration responded that since Soviet military aid to the Kabul regime continued, U.S. aid to the Afghan resistance should also continue. Following the Reagan-Gorbachev Moscow summit in June 1988, Gorbachev used his postsummit news conference to warn that there would be far-reaching consequences if the Geneva accords were "ruined" by continued fighting as the Soviets withdrew. He also said that Moscow would respond to the so-called provocations caused by Pakistan's continuing to provide weapons to the resistance.

In early June, however, the UN monitoring officials indicated that the Soviets were not slowing their troop pullout despite threats to do so. On June 7, 1988, Najibullah appeared with the Soviet deputy foreign minister at the United Nations and condemned continued Pakistan violations of the accord, charging that "camps and centers for the training of the extremist Afghan opposition still exist in the territory of Pakistan. . . . We would certainly reconsider the timetable of the withdrawal if the violations take on a permanent character and take proper action together with the Soviet Union."[115]

In late May, President Zia suddenly dismissed Prime Minister Junejo. The reason, according to Selig Harrison (who quotes UN negotiator Diego Cordovez as his source), was that Junejo had failed in the preceding weeks to clear the details of the final negotiations in Geneva with the president.[116] In early June, Zia named a caretaker cabinet and indicated that new legislative elections would occur at an unspecified date.

Najibullah went from the United Nations to Cuba, where he signed several agreements with Castro and returned to Afghanistan via Moscow, where he met with Gorbachev. On June 13, 1988, Gorbachev, with Najibullah standing beside him, warned that it would be "necessary to undertake the most resolute retaliatory steps" if the United Nations failed to take effective measures to stop Pakistan from aiding the Afghan guerrillas.[117] By late June the Soviet news agency Tass reported that the Afghan Foreign Ministry had sent no fewer than thirty-four notes to the UN observer group in Kabul protesting violations by Pakistan. It went on to condemn "the smuggling to Afghanistan from Pakistan of advisers of all types and ranks by western and other secret services."[118] Pakistan and the United States, in turn, accused the Soviet Union of failing to meet its 25 percent pullout deadline in June.

In early July, the official Soviet newspaper Izvestia quoted the chief of the Afghan army general staff as saying: "For the time being Pakistan and the United States continue to grossly violate the Geneva agreements."[119] This was followed a few days later by an official statement from the Soviet Foreign Ministry:

We are compelled to note that Pakistan in violation of the Geneva agreements continues actively assisting and transferring elements of the alliance of seven to the territory of Afghanistan, new units of opposition, and also armaments and ammunition. Pakistani advisors participate in forming caravans.[120]

By mid-July, the Afghan government had filed forty-six protest memorandums with the UN observer group accusing Pakistan of some 250 violations of the accords. Supporters of the Afghan resistance in the United States were surprised that this series of Soviet protests was followed on July 16, 1988, by this headline in the *Washington Post:* "Pakistan Halts Arms for Afghans: U.S. Approves Action." The story by David Ottaway, a State Department correspondent, went on to cite unnamed U.S. government sources as saying: "Pakistan, under heavy Soviet and UN pressure and with US approval has halted the flow of almost all arms . . . to the Afghan resistance. . . . The supply of US-made Stinger anti-aircraft missiles and such heavy arms as mortars has virtually stopped." The administration, however, reassured congressional supporters of the Afghan resistance that adequate supplies of weapons continued to be provided. (A year later Sen. Gordon Humphrey and Rep. Bill McCollum, Republican of Florida, said that probably few U.S. military supplies had continued.)

A series of ever-sharper threats from Moscow and Kabul followed in subsequent weeks. On July 19, 1988, the Kabul regime declared: "The U.S. intention to support counterrevolutionary groups constitutes not only flagrant violations of the Geneva accords but also an attempt to push Pakistan to the non-observance of these accords."[121] A few days later a deputy Soviet foreign minister blamed Washington directly for violations, charging that the United States was behind the Pakistani action. After visiting Washington in late July, the foreign minister of Pakistan discussed the Geneva accords in Moscow with the Soviet foreign minister and reported that the Soviets emphasized that the Afghan accords were as important as the 1987 U.S.-Soviet INF treaty.

Military Actions against the Resistance. In mid-August the United States released a study stating that between 10 million and 16 million land mines remained hidden in Afghanistan, posing dangers that could delay the return of Afghan refugees. At about the same time, the Afghan resistance fired rockets into a major Soviet base near Kabul, hitting a fuel dump that started a chain reaction killing 710 persons and destroying Afghanistan's main ammunition depot. Almost simultaneously, resistance forces took control of Kunduz, a provincial capital, but Soviet bombers flying from bases in the USSR immediately hit that city, causing major damage and heavy civilian casualties. The bombing attack forced the resistance to withdraw and sent a stark message to strategic towns—if the resistance moved in, the Soviet air force would bomb them heavily.

By August 15, 1988, the Soviet Union declared that it had met its commitment to withdraw half its combat troops. At the same time, Moscow asserted: "The Soviet government most resolutely declares that the continuation by Pakistan of its obstructionist policy vis-a-vis the Geneva accords cannot be further tolerated. . . . The Soviet Union reserves for itself . . . the right to take such measures that are necessitated by the situation."[122]

Then, on August 17, 1988, President Zia, U.S. Ambassador to Pakistan Arnold Raphel, General Herbert Wassom (head of the U.S. military aid mission), and almost the entire top Pakistani military command were killed when the Pakistani leader's airplane mysteriously lost control and crashed. A Pakistani investigation into the cause of the crash concluded that sabotage, probably involving an explosive device, was the most likely cause of the crash. All but one of six Pakistani and American investigating teams that visited the crash scene reached a near consensus that sabotage caused the crash.[123]

Until the official Pakistani report was released in October, however, some U.S. officials resisted this interpretation. In mid-September unnamed officials told the *New York Times* that a mechanical malfunction appeared to have caused the disaster, although they admitted that the United States had no definite knowledge and refused to say whether sabotage might have caused the supposed malfunction.[124]

Lack of conclusive data was not surprising, since State Department officials had blocked FBI terrorism specialists from participating in the on-site investigation, even though FBI officials wanted to participate, U.S. law permitted it, and Pakistan had no objection. Apparently the State Department sought to conceal any evidence of Soviet involvement in Zia's death: it repeatedly suggested, based on less than convincing evidence, that the crash did not result from foul play, and it prevented FBI experts from discovering any evidence that might have suggested otherwise.[125]

When evidence that incriminated the Soviets finally came to light, some U.S. diplomats seemed to suppress it. In January 1989 American chemical experts reported that chemical traces had been found in the cockpit of the Zia plane. They concluded that the chemicals had been released moments after the aircraft took off, incapacitating the pilots. Since such an operation would have required terrorist capabilities far beyond those of Zia's domestic opposition, the Afghan regime, or even India, Soviet complicity was the natural conclusion. "That probably was what Secretary of State George Shultz feared," remarked the columnists Evans and Novak, "when he vetoed FBI participation" in the investigation in the autumn of 1988.[126] Lally Weymouth speculated on the motive for this State Department action: "Many in the U.S. government may be reluctant to press the issue [of a Soviet role] vigorously—for fear of interrupting the START talks, the talks on regional settlements in Angola and Cambodia and the new era of good feeling between the two superpowers.[127]

In May 1989 Congress began hearings to discover why the State Department had blocked an FBI role in the Zia crash investigation. Robert Oakley, U.S. ambassador to Pakistan and formerly the National Security Council official responsible for Near East and south Asian affairs at the time of Zia's death, admitted to the House Judiciary Subcommittee on Crime that the Reagan administration had erred in excluding the FBI. At the time, Oakley averred, the security of Pakistan and the survival of its fragile government had been paramount in the minds of administration officials. "Given the fact that the army was going to be playing a very important role in the evolving future of Pakistan," he testified, "we wanted to do what we could to engender stability during this situation," explaining that it did not occur to him that the FBI should participate in the investigation, although it was assigned to do so by law.[128]

In June 1989, ten months after the crash but shortly after these hearings opened, FBI investigators were finally allowed to go to Pakistan. The Pakistani ambassador to the United States at the time of the crash, Jamsheed K. A. Marker, said after his retirement in mid-1989 that he had known what the investigation would find: "I am convinced that the cause of the crash was not any type of mechanical failure or accident, but an act of sabotage."[129]

A renewed campaign of threats and intimidation accompanied a new Soviet military offensive. On November 1 the regime paraded Soviet-built medium-range SCUD surface-to-surface missiles through the streets of Kabul. Formally suspending the troop withdrawal from Afghanistan on November 4, the Soviets acknowledged that they were giving the Afghan regime more powerful weapons than those deployed before the Geneva agreement and that they themselves had been using Soviet-based long-range Tu-26 bombers and MiG-27 jet attack aircraft against the resistance. They defended the new arms shipments as a response to aggression from the other side, notably American-backed Pakistani aid to the resistance.[130] The following day Soviet ambassador Yuli Vorontsov, accusing the United States and Pakistan of flagrantly violating the Geneva accords, called for renewed talks on a political settlement.

Despite this juggernaut of simultaneous threats and blandishments, the resistance leaders refused to enter into a coalition with the Communists and rejected an invitation to visit Moscow for further talks. They continued to insist on forming a new, independent, non-Communist government to replace the existing Najibullah regime.

By early February 1989, it was clear that neither the death of Zia and ten other senior Pakistani generals nor all the Soviet maneuvers and military pressures had been able to win the acquiescence of the Afghan resistance in a coalition with the Communist regime in Kabul. In February 1989—on the eve of the deadline for the completion of the Soviet troop withdrawal—the State Department again condemned the massive military attacks on Pakistan and called for a halt to the widespread destruction that the Soviet Union was still inflicting inside Afghanistan even though the resistance was restrained.

The Soviet Withdrawal. By February 5, 1989, according to *Pravda*, the last Soviet soldier had left Kabul. The Western media reported that Soviet convoys and aircraft were removing thousands of Soviet troops and that the Soviet commander in Afghanistan had said that all troops would be out by the February 15, 1989, deadline. Since the embassies of the United States and most Western countries had closed, however, and virtually all Western journalists had also left Kabul, news of the Soviet withdrawal was based essentially on reports from Moscow and Islamabad, plus those of Moscow correspondents flown to Dushanbe and Kabul for a few hours to witness troops departing Kabul or arriving in the Soviet Union.

Were all Soviet combat forces withdrawn? Although many observers believe so, private citizens lacking access to government information have no independent way to be certain. In May 1989 Congressman McCollum asserted publicly that Soviet forces in Afghanistan had not been completely withdrawn. He claimed that by December 1988 about 11,000 Soviet Uzbek, Tajik, and Turkomen elite troops had been secretly enrolled in the Afghan army. In addition, he contended that 20,000 Soviet elite forces operated in unmarked KGB uniforms in late 1988 and that the Soviets had "donated" Soviet citizens from the Far East to the Afghan army.[131]

In addition, according to McCollum, the Soviet Union directly controls one element of the Kabul regime's army consisting of

> some 20,000 young Afghan males who were taken from their villages in the early 1980s and then trained in the USSR. In other words, as the "official" Soviet army left Afghanistan, the clandestine Soviet army—better trained and more reliable—tiptoed into Afghanistan with supplies and new equipment awaiting them.[132]

Rosanne Klass had predicted such possible Soviet evasions of the accords in February 1988.[133]

Even if we assume that all or nearly all Soviet combat military forces were out by February 15, 1989, an overview of both sides might

87

suggest how the future might evolve. Table 3–8 summarizes the estimated combat forces available to both sides.

At the end of 1988, the U.S. government concluded, the Kabul regime's armed forces were:

> reeling under the pressure of an unbroken series of defeats, retreats and consolidations. . . . It is a demoralized force. . . . The army has not expanded its control anywhere in the country over the last year [1988]. Most experts agree that it probably can survive for no more than a matter of months after a complete Soviet withdrawal.[134]

But in 1989, following the Soviet withdrawal, according to official U.S. government published estimates, the Kabul regime had an estimated 130,000 total armed personnel fully equipped with armor, an air force, and SCUD missiles with the acknowledged presence of Soviet military "advisers."

If Congressman McCollum's report is correct, it would be necessary to add 50,000 fully trained and equipped troops to those of the Kabul regime (including 30,000 disguised Soviet ethnic troops) and perhaps another 35,000 Soviet air and land forces based just across

TABLE 3–8

ESTIMATED FORCES OF THE AFGHAN COMMUNIST REGIME AND THE RESISTANCE, AFTER FEBRUARY 15, 1989

	Regime	Resistance
Army	40,000	—
Secret police and Ministry of Interior police	35,000	—
Total militias	25,000	—
Armed Communist party	30,000	—
Official total	130,000	350,000 (half in combat)
Secret Soviet ethnic troops	30,000	—
Soviet-trained Afghan units	20,000	—
Soviet air and land forces on the Afghan border helping Kabul	35,000	—
Alternative total	215,000	350,000

SOURCES: State Department, *Afghanistan: Soviet Occupation and Withdrawal*, p. 7; *New York Times*, February 8, 1989 (claims by regime); and Rep. Bill Mc-Collum, "A Hollow Accord in Afghanistan," *Washington Times*, May 9, 1989.

the Soviet border, which reportedly also continue to provide bombing strikes and other military support.

They face a resistance that numbers about 350,000 (of whom about half are in combat at any one time—more in the summer and autumn, fewer in the harsh winter). Most of these guerrillas are untrained for conventional combat; they have no air force, no heavy artillery, no armor, often no shoes. They are short of Stingers and other needed weapons. One resistance leader told members of Congress in July 1989 that few external supplies had been received since January 1989.[135]

But the Afghan regime also had to contend with the continuing internal rivalry between the two Communist factions and, within the Parcham faction, between supporters of Najibullah and Babrak Karmal. Further, the Kabul regime faced the almost universal public expectation that it would be defeated. Some in the resistance may have counted on that sense of doom as a trigger to begin the unraveling process through internal dissension and defections on an ever-larger scale in the wake of the Soviet pullout.

Despite the optimistic expectations of so many U.S. government officials and much of the Western media when the Soviet troop withdrawal began, the Kabul regime continued to function and maintain control over all major cities and parts of the countryside after the withdrawal had been completed. In fact the official U.S. government assessment at the end of 1988 showed the regime at least contesting much of the Afghan countryside, although the resistance was estimated in firm control of some provinces (see figure 3–2).

The military progress of the resistance had continued steadily during 1988. By mid-November five provincial capitals were under resistance control, and by mid-February 1989, their forces had surrounded most of the major Afghan cities, including Kabul.

Problems of the Resistance. The next stage of military operations, however, posed new and different political and military challenges. Many resistance commanders were reluctant to attack the cities directly for fear of causing severe civilian casualities. They also feared the inexperience of the resistance in this kind of battle and its lack of the needed weaponry. The leaders knew that frontal assaults on heavily defended urban areas were sure to produce heavy casualties. Kabul, for example, reportedly is surrounded by a triple ring of fortifications and heavy artillery emplacements extending thirty kilometers around the city. Those forces loyal to the regime were well equipped, dug in, and likely to fight with the furious desperation of men who see no hope if they lose.

FIGURE 3–2
CONTROL OF THE PROVINCES BY THE AFGHAN REGIME AND THE RESISTANCE, LATE 1988

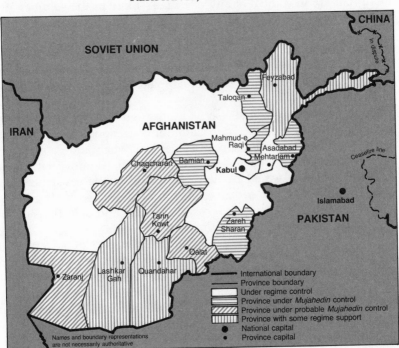

SOURCE: Adapted from U.S. Department of State, *Afghanistan: Soviet Occupation and Withdrawal*, Special Report no. 179, December 1988, p. 6.

In early 1989 one resistance commander outlined the need for entirely new combat tactics, far better coordination and control, and far heavier weapons. And this, he said, would require the resistance to train for and learn about conventional warfare—a task requiring time and increased external military support.[136]

An alternative siege strategy of cutting off the cities from supplies also posed the political and moral problem of inflicting suffering on the civilian populations. These, after all, were the very people the resistance was fighting to liberate.

To help civilians in the towns, the mujahedin set up food depots near the cities. In February 1989 a resistance commander near the city of Jalalabad told a reporter, "The people of Jalalabad know it [the food] is there. We have told them we will give them security and feed them, but we are not in a position to enter Jalalabad and give it to them. The people are in a way imprisoned.[137]

Near the same city a Western relief worker noted that "the people know the flour is there just a few miles from their homes. . . . They are hungry and can't get food, and therefore, they'll blame the regime. Ultimately, the goal is that this will weaken the regime."[138]

Cooperation and Dissension in the Alliance. Political cooperation among the groups making up the resistance alliance groups increased during 1988. By early 1989, the seven members of the alliance based in Pakistan had agreed to include the much smaller resistance grouping of Shiite Moslems based in Iran. These, however, continued to demand a larger representation in the interim government than the Pakistan-based Sunni majority was willing to provide. Negotiations over many weeks produced agreement on a three-part governance structure to include the seven-party resistance leaders as a supreme council with one resistance leader as prime minister of the government and the *shura* as a group composed of more than 500 representatives of all resistance organizations and others, as the representative decision-making body. Despite this progress in establishing the institutions for governance, differences and rivalries among the resistance groups continued—as starkly demonstrated by the Hekmatyar group's killing in July 1989 of thirty Jamiat Islami commanders.

In addition to the differences among the resistance organizations at headquarters, there have always been some tensions between the political organizations of the resistance and the combat commanders in the field. Over the years the combat commanders inside Afghanistan have established and operated local administrations to provide services such as schools and hospitals, usually working closely with traditional religious and tribal leaders. In early February 1989, some resistance commanders said that if the Pakistan-based parties could not form a provisional government, they could create one themselves inside Afghanistan by bringing together the existing regional administrations. One told a journalist that this would "take more time than if a government is chosen in Pakistan, but we can do it."[139]

As usual, many of the most serious disagreements concerned the Islamic party of Hekmatyar. His organization had long been favored by the government of Pakistan in the distribution of aid and supplies. Informed observers speculated about why Hekmatyar got a disproportionate share of military and other support. Among other reasons, it is widely believed that he had promised Pakistan's military establishment that if he gained power in Afghanistan he would not raise the issue of Pushtunistan.

Commanders from other parties have accused Hekmatyar of opportunism. Said one, "Hekmatyar is very good at publicity, but he

91

leaves the fighting to the others and then his men come out of their warm quilts to take the credit." A number of field commanders feared that Hekmatyar's fighters might attack major cities after the Soviet troop withdrawal (as he threatened), in which case other groups might be forced to follow suit even though they considered it bad strategy. Pakistan was reportedly urging resistance commanders to go on the attack because "that way [Pakistan liaison officials] hope they can coordinate our fighting and push the mujahideen they want to the front."[140]

Since the resistance groups will need continued support from Pakistan for some years (until they can overthrow the Communist regime), a situation in which most resistance groups preceive that Pakistan favors a party that is hated, feared, and distrusted contains the seeds of serious future problems. As of July 1989, however, the failure of the siege of Jalalabad and changes in Pakistan's military leadership may have reduced the disproportionate aid to Hekmatyar's group.

Alternative Futures for Afghanistan

The conflict in Afghanistan could be resolved in three possible ways:

• A pro-Soviet regime survives, possibly modified with cosmetic changes of leadership personnel but still under Communist (and Soviet) control.

• The pro-Soviet regime moves from Kabul and reestablishes itself in the northern part of Afghanistan (adjacent to the Soviet border), probably in the city of Mazar-i-Sharif, while the devastated and overwhelmingly Pushtun south and west come under the control of the resistance.

• The resistance alliance establishes an independent non-Communist government and overthrows and displaces the Communist regime.

Many in the free world may simply assume that the resistance has won the war and that the people of Afghanistan are free before this actually happens, while the Soviet Union will continue its efforts to sustain a pro-Soviet regime in control of as much of Afghanistan as possible. Since February 1989, Moscow has continued full political and military support to the Afghan Communist regime, mounting bombing raids from Soviet territory against resistance targets inside Afghanistan. As the resistance units mass for attacks on fixed targets, they are and will be far more vulnerable to precisely the kind of bombing and other attacks that the Soviet Union could launch from its territory, including toxic weapon attacks.

92

In June 1989, journalist David Ottaway summarized the new military tactics used by the Soviet-backed Kabul regime to hold off the resistance in a number of cities: high-altitude bombing from Soviet territory above the range of the Stingers, launching of Soviet surface-to-surface missiles, massive artillery attacks, and continuing Soviet military resupply of the Kabul regime.[141] The Soviets themselves have confirmed delivery of twenty-five military cargo planes per day of supplies, with reports of 120 tanks and armed military vehicles in one convoy. In June 1989 U.S. Defense Department officials estimated that large quantities of Soviet tanks, armored personnel carriers, and guns continued flowing into Kabul.[142]

The Propaganda War. The Soviets and the Kabul regime have launched a major propaganda effort aimed at creating the perception that the resistance is needlessly continuing the war in Afghanistan. With its extensive international propaganda resources, the Soviet Union is suggesting that no further reason exists for war in Afghanistan, that the Kabul regime, anxious to end the bloodshed, is ready to work peacefully and cooperatively with its opponents in a policy of reconciliation but that the resistance is fanatical and driven by its aggressive backers, Pakistan and the United States. This campaign is combined with an effort to raise humanitarian concerns about suffering inflicted on civilian populations by mujahedin attacks.

In fact, even before the pullout of overt Soviet forces was completed and while Moscow was still intensifying its attacks in the countryside, the Western media were finally invited to Kabul, where their attention was skillfully directed to the plight of civilians, especially children, in the cities. The Soviets portrayed themselves as humanitarians sending in emergency food supplies to stave off starvation while the resistance was blamed for suffering inside the besieged cities.[143] In the autumn of 1988, when a resistance group ambushed a UN relief convoy en route to Kabul, Prince Sadruddin Aga Khan, head of the special UN program for Afghanistan, told the press: "The shortages which have been compounded by the coldest winter Afghanistan has faced in sixteen years have affected nursing mothers and children, the aged, the sick and people who are usually forgotten in situations of this kind."[144]

In addition to painting the resistance as blindly set on continuing the conflict regardless of its cost in human suffering, Soviet propaganda and Soviet Kabul agents also accentuate the differences among the resistance organizations, suggesting that they are indifferent to the future of Afghanistan and its people. According to this view, the groups are fighting simply to seize power for themselves; their refusal to join a "broad-based government of reconciliation" is purely a matter of self-interest.

The Soviet Union is also likely to continue painting Hekmatyar's extremist Islamic party as typical of the entire resistance, using and exaggerating its actions and policies to discredit the entire resistance with its external supporters, especially in the West.

Selig Harrison, an observer who supports the idea of a "government of reconciliation," has repeatedly raised the specter of a pro-Khomeini, anti-Western fundamentalist Afghanistan as the result of a resistance victory. While the Soviet Union supplies steady political and military help to the Communist regime, and works incessantly to discredit, divide, and weaken the Afghan resistance, it will also be very active diplomatically and politically through the media, trying to persuade the world community to cut off aid to the resistance. The methods and elements of this campaign will vary from country to country.

Pakistan is obviously key. In its first months in office, the new government of Prime Minister Benazir Bhutto, established by elections in November 1988, continued Zia's policy of helping the resistance. Quite understandably, the new prime minister perceived that an attempt to contradict the views of the Pakistani military on such a major question of national security policy—as they see it—would risk a military coup against her new and fragile government. Yet Bhutto and her Pakistan People's party, long calling for a negotiated settlement recognizing the Kabul regime, modified their position during the fall 1988 election campaign to support compliance with the Geneva accords.

Selig Harrison argues that the Soviet Union explicitly rejected the Zia government's statement that, while signing the Geneva accords, Pakistan—like the United States—would reserve the right to aid the resistance under the doctrine of positive symmetry. Harrison argues that, contrary to what the State Department has said, the Soviet Union did not accept the U.S. position on positive symmetry, but only took note of it. The Soviet Union, he says, assumed that, by signing, Pakistan would be bound to stop helping the resistance in any way, as specified in detail in the accords. According to Harrison, "Soviet diplomats say that Moscow would not have signed the settlement if [Pakistan] had not assumed a clear legal obligation to stop aid."[145]

Given the fate of President Zia, and the international unwillingness to hold Moscow or Kabul to account, the Soviet Union is in an even stronger position to insist that Pakistan must finally comply with the letter of the Geneva accord, since the (overt) Soviet ground forces have been withdrawn.

94

Inter-Services Intelligence (ISI), reported to be the principal agency of the government of Pakistan concerned with help for the Afghan resistance, is a stronghold of military intelligence and of the military institution. Both Prime Minister Bhutto and the Soviet Union thus share an interest in restructuring the ISI to reduce its influence on Pakistan's internal politics, which the Soviets assume will reduce its ability to thwart Soviet goals by helping the Afghan resistance.

In early February 1989, a Pakistani government-owned newspaper published an attack on ISI. This nearly unprecedented article called ISI an "invisible government" and accused it of having a "hand in the making and unmaking of persons, policies, and even governments. The succession of despotic rulers . . . lacking public sanction could only govern through loyal agencies that could manipulate . . . the informed and (misinformed)" friend and foe.[146] This dramatic article went on to charge the ISI with following a "militarist" Afghan policy often different from that of the Foreign Ministry.

Soon after, the Bhutto government began a review of the ISI, which led to the removal of its director, General Mohammed Gul, and the transfer of many of its responsibilities to the Intelligence Bureau, which is reportedly staffed by many former friends of Bhutto's father, the late prime minister whom Zia had overthrown and executed. These changes increase the possibility that under the rubric of a future Afghan political settlement, the Bhutto government could decide to change Pakistan's position markedly vis-à-vis the Afghan resistance.

In 1989 the Soviet Union, having sent a massive quantity of weapons to Kabul, proposed to the United States a policy of negative symmetry—a joint moratorium on arms deliveries to both the Kabul regime and the resistance. (A year earlier, Moscow had rejected the same idea when the State Department proposed it.) This is exactly the kind of agreement the Kremlin could secretly violate, however, because of its thousand-mile border with Afghanistan, while using such an agreement to obtain a cutoff of U.S. arms to the resistance. The State Department could also possibly use the issue of the waiver required for continuing U.S. aid to Pakistan to press Pakistan to reduce its military support to the resistance in the interests of the "peace process."

On February 8, 1989, the Bush administration initiated a review of America's Afghanistan policy. The Soviet propaganda apparatus continues doing all it can to bring about the widespread perception in the United States that the Afghan conflict is degenerating into internecine combat among various rival resistance factions, killing many civilians for no good purpose. If successful, this could well lead to pressure in Washington to reduce sharply or terminate military aid

95

to the resistance. The same thing might happen if the perception that the conflict in Afghanistan had already been "won"—before the resistance forces had actually succeeded in establishing a fully independent Afghanistan—became the consensus view among the U.S. and Pakistani leadership.

With respect to China, Beijing had demanded Soviet withdrawal from Afghanistan as a precondition for a rapprochement with Moscow. The announced completion of the withdrawal on February 15, 1989, cleared the way for the Soviet-Chinese summit in May 1989. The Soviet Union's careful process of détente and diplomatic fence mending could produce a package of mutual concessions that might include the termination of Chinese aid to the resistance.

As for Iran, the Soviet Union began to make diplomatic overtures to Tehran as early as 1987. They resulted in some reduction of Iranian support for the resistance and a perceptible warming toward the Soviet-backed Kabul regime, signaled when Iran's ambassador in Kabul attended an official function for the first time since the Soviet invasion. As a result of a visit by representatives of Iranian ruler Khomeini to Moscow in 1988, commercial ties between the two countries were strengthened. In early 1989 Tehran reportedly encouraged the Iran-supported resistance organizations to make unreasonable demands for participation in the *shura* and the new interim government. Then on June 22, 1989, following Khomeini's death, Iran and the Soviet Union held a summit meeting, agreeing to military, economic, and technical cooperation. This cooperation specified an estimated $15 billion in new transactions, including several billion dollars worth of Soviet military sales to Iran, for example, the top-of-the-line MiG-29 aircraft. Herbert Meyer, a senior CIA official from 1981 to 1986, compared this alliance to the Hitler-Stalin pact and expressed his shock that "the Bush administration has said nothing, offered no explanations, provided no direction."[147] Whatever the ultimate effect of this Soviet-Iranian agreement, it will probably reduce if not eliminate the willingness of the current Iranian regime to help the anti-Communist resistance in Afghanistan vigorously.

Soviet Objectives. The Soviet Union has been and remains plainly committed to using every means at its disposal to bring about a cutoff of aid to the resistance by Pakistan, the United States, Iran, and China. Moscow's success would greatly enhance its prospects for keeping the Kabul regime in power for some time to come, or at least of ensuring its control in northern Afghanistan, while leaving an unviable south to collapse.

In early February 1988 officials in Moscow reportedly stated that if Kabul came under heavy attack, the regime might relocate north-ward to Mazar-i-Sharif. This town has received a new physical and bureaucratic infrastructure in preparation for its possible use as a fallback location for the government. As noted earlier, the option of detaching the north from the rest of Afghanistan was apparently prepared carefully by Moscow during the many years it pursued a highly differentiated policy in that region. Northern Afghanistan, with the natural resources that the Soviet Union wants to exploit, has a far more defensible topography immediately adjacent to the Soviet border and readily accessible to Soviet military reinforcement.

In this scenario the Soviet Union and the Afghan Communist regime (including the secret police, KhAD) would also continue to do everything they could to end external aid to the mujahedin, while at the same time stirring up as many problems as possible among whatever elements of the resistance remained in the territory under Communist control.

Toward an Independent, Non-Communist Afghanistan

In the months after the Geneva accords entered into force on May 15, 1988, the stratagems of the Soviet Union and the Kabul regime failed to eliminate external aid to the resistance and entice it into a coalition with the Kabul regime. The Afghan resistance and most of the countries supporting it continued to press toward an independent Afghanistan. Quite possibly the Soviet tactics and maneuvers following the February 15, 1989, pullout of its overt troops may also fail. In that case if their supporters hold firm, the Afghan resistance might, after some time, be able to establish a new, independent government for Afghanistan replacing the Communist regime. While some degree of differences and jockeying for position will certainly remain among the various resistance groups, their years of cooperation may enable most if not all of them to work together in a practical way. The biggest questions remain the effect of manipulation by outside interests, Soviet subversion, and the Islamic party under Hekmatyar. Once the Kabul regime has been removed as a major threat, however, if the six other resistance organizations are unified, they might be able to remove the Hekmatyar faction and persuade many of his followers to work with the new coalition or disband.

The ultimate success of the Afghan resistance in liberating its country from communism will mean a long, difficult period of reconstruction, but eventually a far brighter future for the people of Afghanistan will emerge if the Soviet grip on all its economic resources can be broken. It could also have an important effect in helping to stabilize the entire region, including India and Pakistan.

Moreover, an independent Afghanistan would provide a positive example to the Islamic peoples of the Soviet Union—especially during this time of *glasnost* and the revival of national feeling among non-Russians in the Soviet Union.

Because of the Soviet military power, any new non-Communist government in Kabul is likely to avoid any direct attempt to agitate or mobilize the millions of Moslems living within the Soviet Union. Any such attempt would likely be met by very strong Soviet countermeasures, and the new Afghan government would know beforehand not to risk Soviet threats or pressure. Nevertheless, the very fact that the people of Afghanistan after a long struggle were finally able to liberate themselves from the same Communist political system that has suppressed Islam in the Moslem regions of the Soviet Union since 1922 would be bound to add to the demands for greater regional autonomy and religious expression.

The chances of such a positive outcome in Afghanistan are not strong unless the United States acts with energy and constancy to help the resistance succeed. Among the most important contributions, the United States could use all its means of diplomatic persuasion to ensure continued external support to the resistance, especially from Pakistan. The military stalemate experienced by the resistance until the end of 1989—notably its failure to capture the strategic town of Jalalabad—was due at least partly to inadequate supplies from the West.

By late June 1989, the optimistic U.S. estimate that the Kabul regime would collapse in six to twelve months after the final Soviet withdrawal was being seriously questioned. As a result, according to the *Washington Post:* "The question now is whether the United States can get the necessary artillery and munitions to the resistance in time for its offensive this summer, which may well be its last opportunity to gain a military victory before U.S. and Pakistani support fades."[148]

In early July 1989 U.S. officials again promised that new supplies would reach the resistance soon. Only the right weapons in adequate quantity can make the guerrillas an equal match to the well-supplied Afghan army: such military support would include secure communications, improved intercept and tactical intelligence capabilities, mine-clearing and breaching equipment, long-range mortars, and adequate supplies of anti-aircraft missiles.

Many believed that Prime Minister Benazir Bhutto of Pakistan, during a state visit to Washington in June 1989, provided important backing for increased military and political support for the resistance. Invited to address a joint session of Congress, Bhutto said:

> Both our countries have stood alongside the Afghans in their struggle for more than a decade. For ten long years the

people of Pakistan have provided sanctuary to our Afghan brothers and sisters. . . . And for ten long years, the United States, in a united bipartisan effort of three Administrations and six Congresses, has stood side by side with Pakistan, and the brave Mujahideen. . . . Even now the Soviet government is giving full backing to the Kabul regime's efforts to cling to power. It left in its possession vast quantities of lethal weapons—weapons supplemented by a regular supply of hardware including Scud missiles, some of which have already hit Pakistan territory. More threats have been received, threats to supply new weapons "never before seen in the region." The Soviets have gone. But the force of foreign arms continues to deny Afghanistan the ultimate fruit of victory—self-determination. . . . Our concerns are for a stable, independent and neutral Afghanistan. An Afghanistan where the people can choose their own system, their own government in free and fair elections. . . . Pakistan and the United States have travelled a long road with the Afghans in their quest for self-determination. Let us not at this stage, out of impatience or fatigue become indifferent. We cannot, we must not abandon their cause.[149]

This speech followed disturbing signs of diminishing bipartisan congressional support for the Afghan resistance. The chairman of the House Permanent Select Committee on Intelligence, Democratic Congressman Anthony Beilenson of California, published an article that "shocked the mujahedeen by suggesting that Washington and Moscow negotiate 'a mutual cutoff of all military aid to Afghanistan.' "[150] That would virtually ensure the permanence of the Kabul regime.

Even former stalwart supporters among Democratic senators such as Bill Bradley (New Jersey), Robert Byrd (West Virginia), and David Boren (Oklahoma), chairman of the Senate Select Committee on Intelligence, all seemed to question the goal of helping the resistance until it had achieved victory. Senator Bradley, for example, said the Bush administration should make an attempt to reach a negotiated settlement. Democratic Congressman Robert Torricelli of New Jersey gave the best reply: "It would be an error to undertake a change in policy at this point. A traditional weakness of American foreign policy is a lack of patience. The best plans often fail: because we don't have the patience to see them to conclusion."[151]

Victory for the resistance will take much longer. The doubts among some in Congress might well grow with time—unless the Bush administration keeps Congress and the public informed about what is really occurring in Afghanistan and maintains the bipartisan congressional coalition that is committed to a free, independent Afghanistan. The United States must also work vigorously in the international arena and through bilateral diplomacy, as well as use its foreign aid programs, to reinforce the support given to the resistance by our allies and others in the region, especially Pakistan.

Continued Threat. After having probably been responsible for President Zia's mysterious death, the Communists continue to threaten Pakistan. In early July 1989 an Afghan government spokesman blamed Pakistan for mujahedin rocket attacks against Kabul and issued an ominous and direct threat: "Pakistan is directly involved in killing the innocent people of Afghanistan by violating the Geneva Accords."[152]

The United States should also use its political and economic influence with India to reduce its willingness to cooperate with Moscow and the Kabul regime against the resistance and Pakistan—especially to indicate that any coercive Indian actions against Pakistan on this issue would entail loss of Indian access to U.S. foreign assistance and to U.S. markets. The gradual normalization of relations between Pakistan and India as evidenced by the July 1989 summit meeting between the leaders of both countries, Bhutto and Gandhi, offered the prospect of reduced coercive actions by India.

Besides continuing our aid to the resistance and taking the lead in seeking more humanitarian assistance for the long-suffering people of Afghanistan, the United States should recognize the government established by the resistance as the new and legitimate government of Afghanistan and encourage our allies and friends to do the same. Moreover, the United States should ensure that all humanitarian aid which it contributes for Afghan reconstruction and all free world aid will be dispensed by the new resistance government, not the current Communist regime.

Any additional diplomatic negotiations or settlements on Afghanistan must be predicated on the full participation and approval of the Afghan resistance, which along with the Afghan people has the most at stake. A superpower-negotiated agreement would ultimately serve neither our interests nor the resistance's. Consistent with their long-standing refusal to deal with the Soviet puppet Najibullah, resistance leaders rejected a diplomatic plan proposed in June 1989 by PLO Chairman Yasser Arafat. This plan called for a cease-fire and talks between the regime and the resistance, followed by elections—which could not be fair or free since the Kabul regime would still be in power. No such unacceptable "political solution" must be imposed upon the Afghan freedom fighters.

The leaders and peoples of the free world must also receive a continuous flow of accurate information about events in Afghanistan.

This requirement is especially important because the free world will have to cope with a great deal of speculation, misinformation, and deliberate Soviet-inspired disinformation. Further, to sustain sympathy and support for the postliberation government, the peoples and leaders of friendly nations will need access to timely and comprehensive information that puts into context the inevitable frictions and problems that any post-Communist government will face.

Finally, the United States should provide administrative, diplomatic, and political training to the Afghan resistance government that will far better enable it to help the people within its control, continue the battle against the Kabul regime, and present its case to the free world.

All of these measures are well within the capabilities of the United States and other free world allies if the right decisions are made and if there is a commitment to helping the people of Afghanistan regain their freedom.

4
Angola

Angola and Mozambique were part of Portugal's overseas empire for nearly five hundred years, from 1482 until 1975. The Kingdom of Portugal had achieved sovereignty in 1143 and established an alliance with England in 1373. In the fifteenth century Portugal began a period of overseas expansion, establishing colonies in Africa, Asia, and America. This expansion ended when Spain occupied Portugal, between 1580 and 1640.

Portugal gained effective occupation of its African colonies only in the early twentieth century, although its largest colony, Brazil, had become an independent republic in 1889. In 1910 the king of Portugal was overthrown and the second Republic of Portugal was proclaimed. It lasted until 1926, when an army coup led to the establishment of the Salazar regime, which held power until 1974.

Beginning as finance minister, Dr. Antonio Oliveira Salazar ruled as prime minister from 1932 until his health deteriorated in 1968. In World War I, Portugal fought with the Allies and in World War II it stayed neutral, although it granted the Allies bases in the Azores, a Portuguese territory. In 1949 Portugal was a founding member of the North Atlantic Treaty Organization, for which it provided strategically important basing facilities.[1]

Anticolonial Movements

After World War II, a movement for national independence from the long-established European empires gained force throughout the third world. In the 1940s the Philippines, India, and Indonesia gained their independence. In the 1950s African countries began to win independence from the United Kingdom and France, usually through negotiation and political action but sometimes through armed conflict. But the Salazar government had no intention of granting independence to Portugal's colonies.

The Soviet Union had for decades used the anticolonial cause as a means of weakening what it called the imperialist world. In the late 1950s the post-Stalin Soviet Union developed close relations with African independence movements and the newly independent regimes, intending to encourage formal cooperation and perhaps eventually establish pro-Soviet regimes. Moscow often worked through the Communist party in the Western colonial powers (France, the United Kingdom, Portugal) to establish these links (see table 4–1).[2]

In December 1956, in the words of a Rand report, "a small group of African intellectuals and whites under the strong influence of the communist party of Portugal" founded the Popular Movement for the Liberation of Angola (MPLA).[3] Its social base consisted primarily of left-oriented urban elites (some of whom were *mestico* or mixed-blood), Angolan students in Europe, and middle-class groups in some Angolan cities. Most MPLA followers came from the Kimbundu people in the slums of Luanda and then in rural areas. From the beginning, the MPLA was under strong Communist influence, sending its first delegation to Moscow and receiving Soviet assistance as early as the summer of 1960. According to Soviet sources, the Khrushchev regime gave the MPLA political and military training, medicine, food, clothing, money, and weapons. The MPLA's armed attacks against Angola's Portuguese administration began in early 1961 with an unsuccessful attempt to free cadres from a Luanda prison.

Soon after Holden Roberto's armed anticolonial movement began its military operations against the Portuguese in Angola's northern provinces. Founded in 1954 as the Union of the Peoples of Northern Angola, it was renamed in 1958 the Angola People's Union and in

TABLE 4–1
ANGOLA'S ANTICOLONIAL MOVEMENTS

Group	Ethnic Base	Percentage of Angolan Population	External Support from
MPLA (1956)	Kimbundu	15–20	Soviet bloc, Cuba, Zambia, Congo (Brazzaville), Tanzania
FNLA (1958)	Bakongo	20	Zaire; U.S. until 1976
UNITA (1966)	Ovimbundu	40	Zaire, Kenya, Nigeria, Morocco, various Middle Eastern countries, Ivory Coast; U.S. since 1985

SOURCES: Alexander R. Alexiev and Nanette C. Brown, "UNITA of Angola: Profile of an Anti-Marxist Resistance Movement," Rand Working Draft 2745-USDP, October 1985, pp. i–v, and 20; and Peter Vanneman, "The USSR and the Angolan Conflict," paper presented to conference on Soviet policy toward southern Africa, University of Miami Graduate School of International Studies, December 1988, p. 21.

1962 the National Front for the Liberation of Angola (FNLA). The FNLA received its support mainly from the Bakongo people of northern Angola, about one-fifth of the country's population. In 1963 the FNLA formed a government-in-exile based in neighboring Zaire, which the newly established Organization of African Unity recognized as the sole authentic representative of the Angolan people.[4]

In 1961 the Portuguese empire came to an end in two places. The former French territory of Dahomey, now independent, asked Portugal to withdraw its governor from what was once a small Portuguese enclave within its territory but had become just a residence and garden. The Portuguese government refused but, when given an ultimatum, decided to burn down the residence and withdraw. Thousands of miles away, the Indian government used military force to take over three small territories, including the Portuguese-ruled enclave of Goa.

Nevertheless, the Salazar regime refused to recognize the expulsions. In official Portuguese literature Goa remained a Portuguese territory that was temporarily occupied. The Salazar regime responded to the 1961 Angolan rebellion and to a simultaneous armed uprising in the Portuguese colony of Guinea (now Guinea-Bissau) by substantially increasing its military forces and trying to strengthen its political and economic control. In 1964 an armed independence movement began operations in the Portuguese colony of Mozambique. For the next decade, as a result, Portugal fought three colonial wars in Africa.

In 1966 Jonas Savimbi established the third major anticolonial movement in Angola. Savimbi had left Angola in 1959 at the age of twenty-five to study medicine in Portugal. Because of his militant anticolonial activities, he was forced to leave Portugal in 1960. Savimbi went to Switzerland, where he changed his field of study and in 1965 obtained a doctorate in political science.[5] During these years he belonged to Holden Roberto's FNLA, becoming general secretary and then foreign minister of the revolutionary government in exile that Roberto established in 1962. After Savimbi left the FNLA in July 1964, apparently because he objected to its tribalism, he

> started looking for support, and, on the advice of Nasser, a long-time patron, visited both the Soviet Union and China in late 1964 and early 1965. While the Soviets responded with hostility to his ideas and urged him instead to join the MPLA by promising him the vice-presidential position, the Chinese were much more forthcoming. As a result, Savimbi was provided with some funds and allowed to bring eleven of his closest associates for four months of military training at Nanking in the summer of 1965. Armed with the acquired

knowledge and a limited supply of weapons, Savimbi and his comrades returned to Angola and founded UNITA [National Union for the Total Independence of Angola] on March 25, 1966.[6]

Since Savimbi believed strongly that the anticolonial movements must be based in Angola, he criticized the MPLA for operating mainly from Congo-Brazzaville and the FNLA for operating from Zaire. Working initially within his own Ovimbundu tribe (the largest in Angola, accounting for about 40 percent of the population), Savimbi

> began building a vertical political hierarchy party structure based on popular horizontal organizations coupled with an infrastructure of population support services such as schools and clinics. . . . This system proved highly effective, and by the early 1970s UNITA enjoyed far greater popularity among rural Angolans than its rivals.[7]

In 1968, after the Portuguese ruler Salazar suffered a cerebral hemorrhage, Dr. Marcello Caetano succeeded him as premier. In one of his first speeches, the new premier reaffirmed the regime's determination to continue Portugal's policy in Africa: "Angolan Portugal has a brilliant future before it," he declared. "Angola is quite firmly determined to remain Portuguese. . . . The secret of triumph lies in the strength of one's will to conquer."[8] By 1974, after thirteen years of war, Portugal seemed to have the situation in hand:

> At the end of 1973, there was no evident sign of any weakening in Portugal's determination to remain in her overseas provinces, nor was there any evidence that her armed forces could not contain the guerrilla incursions. . . . Foreign observers who wished to prove this for themselves could travel throughout the territories and observe the Portuguese presence in all the populated areas, and could see the massive economic, social and educational developments that [had] radically changed the face of Angola and of little Guinea, and that were beginning to change that of Mozambique. Few would deny that the chief impetus for the rapid social and economic changes came from the guerrilla wars. . . . Except in the Tete and Zambezia districts of Mozambique, the struggle—after thirteen years—was still being fought (and sporadically at that) in these same border areas, none of which contained any important urban or industrial centre.[9]

In early 1974 the MPLA had about 1,400 armed guerrillas; UNITA, about 1,000; and the FNLA, an estimated 12,000.[10]

Events of 1974 and 1975

The military stalemate in the African colonies was broken by a series of unexpected events in Portugal, which had become weary of war after thirteen years. In addition, the Portuguese military leadership had come to understand that success against the anticolonial movements in Guinea-Bissau, Angola, and Mozambique would require not only effective military tactics but also changes in the social and economic policy of Portugal. After experience in the African wars, a group of middle-level Portuguese military officers became committed to political and economic liberalization. In February 1974, one of the best known and most effective combat officers, General Antonio de Spinola, published a book, *Portugal and the Future*, in which he expressed these ideas.

The Coup in Portugal. For some years the Moscow-backed and clandestine Communist party of Portugal (PCP) had become increasingly active. Building on disaffection with the colonial wars, it had made efforts to obtain recruits within the Portuguese military. Some of the most intelligent and best educated of them were influenced by Socialist and Communist ideas. In the summer of 1973, the armed forces movement (MFA)—consisting of reformist military leaders, such as General Spinola, and a smaller group of officers who had been influenced toward communism—began planning for a new regime in Portugal.

Publication of General Spinola's book evoked enormous interest among the reading public and in Portuguese military circles. In March 1974 the Caetano regime relieved both Spinola as army deputy chief of staff and his friend and superior as the army chief of staff. The Portuguese secret police purged the army; many officers were imprisoned, suspended, or reassigned to the Azores.[11]

On April 25, 1974, the armed forces movement overthrew the Caetano regime in a nearly bloodless coup. General Spinola, who led the coup, became president of the new junta. This coup by a coalition of reformist and Communist-oriented military officers, assisted by the Soviet Union and the PCP, nearly led to the establishment of a Communist regime in Portugal in 1975. While democratic-oriented and Communist-oriented elements fought a complicated and largely invisible struggle for the future of Portugal, the new regime made important decisions that resulted in the establishment of pro-Soviet regimes in Guinea-Bissau, Mozambique, and Angola.

The manifesto of the armed forces movement had called for a democratic process to bring about a transition to new government in these three Portuguese colonies. In Angola, Portugal suspended military operations in May 1974 in order to "allow the emergence of a peaceful ceasefire" with the three anticolonial movements.[12] The next month UNITA signed a truce with the Portuguese, and the FNLA began receiving additional weapons and some reported Chinese instructors.[13] After the three factions of the MPLA failed to forge unity at a party congress in Zambia in August 1974, a second MPLA congress the next month did achieve greater unity and restored leadership to Agostinho Neto.

Once Portugal decided to grant independence to Angola, the Soviet Union gave more direct help to its client, the MPLA. According to U.S. government sources the Soviets sent about $6 million worth of weapons to Angola in August 1974. In addition, significant quantities of Soviet weapons began to reach the MPLA through Congo-Brazzaville in October and November 1974, while some 250 MPLA members went to the Soviet Union for military training. The presence of Cuban military advisers also began to increase. This Soviet aid allowed the MPLA to expand its armed troops from an estimated 1,400 in mid-1974 to some 5,000–7,000 by January 1975.[14] While the MPLA was conducting this military buildup in the autumn of 1974, it joined with the FNLA in signing cease-fire agreements with the Portuguese. In November 1974 UNITA and the FNLA agreed to negotiate jointly with Portugal for the independence of Angola. The following month the Organization of African Unity recognized UNITA.

The Alvor Agreement. In December 1974 the Portuguese high commissioner for Angola, Admiral Rosa Coutinho, met with UNITA and MPLA leaders. This meeting led to an agreement to negotiate jointly with Portugal to form a transitional government that would also include the FNLA. UNITA then proposed that all three anticolonial movements establish a joint position for their negotiations with Portugual. In early January 1975 the president of Kenya invited MPLA, UNITA, and FNLA leaders to meet in Kenya, where they negotiated an agreement on the terms of independence from Portugal. On January 15, 1975, leaders of all three movements and the Portuguese government met at Alvor, Portugal, and signed an agreement calling for the establishment of a transitional government of national unity in Angola by the end of January 1975. It set November 11, 1975, as the date for independence.

The Alvor agreement has provided the only basis for political legitimacy in postindependence Angola. It acknowledged that the three anticolonial movements—MPLA, FNLA, and UNITA—were the representatives of the Angolan people; it provided a framework for

Angola's transition to independence; and it focused on peaceful political competition among the three groups in elections to be conducted by the transitional government, composed of these groups and Portugal. The agreement stated explicitly: "The Transitional Government shall organize general elections for a constituent assembly within nine months from the 31st day of January 1975, the date of its coming into power."[15] It also required that the three anticolonial movements and Portugal each contribute an equal number of its armed forces to maintain law and order in Angola.

Though the MPLA participated in the transitional government, it continued its military buildup and its planning for seizing power. In February 1975 a nationwide Angolan poll showed that UNITA enjoyed the support of about 45 percent of the population and the MPLA and FNLA about 20 percent each. These proportions coincided roughly with the size of each movement's ethnic support base, of which the MPLA had the smallest.[16]

Civil War. In late February 1975 fighting broke out between the MPLA and the FNLA. A brief truce was arranged but more fighting occurred in March 1975, as the Soviets continued to ship weapons to the MPLA. As Professor Jiri Valenta, an expert on Soviet actions in developing countries, concluded, "The massive Soviet military supplies to the MPLA reached Angola in March and April [1975] several months before U.S. shipments of military supplies began to reach the FNLA through Zaire."[17] In April 1975, 100 tons of weapons were reported to have been flown to MPLA bases in Angola, while Soviet, Yugoslav, and other ships arrived with heavy weapons, such as multiple rocket launchers and armored personnel carriers.[18]

By June 1975 MPLA forces had established their control over Luanda, the Angolan capital, and most of the Kimbundu tribal territory in northern Angola. Although UNITA had refrained from military action, the MPLA began to attack it, in June 1975. After the MPLA demonstrated its intention to achieve military victory, the United States decided to provide military aid to its rivals.[19]

After the signing of the Alvor agreement, the *London Observer* reported that "Admiral Rosa Coutinho (. . . the Portuguese high commissioner) and most other Portuguese officials here appear to be still backing the MPLA, and this has led to suspicion . . . that the administration plans to prop up the MPLA."[20] In 1987 Rosa Coutinho admitted that he and the Communist faction within the Portuguese government had helped the MPLA take power in Angola. "I knew very well that elections could not be held in the territory during the time that had elapsed," he said. "I had stated at that time that the only solution was to recognize the MPLA as the only force capable of directing Angola, and that Portugal should make a separate agreement with the MPLA and transfer power to the MPLA on the fixed date of 11 November."[21] In a later interview Rosa Coutinho stated that he gave the MPLA needed funds and allowed Soviet weapons and Cuban advisors to enter Angola. As he put it, "I gave the MPLA the opportunity—otherwise they wouldn't have won."[22]

While the MPLA was being helped by Communist sympathizers within the Portuguese government and by the Soviet Union and Cuba, events in Southeast Asia were having an impact on Angola. In 1973 the United States had persuaded South Vietnam to sign a peace treaty with North Vietnam, even though this permitted 120,000 North Vietnamese troops to remain on South Vietnamese territory. Although the United States promised military assistance to South Vietnam if this treaty were violated, North Vietnam immediately began infiltrating thousands of additional troops and tons of military equipment into South Vietnam.[23] In the spring of 1975 North Vietnam launched a major invasion of South Vietnam, violating both the 1973 treaty and international law. By the end of April 1975, Communist movements had gained full control of South Vietnam, Cambodia, and Laos and were beginning the massive repression that would result in the death of several million civilians in those countries.

The failure of the United States to help South Vietnam in the face of an invasion and a breach of the peace treaty apparently emboldened the Soviet Union to press for a rapid MPLA victory in Angola. In May 1975 after heavy fighting broke out in Angola, additional Cuban military personnel began arriving to train MPLA troops. During this time, the United States was providing a small amount of political—but not yet military—aid to the FNLA.[24]

In June 1975 the president of Kenya again convened a meeting of the three anticolonial groups, which called for an end to fighting among them and reaffirmed the need to implement the Alvor agreement and to hold elections before independence. The MPLA, UNITA, and FNLA signed the Nakuru agreement on June 21, 1975, declaring: "Because of the little time left until the 11th of November and because of the complexity of the electoral process, the liberation movements promise to make every effort to hold elections."[25]

Soviet weapons continued to flow to the MPLA, which in July 1975 broke this agreement and resumed fighting to take control of as much Angolan territory as possible. Condemning this renewal of combat, in August 1975 the Organization of African Unity proposed that an all-African peace-keeping force restore order. At the same time thousands of additional Cuban military officers and combat troops began arriving to help the MPLA. From an increase in the number of its advisers for the MPLA in 1974, the Cuban presence had grown to organized training contingents in March 1975, to staffing for at least four training centers by June 1975, to the arrival of thousands of Cuban combat troops and generals (including the chairman of the joint chiefs, and the heads of the three armies and of the Cuban air force) in September 1975.[26] By the end of September 1975, the combined MPLA and Cuban offensive had brought twelve of Angola's sixteen provinces under MPLA control.

According to the testimony of former Secretary of State Kissinger and to most published estimates, the United States began giving military support to the FNLA in the summer of 1975, several months *after* the Soviet Union sharply increased its buildup of the MPLA's military force. South Africa sent its small contingent of about 2,000 troops into the conflict in mid-October 1975, when thousands of Cuban troops were already operating in combat formations with the MPLA. On October 23, 1975, a small mechanized force composed of about 2,000 South African soldiers and UNITA and FNLA guerrillas began operations against these Cuban-MPLA troops in southern Angola. By early November this UNITA-FNLA-South African group had moved more than 500 miles north and was making steady progress. The Soviet Union reacted by staging an airlift of additional weapons, including tanks and jet fighter aircraft along with thousands of additional Cuban troops.[27]

The People's Republic of Angola. Having captured the capital when it first broke the Alvor agreement months earlier, the MPLA on November 11, 1975, proclaimed the People's Republic of Angola and declared itself the new government. Immediate diplomatic recognition came from the Soviet Union, its allies in eastern Europe, Cuba, North Vietnam, and several Soviet-aligned African countries, including Congo-Brazzaville, Mozambique, Guinea-Bissau, Tanzania, and Algeria. Rejecting the MPLA declaration, UNITA and the FNLA declared that their coalition continued to be the legitimate transitional government mandated by the Alvor agreement, as fighting continued. Shortly after in Portugal, the Communist party "in alliance with radical elements of the armed forces precipitated . . . a violent escalation of the struggle for power." This culminated on November 25, 1975, as an attempted Communist coup, which was "put down . . . with only four casualties after most units surrendered without a fight."[28]

The Soviet Union, Cuba, and the MPLA regime have said that Cuban troops intervened in Angola after South Africa intervened, at the invitation of the new MPLA regime. Another allegation is that the Alvor agreement was broken not by the Communist side but by the small U.S. aid program for the FNLA. The historical record refutes both of these theories.

On December 19, 1975, the U.S. Senate voted 54 to 22 to block any new funds for support to military or paramilitary operations in Angola. This action resulted partly from a misperception of events inside Angola, and partly from a post-Vietnam concern about U.S. involvement in a prolonged conflict with Soviet-backed elements. In early January 1976, an extraordinary session of the Organization of African Unity declined by a tie vote to recognize the MPLA as the legitimate government of Angola. Later the same month, however, the U.S. House of Representatives voted 323 to 99 to prohibit U.S. aid for military or paramilitary activities in Angola as the Senate had. Since Senator Dick Clark, Democrat of Iowa, had led the opposition to U.S. military aid to the anti-Communist groups this prohibition became known as the Clark amendment.

On February 9, 1976, a joint MPLA-Cuban force captured the Angolan capital of UNITA and the FNLA, forcing both to retreat to remote areas. The next day, the secretariat of the Organization of African Unity recognized the MPLA government as the forty-seventh OAU member, and a few days later Portugal recognized the MPLA as the government of Angola.[29]

In congressional testimony at the end of January 1976, Secretary of State Kissinger summed up what had occurred:

Angola represents the first time that the Soviets have moved militarily at long distance to impose a regime of their choice. It is the first time that the United States has failed to respond to Soviet military moves outside the immediate Soviet orbit. And it is the first time that Congress has halted national action in the middle of a crisis. . . . An ominous precedent is set. . . . If the pattern is not broken now, we will face harder choices and higher costs in the future.[30]

During the spring of 1976, the Cuban and MPLA forces drove the FNLA into the far north of Angola. Savimbi and his remaining 2,000 UNITA troops fled 1,200 miles in four months to far southeastern Angola near its present headquarters at Jamba. The MPLA now had control of Angola.

The MPLA Regime

During the first few years after these victories, the MPLA regime faced no serious military resistance. It established its pattern of governance and did what virtually all Communist movements do,

111

constituting itself as a vanguard Marxist-Leninist party holding all political, economic, and military power. With help from the Soviet bloc and Cuba it established a secret police and internal security apparatus, propaganda and censorship organizations, and an array of regime-controlled groups to mobilize and control the population.

Oppression soon became widespread, especially against the tribes of the MPLA adversaries, such as the Bakongo and the Ovimbundu, who constituted about 60 percent of the population. By 1980 this repression and the clear Marxist-Leninist character of the regime had driven virtually all of the white population of several hundred thousand out of the country. More than 250,000 black Angolans also took refuge abroad.

During these early years of MPLA rule thousands of persons disappeared and were presumed killed by the regime, and many thousands were imprisoned. In 1977 one MPLA faction tried to overthrow the MPLA leader Agostinho Neto, who put down the coup attempt with help from Cuban troops. Afterward, thousands were arrested, including many MPLA officials, and many were executed.[31] By the end of 1987 the State Department estimated that more than 400,000 Angolans had fled (300,000 to Zaire, about 94,000 to Zambia) and an additional 700,000 persons had been displaced internally.[32]

The Decline of the Economy. Before the MPLA victory, the Angolan gross domestic product had averaged about 10 percent growth per year between 1966 and 1975. Angola produced enough food for its people and exported large amounts of food, oil, and diamonds. From the start, the MPLA had declared its intention to take control of the means of production. In May 1976 it began the nationalization process and within four years had taken control of 71 percent of all productive units with the state sector employing 83 percent of the work force.[33] The regime imitated the Soviet system of collectivized agriculture—mostly on agricultural property abandoned by the departing Portuguese—and began to regulate agricultural production and to require delivery of agricultural products to the state at fixed prices.

The result was a sharp disruption of what had been a highly productive agricultural economy. Angola had been a large net food exporter with only 2 to 3 percent of the land under cultivation. As a result of MPLA policies and the decline of agricultural production, by the early 1980s Angola had to import about 90 percent of its food requirements. Exports of coffee, a major Angolan commodity, declined, however, from 250,000 tons in 1974 to only 25,000 tons in 1983. Reliable economic data are hard to obtain because in 1983 Angola declared all economic data a state secret. This agricultural decline preceded the expansion and intensification of the anti-Communist guerrilla struggle.[34]

By 1987 the regime itself reported that half the population faced acute food shortages. That same year, UNICEF reported that Angola's child mortality rate was the highest in the world and that up to 45 percent of Angolan children suffered from malnutrition. For many years Angola has been one of the largest per capita recipients of food assistance from the International Red Cross.

From the pre-MPLA year 1975, during the years 1976 to 1979— years in which the regime faced virtually no armed resistance—there was a drop in per capita gross national product (in constant 1984 dollars from $1,276 to $1,146). Table 4–2 provides an overview of Angola's economy, armed forces, and arms imports from 1977 to 1987. The MPLA increased its armed forces by 50 percent between 1975 and 1977, to 47,000, and imported nearly $1.8 billion in weapons during those first several years. GNP remained at the same level during the 1980s as combat intensified. These figures suggest that most of the damage sustained by Angola's economy resulted from policies the MPLA regime pursued soon after it took power.

Having a small population and rich oil and mineral resources, Angola could enjoy a much higher standard of living. The MPLA earned an estimated $12 billion in oil revenues between 1976 and 1987. The Castro regime required the MPLA to pay an annual fee of $17,000 to $22,000 for each Cuban soldier in Angola. From 1976 to 1988 Castro probably earned about $7.4 billion for his troops. Moscow has probably required payments in hard currency and in commodities (diamonds, fish, other food) for its estimated $8.2 billion in weapons. Virtually all of this oil income, earned in hard currency, plus several billions more in cash or commodities, has probably gone to Cuba and the Soviet bloc countries to pay the estimated $16 billion for military and other personnel and for Soviet military equipment (see table 4–3).

MPLA Military Aid. Soon after taking power in 1976 the MPLA regime gave assistance to armed organizations seeking to attack three neighboring countries: Zaire, Namibia, and South Africa.[35] Cuban and other Soviet bloc personnel established guerrilla and terrorist training camps on Angolan territory. These bases served elements from the South West Africa People's Organization (SWAPO) targeted against Namibia, the Katangan secessionist movement targeted against Zaire, and the Communist-led African National Congress (ANC) targeted against South Africa. In March 1977 a force of Katangan rebels, reported to be led by Cuban troops, invaded Zaire from bases inside Angola and were repulsed. In May 1978 another large

113

TABLE 4-2
Angola's Economy, 1975–1987
(U.S. dollars)

	GNP ($ millions)		Population (millions)	GNP/Capita ($ constant '87)	MPLA Armed Forces (thousands)	Arms Imports ($ millions, constant '87)
	Current	Constant '87				
1975	—	—	6.0	—	30	—
1976	—	—	6.0	—	35	—
1977	4,639	8,114	6.2	1,312	47	595
1978	5,192	8,460	6.3	1,340	47	684
1979	5,778	8,654	6.5	1,332	47	554
1980	6,658	9,139	6.8	1,345	47	590
1981	7,194	8,953	7.0	1,288	53	845
1982	8,022	9,439	7.1	1,326	54	853
1983	8,456	9,580	7.3	1,319	54	1,246
1984	8,991	9,820	7.4	1,324	60	1,638
1985	9,741	10,330	7.6	1,365	66	822
1986	—	—	7.7	—	70	1,343
1987	—	—	8.0	—	74	1,600
Total						10,770

SOURCE: U.S. Arms Control and Disarmament Agency, *World Military Expenditures and Arms Transfers, 1988*, pp. 32, 74.

TABLE 4-3
ANGOLA'S ESTIMATED OIL REVENUES AND PAYMENTS TO CUBA AND THE SOVIET UNION, 1976–1988

	Oil Revenue ($ millions)	Cuban Troops in Angola (thousands)	Payments to Cuba ($ millions)[a]	Arms Imports ($ millions, constant '87)	Cost of Soviet Weapons ($ millions)
1976	—	12	216	—	600 ('74–'76)
1977	—	14.5[b]	261	595	—
1978	—	17	306	684	—
1979	—	21[b]	378	554	—
1980	1,390	23[b]	414	590	900 ('78–'81)
1981	1,345	26[b]	468	845	—
1982	1,234	30	540	853	—
1983	1,526	33.5[b]	603	1,246	3,500 ('82–'84)
1984	1,748	37	666	1,638	—
1985	1,906	42[b]	756	822	2,000 ('85–'86)
1986	1,134	47	846	1,343	1,500
1987	2,065	48	864	1,600	—
1988	—	60	1,080	—	—
Totals	12,348 ('80–'87)		7,398	10,770 ('77–'87)	8,500 ('74–'87)

a. Alexiev and Brown estimate $14,000 to $22,000 per Cuban soldier annually.
b. Extrapolated from available data.

SOURCES: *Angola: The Long Road to Freedom* (Washington, D.C.: Free Angola Information Society, 1988), pp. 4–5; *Washington Times*, December 8, 1988; Economist Intelligence Unit, *Angola Country Profile, 1988–1989*; Alexander R. Alexiev and Nanette C. Brown, "UNITA of Angola: Profile of an Anti-Marxist Resistance Movement," Rand Working Draft 2745-USDP, October 1985; U.S. Arms Control and Disarmament Agency, *World Military Expenditures and Arms Transfers, 1988*, p. 74.

force of Katangans invaded Shaba province in southern Zaire. The Mobutu government, which had to call in international assistance to repel the attack, formally accused Angola of supporting the invasion. The Carter administration seconded the charge and accused Cuban forces of helping to train the Katangans. Calling Carter a "liar," Castro denied any Cuban involvement.

By 1987 SWAPO maintained an estimated 7,000 armed personnel on Angolan territory, the ANC about 1,200, and the Zaire-Katangan secessionists about 1,400.[36] SWAPO and ANC guerrillas continued to operate from Angolan territory at least until December 1988, when a diplomatic settlement required a definitive end to such operations.

The MPLA regime clearly agreed with the Soviet Union and Cuba that its victory in Angola should be only a prelude to the victory of other pro-Soviet groups throughout the region. In reply to U.S. protests against the Soviets' and Cubans' massive supply of weapons and troops to help the MPLA take power in late 1975, an *Izvestia* editorial said:

> Some would like to convince us that the process of detente in the world and support of the National Liberation struggle are incompatible things. . . . The process of detente does not mean and never meant the freezing of the sociopolitical status quo in the world and the cessation of anti-imperialist struggles of the people.[37]

The Second War for Angola

After the MPLA regime took power, the second war for Angola pitted the MPLA regime (backed by the Soviet bloc, Cuba, and some African countries) against the UNITA resistance movement (backed by South Africa, Morocco, and a few other Arab and African countries and, after 1985, by the United States). By 1985, this war involved massive combat operations, including hundreds of tanks, artillery, and jet fighters.

The Cuban and Soviet-bloc presence in Angola had increased from some 14,000 troops in 1976 to more than 67,000 by the end of 1988. Estimated Soviet-bloc military deliveries to the Angolan armed forces totaled more than $8.5 billion by the end of 1987 (see table 4–3).

UNITA forces grew from an estimated remnant of 1,000 in 1976 to between 40,000 and 65,000 by 1988. In late 1988, UNITA was estimated to control and administer about 40 percent of Angola and to exercise significant influence in much of the remaining territory.

Early Phases of the War. The second Angolan war involved five phases, as the MPLA regime and its allies intensified combat operations against the growing UNITA movement.

During the first phase (1976–1979), the MPLA regime showed exceptional brutality in its effort to consolidate power. It alienated large portions of the Ovimbundu, the main social base of the UNITA movement, and other tribal groups. An estimated 30,000 of the refugees who fled Angola during these years settled just over Angola's southern border, in Namibia.

In these first years, Savimbi, whose guerrillas had retreated to southeastern Angola after the MPLA victory, established political support among the peasants and recruited followers. His program called for a mixed economy, with maximum opportunities for private ownership, especially in agriculture, and for minimal state intervention. On social issues UNITA called for government-provided health and education to accompany private health and education services. In the political realm, UNITA advocated multiparty democracy with competitive elections. Its program said:

> UNITA objectives remain those embodied in the 1975 Alvor accord. . . . These include the withdrawal of all foreign forces, the formation of a government of national reconciliation and the holding of free and fair elections to establish a pluralistic political system to guarantee the freedom of expression, religion, speech, assembly and the press.[38]

Within its areas of control, UNITA attempted to provide education, health, and other services to the population and found increasing support.

In the second phase (1979–1980), UNITA began occasional insurgent operations on a small scale. By 1980 it had an estimated 10,000 guerrillas. Four operational objectives marked UNITA's strategy throughout its insurgency:

1. Deny as much territory as possible to government control.
2. Isolate government-controlled towns from the countryside.
3. Disrupt the economic structure of the country.
4. Deny the regime the economic means it needs to stay in power by disrupting the export industry.[39]

The third phase (1980–1983) began when the UNITA forces conducted their first major successful conventional operations—the capture of an MPLA garrison by more than 2,000 UNITA fighters in September 1980. The Cuban presence began to increase, but the Cubans mainly performed garrison duties, guarding towns and MPLA facilities. Regime forces for the most part made only occasional patrols into the countryside and worked mainly to keep control of

117

the towns, cities, and strategically important regions. Territory under UNITA control, its forces, and its political organization all grew steadily.[40]

In 1984 the MPLA adopted a military offensive strategy. After joint Soviet-Cuban and MPLA consultations, supplies of Soviet weapons and Cuban combat personnel to the MPLA significantly increased, and the MPLA forces were reorganized.[41] For the first time, the MPLA staged medium-size attacks to drive UNITA back from its zones of control, but failed. Forced recruitment, food shortages, and mass desertions have been cited as causes of the failure.

The 1984 offensives followed and complemented a more active diplomacy by the Soviet Union and Angola. In late 1983 the Soviet Union arranged through the UN secretary general a meeting with South African representatives in New York, which failed to deter a major South Africa incursion into Angola against SWAPO bases in December 1983. The Soviet Union issued a public warning in January 1984 that South Africa should cease aiding UNITA and convened a conference with Cuban and Angolan representatives. This was followed by a more aggressive Soviet-Cuban-MPLA strategy, buttressed by a large increase in weapons. For example, weapons and weapon parts delivered to the MPLA in Angola from January 1 to October 10, 1984, included the following:[42]

25 armored cars
34 57mm anti-aircraft guns
100 other AA guns
96 T-34 tanks
34 T-54 tanks
 3 T-62 tanks
46 personnel carriers (BTR-60)
140 cargo trucks
211 other military vehicles
160,000 tons small arms and ammo
30 MiG-21s (Fishbed) [combat aircraft]
 7 MI-8 helicopters [combat aircraft]
 2 MI-24 rotary wings [combat aircraft]
12 MiG-21 fuselages [combat aircraft]
 5 SU-22 (Fitter) fuselages [combat aircraft]
 5 SU-22 (Fitter) wings [combat aircraft]
 2 MiG-23 (Flogger) fuselages [combat aircraft]
 6 MiG-23 (Flogger) wings [combat aircraft]

This military buildup and offensive continued through 1984, despite the signing in February 1984 of the Lusaka agreement between South

Africa and the MPLA regime. That agreement and the Nkomati accord between Mozambique and South Africa had signaled a turning point to many observers. The Lusaka agreement required the MPLA regime to prohibit SWAPO guerrillas from taking sanctuary on Angolan territory, and it required South Africa to cease military incursions into Angola. It also included acceptance of a Cuban troop withdrawal. Ultimately the agreement collapsed because the MPLA regime demanded that South Africa end all support to UNITA before any Cubans would leave Angola.[43]

Gorbachev's Four Offensives

The fourth phase of the war for Angola began after Gorbachev came to power in the Soviet Union in March 1985. Soviet military support to the MPLA regime increased sharply, and the Cuban troop presence doubled. Each year from 1985 through 1988, the MPLA, Soviets, and Cubans launched a major offensive during the dry season (from May to October) intended not just to contain the UNITA insurgency but to destroy it.[44]

Thousands of Cuban combat troops participated in the 1985 offensive, backed up by Soviet bloc pilots and other personnel. The advancing MPLA Cuban forces:

> were constantly resupplied through a network of Soviet-built air fields, guarded by Soviet planes and an elaborate radar network constructed by the Soviets. There may have been between 9 and 14 Soviet advisers with each battalion and the reason none were killed was that they were withdrawn by helicopter when things went badly. The Soviets commanded most of the air force, artillery and armored units.[45]

After this first offensive failed, President Reagan's administration decided to provide military aid to UNITA (Congress having repealed the Clark amendment). In January 1986 Savimbi visited the United States and met with senior officials, including President Reagan. In February 1986, published reports stated that the Reagan administration would provide military aid to UNITA, including anti-aircraft weapons such as the highly effective Stinger shoulder-fired missile.[46] In May 1986 the Soviet Union and the MPLA issued a joint statement professing readiness "to undertake concerted action in the defense of the independence, sovereignty and territorial integrity of Angola."[47] In the summer of 1986, the MPLA regime with full Cuban and Soviet military support began another major offensive against UNITA, which was also stalemated and turned back.

For the 1987 offensive, planned by Konstantin I. Shaganovitch, a four-star Soviet general, the Soviets delivered more than $1 billion in additional military equipment to Angola "by Soviet AN-24 flights, as many as twelve per day over a six month period":

> Extraordinarily large numbers of Soviet advisers appeared with each of the Angolan Army brigades. . . . Soviet advisers were fighting along with Cubans. . . . The Soviet Foreign Ministry admitted that Soviet troops were manning much of the hardware with Angolan units, including tanks, helicopters, and ground to air missiles. . . . Soviet, Cuban and Angolan pilots reportedly engaged South African jets.[48]

With South African assistance, UNITA halted the offensive and launched a counteroffensive in the fall of 1987, when it destroyed seven Soviet tanks, nineteen armored vehicles, two jet fighter aircraft, and one helicopter gunship. In November 1987 it displayed 220 captured military vehicles along with captured anti-aircraft missiles and two Cuban pilots.[49]

The 1988 Offensive. Preparations for a renewed MPLA regime offensive in 1988 began almost immediately. While attending celebrations in Moscow in November 1987, on the anniversary of the Bolshevik Revolution, Fidel Castro, Angolan president José Eduardo dos Santos, and Soviet leaders may have planned the next moves. Within five months, Angola received about 15,000 additional Cuban troops—Castro's elite military forces, commanded by the experienced General Ochoa Sanchez. A member of the central committee of the Cuban Communist party and a deputy minister of defense, he had commanded the Cuban forces during the MPLA seizure of power in 1975 and had combat experience with Cuban forces in Ethiopia and Nicaragua.[50] (Castro had Ochoa Sanchez and three other Cuba officers executed on July 13, 1989, after they confessed at a staged trail to smuggling narcotics, diamonds, and ivory—most likely Castro feared a military plot against his rule.)

On December 10, 1987, Dos Santos announced he had authorized Cuban forces to begin patrolling to the Namibian border and to attack South African forces. About the same time Vietnamese military advisers arrived in Angola. On January 13, 1988, UNITA and South African troops attacked Cuito Cuanavale, the airbase from which the MPLA, Cuban, and Soviet forces launched their annual offensives.

> General [Ochoa] Sanchez directed the defense. . . . Cuban pilots flew MiG-23 ground attacks . . . against the besieging forces. ANC and SWAPO forces acted as scouts, and the defenders used mobile radar stored in underground bunkers to direct the Soviet planes and the Cuban piloted attack

helicopters. The newly arrived North Vietnamese officers advised on how to resist siege tactics. Privately Soviet strategists boasted of Cuito as "Angola's Stalingrad." This extraordinary combination of Soviet clients was able to hold Cuito Cuanavale despite massive bombardment, leaving a military stalemate in south central Angola.[51]

About 8,000 UNITA soldiers with some South African support met the estimated force of 18,000 MPLA and Cuban troops. According to UNITA, the MPLA forces were caught in a series of ambushes and flanking attacks, which led to their defeat and retreat. UNITA estimated that the Communist side suffered about 2,000 dead and 5,000 wounded, while UNITA lost 150 dead and 600 wounded.[52]

On March 17, 1988, the Cuban armed forces ministry issued this statement: "Every effort by the South African troops and their allies to capture Cuito Cuanavale has been countered with a rain of artillery fire and air strikes. Cuban/Angolan planes have played a brilliant and heroic role in the combats. . . . Their action has been decisive." The Cuban government press agency reported that Castro told a group of foreign diplomats that "Cuban/Angolan/SWAPO forces had advanced [150 miles] south and were now [thirty miles] from the border with Namibia."[53] Military operations in early 1988 now shifted toward Namibia and the South African forces in southern Angola.

Castro had said in 1987 that Cuban troops would remain in Angola until Namibia was independent under the terms of UN Security Council Resolution 435 and until apartheid had been defeated in South Africa. As of 1985, as a result of South African attacks and UNITA's expanded control, SWAPO's estimated strength based in Angola had declined from about 16,500 in 1978 to about 6,500. Over the years Cuba and the Soviet bloc not only gave SWAPO political support, money, weapons, and guerrilla training but also trained SWAPO personnel in conventional military operations. During the 1980s these SWAPO conventional military units had been attached to the Angolan armed forces. Now in early 1988, Cuba moved to integrate them into joint Cuban-SWAPO combat units comprising about 200 to 250 SWAPO guerrillas with some 200 Cuban personnel.

In April 1988, SWAPO leaders met with senior officials in Moscow and then with senior officials in Cuba, Nicaragua, and the United States. One analysis concluded: "It would appear that the decision to rebuild and mobilize SWAPO . . . involved the highest levels of government and the military in both the Soviet Union and Cuba."[54] In the spring of 1988, Cuba deployed an additional 10,000 elite troops into the southern Angolan region along the Namibian border, from which SWAPO had long operated.

The Cuban official daily newspaper, *Granma*, praised the "audacious and unstoppable movements of Cuban/Angolan/SWAPO forces."[55] Responding to a South African warning against any attack on Namibia, Castro said that South Africa was "in no position to demand anything." Another Cuban official said, "We are not saying that we will not go into Namibia."[56] By June 1, 1988, the Cuban press agency described how Castro saw the new balance of forces:

> We now have air and anti-aircraft superiority; the best Cuban anti-aircraft weapons are in southern Angola; and we have the means to face any South African advance. The correlation of forces has totally changed. . . . South Africa . . . must be asking itself if we will advance, seize control of the water reservoirs near and within the Angolan border. . . . This must be part of a negotiated solution. . . . [W]e are in a position to take more [military] risks because if the enemy wants a confrontation he can suffer a serious defeat.[57]

This Communist military buildup and confident political rhetoric all coincided with the U.S.–Soviet summit in Moscow—the fourth Reagan-Gorbachev meeting—in late May and early June 1988. That summit concluded with a joint Soviet–U.S. statement calling for negotiations to reach an accord on Angola and Namibia by the end of September 1988. Simultaneously, the Soviet-Cuban-MPLA coalition increased its military attacks.

Near the Namibian border in Angola, the Calueque Dam, which provided water and power to Angola and northern Namibia, had been exempted from combat throughout the war. On June 27, 1988, a Cuban-MPLA-Soviet infantry and armored force attacked the dam while Cuban aircraft bombed it. These attacks violated promises not to bomb the dam made by Cuban envoys at recent negotiations in Brazzaville. To intimidate UNITA and South Africa further, "Cuban and Angolan pilots flew reconnaissance over northern Namibia where key South African bases are located" and "Soviet 'Frog' surface-to-surface missiles capable of hitting South African bases [in Namibia] [were] deployed."[58] With both sides inflicting substantial casualties, a stalemate resulted.

In July 1988 it was reported that 150 Soviet anti-aircraft missiles (of the advanced SAM-8 type) and advanced radar systems had been deployed against South African air power. Two Cuban-built air bases and military supply and command facilities in southern Angola also posed a direct threat to Namibia. In September 1988, Cuba was reported to have sent 5,000 more troops to Angola. These actions were intended to shift the balance toward the Communist side in the ongoing, intensive negotiations in the summer and fall of 1988. It is well-established Communist practice to increase military operations and threats in conjunction with negotiations.

The Soviet-Cuban-SWAPO Alliance

Much of the diplomacy and international political activity regarding Angola has also involved Namibia, the region to its south. This South African–administered territory is sparsely populated, with about 1 million people. About three times the size of Texas, it is rich in minerals and agricultural potential.

After Germany's defeat in World War I, the League of Nations delegated administrative authority over this former German colony to South Africa. In 1966 the UN General Assembly voted to end South Africa's mandate, and in 1969 the UN Security Council voted for South Africa's withdrawal from Namibia (with Britain and France abstaining). In 1971 the International Court of Justice ruled that South Africa's continued presence in Namibia was illegal. And in 1973 the UN General Assembly voted 107 to 2 (South Africa and Portugal), with 17 abstentions, to recognize SWAPO as "the authentic representative of the Namibian people."

In July 1978 Donald McHenry, the Carter administration's UN ambassador, met with SWAPO leaders in Angola to discuss Western proposals for Namibia, which eventually became the UN secretary general's plan for elections in Namibia.[59] In September 1978 the Security Council passed UN Resolution 435 outlining a program leading to independence for Namibia, including the establishment of a UN force to replace the departing South African troops.

More than half of Namibia's indigenous peoples are members of the Ovambo tribe. In 1957 the Ovamboland People's Organization was established to seek independence for Namibia. By 1960 SWAPO emerged out of this organization under the leadership of Sam Nujoma. By 1962 he was no longer willing to work with the South West Africa National Union (SWANU), based on the Herero tribe, the third largest ethnic group in Namibia with nearly 90,000 members.[60] Nujoma eventually took full control over SWAPO by arranging for the expulsion of moderates, such as Professor Kerina, who returned to Namibia in 1989 as an opponent of SWAPO.[61]

The Soviet Union began a close relationship with SWAPO and Nujoma in the early 1960s.[62] According to Vanneman, "Since 1963 the centerpiece and chief instrument of Soviet policy for Namibia has always been the insurgent South West Africa People's Organization."[63] In 1965 SWAPO announced the start of armed struggle for Namibian independence.

In response to international pressures, South Africa took steps in the early 1970s to establish multiracial self-government in Namibia. These included establishment of the Advisory Council of 1973 and of the Multi-Racial Constitutional Conference of 1975 and a series of elections in the late 1970s. SWAPO refused to participate in any of these political activities. Nujoma expelled dissenting SWAPO leaders as agents of the South African regime. In August 1976—after the establishment of pro-Soviet regimes in Angola, Mozambigue, and Guinea-Bissau—a SWAPO delegation met with Soviet leaders in Moscow to discuss strategy on the future of Namibia. After an October 1976 meeting with Castro, Nujoma affirmed that Cuba was providing support to SWAPO, and in early 1977 he admitted receiving "large donations from Soviet Russia."[64]

The shift toward the Marxist-Leninist domination of SWAPO was evident in its 1976 political program. It called for uniting "all Namibian people, particularly the working class, the peasantry and progressive intellectuals into a vanguard party . . . based upon the ideals and principles of scientific socialism," and ensuring "that all the major means of production and exchange of the country are [in the] ownership of the people."[65]

The MPLA regime in Angola provided significant new support to Nujoma and SWAPO, which was given bases and sanctuary near Ovambo tribal lands in Namibia. In March 1977 Castro visited Angola and met with Nujoma and other African guerrilla leaders. The Soviet Union, Cuba, and East Germany increased their training of these guerrilla forces. In 1978 Nujoma declared, "We are not fighting for majority rule. We are fighting to seize power in Namibia for the benefit of the Namibian people. We are revolutionaries."[66] Shortly thereafter, Chief Kapuuo of the Herero tribe, whose movement was willing to work within the political framework for transition and was opposed by SWAPO, was assassinated.

In December 1978 Nujoma participated in a meeting of world Communist and allied parties in Bulgaria, held to take stock of the world Communist movement. That same month, in elections held under universal adult suffrage for a constituent assembly for Namibia, 80 percent of those eligible voted and forty-one of fifty seats were won by the Democratic Turnhalle Alliance—a multiracial coalition of eleven parties. Supporters of SWAPO contended that it was excluded from the election, so SWAPO's vice president, Mishake Muyongo, appealed to the Soviet Union, East Germany, and Cuba for "all out military assistance [against] the maneuvers of the racists in Pretoria and their American patrons."[67] But the close relationship between SWAPO leader Nujoma and the Soviet Union had begun years earlier. The 1978 elections were not regarded as valid by

Western powers because Namibia remained under South African control.

In 1980 another round of elections was held under universal suffrage for administrative assemblies. Although many multiracial parties participated in these elections, SWAPO boycotted them and subsequent ones. In a speech to the Twenty-sixth Congress of the Communist Party of the Soviet Union in March 1981, Nujoma praised Soviet ruler Leonid Brezhnev as "a devoted, staunch fighter for peace, detente, freedom, and human dignity of all the world's people. . . . Without the support of the Soviet Union, we would not have been able to achieve those results that we have achieved today."[68]

SWAPO's relationship with Cuba and the Soviet Union became closer in the 1980s. One of Eduard Shevardnadze's first acts after being named Soviet foreign minister in 1985 was to meet with Nujoma in Algeria. Some months later, on a highly publicized visit to Moscow, Nujoma told *Pravda:* "The only way out is to seek independence by force of arms."[69] In 1988 SWAPO opened a mission in Moscow and, as we have seen, received a significant increase in weapons, after the joint Soviet-Cuban-Angolan decisions of April 1988. Conventional SWAPO forces began operating with Cuban units in early 1988.

SWAPO's Human Rights Violations. In 1986 a leader of SWAPO-Democrats, a competing organization committed to a peaceful democratic transition to independence for Namibia, said: "SWAPO's atrocities are targeted against members of other ethnic and tribal groups . . . and they [SWAPO victims] number in the thousands."[70] An estimated 10,000 Namibians have died as a result of SWAPO's operations.[71]

In 1986 Amnesty International accused SWAPO of holding and torturing prisoners in Angola.[72] Using the accounts of the parents of SWAPO members who had been killed or imprisoned in SWAPO bases in Angola and Zambia, a West European human rights group wrote in 1988, "The number of SWAPO victims . . . is now certainly a four digit number: today there are at least a few hundred, possibly more, prisoners in SWAPO prisons."[73]

In July 1989 as the United Nations began to return an estimated 41,000 Namibian exiles to their country, further eyewitness accounts of "SWAPO torture, imprisonment and killings of SWAPO members were revealed by Namibians freed from SWAPO prisons." Those released "charged that dozens, perhaps hundreds of SWAPO members accused of spying for South Africa were killed at SWAPO prison camps in Angola." A former labor union official said: "I was beaten every day, I know many people who were beaten to death." And another released SWAPO prisoner said: "I lived in a pit underground. We were beaten, we had no medicine and we feared for our lives every day."[74]

The 1988 report of the International Society for Human Rights described the terrible conditions in the SWAPO central prison, where the inmates were "held in a large hole in the ground" and there were no medical facilities. Death sentences were carried out by firing squad or by throwing the prisoner into a deep hole. In Nyango Prison, the prisoners were chained to posts anchored in the cement.[75]

According to one estimate, the United Nations since the late 1970s has provided tens of millions of dollars in aid to SWAPO, including assistance in making propaganda films.[76] Some Western countries have also provided millions of dollars in assistance, although more than twenty-five years of actions and words show that SWAPO's goal is to establish a pro-Soviet dictatorship to rule the people of Namibia.

U.S. Policy and International Diplomacy

Four U.S. presidents have presided over policy toward Angola since the Communist takeover. After Congress prevented the Ford administration from continuing aid to the pro-Western independence movements in 1975 and in early 1976, the White House accepted the Marxist regime and terminated efforts to influence events there. Although the MPLA and Cuban forces had failed to suppress the UNITA and FNLA independence movements, the Ford administration permitted U.S. corporations such as Gulf Oil to resume activities in Angola, which immediately transferred at least $100 million to the regime.[77] Despite the massive Soviet and Cuban military intervention, and despite Secretary of State Henry Kissinger's strong condemnation of Soviet actions in Angola, President Ford said in January 1976 that he was still enthusiastic about détente.

Some Democratic members of Congress proposed economic assistance to the new MPLA regime. Senator Dick Clark wrote that he believed MPLA President Agostinho Neto was "an African Socialist, not a Soviet Marxist" and quoted Neto as saying, "I am not a Marxist. I never have been. My movement is not Marxist." Democratic Senator John Tunney of California, a strong supporter of the Clark amendment, described the MPLA as "basically pro-Angolan, Socialist and highly nationalistic and involved with the Soviet Union because of U.S. policy mistakes."[78]

The Carter administration's views on Angola were expressed by Jimmy Carter during his 1976 campaign: "The Russian and Cuban presence in Angola, while regrettable and counterproductive of peace, need not constitute a threat to the United States' interests nor does that presence mean the existence of a Communist satellite on the continent."[79] His administration ignored the opportunity to challenge the MPLA regime given by the growing UNITA movement and focused instead on Namibia and Rhodesia, which made the transition to independence under a one-party regime in 1979. Savimbi visited the United States in 1979, with little effect, and described U.S. policy as one of "total absence of resistance to Russian and Cuban aggression" in Africa.[80]

As a presidential candidate, Ronald Reagan supported U.S. aid for UNITA, and in 1981 he appointed as assistant secretary of state for Africa Chester Crocker, who had been critical of Carter administration policy.[81] Under him the State Department took the lead in formulating the Reagan administration's policy of constructive engagement for southern Africa. It had three objectives: independence for Namibia on the basis of UN Security Council Resolution 435; halting the spread of Soviet influence and then reducing it in the region; and progress toward ending apartheid in South Africa.[82]

As the State Department saw constructive engagement, South Africa would grant independence to Namibia in return for withdrawal of Cuban forces from Angola. South Africa was reported to have accepted this linkage in June 1981. The State Department began discussions with the MPLA regime in late 1981, promising diplomatic recognition and U.S. economic assistance in return for its acceptance of the linkage.

From the start, this linkage concept omitted any effort to implement the Alvor agreement in Angola. The parties seemed to assume that the MPLA and UNITA would resolve their conflict once Cuban troops were withdrawn. The United States may have underestimated the prospects of a UNITA victory and overestimated the readiness of the MPLA to conciliate.

In 1981 by a vote of sixty-six to twenty, the Senate repealed the Clark prohibition on U.S. aid to UNITA, though the State Department offered no support for this position. But subsequently, after a House-Senate conference committee approved a new U.S. aid authorization bill retaining the Clark prohibition, it passed both the House and the Senate.

As a result of several years of diplomatic effort, the Lusaka agreement, signed in February 1984, provided for the removal of all SWAPO guerrillas from Angolan territory, the withdrawal of South African troops from Angolan territory, and a timetable for the withdrawal of all Cuban forces. Although the MPLA regime accepted the principle of Cuban withdrawal, it changed its naturalization law to allow Cuban troops to become Angolan citizens, who would not be subject to any withdrawal agreement.

Events of 1985–1987. In mid-1984 the State Department approved U.S. Export-Import Bank credits of $130 million for Angola's national oil company, even though the regime had not lived up to the withdrawal agreement. This credit may have violated the Cuban Assets Control Regulation Act, which prohibits U.S. assistance to Cuba or countries controlled or occupied by Cuban forces. In late November 1984, the MPLA regime outlined its new proposals in a letter to the UN secretary general: Cuban troops stationed in southern Angola would be withdrawn within three years, and the rest would be withdrawn only when "Angola's territory and security have been totally guaranteed," that is, when UNITA had been defeated. In mid-March 1985, UNITA sources noted and deplored the State Department's acceptance in principle of this approach.[83]

South African troops began their withdrawal from Angolan territory, and a joint South African-MPLA monitoring commission was formed in 1985. Although MPLA compliance presented difficulties from the start, Secretary of State George Shultz exemplified State Department thinking by saying in April 1985 that the Lusaka agreement had worked and "the war between South Africa and Angola is over."[84] Shortly after this optimistic statement, the Lusaka agreement collapsed because the MPLA demanded that South Africa withdraw and stop supporting UNITA before any Cubans left. Even after UNITA had defeated the massive MPLA-Cuban-Soviet military offensives of the next four years and contained the Communist military buildup, in the 1988 final accords the State Department accepted the MPLA approach and essentially met many of the MPLA's 1984 demands.

Four major events occurred in 1985: the first of four annual Soviet-Cuban-MPLA military offensives; President Reagan's public proclamation of the Reagan Doctrine; congressional repeal of the Clark amendment; and the decision of the African National Congress to make South Africa ungovernable through a campaign of violence and terror and to bring about economic sanctions against South Africa. The first and fourth events favored the MPLA regime and led ultimately to the accords signed in 1988.

Following his overwhelming reelection victory, President Reagan proclaimed the Reagan Doctrine in his January 1985 state of the union address. He declared that the United States would "not break faith with those who are risking their lives—on every continent, from

Afghanistan to Nicaragua—to defy Soviet-supported aggression and secure rights which have been ours from birth. . . . I want to work with you to support the democratic forces whose struggle is tied to our own security."[85] In the spring and summer of 1985, Republican senators Steve Symms (Idaho), Malcolm Wallop (Wyoming), and Jim McClure (Idaho) led the successful effort to repeal the Clark amendment. In the House, after enough Democrats joined the Republican minority to repeal the prohibition on military aid to UNITA, Congressmen Jack Kemp (Republican of New York) and Claude Pepper (Democrat of Florida) introduced an aid proposal for UNITA. The central committee of the MPLA reportedly concluded that the repeal of the Clark amendment "confirms the criminal nature of Washington's policy of constructive engagement."[86]

In October 1985, Secretary of State Shultz wrote House Republican leader Robert Michel (Illinois): "I understand that Congressmen Pepper and Kemp have introduced legislation which would provide $27 million in non-lethal assistance to Dr. Savimbi's movement, UNITA, in Angola. . . . The suggested legislation should be opposed." On October 18, 1985, Michel responded to Shultz that aid to UNITA was "not only a geostrategic but a moral necessity. . . . I cannot see how we can argue that aid to the democratic forces in Nicaragua helps the chance of negotiations while aid to UNITA somehow damages the negotiating process."[87]

After this exchange of letters became public, the *Washington Times* reported on October 23, 1985, that Republican Congressman Jim Courter of New Jersey had "gathered twenty-seven other Republicans to sign a letter to President Reagan urging aid to UNITA." At the same time the six Democratic members of the House Subcommittee on Africa wrote their colleagues: "Any U.S. aid to UNITA would ally us with South Africa in its regional aggression and effectively undermine our ability to pressure South Africa to dismantle its internal system of apartheid. . . ." Within the Reagan administration, CIA Director William Casey and other members of the foreign policy cabinet tried to get a presidential decision on the UNITA aid issue. After some weeks, President Reagan revealed that the United States would provide military aid to UNITA.[88]

South African Sanctions. Events concerning South Africa moved in the opposite direction during 1985. The African National Congress, an anti-apartheid organization with Communist elements in its leadership, has since 1961 used violent as well as political means.[89] In 1985 it initiated a campaign that included the use of gasoline-filled tires to burn alive hundreds of black persons accused of working with or for the South African government. Gangs of teenagers called "comrades" usually conducted these terrorist attacks.

This violence and the countermeasures by the South African government resulted in increased media attention in the industrial democracies and in a campaign for sanctions against South Africa. While daily protests were being held in front of the Embassy of South Africa in Washington, D.C., Democrats in Congress planned for economic sanctions against South Africa to be enacted in 1985.[90] In an effort to put events in South Africa in some perspective, Secretary of State Shultz said in early 1985:

> There has been more reform in South Africa in the past four years than in the previous thirty. . . . South Africa is not a closed totalitarian society. . . . There is in that system a significant degree of openness of political activity and expression—a generally free press, independent judiciary, vigorous debate within the governing party and in Parliament, and vocal critics from all viewpoints. We have consistently called for an end to apartheid.[91]

Nevertheless, after the House of Representatives passed a tough sanctions bill and the Senate began to consider it, the State Department persuaded President Reagan to enact limited economic sanctions in September 1985. It contended that they would both delay more severe sanctions and make clear the administration's opposition to apartheid.

The ANC-initiated violence in South Africa continued during 1986. In June, on the tenth anniversary of the 1976 Soweto uprisings, the House passed a comprehensive sanctions bill. In September 1986 the Senate approved less severe sanctions and then overrode President Reagan's veto of this bill. Subsequently, after Secretary of State Shultz met with ANC leader Oliver Tambo, the State Department announced that U.S. officials would continue these contacts.

These developments led to profound insecurity in the government of South Africa over its important relations with the United States and other major free world countries. The Soviet Union might have reiterated the threats it had made in 1983 and 1984 of dire consequences if South Africa continued to support UNITA. In any case, the U.S. economic sanctions of 1986 were fresh in the memories of South African leaders, and the threat of additional U.S. economic sanctions was a means of pressure the U.S. State Department could use when in the midst of the 1988 final negotiations the House of Representatives again had passed even more severe sanctions and the Senate prepared to consider them.

Early in 1987, while the MPLA-Cuban alliance increased its

military and political efforts, U.S. Assistant Secretary of State Chester Crocker met a number of times with MPLA officials, and in July 1987, he traveled to Luanda for negotiations. MPLA ruler Dos Santos had already declared—as had Castro—that Cuban troops would remain in Angola until apartheid was abolished in South Africa. After several days in the Angolan capital, Crocker terminated the talks, calling them a waste of time.

But after conferring with Castro in Havana in August 1987, Dos Santos presented new and seemingly more flexible proposals. The MPLA proposed that Cuba participate in the talks, that Namibia be granted independence within one year, and that some Cuban troops leave Angola within two years, with the rest remaining longer. Although the United States immediately rejected this proposal, it was similar to the final agreement reached in December 1988.

During this diplomatic activity, the MPLA and Cubans were preparing their 1987 autumn military offensive. After UNITA success-fully turned back this offensive, a number of other African states, including Kenya, Zambia, and the Ivory Coast, offered to mediate negotiations between UNITA and the MPLA. Nigeria offered to contribute 15,000 troops to a peacekeeping force to supervise the establishment of a transitional government in Angola.

1988—The Decisive Year

Activity in Angola in 1988 can be divided into two periods: in the first half of 1988, Cuban forces were being increased, and the Cuban-MPLA axis undertook significant new military actions; the last six months were marked by intense formal and informal diplomatic negotiations. Throughout 1988, the United States and South Africa made significant retreats from previous negotiating positions, while the Communist position changed only slightly.

At the end of January 1988, when Assistant Secretary of State Crocker went to Angola for bilateral talks, Cubans participated as members of the Angolan delegation. In these talks, the United States accepted the concept of Namibian independence and withdrawal of all South African troops from Namibia *before* all Cuban troops had withdrawn from Angola. Thus the United States failed to take advantage of the position of strength that resulted from UNITA's victories.

The Cuban military buildup and the impending U.S.–Soviet summit led a bipartisan group of senators to write President Reagan on May 12, 1988, shortly before his summit meeting with Gorbachev.

> There can be no peace without national reconciliation and there can be no national reconciliation without UNITA. . . .
> This letter is intended to send a strong signal to Moscow

131

> that there is broad bipartisan support for those U.S. policies which will facilitate a negotiated settlement and the holding of free and fair elections in Angola. . . . We are also bothered by recent press reports that suggest the State Department might accept a settlement in Angola that falls short of the stated U.S. policy goals. . . . We hope that you and the Secretary of State might convey to the Soviets . . . that the U.S. is committed to achieving a democratic outcome and free elections in Angola.[92]

Forty-eight members of the House of Representatives sent the president a similar letter on the same day.

During a June 1988 visit to the United States to meet with President Reagan, senior officials, and a broad range of citizens' groups, Savimbi addressed the bipartisan Angolan task force of the U.S. Congress. Repeating his call for the implementation of the Alvor agreement as the solution for Angola, he said, "Let free and fair elections determine the government of Angola! Let's replace bullets with ballots."[93]

Some members of Congress and private citizens warned Savimbi that the State Department's agenda might undermine his movement. They urged him to ask President Reagan for direct UNITA participation in the negotiations and for a clear statement that Angola would have to implement the Alvor agreement for free elections and remove all Cuban troops before the independence of Namibia would occur.[94] The State Department, however, apparently had already made the basic decisions: Namibia would become independent before all Cuban troops had left Angola; the timetable of the final Cuban withdrawal was all that remained for negotiation; and free elections in Angola would not be part of the accords.

Beginning of Four-Party Talks. The final negotiations began on May 3, 1988, with the first of eight rounds of four-party talks. The participants included South Africa, Angola, Cuba, and the United States, as mediator, with the Soviet Union as an observer; UNITA was excluded. Before the U.S.–Soviet summit in May–June 1988, Under Secretary of State Michael Armacost expressed optimism about the negotiations on Angola and Namibia, saying that the United States would ask the Soviets to "utilize influence they have with Luanda and Havana to encourage a realistic and prompt timetable for the Cuban withdrawal. And secondly, that they encourage a process of national reconciliation within Angola." He said further that the Soviets had "lent some encouragement on the issue of internal reconciliation between the MPLA and UNITA." But these State Department perceptions were contradicted by events days later, when the Soviet deputy foreign minister representing Moscow was reported to have "strongly rejected the idea that Moscow would press the Angolan government in Luanda to share power with the rebels [UNITA]."[95]

Thus, free elections as a means of internal reconciliation were agreed by the Soviet Union, Cuba, and the MPLA regime—the subsequent talks never focused on them. By late September, the Soviet representative in the negotiations, Deputy Foreign Minister Anatoly Adamishin, had achieved much of what Moscow sought. Again he said that the Soviet Union would not press the MPLA government to reach agreement with UNITA in order to facilitate the peace settlement.

Thus the United States conceded that Namibia would achieve independence before all Cuban troops had left Angola and allowed the issue of free elections—for internal reconciliation—to be shelved. Subsequent negotiations focused on the timetables for South African and Cuban troop withdrawals from Namibia and Angola respectively and on verification of the agreements (see table 4–4).

Through these rounds several types of pressure weighed on South Africa. First, military pressure from Cuba and the MPLA raised the prospect of heavy South African casualties; Castro boasted in June 1988 that South Africa had been defeated. Second, on May 3, 1988, the day of the first round of four-party talks, the House Foreign Affairs Committee approved virtually full economic sanctions against South Africa. Throughout the summer and fall, the South African government seemed to use its Angola-Namibia diplomacy to forestall further sanctions.

Third, in the spring and summer of 1988 U.S. public opinion polls showed the Democratic presidential candidate, Governor Michael Dukakis of Massachusetts, far ahead of the likely Republican nominee, George Bush. Governor Dukakis had taken strong positions against continued U.S. aid to UNITA and in favor of complete economic sanctions against South Africa. These views and his early lead in the polls could have emboldened the Communist side and encouraged South Africa to judge that it had better complete an agreement during the Reagan presidency. The State Department also strongly desired a settlement and did not want South Africa to stand in the way.

UNITA's Ebbing Support. In the spring and summer of 1988 the African supporters of UNITA had made several efforts to put the issue of UNITA-MPLA negotiations for "national reconciliation" on the negotiating agenda. In May 1988, the secretary general of the

133

TABLE 4–4
CHRONOLOGY OF FINAL NEGOTIATIONS ON ANGOLA AND NAMIBIA,
MAY–DECEMBER 1988

Date	Place	Event
May 3	London	First round of exploratory four-party talks among U.S., South Africa, Angola, and Cuba
May 3	U.S.	House Foreign Relations Committee approves nearly full economic santions against South Africa
May 12–13	Brazzaville	South Africa–Angola talks
May 18–19	Lisbon	U.S. (Crocker) and USSR (Adamishin) meet and hope to establish a general framework for Cuban withdrawal
June 1	Moscow	U.S.–USSR summit concludes with a call for an agreement by September 29, 1988
June 24	Cairo	Second round of four-party talks; communiqué says that progress has been made
June	U.S.	Savimbi and MPLA groups visit U.S.; Savimbi received by Reagan
July 13	New York	Third round of four-party talks results in agreement on fourteen principles
August 2	Geneva	Fourth round of talks: South Africa offers withdrawal from Namibia within nine months provided all Cubans leave Angola by then, and if ANC bases are dismantled; MPLA and Cuba reject it
August 8	Geneva	South Africa, Cuba, Angola announce cease-fire; South Africa offers to begin Namibian independence November 1988, if Cuba and Angola present an acceptable timetable for Cuban withdrawal
August 11	U.S.	House approves nearly full economic sanctions against South Africa
August 30	Angola	South Africa completes troop withdrawal one day early
September 7	Brazzaville	Fifth round of talks: Angola and Cuba insist on 36 months for withdrawal, the United States insists on 24, South Africa insists on 12

TABLE 4–4 (continued)

Date	Place	Event
September 14	U.S.	Senate Foreign Relations Committee approves economic sanctions against South Africa
September 26	Brazzaville	Sixth round: No agreement
October 8	New York	The four parties have "informal consultation"
October	U.S.	Congress adjourns without having passed economic sanctions
November 8	U.S.	Vice-President George Bush elected president
November 11	Geneva	Seventh round: preliminary agreement reached, subject to approval by governments
November 18		Angola and Cuba approve
November 22		South Africa approves
November 30		UNITA Vice-President Chitunda criticizes the accord
December 4	Brazzaville	Talks on verification suspended by South Africa
December 13	Brazzaville	Eighth round: agreement reached with verification to be worked out by signing date December 22, 1988
December 21	New York	Agreement on verification reached
December 22	New York	Signing of both accords on Angola and Namibia

Organization of African Unity referred to an "MPLA government rather than the Angolan government."[96] In June 1988, King Hassan of Morocco and President Mobutu of Zaire announced a joint campaign to begin MPLA-UNITA détente. In mid-August 1988, the leaders of Gabon, Zaire, Niger, the Ivory Coast, Zambia, and Mali (whose president was also chairman of the Organization of African Unity) voiced their strong support for reconciliation between the MPLA and UNITA.

At the same time, a group of Republican foreign policy experts and political leaders warned President Reagan that the "planned settlement contains serious flaws that will allow the Communist side to manipulate it," leading to the neutralization of UNITA and a victory for the MPLA and SWAPO.[97] Reagan replied a few weeks later that "your concerns are understandable. . . . It can't be said . . . that

135

the Namibian independence process will be set in motion long before the Cubans have gotten completely out of Angola."[98] Despite that and other assurances, virtually all the items the Republican signers warned against were in the final agreement.

There is no evidence that the United States encouraged African support of UNITA and an internal political settlement through free elections within Angola. In fact, Savimbi told President Reagan in a personal letter in September 1988 that the State Department was discouraging African countries from helping UNITA bring about national reconciliation. Savimbi asked President Reagan to reassure the African heads of state that the United States still sought national reconciliation through free elections within Angola.[99] But this did not occur.

Faced with this situation, South Africa retreated in the negotiations. At the third round of four-party talks, South Africa accepted agreement on fourteen principles, including the termination of its aid to UNITA and implementation of the Namibian settlement at the beginning of the process rather than at the conclusion, when all Cuban troops would have been withdrawn from Angola. At the fourth round in August, South Africa proposed the simultaneous withdrawal of its troops from Namibia and all Cuban troops from Angola within nine months. After Cuba and the MPLA immediately rejected this, South Africa dropped its proposal.

On August 8, 1988, South Africa announced a cease-fire with Cuba and the MPLA and declared that it would withdraw all its troops from Angola by the end of August. It conditioned this withdrawal only on the Cubans and Angolans presenting an acceptable timetable in subsequent talks. South Africa felt most vulnerable at this time to the prospects of congressional sanctions and a Democratic victory in the U.S. presidential election, since the Democratic candidate led by seventeen percentage points in the polls. Three days later—despite South Africa's concessions—the House of Representatives approved nearly total economic sanctions against South Africa.

At the fifth round of negotiations in September, Angola and Cuba insisted on a thirty-six month timetable for the Cuban withdrawal, South Africa proposed twelve months, and the United States suggested twenty-four months. On September 3, 1988, Savimbi publicly suggested that U.S. Assistant Secretary of State Crocker was "playing into the hands of my own enemies. . . . What is Crocker trying to do, save the face of his enemies and dig the graves of his friends?"[100]

The MPLA leader had revealed his objectives clearly in late August 1988 by saying that UNITA's "neutralization will demand that additional and final sacrifice by our people and by our armed forces combining political action with military action . . . to once and for all annihilate the puppet gangsters in the pay of imperialism and racist South Africa."[101]

On September 14, 1988, the Senate Foreign Relations Committee voted along party lines to impose new economic sanctions against South Africa. This set the stage for the sixth round of four-party meetings in late September, and for continuing consultations in New York in early October. By this time the prospects for the full Senate enacting economic sanctions had been reduced, since Congress would adjourn by the third week in October for the presidential election campaign. South Africa could now observe that George Bush, who was believed to be more moderate on sanctions than Governor Dukakis, seemed likely to win the election. Taking the diplomatic initiative South Africa's president met with several black leaders in southern Africa, while the negotiations halted until after the U.S. presidential election.

In late September 1988 Soviet Deputy Foreign Minister Adamishin expressed irritation at U.S. insistence on a Cuban troop withdrawal within twenty-four months. "It was no other person than Crocker who told them [the MPLA], 'if you agree to three years, I'll ensure a pullout of South African troops from Namibia.' . . . Why were the three years good enough for Chester Crocker when he convinced them to enter the negotiations and now these three years are not good?"[102]

The seventh round of four-party talks convened in Geneva on November 11, 1988, three days after George Bush had been elected president. South Africa now made its next concession: it agreed to thirty months for a Cuban withdrawal from Angola and offered to withdraw totally from Namibia within nine months. The issue of verification was to be decided by subsequent talks—another concession.

On November 25, 1988, three days after South Africa approved the final terms of the settlement, Savimbi publicly criticized this action. In a filmed interview, he said:

> You have to understand that when the Russians and Cubans, the Communists, when they negotiate they negotiate to have peace and victory—not because they want peace, but victory also. . . . The South Africans . . . have taken a course where they felt . . . you [the United States] make concessions. . . . The MPLA and the Cubans and Russians have tested the South Africans and they have found that there was weakness. . . . In the past every time President Botha wanted to decide a major issue he consulted with me. . . . This time I

was not consulted at all. . . . When I went there, the deal was done.[103]

In the same discussion Savimbi referred to the discouragement he found among conservatives during his June and July 1988 visit to the United States:

I saw that all my conservative friends were just trying to advise me to get a contact with the blacks, get a contact with the Democrats . . . because [they] think that the next president will be Governor Dukakis, but I said to them, "listen, now we are in July. We have August, September, October— the election is in November."[104]

Perhaps Savimbi's most poignant reaction to the accords were these words:

How are we going to accept . . . to destroy a victory that was in our reach . . . ? Last year they were defeated—the Russians and the Cubans were defeated. How it comes that this year we are going to be defeated at the negotiating table? We cannot accept it.[105]

The discussions on verifications were held in Brazzaville on December 4, and were suspended when South Africa found the Angolan and MPLA position unsatisfactory. While in Mexico City for the inauguration of the new Mexican president, Castro said that "verification [of Cuban troop withdrawal from Angola] was none of South Africa's business" and threatened to keep his troops in Angola for an additional ten years.[106] The MPLA and Cubans were being consistent in separating the issues of Namibian independence and Cuban withdrawal from Angola.

The Final Accords. On December 13, 1988, the eighth round of four-party talks were held. South Africa agreed to the terms as contained in the final accords, with the verification issue to be worked out before a final signing ceremony at the United Nations in New York on December 22, 1988.

The immediate pressure of further U.S. economic sanctions was removed by the adjournment of Congress in October, and the possibility of a Democratic president who would view them unfavorably ended with the election in November. Nevertheless, South Africa continued to move back from its original positions and finally acceded to the terms proposed by the U.S. State Department. Perhaps this reflected a concern over further military casualties in the face of the 1988 MPLA-Cuban military buildup, along with a belief that Soviet foreign policy had changed and that the Cubans would honor the withdrawal terms. If the accords were violated, South Africa may have thought it could defend its interests in the region unilaterally.

Although President-elect Bush made no public statements on the negotiating approach, Assistant Secretary of State Crocker may have told the South African government that the State Department policy would remain the same. UNITA Vice-President Dr. Jeremias Chitunda publicly objected to the accords in late November, charging that Cuba had not just 50,000 troops in Angola as stated in the draft accords but 60,000 troops, with another 20,000 Cuban military personnel inside various MPLA organizations.[107]

The final accords on Angola and Namibia were initialed on December 13, 1988, and signed in New York on December 22, 1988. The accord on Namibia provided that South Africa would permit the United Nations to begin implementing the independence process on April 1, 1989, and that all but 1,500 of South Africa's estimated 20,000–30,000 troops in Namibia must be withdrawn by July 1, 1989. The second accord was a bilateral agreement between the governments of Cuba and Angola. It assumed a total Cuban troop presence of 50,000, in spite of the UNITA contention that there were at least 60,000. Cuba would remove 3,000 of them by April 1, 1989, move the remainder north of the fifteenth parallel by July 1, 1989, remove half of those remaining troops by November 1, 1989, and remove the rest in stages with all to be out of Angola by July 1, 1991 (see table 4–5).

The two accords have different verification mechanisms. The Namibia accord was verified, monitored, and implemented by a United Nations Transition Assistance Group (UNTAG) to involve nearly 5,000 UN officials and troops. The bilateral Angolan-Cuban accord is to be monitored by a United Nations team of approximately ninety persons dependent upon Cuban and Angolan military authorities for access throughout Angola.

No provision was made for the implementation of the 1975 Alvor agreement or for any other mechanism for internal reconciliation through free and fair elections between the MPLA and UNITA in Angola. UNITA was excluded from the negotiations, and its future is not addressed directly, except that the accords required South Africa to terminate its aid to the resistance group. The accords do not prohibit the United States and other countries from continuing this assistance.

The accords ensured that Namibian independence was irreversible before the withdrawal of any significant number of Cuban troops from Angola. Once the UN-administered process began on April 1, 1989, and all but 1,500 South African troops were withdrawn by July 1, 1989, the accords still permitted Cuba to have 47,000 (or according

139

TABLE 4–5:   ANGOLA-NAMIBIA ACCORDS OF DECEMBER 13, 1988

	Namibia	Angola	Cubans Remaining "Official"a	Cubans Remaining UNITAb
1989: Jan. 1	UN advance teams begin arriving		50,000	80,000
Jan. 22	Joint commission to monitor UN Res. 435 begins operations			
April 1	UN force to reach 9,000; RSA to begin withdrawing troops.	Cuba to remove 3,000 troops	47,000	77,000
July 1	RSA has withdrawn all but 1,500 troops.	Cuba to have moved its remaining forces north of 15th parallel		
Nov. 1	UN-supervised elections for constitutional assembly.	50% of 50,000 Cubans to have left. All remaining troops north of 15th parallel	25,000	55,000
1990: March		Independence under elected government		
April 1		67% of 50,000 Cubans to have left	16,500	46,500
Oct. 1		75% of 50,000 Cubans to have left	12,500	42,500
1991: July 1		100% of Cubans to have left	0	30,000c

NOTE: Accords were formally signed December 22, 1988, in New York along with UN Security Council enabling resolution specifying verification. RSA = Republic of South Africa.

a. Based on assumption that December 1988 Cuban strength was 50,000.

b. According to Jeremias Chitunda, UNITA vice-president, quoted in the *New York Times*, November 30, 1988; and Jonas Savimbi, UNITA president, panel discussion on Angola, American Enterprise Institute, Washington, D.C., June 29, 1988.

c. Plus 6,500 other Soviet-bloc personnel (1,000 East Germans, 2,500 Soviets, 3,000 North Koreans) = 36,500 total Communist personnel remaining.

140

to UNITA 57,000) Cuban troops in Angola until November 1, 1989. Moreover, Cuban troops were not required to return to Cuba. They could be sent to neighboring Mozambique, to Congo-Brazzaville, or even to Namibia after independence. Nor do the accords prohibit the MPLA regime from asking other pro-Soviet countries to send additional troops to replace the departing Cuban forces.

The bilateral Angolan-Cuban accord on Cuban troop withdrawal is reversible if the two governments decide that conditions have changed. Article III states that in case of blatant violations by South Africa—in the sole determination of Cuba and Angola—the two Communist governments can change the terms of the Cuban troop withdrawal.

The verification process is questionable in a number of ways. Since the United Nations endorsed SWAPO in 1973 as the "sole authentic representative of Namibian people," the UN monitoring and verification effort might be expected to favor it. The joint commission established to settle disputes about verification consists of the MPLA regime, Cuba, the Soviet Union, the United States, South Africa, and post-independence Namibia. Political realism suggests that the Communist regimes will work together and oppose South Africa on most issues.

Verification of the Cuban troop withdrawal from Angola is hampered by the lack of a verified initial count. In a country twice the size of Texas, UNITA's count of 60,000 regular Cuban forces with an additional 20,000 dispersed in other Angolan organizations may be credible. UNITA also counts an additional 6,500 Soviet bloc personnel from East Germany, the Soviet Union, and North Korea. Ninety UN officials could hardly verify Cuban troop strength—especially if the Cuban and Angolan regimes tried to conceal the true numbers—for example, by integrating Cuban units into Angolan forces with Angolan uniforms.

The Brazilian general leading the UN verification team in Angola said in early 1989, "When they [Angola and Cuba] tell us there are no more troops we will tell the United Nations they have gone. We will trust the information given by both countries. It would not be normal for two countries to sign an agreement and not fulfill it."[108]

Alternative Futures for Angola and Namibia

Most reactions to the final accords were positive. The chief U.S. negotiator, Assistant Secretary of State Crocker, said that the signing "signifies the end of a sad chapter in Africa's modern history and the beginning of a new chapter." The *Washington Post* called the accords "a historic peace agreement," and the *New York Times* was also enthusiastic.[109]

An American expert on southern Africa, Gerald Bender, commented that Castro's military victories in the spring of 1988 made it possible "to bring his troops home with pride. And Moscow encouraged Angola and Cuba to persist with negotiations." He concluded: "The terms of agreement are not that different from . . . the Cuban-Angolan declaration in early 1982. What is new is that after eight bloody years, South Africa finally has decided to implement U.N. Security Council Resolution 435 calling for the independence of Namibia."[110] And an academic expert on the Soviet Union, Vernon Aspeturian, called the accords "part of an overall package designed to lay the foundations for a long period of Soviet-American and Soviet-Western cooperation and even collaboration."[111] The Reagan administration also praised the accords. At the signing ceremony Secretary of State Shultz said:

> This is a moment for celebration of achievement and dedication to a better future in southern Africa. . . . We have just witnessed the signing of an unprecedented agreement that will bring long-awaited peace to southwestern Africa and independence to Namibia. . . . The regional settlement concluded here today represents a momentous turning point in the history of southern Africa.[112]

These positive expectations rested on several assumptions. The first was that the people of Namibia would be able freely to choose their postcolonial governments, rather than find themselves intimidated and coerced by SWAPO. A second assumption was that Cuba would withdraw all of its combat forces as scheduled. The third assumption was that as the Communist MPLA regime had fewer and fewer Cuban troops to protect its security, it would open negotiations with UNITA. According to the optimistic view, that process would result in a transitional government of national reconciliation and eventually in a government of Angola chosen by free elections.

Unfortunately, events since the signing of the accords in December 1988 suggest a darker future for both Namibia and Angola—with the pro-Soviet SWAPO regime in power in Namibia, the MPLA regime in power in Angola, and UNITA ever more isolated and weaker militarily.

Namibia's Prospects. In signing these accords and giving independence to Namibia, South Africa might have expected that the free world would reduce pressure to end apartheid, that the economic dependence of Namibia might prevent it from being hostile, and that other sources might provide aid for the survival of UNITA. It might also have hoped that South African military actions, if absolutely necessary, could reverse any negative trends in Namibia.

In Namibia SWAPO is the only organization with both a political and a military capability. It has years of experience in coercion and intimidation as well as political action, and it has the full support of the Soviet bloc and Cuba, and the acquiescence of a number of other African states. It would be virtually impossible for South Africa to reestablish its control there.

SWAPO's logical tactics would be to emphasize its intended moderation, conceal its Marxist-Leninist political and economic program and to avoid any overt use of violence. SWAPO can use its political and armed cadres to expand its area of authority. The United Nations monitoring group is unlikely to prevent coercive SWAPO activities, since they would be denied.

The substantial expansion of SWAPO's conventional military capabilities in 1988, and the joint SWAPO-Cuban-MPLA military actions prepared the way for SWAPO to establish its military forces. The accords do not prevent the newly independent government of Namibia from inviting whatever foreign troops it might want—including Cubans—to protect it from real or alleged South African pressures.

SWAPO, assisted by the Soviet Union, Cuba, and the MPLA regime, can cast doubt on South Africa's good faith in implementing the accords on Namibia, as Cuba's vice foreign minister did just after signing the accords. The MPLA leader Dos Santos said after the signing that SWAPO "will need support to win the elections against the South African puppets who will undoubtedly be supported by the Pretoria regime." Before the final accord was signed, the secretary general of SWAPO said:

> The racist regime [in South Africa] is under great pressure. From a historical point of view its days are numbered. . . . We totally trust our friends from Angola and Cuba. . . . No African country will be really free as long as imperialism and racism exist on the continent. Therefore, independent Namibia, under SWAPO's leadership, will continue to render political and diplomatic assistance to the African National Congress. . . . We must destroy the system of apartheid once and for all.[113]

An independent Namibia under SWAPO is likely to work against both the West and South Africa under the anti-apartheid banner. Although South Africa assumed that Angola would dismantle the six admitted ANC bases on its territory, an ANC spokesman said in late

143

December 1988: "That is not the way I interpreted the protocols. . . . I do not think anybody else outside of the three parties concerned has got that impression except for the Americans."[114] In January 1989, at the seventy-seventh anniversary of the ANC, its leader, Oliver Tambo, said that the Angola-Namibia accords constitute

> an advance of great strategic significance. . . . It is against this background that the African National Congress, in consultation with the fraternal government of the People's Republic of Angola and other friendly countries, has readily agreed to move our military personnel from Angola so as not to allow the racists [South Africa] and their allies to use the presence of ANC military facilities as an excuse for blocking or otherwise delaying the process now in motion. . . . The armed struggle is more vital than ever before. Our approach must be of militant mass defiance.[115]

The ANC can move those camps and operate militarily from other countries bordering South Africa while continuing to receive full support from the Soviet bloc and Cuba. The Angolan foreign ministry declared that the MPLA regime gave "support and solidarity" to the "just struggle of the ANC."[116]

The Future of UNITA. The Communist side repeatedly made clear its optimism that UNITA would be isolated and defeated with the help of the accords. In October 1988 MPLA leader Dos Santos said that "from a strategic point of view UNITA is militarily defeated. . . . Political reconciliation would start in Angola after foreign military aid to UNITA ends."[117] The MPLA's view of reconciliation is amnesty for UNITA members who surrender rather than Savimbi's meaning: free and fair elections to decide who governs. Cuban and Angolan officials repeatedly said that the two accords are separate and that implementation of one is not linked with the other.

With the accords preventing South Africa from aiding UNITA, foreign assistance would have to come through other African states, notably Zaire. In the spring of 1988, Cuba and Angola began pressing the Mobutu regime in Zaire to cease cooperating in providing aid to UNITA. Angola's defense minister warned Zaire that UNITA's supply flights from Zaire were not conducive to a "climate of good neighborliness along the common border," and the MPLA regime threatened that continued help for UNITA could cause problems for Zaire's political stability.[118] In the fall of 1988, the president of Zaire was reported to have been threatened by top Cuban political leaders with an invasion if he did not stop aiding UNITA.[119] Given the assassination of Pakistani President Zia after Soviet and Afghan regime warnings against his aid for the anti-Communist resistance, African leaders are likely to take Communist warnings and pressures all the more seriously.

In late March 1989 Savimbi responded to months of hostile statements from SWAPO: "If they cannot give me a guarantee they will not attack UNITA forces, we will fight them from Luanda to Windhoek." He added that SWAPO was "trying to infiltrate Namibia."[120] On the day the UN transition process was to begin, April 1, 1989, during the first Cuban-Soviet summit meeting in Havana since 1974, several hundred heavily armed SWAPO guerrillas crossed the border from Angola into Namibia, saying later that they were seeking to turn themselves in to UN forces. South Africa took immediate military action with UN approval; SWAPO had promised the United Nations to keep its armed forces north of the sixteenth parallel in Angola (several hundred miles north of the Namibian border) until after the November 1989 elections. After several hundred SWAPO infiltrators were killed in combat during the first weeks of April, SWAPO promised that the rest would leave Namibia.

About the same time, UNITA provided evidence that Cuban and MPLA military forces were augmenting their chemical warfare capabilities and again proposed a cease-fire and negotiations with the MPLA. To facilitate negotiations, Savimbi offered to exclude himself from the delegation and from the transitional government that would—in UNITA's proposal—prepare for elections. Savimbi would, however, lead UNITA in those elections.

The MPLA-Cuban axis probably hoped that any increase in U.S. aid to Savimbi would be discouraged by the December 1988 accords, by allegations that UNITA committed human rights abuses, and by the opposition of prominent Democratic congressmen. But even critics of U.S. support for UNITA said that the MPLA had to do more than grant amnesty to UNITA or risk an increase in covert aid. On May 16, 1989, at a conference with heads of state from Zambia, Zimbabwe, Congo, Mozambique, Gabon, São Tomé, and Zaire, the MPLA presented its peace proposals, which repeated the call for a halt to aid for UNITA but made no provision for free elections or for a transitional government with a role for UNITA. Zaire's participation—despite Mobutu's many years of support for UNITA—was a sign of events to come.

In June 1989 a bipartisan coalition led by Senators Dennis DeConcini (Democrat of Arizona) and Jesse Helms (Republican of North Carolina) showed support for UNITA by the conditions they attached to the appropriation of $80 million in U.S. funds for the UN implementation of the Angola-Nambia accords. Their effort to condition

145

the release of these U.S. funds on Cuban-MPLA-SWAPO compliance with the accords was opposed by the Bush administration as too broad and unverifiable. Secretary of State James A. Baker urged the Senate not to enact these conditions. Describing the regional settlement as one of our country's outstanding diplomatic achievements, he wrote, "A major source of East-West tension in the Third World has been defused and converted to an arena of cooperation." Rep. Howard Wolpe of Michigan, chairman of the House Foreign Affairs subcommittee on Africa, published an article that opposed any U.S. military aid to UNITA.[121]

The Role of Zaire. After the pro-UNITA coalition in the U.S. Congress overcame the opposition of both the Bush administration and the anti-UNITA Democrats in Congress, the MPLA must have realized it would have to show more progress toward national reconciliation. When the MPLA informed him it would be willing to meet with UNITA, Mobutu convened a conference in Zaire of seventeen African leaders. Savimbi and MPLA leader Dos Santos met there for the first time and agreed on the following: a ceasefire to take effect June 24, 1989; the creation of a UNITA-MPLA group to begin direct negotiations; the formation of a verifications commission comprising MPLA, UNITA, and Zairian officials to work out "ceasefire details and reinforce them."[122]

But the MPLA regime described this agreement in terms quite different from those used by Zaire and UNITA. Dos Santos stated that the negotiators had agreed upon four main points: the "special case" of Savimbi not to be publicly announced; a cease-fire; the integration of UNITA's "members into the existing institutions" (a long-standing MPLA offer to elements of UNITA to accept MPLA amnesty by surrendering); and the end of outside "interference," meaning no further aid to UNITA. Taking issue with this description of the Zaire agreement, Savimbi said: "We have rejected that. No one will be integrated."[123]

Mobutu convened his peace conference just before visiting the United States to meet with President George Bush. The apparent public relations benefits for Mobutu were illustrated by this account of June 29, 1989, in the influential *Washington Post:*

> Publicly reviled only months ago by his fellow black African leaders as the heavy-handed strongman of one of the continent's most corrupt countries, Zairian President Mobutu Sese Seko is seeking to create a new image as a bold peace broker as he begins a visit to Washington. Mobutu goes fresh from a stunning diplomatic breakthrough . . . to meet with

President Bush to report on the historic handshake last week between . . . Dos Santos and . . . Savimbi. . . . "If this had been Henry Kissinger, he'd be certain to win the Nobel prize," an ebullient senior adviser said as Mobutu began his journey to Washington.

After their two-hour meeting, Bush praised Mobutu as "a peacemaker whose diplomacy was helping to bring an end to fourteen years of war in neighboring Angola."[124] Even the conservative *Washington Times* on June 26, 1989, hailed the Zaire agreement as a "triumph" for the Reagan Doctrine. In a letter published three days later in the same newspaper, however, the conservative leader Howard Phillips raised the critical question of whether the Zaire cease-fire agreement would lead to "genuine national reconciliation and free elections in Angola or was merely a tactic by the MPLA government designed to secure membership for Angola in the IMF and the World Bank, something the Bush administration has proffered as a 'quid pro quo' when there is progress toward national reconciliation."

After several days of meetings in the United States, Mobutu was described by the *Washington Post*, on July 1, as opposing "continued covert U.S. military assistance to rebel forces in Angola now that national reconciliation talks have begun." He was quoted as saying that while the Bush administration

> should do as it sees fit . . . you could ask the question, "Do UNITA and (the MPLA) still need military equipment and weapons systems?" My answer would be that the people of Angola should think about one thing and one thing only: the economic and social development of their country.[125]

If Mobutu holds to this, other countries will have much more difficulty providing material support to UNITA. The MPLA will have accomplished one of its major goals.

The evidence since the June 22, 1989, Zaire agreement suggests that the MPLA is still intent on attaining its objective of defeating UNITA. On the day Mobutu met with Bush, it was reported that the MPLA politburo had stated, falsely, that Savimbi agreed to its conditions for a "one party state and accepted Mr. Dos Santos' authority."[126] Then, on June 30, 1989, the first day of the much heralded MPLA-UNITA negotiations, as Dos Santos accused UNITA of violating the cease-fire, the MPLA regime suddenly broke off the talks. Although UNITA immediately issued a formal denial of the MPLA allegation, Crocker's former deputy and then successor as assistant secretary for African affairs, Ambassador Herman Cohen, nevertheless, went on a scheduled visit to the MPLA capital a week later. Then came the announcement that the Bush administration was considering switching its vote against admitting Angola to the financial benefits of the International Monetary Fund.

Negative Trends. When the MPLA regime talks about talking with UNITA, it receives tangible benefits, even though it deals duplicitously with UNITA. A report indicated for example, that several battalions of Cuban troops "massed at the southern town of Cuito Cuanvale for what . . . could be a new offensive against the UNITA position in . . . Mavinga (gateway to Savimbi's headquarters) if the peace talks do not develop favorably for MPLA."[127] If the report is correct, Cuban forces violated the requirement that all would have moved north of the fifteenth parallel by July 1, 1989.

If the MPLA regime uses desultory negotiations with UNITA to manipulate both Mobutu and the United States, then UNITA will lose its ability to obtain support. When it stopped the four major Gorbachev-era offensives between 1985 and 1988, UNITA had obtained increasing, though discreet, African support. African states supportive of UNITA, however, are now likely to be the focus of pressure from the Soviet Union, Cuba, and other Communist and left-leaning governments.

UNITA's future relationship with the United States is also unclear. In early January 1989, President-elect Bush sent Savimbi a letter promising to continue U.S. military aid to UNITA. Nevertheless, reports continued to circulate that the State Department favored the normalization of relations with the MPLA regime in Angola, including its admission to the World Bank and International Monetary Fund, where it could obtain Western aid and credits. On January 27, 1989, the *New York Times* reported that U.S. and Angolan officials discussed low-level diplomatic representation, such as a liaison office, in each other's capitals.

In February 1989 Savimbi himself expressed concern that the accords might contain a secret clause pledging the United States to recognize the MPLA regime. At the same time he expressed deep disappointment with the accords and with the United States for excluding UNITA from the negotiations: "The U.S. held all the cards; why did the U.S. not include peace in Angola in the settlement? Is the U.S. saying any ally of the U.S. is destroyable, is expendable. . . . Will we be part of that group of U.S. allies which has been betrayed?" Savimbi asked that U.S. aid for his movement be provided through open congressional appropriations rather than through covert action procedures. "A commitment from Congress is difficult not to implement. A secret executive order can be countermanded at any time," he explained.[128] This lack of confidence in the executive branch and more specifically in the Department of State may well increase if the accords move in a negative direction.

Before the accords took effect on December 22, 1988, UNITA said that South Africa had provided enough military equipment and spare parts to supply its 30,000 regular troops and 45,000 guerrillas for about two years. In announcing this, UNITA expressed its concern that a period of military danger would come during the 1989 dry season. From July to November 1989, Cuba would still be permitted to have 47,000 (UNITA claimed it had 57,000) troops in Angola; South Africa would have essentially withdrawn from Namibia; and the MPLA regime could launch a major offensive against UNITA which would not be prohibited or precluded by the accords. As it turned out, UNITA was correct to view August through October 1989 as months of great danger, since the MPLA did launch offensives during those dry months. UNITA turned them back as it did a larger attack with direct Soviet military participation in December 1989.

Will the Cuban troops actually complete their required withdrawal from Angola? Cuba and the MPLA violated the 1975 Alvor accords, and they have said repeatedly that the security of the MPLA regime must be guaranteed and that it must remain in power. The MPLA regime repeatedly rejected the concept of a transitional government of genuinely shared responsibility and power with UNITA. On the day the accords were signed, December 22, 1988, the MPLA deputy foreign minister called UNITA a "puppet organization," and the Cuban foreign minister said that the United States was playing the "paradoxical" and "interfering role South Africa has now waived by the signing."[129]

Cuba could withdraw and redeploy some thousands of its troops, to create the impression of compliance while retaining as many troops as necessary to ensure the continued existence of the MPLA regime. Angola could either conceal these forces in its army or invoke the terms of the accord permitting a change in the withdrawal schedule, and then blame South Africa for violating the accords.

These negative trends could occur within the context of the accords, especially as interpreted by the pro-MPLA majority on the joint commission. In addition, Soviet U.N. personnel are likely to play an important role in dealing with Namibia and SWAPO. As a 1985 report by the U.S. Senate Select Committee on Intelligence put it:

> The Soviet Union is effectively using the UN Secretariat in the conduct of its foreign relations, and the West is paying for most of it. The 800 Soviets assigned to the United Nations as international civil servants report directly to the Soviet

missions and are part of an organization managed by the Soviet Foreign Ministry, intelligence services, and the Central Committee of the Communist Party through their comprehensive approach to the strategy and tactics of personnel placement and their detailed plans for using the United Nations to achieve Soviet foreign policy and intelligence objectives.[130]

Such negative developments are likely to emerge gradually, almost imperceptibly, over many months, commanding little attention at top levels in free world governments. South Africa would have difficulty confronting such an evolution because of its concerns about international pressures, about probable allegations of South African violations, and about its own misjudgments in signing the accords.

Signing the accords may have several negative effects for South Africa. First, the regional balance might shift strongly toward the Communist side and toward the pro-Soviet African National Congress, while weakening UNITA. Second, the removal of the Namibia issue may increase, rather than reduce, pressures against South Africa from countries eager to see apartheid end. Third, the genuinely democratic anti-apartheid groups within South Africa will be attacked both by the strengthened ANC and by the ultra-right, just when a transition to multiracial democracy might be possible.

By early 1988—after thirteen years of MPLA failure—UNITA had the momentum in Angola. At the same time a number of multiracial democratic organizations existed in Namibia that could have succeeded in establishing an independent democratic government. If SWAPO rules Namibia and the MPLA defeats UNITA, the setback for those people and the United States will be the result in part of incompetent diplomacy.

Future U.S. Policy in Angola and Namibia

The following actions could increase prospects for a free and independent Angola and Namibia:

• The United States should reaffirm its objective of helping the people of Angola have free and fair elections in accord with the Alvor agreement of 1975.

• The United States should recognize UNITA as a belligerent and substantially increase political, diplomatic, and military support until these elections are held.

• The United States should encourage all its allies to isolate the Angolan Communist regime politically and economically (with the exception of humanitarian assistance) until it opens good-faith negotiations with UNITA and conducts elections under international democratic supervision.

• The United States should work with its allies and with African countries that share these objectives in a concerted strategy to bring real peace to Angola through implementation of the 1975 Alvor agreement.

• A monthly report should be made by the administration to Congress on compliance with the agreement on Cuban troop withdrawal. If Cuba does not withdraw its forces, the administration should sharply increase its military aid to UNITA and take other actions to isolate the MPLA and Castro regimes.

• Should the MPLA and Cuban forces launch military offensives against UNITA, the United States should immediately increase military aid to UNITA and prevent the MPLA regime from benefiting from oil exports to the United States or from U.S. oil technology, as was done with Libya in 1986.

• The same counteractions should be taken if the president certifies that Cuban or MPLA forces are continuing to use chemical weapons against the people of Angola and UNITA. The United States should provide UNITA with means of self-defense against such attacks and publicize them, as was done in the early 1980s with Soviet and Vietnamese chemical warfare.

• Unless Cuba withdraws its troops on schedule, the United States should provide full diplomatic recognition to UNITA as the government of Angola and provide substantially increased assistance so that the UNITA government can bring about the independence of Angola as agreed upon in the Alvor accord.

• The United States should use radio broadcasts into Angola as well as Cuba (the authorizing legislation permits Radio Marti to broadcast to the "people of Cuba," thousands of whom are in Angola), to inform the Cuban troops of the withdrawal commitments made by the Castro regime.

• The U.S. ambassador to the United Nations should demand that the estimated 4,500 Angolan children held on Cuba's Isle of Youth for ideological indoctrination be returned to Angola.

Verification must also be improved. An independent estimate must be made by the United States and other UN member states of the actual number of Cuban and Soviet-bloc personnel in Angola, including those Cubans who have received Angolan citizenship. The estimated ninety UN personnel are insufficient to verify the Cuban withdrawal. Their number should be increased to a level commensurate with the difficulty and seriousness of their mission. Membership of the Angola verification force should include only genuine democracies—that is, governments freely elected at regular intervals. They should have immediate access, using their own air and land transportation to all suspect sites. Denial should be deemed a confirmation of a violation. Current UN guidelines suggest that the Angolans and Cubans provide transport for the verification force when it lacks its own means. This provision allows the Communist side to control the verification group and to increase risks of evasion. Verification teams should be stationed at all Angolan military bases, ports, airfields, and major road and rail entry points, as well as at MPLA and Cuban military facilities. They should have access to all incoming air, sea, and land vehicles. These groups should have access to information from any UN member government, including the United States.

The United States and other free world countries should also help increase the effectiveness of the genuinely democratic people and organizations of Namibia. Among such groups are the SWAPO-Democrats, the leftist but avowedly democratic South West Africa National Union (SWANU), and the Democratic Turnhalle Alliance, a multi-ethnic coalition of eleven political parties and ethnic groups. Free-world countries including the United States should do the following in Namibia:

• carefully monitor political trends in Namibia and provide objective information about the true political character and actions of SWAPO and all competing political groups
• provide encouragement along with financial and material assistance to genuinely democratic political groups in Namibia
• send official delegations at least three months before scheduled elections to verify that adequate preparations for a democratic election are being made, including full freedom of speech, assembly and organization for all competing political organizations; also to assess whether SWAPO is secretly using its cadres and armed component to intimidate and coerce the people of Namibia
• send official delegations from genuine democracies to monitor the actual election and vote-counting procedures—in addition to any UN monitoring
• consider providing funds for broadcasts in tribal dialects giving information about SWAPO and about democratic groups, leaders and procedures

The peoples of Angola and Namibia did not want to move from colonialism to oppression by pro-Soviet dictatorships, but the years of struggle by UNITA to end MPLA rule have been sharply set back by the Angola-Namibia accords. These actions would strongly increase prospects for freedom in Angola and Namibia, which in turn would improve the prospects for a transition to multiracial democracy in South Africa.

5
Mozambique

Mozambique's history and recent conflicts parallel those of Angola. Like Angola, it became a Portuguese colony in 1498. Portuguese colonial officials exercised rather nominal authority over both countries until the late nineteenth century. Attempts to control most of the territory succeeded in the 1930s.[1] The armed struggle for independence from Portugal began in 1964. Slightly more than ten years later, in 1975, Mozambique gained independence—under a Communist regime. As that regime implemented its radical program with repression, an armed resistance movement arose and continues to the present.[2]

Background

Located on the southeastern coast of Africa, Mozambique borders the Indian Ocean on the east and, from north to south, Tanzania, Malawi, Zambia, Zimbabwe, South Africa, and Swaziland.

With 304,000 square miles—about twice the size of California—it is lightly settled; more than 85 percent of Mozambicans live in the countryside. Several tribal groups are indigenous. Religious affiliation is divided among Islam (about 30 percent, especially in the north), Christianity (15 percent), and African beliefs (50 percent).

The climate varies from tropical to subtropical. Although the country has many natural resources such as minerals and natural gas, its economy has been primarily agricultural. Lacking Angola's diamonds and oil, Mozambique's exports include cashews, shrimp, sugar, tea, and cotton, mainly to Western countries.

The Portuguese colonial administration had sought to work with traditional village headmen and chiefs in establishing its control. By the 1960s, the population of about 9 million people was still overwhelmingly rural. About 230,000 persons of Portuguese descent lived primarily in towns and cities. Although agriculture was by far the largest part of the economy, by the early 1960s general economic development showed a slight upswing, particularly with cash crop farms and light industrial plants. Portugal had also installed the rudiments of modern transport and social services.

Until the late 1970s a major source of employment and income to Mozambique had been the rail lines, roads, and pipelines that linked its landlocked neighbors with the Mozambican ports of Maputo and Beira. Early in the twentieth century Portuguese colonial administrators had permitted large private companies, controlled and financed mainly by British interests, to establish such rail lines and thereby improve commercial opportunities for the mines and plantations in the British colonies of East Africa. Perhaps these long-established commercial relationships may partly explain Great Britain's diplomatic support for the Marxist-Leninist Mozambique regime established in 1975.

Emergence and Victory of Frelimo

In the late 1950s the example of independence movements in a number of other African countries stimulated similar aspirations among the educated groups in Mozambique as well as in Portugal's other African colonies, such as Angola. Several Mozambican independence movements were established; these merged in June 1962 in Tanzania to form the Frente de Libertacao de Mocambique (National Front for the Liberation of Mozambique), or Frelimo. Unlike the MPLA in Angola, which from the start was guided and influenced by the Portuguese Communist party and Angolan Communist elements, Frelimo was originally a coalition which included but was not dominated by the Communists of Mozambique.[3] Its initial operational bases were in recently independent Tanzania.[4] In 1964 Frelimo initiated its decade-long war against Portuguese colonial rule.

The movement's first leader was Eduardo Mondlane, a member of the southern Shagaan tribe. After receiving a doctorate from Northwestern University, he lived in the United States while working for the United Nations. Mondlane was teaching anthropology at Syracuse University at the time Frelimo was established. Mozambique scholar Thomas Henriksen notes that Mondlane's book, *The Struggle for Mozambique* (1969), "is free of much of the Marxist jargon that characterized the writings of his contemporary revolutionaries . . . in the sister Portuguese colonies."[5]

During the 1960s Frelimo was "the only African liberation movement in Portuguese Africa to receive assistance from both Peking and Moscow."[6] Its leaders found the Chinese Communist doctrine of peasant-based guerrilla warfare suited to conditions in Mozambique, but they also welcomed the Soviet Union's more significant levels of military and other aid. By its second congress in 1968, Frelimo had moved far to the left and "adopted many aspects of a standard

154

Communist movement, including a cell structure, democratic central-
ism, self-criticism, and a pervasive use of Marxist idiom."[7]
The transition from a broad coalition to a Communist-dominated
movement took place in two stages. First, between 1966 and 1968
several non-Communist Frelimo leaders were assassinated by persons
still unknown. Among the victims were Frelimo's popular military
commander, Philip Magaia, and his deputy. According to Henriksen,
"Frelimo blamed [these assassinations] on Portugal . . . but they are
probably another instance of a revolution devouring its own children."[8] Samora Machel, a Communist, took over as head of the army
and also began to live with Magaia's widow.

In 1969 Frelimo leader Mondlane was also assassinated. After a
brief interlude of power sharing, Machel took leadership of Frelimo.
From that time on, Communist control of Frelimo was assured, and
Soviet military aid to Frelimo was reported to have increased.[9] Machel
consolidated his position and Frelimo's leftward direction with murders and expulsions from Frelimo. During the early 1970s several
former Frelimo leaders publicly denounced the Communist takeover
of the movement.

The April 1974 coup in Portugal had profound implications for
Mozambique, as it did for Angola. The pro-Communist elements
within the new Portuguese governing coalition worked diligently to
legitimate Frelimo; in September 1974 they succeeded with the signing of the Lusaka agreement. Without giving the people of Mozambique any opportunity to express their political views through an
election or referendum, the agreement provided for Frelimo to govern
in a transitional arrangement with Portugal for nine months and then
to form the new government when Portugal granted independence
in June 1975.

This accord was a major political achievement for the Communists since it established a political process that would deliver Mozambique to Frelimo control. It may also have encouraged the Soviet
Union and Cuba to increase their activities on behalf of the MPLA in
nearby Angola, which occurred only after the September 1974 Lusaka
agreement. Also in 1974 the Communist-led and controlled anticolonial movement of Portuguese Guinea took power and established its
pro-Soviet dictatorship in the renamed Guinea-Bissau.

U.S. Reaction. In 1974 and 1975, as Mozambique moved toward rule
by a clearly Communist movement, the Ford administration paid
virtually no attention. There was also very little U.S. media reporting
of events in Mozambique. What little coverage there was focused on
themes favoring a Frelimo perspective. On April 27, 1974, for exam-

ple, the *New York Times* reported that the United Nations World Food Program would make food available to Frelimo and to "peoples in the liberated areas" in Mozambique and Angola. On the same date that newspaper discussed a pro-Frelimo documentary filmed in Mozambique in 1971 "on location in the Portuguese territory with cooperation of the Mozambique Liberation Front." This news story reported that "the movie shows organized health care units, schools, and agricultural communes under revolutionary control, as well as combat recorded by the two Americans during their six-week stay in Africa."[10]

The same influential newspaper reported on April 29, 1974, that Machel said that military aid from the Soviet Union did not "make us Communists. . . . Frelimo is a Mozambique party." On May 11, 1974, the *New York Times* wrote that missionaries had accused Portugal of a massacre in Mozambique; on June 28, after a five-member UN commission investigated the charges—without actually going to Mozambique—the *New York Times* reported that the UN panel backed the claim.

Following the September 1974 agreement giving power to Frelimo, the *New York Times* said in a September 11 editorial headlined "Sunrise in Mozambique":

> It is an occasion for great relief if the rebellion by a group of white settlers against the agreement for the independence of Mozambique has been quashed. . . . Frelimo, which has wrested large areas of Mozambique from Portuguese forces . . . appeared to be the only viable representative of the country's seven million blacks.

Such coverage served to reinforce the claims of Frelimo supporters. Only on September 21 after the Lusaka agreement did the *New York Times* publish an analysis that came close to the truth about Frelimo; its reporter on the scene, Charles Mohr, called Frelimo

> perhaps the most disciplined and militant revolutionary organization in the short history of independent black Africa. It will almost surely bring great changes to Mozambique and may cause serious shocks to white-ruled southern Africa. Its leaders are austere Marxists with ideas bearing distinct resemblance to the Maoist principles in China. . . . The Front has already been supporting black guerrilla units operating in northeastern Rhodesia. . . . One of its most often-repeated goals is the "extinction" of not only Portuguese power in the territory, but also all "imperial" economic influence.

There is little if any sign that the Ford administration was concerned about or even aware of any of these events. During the spring of 1975 it seemed preoccupied on the one hand with summit meetings and negotiations with the Soviet Union and on the other with Communist violations of the 1973 Vietnam Paris agreements, which led to Communist victories in Vietnam, Cambodia, and Laos in April of 1975. Among the first governments to recognize independent Mozambique on June 25, 1975, were the Soviet Union and the Communist government of Vietnam, which sent a congratulatory message to President Machel. President Gerald Ford also wrote to President Machel, on June 25, 1975:

I am pleased to inform you that the United States government extends recognition to Mozambique. . . . We congratulate your leaders and their Portuguese colleagues on the wise statesmanship that has led to Mozambique's independence. The American people share with the people of Mozambique the view that hard-won individual liberty and national independence can be preserved only by unremitting labor and sacrifice. As we strengthen and multiply our bonds of mutual friendship, I am confident of a future in which our two peoples will work together for the freedom, peace and security of all mankind.[11]

The president seemed to have little or no idea that Frelimo was a Communist movement and had long received support from the Soviet bloc. Yet at the same time the Ford administration was working to prevent the MPLA from continuing its violations of the Alvor agreement in Angola and from establishing another pro-Soviet regime.

On July 21, 1975, Nathaniel Davis, the assistant secretary of state for African affairs, offered sentiments about Mozambique similar to President Ford's letter in testimony before the Senate Committee on Foreign Relations. In August the United States voted to admit the People's Republic of Mozambique into the United Nations. The following month Secretary of State Henry Kissinger and Mozambican Foreign Minister Joaquim Chissano (who became president in 1987) initiated diplomatic relations.[12]

Immediately after independence, the New York Times editorialized on June 28, 1975:

Frelimo and Mr. Machel displayed strong traits of intelligence, tenacity, and creativity both in waging the war and in governing the areas liberated in the fight. The new rulers have already confounded some doomsayers by refraining from mass arrests, executions or any semblance of a reign of terror. Mr. Machel has promised his country an end to oppression and a socialist future.

But on July 7, only days later, Charles Mohr, in that same paper, reported from Mozambique:

Frelimo is a strongly Marxist party and evidently intends to reshape Mozambique along Communist lines, but it clearly believes that the transformation must be done on a careful, step by step basis. . . . It is apparent to foreign visitors and residents that the 9 million people of Mozambique have already come under intense psychological and political pressure and that this will be unrelenting and intensified soon.

Actions of the Frelimo Regime

Frelimo rule has been marked by political repression, economic mismanagement and failure, increasing deprivation, aggression through indirect means against neighboring countries, and, since 1980, a sizable armed resistance movement. During the first two years of Communist rule—before an armed insurgency arose to threaten Frelimo—the regime had shown the people of Mozambique its true character and political purposes.

Political Repression. The human costs of the Frelimo regime and the subsequent insurgency against it have been enormous:

- 4,500[13]–200,000[14] political prisoners
- up to 75,000 executions[15]
- 1.6 million refugees to other countries[16]
- 2 million displaced within Mozambique[17]
- 100,000 deaths from starvation[18]
- 5 million at risk of starvation[19]

The population of Mozambique has been decimated. The regime's repression and economic policies drove out nearly all of the 230,000 Portuguese, who left behind their property but took their valuable technical skills.[20]

With personnel from the Soviet bloc—especially from East Germany and Cuba—Frelimo established the instruments for totalitarian control over Mozambique. East German personnel, for instance, organized the secret police, Servico Nacional de Seguranca Popular (the National Service for Popular Security), or SNASP. They also directed the many new prisons and concentration camps, called centers for mental decolonization;[21] they were quickly filled. On the night of October 30–31, 1976, for example, SNASP arrested more than 3,000 in Maputo, Beira, and Nacala, with many going to "reeducation" camps. According to Edward Cain, an experienced observer of Mozambique, "SNASP soon became greatly feared by both blacks and whites."[22] As noted above, estimates of inmates in the concentration camps in the 1980s range from 4,500 to more than 200,000. In 1982 Jorge da Costa, a former head of the secret police, stated that fourteen to twenty concentration camps then held about 64,000 persons.[23]

Conditions at the camps were savage. Amnesty International reported that from 1975 to 1978 severe beatings, often leading to death, were commonplace; prisoners were often buried alive. Others were imprisoned in total isolation or suffered weeks or months of paralysis from having their arms tightly bound with wet ropes that contracted as they dried out. The anti-Frelimo armed resistance movement asserted in April 1986 that more than 75,000 died in Frelimo concentration camps. The resistance movement, which liberated many of those camps, found evidence that many thousands of prisoners had been executed by bayoneting, slitting of the throat, hanging, and being bound to trees or partially buried outside the camps to be devoured by wild animals.[24]

Since independence Frelimo persecuted all religions, including Christian and Moslem. All private schools and medical facilities (many operated by religious groups) were nationalized within one month of the Frelimo victory. A 1979 law declared all religious buildings the property of the state and forbade children under eighteen to attend religious services. Instead they were to receive Marxist-Leninist indoctrination.[25]

Economic Failure. In addition to nationalizing independent institutions, Frelimo attempted almost immediately to impose a Communist economy.

At the third Congress in 1977 Frelimo officially transformed the organization into a Marxist-Leninist party. Speaking to the congress in February 1977, Machel said, "Our struggle is to destroy all vestiges of feudalism and colonialism, but fundamentally to crush capitalism, which is the most advanced form of exploitation of man by man."[26] All independent professionals were to be brought under Communist control, and virtually all industrial facilities were taken over by the state. Manufacturing production decreased steadily in response to nationalization and other restrictive policies. During the 1980s these problems were exacerbated by insurgent attacks on transportation and other infrastructure needed by the manufacturing sector.

State farms and agricultural collectives were established "as much to control the rural population as to increase food and cash

159

crop production."[27] In 1975, before independence, agriculture accounted for about half the cash economy, and agricultural products provided most of Mozambique's export earnings. The regime's program in agriculture was "even more devastating than in other sectors of the economy. . . . [It] resulted in starvation, death, and insurrection."[28] Within the first three years of Frelimo rule agricultural production fell almost 50 percent, with food shortages as early as 1977—long before the armed insurgency became a problem for the Frelimo regime.[29] Sugar production, for example, declined from 228,000 tons in 1975 to 23,600 tons in 1986. During the eleven years of Frelimo rule (1977–1987) real GNP per capita declined almost 40 percent (see table 5–1).

Michael Cecil, a British television producer, spent two months with the Mozambique National Resistance (Resistencia Nacional Mocambicana, or Renamo) in the countryside in 1987. He describes how the forced agricultural collectives, or Aldeas Communales,

> make the government deeply unpopular. . . . Peasants were taken whether they liked it or not and placed in the Aldeas 1,500 at a time. Once there, they were made to grow crops which were then taken away, and in return for which they received a small and inadequate ration. For purposes of control some people were moved to Aldeas far from their original homes. Hardly surprisingly, this left many of the people ripe for any alternative.[30]

Military Growth. Despite the economic decline one sector showed significant growth: the military. In 1975 Frelimo's armed forces numbered around 20,000. Within five years they had grown to about 30,000 and by 1986 to 65,000.

In 1976 Machel had visited Moscow and signed a military agreement, and in March 1977 he again visited the Soviet Union. In 1983 he met with Soviet leader Yuri Andropov in Moscow. Their joint communiqué described "relations between the USSR and Mozambique as a model of fraternal, all-around cooperation for peace and social progress."[31] By 1986 Frelimo had imported more than $2 billion in weapons; and more than 98 percent of its weapons imports came from the Soviet Union.[32] Much of this buildup predated the threat of the Renamo insurgency.

This military buildup was partially attributable to Frelimo's desire to ensure control over the people. A related purpose may have been protection from retaliation once its military cooperation with armed movements opposing the governments of Rhodesia and South Africa became evident. At the start of the Frelimo regime Machel spoke of its "natural allies" among other armed movements, includ-

TABLE 5-1
ECONOMIC TRENDS AND MILITARY EXPENDITURES AND FORCES IN MOZAMBIQUE, 1975–1987

	Military Expenditures (millions)		Armed Forces (thousands)	GNP (millions)		GNP per Capita (1987 dollars)
	Current dollars	Constant 1987 dollars		Current dollars	Constant 1987 dollars	
1975	NA	NA	20	NA	NA	—
1976	NA	NA	21	NA	NA	—
1977	31	54	26	831a	1,454a	131
1978	57	93	25	899a	1,465a	128
1979	56	83	30	992a	1,486a	126
1980	80	110	30	1309	1,797	148
1981	100	125	30	1,416	1,773	143
1982	101	118	30	1,447	1,703	133
1983	NA	NA	32	1,294	1,466	112
1984	NA	NA	34	1,372	1,499	112
1985	95	101	35	1,283	1,361	99
1986	NA	NA	65	1,331	1,374	97
1987	103	103	65	1,237	1,237	85
Total	623+	787+	—	—	—	—

NA = not available.

a. Estimate.

SOURCE: U.S. Arms Control and Disarmament Agency, *World Military Expenditures and Arms Transfers, 1988*, Washington, D.C., 1989, p. 54. Armed forces data for 1975–1976 are from 1987 edition, p. 70.

ing those opposing the governments of Rhodesia and South Africa, and he applauded "the heroic and gigantic fight of the people of Indochina, their victory over the most cruel and most bloodthirsty aggressor of our time, American imperialism."[33]

In March 1976 Machel took the initiative to close the border with Rhodesia (renamed Zimbabwe after independence in 1980) and to prevent it from transporting products through Mozambique. The Frelimo regime nationalized all Rhodesian assets in Mozambique and became the main base for one of the major anti-Rhodesian armed groups, Robert Mugabe's Zimbabwe African National Union (ZANU). In 1977 Rhodesian forces began retaliatory commando raids against ZANU guerrilla bases in Mozambique. On one raid Rhodesian commandos were reported to have attacked a camp of 5,250 anti-Rhodesian guerrillas.

Machel's decision to close the Rhodesian border cost Mozambique an estimated $500 million annually in lost rail and transit fees in addition to $18–20 million in remittances from Mozambicans who had been employed in Rhodesia. Some of this loss was offset by about $102 million in UN funds and economic aid from free-world countries. Other major economic costs resulted from the Frelimo regime's foreign policy decisions, including the loss of a once-thriving tourist industry with 500,000 South Africans and Rhodesians annually visiting the coastal areas of Mozambique. The Frelimo regime placed the attainment of its ideological goals far ahead of its economic interests.

Machel also permitted the African National Congress (ANC) to maintain bases and carry out operations against South Africa from its territory. This organization, closely linked to the South African Communist party, conducts political and paramilitary operations against South Africa.[34] After 1980, once Rhodesia had become independent as Zimbabwe and come under the control of Robert Mugabe and his ZANU movement, South Africa became the focus of the ANC and other armed groups operating from Mozambique's territory. Also at this time external support for Renamo shifted from the Rhodesian government to the South African government.[35]

Renamo—The Mozambique National Resistance

In 1987 Chester Crocker, assistant secretary of state for Africa, described Renamo's origins: "Renamo was created by the Rhodesian secret service in 1977 to punish Mozambique for that country's assistance to Zimbabwean liberation movements. With Zimbabwean independence in 1980, sponsorship of Renamo was taken over by the

South African Defense Force."[36] In May 1985 the State Department's *Background Notes: Mozambique* said the following about Renamo:

> Since 1980, an armed insurgency identifying itself as the Mozambican National Resistance has waged an increasingly violent bush war. . . . Renamo does not appear to exercise administrative control over any portion of the country but rather is a guerrilla force that carries out hit-and-run raids. . . . Renamo has publicly enunciated only a vague political program although its broadcasts and publications present an anti-communist posture.

Other sources provide a far more complex and complete picture of the origins and activities of Renamo.

In the 1960s the Frelimo governing elite had consisted of eleven persons, all drawn from the southern part of the country. None came from the northern Maconde tribe, the Macua tribe (the largest in Mozambique), or other tribes in three quarters of the country. In contrast, many of Frelimo's fighters were drawn from the Maconde and, in December 1975, Maconde soldiers were the first to revolt against the Frelimo regime.

Growth of Renamo. By early 1976 three groups had taken up arms against the Frelimo regime. One of these—named after a Frelimo military commander supposedly murdered by Machel himself—denounced Machel's personal extravagance and exposed brutalities in Frelimo concentration camps. By the spring of 1977 Andre Matessangaisse brought several armed anti-Frelimo groups together to establish Renamo. Matessangaisse, a Frelimo member since 1972, was imprisoned by the Frelimo regime in a concentration camp in 1975. He escaped in October 1976 to lead the armed opposition against the Frelimo regime. According to Cain, "rather than the Rhodesian intelligence establishing the MNR [Renamo] it was natural for the opposition to look to [Rhodesia] for help, but there were limits to the Rhodesians' willingness to help the resistance."[37]

By the end of 1978 Renamo had fewer than 1,000 trained and armed personnel. One year later the movement had grown to some 4,500 men and controlled parts of two provinces. In 1980, soon after its ally Mugabe took control of an independent Rhodesia (renamed Zimbabwe), Frelimo launched a major offensive and reduced Renamo resistance forces to an estimated 300 fighters. In June, 1980, after Matessangaisse was killed in combat, Afonso Dhlakama became commander in chief. Dhlakama, now in his late thirties, is described as a "shrewd administrator, good decision-maker and level-headed soldier."[38] The son of a chief of the Ndau tribe, he was educated at a

163

mission school. Conscripted into the Portuguese army, he rose to the rank of lieutenant. He met Mantessangaisse in the Portuguese army; they defected together to join Frelimo. At this time South African forces began occasional raids into Mozambique to attack ANC staging areas for its raids into South Africa. The South Africans gave Renamo some military help as part of this anti-ANC effort.[39] By 1984, Renamo surged to 15,000 men; by 1986, an estimated 22,000.[40]

At a 1981 secret conference in West Germany Renamo adopted a political program calling for an end to the Communist Frelimo government "without any spirit of vindictiveness" and for "the people's right to choose and freely vote on the country's political, social and economic system." The Renamo program called for a parliamentary system with free elections. It viewed the private sector as central to Mozambique's economy and pledged to prevent class or other exploitation. Around 1987, Renamo issued more complete proposals for "politics, economics, justice, health, education, public services, [and] international politics" and repeated its objective to "democratize, liberalize, and create the conditions for the overall progress of . . . Mozambique."[41]

By the late 1980s Renamo forces were active in all ten provinces and enjoyed the support of an estimated 80–90 percent of Mozambique's 15 million people.[42] Within its zones of control Renamo established a civilian government that administers schools, medical clinics, and agricultural programs.[43] The April 5, 1987, Johannesburg *Sunday Star Review* credited Renamo with building

> a traditional system of authority and private property, using village leaders . . . as their go-betweens with the local communities. . . . A controlled administrative program has led to the beginnings of a normal social structure. Schools and churches are being built, teachers trained, food distributed.

The May 1987 *Africa Events* reported that Renamo enjoyed considerable local support, that it respected private property rights, and that small farms in Renamo territory were producing abundant quantities of corn, manioc, rice, peanuts and fruits.

Renamo Organization. Some 80 percent of Renamo military leaders served in Frelimo. The top Renamo leadership consists of Dhlakama and the commanders of four fronts, each from one of the major tribes: the Macua, the Ndau, the Shona, and the Shangaan. After two months with Renamo in 1987, British television producer Cecil described Renamo military operations:

The chain of command starts at the top with the leader of Renamo, Afonso Dhlakama. He controls all Renamo activity country wide, and nothing is done without his say so. Beneath him there is a military staff based at Gorongosa. Through this Dhlakama runs the war. Each province has its own commander and military headquarters from which all operations in that province are conducted. The provincial commander communicates with Gorongosa daily by radio giving a report on the current situation in his area of responsibility. He receives transmitted to him in return any further instructions that might be necessary. The provinces are generally divided into 2 regions, the regions into districts, the districts into localities, and the localities into zones, the number of these depending on local population densities. There are between 1,500 and 2,000 men in each province, but numbers vary according to the local state of affairs. With a presence in all of Mozambique's ten provinces, this makes a total of nearly 20,000 men. Their task is twofold: first to retain control over territory already won from the government, second to conduct largely guerrilla operations against government-held locations and installations. In addition to these men there are a further 3,000 divided into 9 separate "battalion" formations. These are not tied to any particular province and come under separate command. Their role is more conventional, and they are used for all principal offensive action against government forces, such as attacks on towns and military bases.[44]

Cecil also reported on training of Renamo personnel:

Dhlakama outlines a reasonably thorough training programme for Renamo recruits and troops. The recruits start with 3 months basic training. This includes firing and maintenance of weapons, drill, minor tactics, and general inculcation of military discipline. They are also taught about Renamo itself, its goals and its aims. After this, they go into the field for 2 months service to gain combat experience. This is then followed [by] specialist training at their provincial base. The best of the recruits are selected for the battalions and the remainder are then posted to commands within their own province.[45]

Renamo, according to Cecil, worked with traditional authorities:

Recruiting is carried out by the village and district headmen, who were reinstated by Renamo in areas captured from the government. These headmen were in authority from colonial times and before, but were universally dismissed by the incoming Frelimo government. Although they owe the regaining of their positions to Renamo, they are in theory independent. In practice they appear to cooperate fully and whole-heartedly with the guerrillas.[46]

The British observer also commented on Renamo tactics:

> The tactics employed by Renamo are neither new nor complicated. In order to take over a given area they first dominate the rural districts, thus putting any towns into isolation. This process is then continued by destroying all communications linking that area with the rest of the country. Roads are blocked and dug up, telephone lines are torn down, bridges are sabotaged and railway lines are blown up. All collective villages or "Aldeas Communales" are disbanded and their inhabitants allowed to return to their old homes. In the meantime, the garrisons of the towns are kept under constant pressure. Only able to be resupplied by air, they undergo periodic attack, until they are finally driven out. . . . Many towns have changed hands a number of times in this way. This has resulted in a situation where Renamo controls the large majority of the rural areas, while the government still controls the larger towns, and in some cases the immediate surrounding area.[47]

U.S. Policy. In the summer of 1988 U.S. journalists visited Renamo-controlled areas. They reported that the armed resistance had a strength of about 15,000 to 20,000, with "extensive Renamo presence in much of rural Mozambique" and "sufficient support from the war-weary local population . . . to the point where . . . reconstruction is impossible without their cooperation."[48] Renamo leader Dhlakama expressed his strong disappointment with U.S. policy toward his movement:

> [President] Reagan said he would support all anti-communist guerrilla movements when he came into the White House. This he is not doing. . . . Crocker is compromising with Frelimo. He is playing a very dirty game, and Reagan is getting the wrong information. We feel betrayed by Reagan. What he has declared does not rhyme with his deeds.[49]

Despite the Frelimo regime's Communist allegiance and its record of brutal repression, and despite Renamo's reported widespread support from the population of Mozambique, the U.S. Department of State has been consistently negative about the anti-Frelimo insurgency. In 1987 Assistant Secretary of State Crocker accused Renamo of destroying twelve food delivery trucks in the preceding two years, and he seemed to endorse a report by the UN Children's Fund that

Renamo insurgents had destroyed many medical clinics in Mozambique since 1981.

Further, in April 1988 the Department of State released its "Summary of Mozambican Refugee Accounts of Principally Conflict-Related Experience in Mozambique." This report, written by a consultant it had hired, concluded on the basis of interviews with 196 persons that Renamo had been responsible for up to 100,000 civilian deaths. The accuracy of this report was questioned because it was based solely upon interviews through translators with Mozambicans in refugee camps—85 percent of which were under direct control of the Frelimo government and all of which were under its indirect control. One critical analysis of this report said:

> The refugees, living in camps guarded by Frelimo or Frelimo-allied soldiers, are understandably hesitant to speak out against abuses by Frelimo soldiers. . . . Among the report's most serious flaws is the author's extrapolation leading to his conclusion that "it is conservatively estimated that 100,000 civilians may have been murdered by Renamo." From a small sample of no more than eighty interviews, the author conducts a series of worst-case extrapolations, leading to a conclusion that therefore is highly suspect. . . . Declares a high State Department official: [The] "statistical methodology is the most bizarre thing I've ever seen."[50]

Perhaps most telling about the validity of the report is its assertion that among the 196 refugees, 96 percent were very or somewhat negative about Renamo, while only 17 percent were very or somewhat negative about Frelimo and 72 percent had no complaint about Frelimo (despite its brutality and economic failures). Dhlakama denied the charges and insisted that government units were commiting atrocities to frame and discredit Renamo. According to the July 31, 1988, *New York Times*, he said, "If we were just a bunch of bandits, we would have been caught and handed over to government forces long ago."

Frelimo has allegedly staged attacks such as those recounted in the State Department report and then blamed them upon Renamo.[51] One such attempt to discredit Renamo apparently took place in July 1987. Frelimo reported that Renamo soldiers staged a predawn attack on the town of Homoine in southern Mozambique and killed nearly four hundred villagers. Some analysts noted numerous anomalies, such as the absence of any government casualties, indicating government responsibility. In a Renamo communiqué of July 29, 1987, Dhlakama called the attack "a shameful cover-up of the dissension within Frelimo at the cost of Mozambican lives." His Washington representative, Luis Serapiao, noted that Renamo had been accused of staging the attack just as it was seeking U.S. recognition.

The International Dimension

As the Frelimo regime entered the 1980s, it faced a seriously deteriorating economy and a continually growing insurgency. The leadership of the Mozambique regime had three tasks: to maintain its hold on power and its relations with the Soviet bloc; to improve the economy; and to defeat the Renamo insurgency. To maintain itself in power it continued to use the full means of the totalitarian state, including repression and executions, but it also gradually exercised greater pragmatism, including the end of religious persecution. Close relations with the Soviet bloc, Cuba, and other Communist allies were maintained by a continuing series of consultations and the presence of thousands of personnel from these countries working in the Frelimo regime.

Frelimo's concern about the growth of Renamo's power often resulted in a flurry of visits and consultations with Soviet leaders— as in the spring of 1982. In late 1982 and early 1983 Machel visited Moscow for consultations with Soviet leaders just before beginning his negotiations with South Africa. (Was the conventional view that the Soviet Union opposed Machel's negotiations with South Africa merely the result of disinformation intended to be believed by South Africa and Western governments?) Although the Soviet Union refused to admit Mozambique to full membership in its economic arrangements with Eastern Europe (the Council for Mutual Economic Assistance), there has been every sign of continuing Soviet support and cooperation throughout the 1980s.

In 1980 Machel took steps to reduce corruption and improve administrative accountability to remedy the country's worsening economic situation.[52] He deplored the omnipresent "organized red tape; bureaucracy [had been] transformed into a system to paralyze our economy. . . . The state cannot continue to be involved in hundreds of people's shops."[53] In the late 1970s Mozambique had requested and received increasing amounts of economic aid from the West. Between 1976 and 1987 the Frelimo regime received $2.7 billion in bilateral and multilateral economic development aid from industrial democracies, the Organization of Petroleum Exporting Countries (OPEC), and Western multilateral lending agencies. From 1977 to 1987 the Frelimo regime imported about $2 billion in weapons— virtually all from the Soviet bloc. The regime seemed to be converting humanitarian and development aid money from the free world into payments for Soviet-bloc weapons (see table 5-2).

TABLE 5–2

ECONOMIC AID FROM THE FREE WORLD AND IMPORTS OF SOVIET WEAPONS TO MOZAMBIQUE, 1976–1987

	Free-World Economic Aid (millions of current dollars)				Arms Imports (millions of current dollars)		Arms Imports as Percentage of Total Imports
	Bilateral	Multilateral	OPEC	Total	Current	Constant 1987	
1976	34	36	2	72	—	—	—
1977	66	14	NA	80	30	52	9
1978	75	30	NA	105	150	244	29
1979	114	31	10	155	100	150	18
1980	114	34	10	158	170	233	21
1981	110	33	1	144	110	138	14
1982	161	41	6	208	150	177	18
1983	161	50	1	212	400	453	63
1984	190	66	3	259	360	393	67
1985	217	77	6	300	270	286	NA
1986	319	95	7	421	170	176	35
1987	532	115	3	649	120	120	NA
Total	2,093	622	49	2,763	2,030	2,422	—

NA = not available, not applicable, or nil.
SOURCES: *Organization for Economic Cooperation and Development, Geographical Distribution of Financial Flows to Developing Countries, 1975–1985,* Paris, 1986; ibid., *1984–1987;* U.S. Arms Control and Disarmament Agency, *World Military Expenditures and Arms Transfers, 1988,* Washington, D.C., 1989, p. 96 (cumulative total value of Soviet arms shipments to Mozambique between 1983 and 1987 was $1.3 billion, p. 111).

At its fourth party congress in 1983 Frelimo announced a major economic reform to break up state farms into smaller units, encourage private sector farming, decentralize planning, support private industry, and recognize the necessity of private shops. It also specified state industries that were to be sold to private owners. In 1987 Gillian Gunn, a close observer of Frelimo, concluded that "many of the Fourth Party Congress resolutions remained unfulfilled."[54]

Diplomatic Offensive. In 1982 the Mozambique regime increased the import of troops from Zimbabwe and Tanzania to help against the Renamo insurgency. That year an estimated 10,000 to 15,000 troops from Zimbabwe and 1,500 from Tanzania were already helping the Frelimo forces.[55] But also in 1982, Machel began to cultivate Washington "in the hope that the Reagan administration would pressure South Africa to halt its regional 'destabilization' and that U.S. assistance and investment would help rejuvenate Mozambique's flagging economy."[56] Assistant Secretary Crocker interpreted these overtures to mean that Mozambique's leaders had "signaled their desire to explore a new relationship."[57]

Indeed the Communist regime in Mozambique hoped to use diplomacy and overtures to South Africa, the United States, and Western Europe to isolate Renamo from external support and to obtain more economic aid and credits for its ailing economy. International negotiations since 1982 and the subsequent events show that Frelimo (no doubt with Soviet counsel) has been quite successful.

U.S. Secretary of State George Shultz and Frelimo Foreign Minister (and later President) Joaquim Chissano met in the fall of 1982. Negotiations between Mozambique and South Africa began in 1983. These resulted in the Nkomati accord, signed by Mozambique and South Africa on March 16, 1984. Each side committed itself to cease hostile acts against the other and to prevent hostile insurgent groups from operating against each other from their territories. The accord thus required South Africa to end its logistical support for Renamo, and Mozambique no longer to permit ANC units to operate from its territory.

Following the Nkomati accord the Mozambique regime obtained agreements for military training and supplies from the United Kingdom, Portugal, and the United States. This meant a de facto legitimation of the Frelimo regime by those governments and corresponding political isolation of Renamo from those same governments and possibly other NATO countries. British training for Frelimo officers reportedly began in February 1986.[58] Zimbabwe provided an additional 6,000 soldiers to Mozambique in mid-1986. By 1988 there were an estimated 20,000 troops from Zimbabwe and 10,000 from Tanzania, along with Soviet, East German, Cuban, and North Korean "advisers" giving military help to the regime.[59]

Following the Nkomati accord, President Reagan waived a 1977 congressional ban on U.S. bilateral nonemergency aid to Mozambique. In July 1984 Mozambique was made eligible for U.S. investment insurance from the Overseas Private Investment Corporation (OPIC). In September Mozambique joined the International Monetary Fund and obtained a $60 million loan. It also joined the World Bank, the International Finance Corporation, and the Lomé Convention trading group associated with the European Economic Community. The U.S. Congress approved a bilateral aid program (to begin at $8 million). In October 1984 Mozambique signed an oil exploration agreement with an American oil company and rescheduled $300 million of Western debts. In November 1984 the British Petroleum Company signed an oil exploration contract with the Mozambique regime. All of these economic benefits followed Frelimo's signing of the Nkomati accord—even though the terms were never reasonably implemented since both sides continued to aid and facilitate the operations of hostile guerrilla forces.

Demonstrating continued close relations with the Soviet Union, Frelimo concluded additional cooperation agreements in the summer of 1985. Yet in September as the United States imposed limited economic sanctions against South Africa, Frelimo leader Machel met with President Reagan on an official visit to the United States. Just before Machel's visit, Frelimo alleged that documents found at a captured Renamo base proved South Africa's repeated violation of the Nkomati accord. During his discussions with President Reagan, Machel congratulated the United States for imposing economic sanctions against South Africa.

In the spring of 1986, Machel and President P. W. Botha of South Africa met for the first time since the Nkomati accord; they both sought to improve relations. In October 1986, Machel died in a plane crash and was succeeded by Chissano. The normalization of relations was again suspended when South Africa publicly declared that documents found in the wreckage of Machel's plane revealed a plot by Mozambique and Zimbabwe to overthrow the government of Malawi, which Frelimo had accused of helping Renamo. Then in the spring of 1987, after an ANC bombing attack in Johannesburg, South African forces were reported to have raided buildings in the Mozambican capital of Maputo which they believed were used by the ANC.

Renewed Negotiations. Later that summer South Africa and Mozambique held talks on reviving the joint security commission, which had been intended to monitor the Nkomati accord. Following those negotiations Frelimo offered a number of diplomatic initiatives to increase international support for itself and to isolate Renamo.

In October 1987 President Reagan met with Chissano at the White House. Soon thereafter the British Commonwealth heads of government granted the Frelimo regime observer status at their meetings. In November Mozambique, South Africa, and Portugal signed an agreement to restore the Cabora Bassa Dam in Mozambique, which sells 90 percent of its power to South Africa. (The next year South African troops cooperated with Frelimo to prevent Renamo sabotage of power lines running from the dam to South Africa.) In December 1987 Mozambique and Malawi signed a joint cooperation agreement. These steps further legitimated the Frelimo regime and isolated Renamo.

In April 1988, the State Department released its widely publicized, critical report on Renamo. In May, South Africa and Mozambique signed an agreement to reconvene the joint security commission; both sides again pledged to stop aiding insurgents attacking the other's territory. This agreement served the ANC's interest more than Renamo's. The ANC could simply shift its more visible paramilitary operations to several nearby countries. For Renamo, however, South Africa's transformation from a friendly to a neutral or hostile neighbor posed major problems.

In June 1988 South Africa, Mozambique, and Portugal signed another agreement to revitalize the Cabora Bassa Dam, with expected economic benefits for all three.

In September 1988 Botha visited Mozambique on the first state visit by a South African president to any black African country. He promised peace and substantial financial aid. This visit virtually assured that Renamo would receive no more South African support. South Africa followed this agreement by sending the Frelimo regime 139 tons of nonlethal military supplies.

Another event in Frelimo's favor was the September 1988 visit of Pope John Paul II. The pope urged an end to the fighting and called for foreign reconstruction aid for Mozambique. The regime used this visit both to symbolize its professed new tolerance of religion and to increase the prospects for more economic assistance from the free world.

This normalization of relations between the West and Frelimo in 1988 took place as the United States was encouraging South Africa to negotiate with Angola and Cuba. This diplomatic process, begun in May 1988, culminated in the Angola and Namibia agreements of December 1988.

These events had been set in motion by the diplomatic activity of both the Frelimo regime and the United States. A marked shift in international alignments resulted between 1978 and 1988 (see table 5–3). In 1978 Frelimo had the support of the Soviet bloc and its allies, but it faced strong opposition from several southern African countries and hostility or disapproval from some Western democracies. By 1988 that situation had changed in Frelimo's favor. Frelimo diplomacy, U.S. policy, and the decisions of several European and African countries meant support for Frelimo from Zimbabwe, Tanzania, Zambia, Portugal, the United Kingdom, and the United States as well as from the Soviet bloc, Cuba, and North Korea. Malawi and South Africa had become neutral, and virtually no government remained openly opposed to Frelimo or supportive of Renamo.

Analysis of Frelimo Activity. The Frelimo regime has therefore achieved many of its political and economic objectives through the normalization of relations with South Africa and the West. But has the Frelimo regime made fundamental changes in its internal or international political orientation?

The U.S. Department of State under President Reagan concluded that the Frelimo regime had done so. In April 1985 Secretary of State Shultz said, "We helped move Mozambique away from heavy dependence on the Soviet camp and closer to true non-alignment."[60] In June 1987 testimony to Congress, Assistant Secretary of State Crocker summarized the conclusions of the State Department:

TABLE 5–3
INTERNATIONAL ALIGNMENTS TOWARD MOZAMBIQUE, 1978 and 1988

	Anti-Frelimo	Neutral	Pro-Frelimo
1978	Rhodesia South Africa Malawi	United States	Soviet bloc Cuba Tanzania
1988		Malawi South Africa	Soviet bloc Cuba Tanzania Zimbabwe Zambia Portugal United Kingdom United States

By 1983, faced with economic collapse, a suffocating and unproductive link to Moscow, and a growing insurgency, Mozambican leaders made a fundamental decision to reorient their country's foreign and domestic policies. Under the leadership of the late President Samora Machel, the government of Mozambique began to change drastically its economic policies, reduce its dependence on Moscow, reassert its independence and non-alignment and reach out to the West.[61]

Crocker praised Mozambique for signing the 1984 Nkomati agreement and for its "successful bilateral security dialogue" with Malawi in the fall of 1986 (which led Malawi to expel Renamo guerrillas based in its territory). He added, "No country in southern Africa has worked more consistently than Mozambique with the United States to further the cause of peace and stability in Southern Africa."[62]

Yet Frelimo actions during those years can be interpreted in a different light. Just as the Soviet regime under Stalin sought to borrow funds and obtain economic and technical assistance from the West as it carried out its worst repression, and just as the Soviet regime under Brezhnev used the spirit of détente during the 1970s to obtain Western credits and aid, so too has the Frelimo regime sought increased aid from free world countries during the 1980s.

As noted, it has succeeded in obtaining more than $1.7 billion in free world economic aid from 1976 to 1985 (see table 5–2). As with most of its allies and clients, the Soviet Union does not provide economic aid but does export weapons to the Frelimo regime. Since Soviet arms shipments are estimated at about the same amount, $1.7 billion, increased amounts of free-world economic aid, far from reducing Frelimo's dependence on the Soviet Union, may actually have enabled Mozambique to pay the Soviet Union hard cash for its weapons.

In addition, thousands of Soviet bloc and Cuban advisory personnel remained in Mozambique during the 1980s. One experienced observer disagrees with the Shultz-Crocker interpretation of events and concludes that during the 1980s, "despite its overtures to the West, Frelimo strengthened its ties with the Soviet Union."[63] In addition to the wide range of political, military, and economic cooperation agreements implemented and negotiated with the Soviet bloc and Cuba during these years, Mozambique in 1985 established a program of party-to-party exchanges between Frelimo and the Soviet Communist party. Also during the 1980s Soviet personnel suffered casualties in Mozambique; Soviet pilots were reported to have defended the port city Beira from being crippled by Renamo.[64]

As the only example of Mozambique's ostensibly greater independence from the Soviet Union, Crocker noted in his 1987 testimony that "Mozambique no longer votes with the USSR in the United Nations on such international questions of overriding importance to Moscow as Afghanistan and Cambodia."[65] Perhaps, but Mozambique has opposed the positions of the United States in 95 percent of UN votes; its record there is virtually indistinguishable from that of any Soviet-allied country. Crocker failed to mention that in 1984 Mozambique and the Communist regime of Afghanistan signed a mutual cooperation agreement that continued in force.

Chissano has also made his loyalties clear: "The Socialist [Communist] countries are natural economic and political allies of the Third World."[66] He has stressed Frelimo's priority of friendship with the Communist world rather than cooperation with Western countries. In another stark indication of its intention to remain in power and adhere to communism, Frelimo has year after year rejected Renamo's proposals for negotiations leading to elections in which the people of Mozambique can choose their own government. Soon after his accession to the presidency in 1986, Chissano pledged to maintain Frelimo's obduracy: "The continuation of the struggle, without pause, against armed banditry in our country constitutes the most sacred and fundamental of the tasks in this phase of our history. It is a struggle in which there can be no form of compromise."[67] These actions and words of Frelimo leaders confirm, as Henriksen noted, that "from independence Frelimo has never wavered in its view of Mozambique 'as an integral part of the world proletarian revolution' . . . [and] as part of the 'vast anti-imperialist front.' "[68]

The State Department's June 1987 policy statement on Mozambique was also positive and optimistic concerning Frelimo's economic programs and human rights record. It credited Mozambique with a "break with socialism" and a "tough and sensible economic recovery plan."[69] The State Department mentioned the regime's privatization of some light industry firms and its return of some land to private farmers. It also commended the regime for "some impressive positive trends" in observance of human rights, including the reopening of "most churches that were closed after independence."[70]

By 1989 evidence was mounting that the State Department had overaccentuated the positive side of Frelimo's internal record. Although Chissano had in 1986 endorsed some limited steps toward a mixed economy, he made clear that Frelimo still viewed "the construction of socialism [communism] as the objective of Mozambican society. . . . Only a Socialist society guarantees to the people as a whole equal rights and opportunities."[71] Like other Communist regimes that have adopted new tactics to neutralize challenges, Frelimo temporarily lessened some restrictions while maintaining its control over the country and government. In 1989 Frelimo was still a dictatorial regime intolerant of free speech, press, or assembly; concentration camps remain in operation; and state-appointed central planners continue to control the economy.

The Future

During the 1980s the Renamo movement continually grew in armed strength and in its control of Mozambican territory. By 1987 it had an estimated 20,000 combatants and the support, by some estimates, of as much as 85 percent of the population. Yet the Reagan State Department never viewed Renamo as a legitimate opposition movement, much less a possible or desirable alternative to the Frelimo regime. In 1987 the State Department explicitly rejected what it called the "persistent myth . . . that the insurgent movement of Renamo is a democratic alternative to the government of Mozambique." While ignoring the Frelimo regime's continuing repression of all potential opponents, this statement by Crocker cited allegedly "credible reports of Renamo atrocities against the civilian population." The department ignored the appeal of the Conference of Catholic Bishops of Mozambique urging Frelimo to negotiate with Renamo, but to show "that Renamo lacks a credible political identity where it really counts—in Mozambique itself," Crocker did cite the bishops' statement that they have no relationship with Renamo. The Crocker statement further explained that

> the road, rail and pipeline corridors through Mozambique represent virtually the only transport egress for Southern African countries that is not dominated by South Africa. All the independent countries of southern Africa . . . have a vital stake in keeping those transport links open. . . . With the exception of South Africa, Mozambique's neighbors . . . support the government of Mozambique against the insurgents and would regard official contact with them by Western governments as a hostile act.[72]

Do these statements suggest that the Reagan State Department put the economic interests of those owning and using the transport links above political interests and values with regard to Mozambique? Renamo has sought to weaken Frelimo's grip on power by attacking and sabotaging the transportation links through Mozambique in order to prevent the regime from using them to earn revenue. This successful sabotage campaign by Renamo in Mozambique (and by UNITA in Angola) has caused the landlocked southern African states to shift an estimated 85 percent of their shipping during the 1980s through South Africa.

The landlocked southern African states, dependent upon South Africa for the movement of their exports and imports, have been understandably reluctant to press with full vigor for expanded economic sanctions against South Africa. Zimbabwe's thousands of troops are in Mozambique primarily to keep open the transportation corridor between Zimbabwe and the Mozambican port of Beira. In 1986 the State Department asked Congress for several hundred million dollars in economic assistance to repair and improve this transportation route, which it called the "freedom corridor"—meaning freedom from the need to use South African transportation facilities.

The words and actions of the Reagan State Department reveal its active policy of helping the Frelimo regime diplomatically, economically, and militarily and of encouraging increased free world help while isolating the Renamo armed resistance. As the Reagan administration shifted in 1985 toward limited economic sanctions against South Africa and abandoned UNITA's objectives for fair elections in Angola during the diplomacy of 1987 and 1988, the State Department seemed to assume that the Communist regimes in Angola and Mozambique were in power to stay and that U.S. policy should accommodate them while trying to use economic aid to encourage them toward more moderate internal and international actions. This policy represented a continuation of the implicit economic determinism in U.S. foreign policy about which Jeane Kirkpatrick wrote in 1963.

But, there is a puzzling contrast between U.S. policy toward the Communist MPLA movement in Angola and policy toward Frelimo in Mozambique. In the 1970s, as the MPLA was fighting for power in Angola, the Ford administration recognized—belatedly—its Communist loyalties and tried to prevent its victory. Since then, U.S. leaders have recognized in their public statements and policy decisions that the MPLA is Communist and that the UNITA resistance is pro-Western and democratic. Yet although the Communist political orientation of Frelimo became clear in the late 1960s, the U.S. government seemed to ignore it. The Lusaka agreement's nine-month transition, from September 1974 to June 1975, gave the Ford administration the opportunity to urge its NATO ally Portugal not to hand over power to a Communist movement. Ford administration officials never made any such effort or even perceived what was happening.

During the 1980s Reagan administration officials appeared to continue this pattern of selective perception (or self-deception) concerning the Frelimo regime, its close ties with the Soviet bloc, and

177

the real political meaning of its limited internal steps toward moderation and its understandable search for political and economic assistance from the free world. There is no apparent explanation for this contrast in the U.S. government's perception of two similar Communist movements simultaneously taking power in the former African colonies of Portugal. Despite these contrasting perceptions, the result of the Reagan administration policy may well be the same in both countries: reinforcement of the existing Communist regimes.

The year 1988 was as significant a turning point for the regime in Mozambique as for that in Angola. South Africa apparently decided to accommodate the Frelimo regime instead of continuing its opposition. Among the reasons were doubtless many of the ones that affected South Africa's changing policies toward Angola. In particular, South African leaders were probably concerned about the far more severe economic sanctions that influential Democratic members of the U.S. Congress were seeking. Some in South Africa were also clearly anxious to believe that Soviet foreign policy goals had changed in the wake of the Afghanistan accord of April 1988 and the warm spirit of U.S.-Soviet détente.

Prospects for Freedom in Mozambique

Since the 1974 Lusaka agreement, which effectively handed over Mozambique to Frelimo without the consent of the Mozambican people, the United States under four presidents from both political parties has chosen to tilt toward the Communist regime. This preference continued during the Reagan years despite the demonstrated brutality of the Frelimo regime, the wholesale starvation and deprivation caused by forced collectivization and relocation, and the effective challenge mounted by Renamo. In contrast Renamo has proclaimed its goals to be genuine democracy, opportunity for private economic initiative, and respect for freedom of speech, assembly, association, and religion.

If the Bush administration continues the policies of its predecessor in Mozambique, Frelimo's strategy will probably continue to succeed. The regime will probably continue in power and maintain its close relations with the Soviet Union and with Soviet allies such as Cuba. At the same time the Frelimo regime will likely continue receiving free world economic aid and trying to defeat the Renamo movement. Because it receives aid both from the Soviet bloc and from many free world countries, Frelimo has little incentive to negotiate a just peace with Renamo. Therefore the civil war will continue.

The conventional Western view seemed to hold that expanded

political support and economic aid to Frelimo would ultimately benefit the people of Mozambique and improve stability in the region. This optimistic view rested on the regime's protestations that it was moving toward greater pluralism; the July 1989 Frelimo party congress, for instance, took a rhetorical step away from Marxism-Leninism. Yet the record of the Frelimo regime shows that despite tactical adjustments in its foreign policy and internal rhetoric and practices, its core objectives remain unchanged: to reestablish itself as the sole power inside Mozambique by defeating Renamo and to continue its international alliance with the Soviet Union and its support for Soviet strategic objectives in southern Africa.

The historic pattern of Frelimo suggests that if it defeats Renamo, enormous and bloody repression will then be directed against the millions of people in rural areas who backed the resistance. A Frelimo victory will harness the state and the people it controls to anti-Western objectives in Africa. Targets of aggression might include Botswana, Lesotho, Malawi, Zaire, and especially South Africa. The threat that Renamo posed to Frelimo may well cement the regime's resolve to extirpate any possible germ for recurrence—just as the Vietnamese Communists did after they won in 1954 and judged that their repression in 1945–1946 had not been thorough enough.

The United States should consider providing political, economic, and military aid to the people of Mozambique who seek to free themselves from the Frelimo dictatorship and to establish an independent government based on popular consent, respect for civil rights, and an economic program that invites private initiative and the free market. As a first step, the United States should explore whether Renamo acts on the beliefs that it professes. If it does so, then it should immediately receive U.S. support. If it does not, the United States should undertake serious but discreet negotiations with the Renamo leadership to obtain improvements in its practices. These efforts should be monitored, and only nonmilitary humanitarian aid should be supplied to the people through Renamo. The criteria for U.S. support of any armed resistance movement in Mozambique or any other country must include its objective of establishing a free and independent government, its adherence to the laws of war in its combat operations, its humane treatment of prisoners and the people in its zones of control, and its removal from civil or military authority of any persons who act with cruelty toward defenseless people.

Recommendations for U.S. Actions. If objective analysis demonstrated that the current or improved Renamo could and should be supported, what actions should the United States take? First, it should work with friendly countries to find ways of providing Ren-

179

amo with nonmilitary supplies, both for its own forces and for the millions of people in rural areas it controls. Renamo has an administrative structure and distribution system that could dispense necessary supplies such as medicine, food, and clothing; doing so would help the people, increase its capacity to govern and to obtain additional popular support.

Second, the United States should report to the world the history and actions of the Frelimo regime and seek to isolate Frelimo from Western diplomatic and economic support until it agrees to Renamo's three conditions: first, all foreign troops withdraw from Mozambique; second, a council of national reconciliation, with all sides represented is established; third, free and fair elections are held, with international observers. Free world countries must stop military aid to the Frelimo regime. Soviet bloc military aid will continue. The free world, however, should not contribute to maintaining a repressive Communist dictatorship.

Third, the United States should launch a major international diplomatic campaign to have Renamo accepted as a belligerent under international law and accepted as an observer by international organizations such as the Organization of African Unity and the United Nations, much as the Palestine Liberation Organization (PLO) has been accorded this level of international recognition.

Fourth, the United States should provide enough military assistance to Renamo to expand its operations and its area of control until victory. Among its most urgent military needs are anti-aircraft weapons (Soviet-made SAM-7s or the equivalent would be adequate for defense against the random bombing of civilians and against Zimbabwean paratroop commando attacks); secure communications; means for improving Renamo's tactical intelligence; and professional training for Renamo combat leaders, both in the next stage of military operations against Frelimo forces and in humanitarian professionalization regarding the treatment of Renamo's forces, opposing forces, and civilian populations.

Fifth, the United States should encourage the efforts of those African countries that have been helping Renamo and those that fear Frelimo and its Soviet-aided allies in the region but might take more visible anti-Frelimo stands if they actually believed that the United States would do the same.

Taken together, this strategy of political, diplomatic, and military aid could succeed, at a reasonable and sustainable cost, in helping the people of Mozambique free themselves from a failed Communist dictatorship and move into a future of freedom and promise.

6
Cambodia

The people of Cambodia are among those who have suffered most from totalitarian regimes in modern times. The slaughter and degradation inflicted on the Cambodian people during the last quarter century is the direct result of wars for power initiated by the Soviet-aided Communist movements of Vietnam, Cambodia, and Laos. The Khmer Rouge, the Cambodian Communist regime that took power in 1975, was responsible for killing as many as 2 million of its countrymen.

In late 1978 Communist Vietnam, having achieved domination of one Communist neighbor, Laos, invaded Cambodia, its other Communist neighbor, in order to install a puppet government there. Beginning in 1979 the occupation forces faced armed resistance movements, both non-Communist and Communist, as the Soviet Union and Communist China entered the conflict in aid of rival Cambodian Communist factions. The backing by these major powers makes it likely that they along with Vietnam will determine Cambodia's future, unless there is a change in U.S. policy.

Background

Modern Cambodia is bordered on the east by Vietnam, on the north by Laos, on the west by Thailand, and on the south by the South China Sea. It is a fertile country with abundant agricultural and fishing resources. More than 90 percent of the population work in agriculture (rice, rubber, beans, and corn). A small amount of light industry developed in the years after World War II (textiles, cement, and rubber products), along with some mining of phosphates, gemstones, and gold. By 1970, the population was about 7 million, with Phnom Penh, the capital, having about 600,000, and a few other cities about 200,000. The remainder of the population lived in the countryside.[1]

The overwhelming majority of the population are Buddhists. About 90 percent belong to the Khmer ethnic group, with the remainder divided between Chinese and the Chams (Moslems descended from an ancient kingdom). In the thirteenth century the Khmer

181

empire stretched across much of Southeast Asia from the South China Sea into Burma. By the nineteenth century this empire had been reduced to Cambodia's present-day dimensions (about the size of North Dakota) by the conquests of Vietnamese from the east and Siamese from the west. The latter established present-day Thailand.

In 1863 French colonial activity began with the establishment of a protectorate over Cambodia, and in 1887 France incorporated Cambodia into the Union of Indochina, which included Laos and Vietnam. The French approved the traditional Khmer monarchy, and in 1941, at the age of seventeen, Prince Norodom Sihanouk with French support succeeded his grandfather as king. Throughout the next decades, Sihanouk played a major role in the political life of Cambodia.

During the 1930s, an anticolonial movement appeared in Cambodia as well as in neighboring Vietnam. It was led by Khmer members of the civil service establishment, some Buddhist monks, and students. Imperial Japan and Thailand, both opposed to European colonialism, provided some support, as did the emerging Soviet-supported Communist movement in Vietnam, the Indochinese Communist party.

Following the years of military occupation by Japan during World War II, the history of Indochina, including Cambodia, has been shaped by Communist-initiated wars to take power in Vietnam and ultimately in Cambodia and Laos as well. In retrospect a number of distinct phases to this Communist war for power in Southeast Asia are clear. We can also see a series of actions by the leadership of Cambodia that would ultimately have disastrous consequences for its people.

In 1945 imperial Japan, on the eve of its defeat, granted independence to Vietnam under a government led by the Emperor Bao Dai. But Ho Chi Minh, a founder and leader of the Indochinese Communist Party and longtime agent of the Soviet Comintern, organized an armed coalition which, after Japan's defeat, forced the emperor to abdicate. In the autumn of 1945, Ho Chi Minh declared the establishment of the Democratic Republic of Vietnam.[2]

The Vietnamese Communists followed Lenin's admonition to seek broad alliances in preparation for seizing power. They used a coalition called the Vietminh, which included non-Communists, to deceive non-Communist anticolonial Vietnamese and win the approval of the United States and France. In fact, the Vietnamese declaration of independence read by Ho Chi Minh on September 2, 1945, began: "All men are created equal. They are endowed by their creator with certain inalienable rights, among these are life, liberty and the pursuit of happiness." The leadership of the new Vietminh government was careful to restrain those Communists who wanted to move too quickly. One secret directive aimed at overzealous Communists within the Vietminh coalition stated: "Our government, I repeat, is a bourgeois-democratic government, even though the Communists are now in power."[3]

While maintaining a facade of democratic institutions and continuing a complex series of negotiations to maintain a modus vivendi with the French, the Vietminh government moved toward consolidating one-party Communist rule. In November 1946, however, France sought to reassert its control and initiated military action against the Vietminh. The first war for Vietnam had begun. It would continue until the 1954 Geneva accords ratified the Vietnamese Communists' partial victory over France and resulted in partition of the country into a Communist north and a non-Communist south. This division was not without historical example: The northern Tonkinese and southern Annamese had not been united into a single Vietnamese entity until the French formed the Union of Indochina in 1887.

The Vietnamese Communists had learned a great deal from the Maoist emphasis on psychological and political warfare as well as rural insurgency. In 1946, a leading Vietnamese Communist strategist wrote:

Concerning our foreign policy . . . we must isolate the enemy, win more friends. We must act in such a way that the French people and the colonial peoples in the French colonies will actively support us and oppose the reactionary French colonialists, that all peace loving forces in the world will defend us and favor the aims of our resistance.[4]

This is the international strategy for Vietnam, Cambodia, and Laos that was adopted by the Vietnamese Communists.

France had recognized the autonomy of Cambodia within the French Union of Indochina in 1946 and that of Laos in 1949. When Cambodia became fully independent in 1953, a small Cambodian Communist movement already existed, working under the leadership of the Indochinese Communist Party. One part remained in Cambodia and established a political party to participate in the parliamentary governing system, while the other part of the movement went to North Vietnam after the Communist regime was established there by the 1954 Geneva accords. Those accords had also provided for the full independence of Laos but permitted the Communist Pathet Lao movement to occupy two northern provinces. The Communist side manipulated the 1954 Geneva accords with impunity. Quite understandably, in 1989 the Vietnamese Communist regime and its Cambodian ally would point to those accords as a model for a new agreement on the future of Cambodia.

In 1955 King Sihanouk declared that Cambodia would remain neutral, and he refused to join the newly established Southeast Asia Treaty Organization (SEATO). His decision to maintain close relations with Communist North Vietnam and Communist China irritated the anti-Communist governments of Thailand and South Vietnam. Later that year, Sihanouk abdicated in favor of his father and founded a political movement, the Popular Socialist Community, which won all the seats in the National Assembly in the elections of 1955, 1958, 1962, and 1966. Sihanouk's political success was due to the peasants' view of him as the personification of traditional rule and to the forced disbanding or curbing of most competing political movements.[5]

The 1954 Geneva accords had given the Vietnamese Communists control of North Vietnam's 14 million people and 63,000 square miles of territory—about 55 percent of the population and 45 percent of the total territory of Vietnam. For the next four years the Communist regime in Hanoi focused on consolidating its power and carrying out its internal agenda. Almost all the French departed, and 2 million to 3 million Vietnamese, mostly Catholics, unwilling to live under communism fled to the south.[6]

The Vietminh government of 1945–1946 had executed an estimated 10,000 persons in the Hanoi area alone.[7] But this bloodletting was insufficiently thorough in the view of the secretary general of the Indochinese Communist Party, who wrote in 1946:

> We regret only that the repression of the reactionaries . . . was not carried out fully in the framework of its possibilities. . . . For a new-born revolutionary power to be lenient with counter-revolutionaries is tantamount to committing suicide.[8]

Back in power after 1954, the same Communist movement in North Vietnam executed many more thousands of people whom it considered "class enemies." In his definitive study of Vietnamese communism, Turner estimates that during the land reform program between 50,000 and 100,000 owners of small parcels of land who were branded as landlords were executed and their families ostracized. One former North Vietnamese official described the consequences for the families:

> Like leprous dogs they became creatures at whom children were encouraged to throw stones. Nobody was permitted to talk to them or have any contact with them. . . . In consequence the majority of them died of starvation, children and old people first, and eventually the others.[9]

The North Vietnamese were following the example of the Chinese Communists, who after taking power in 1949 had executed millions of "landlords" and other "class enemies." The Soviet Union's de-Stalinization program launched by Nikita Khrushchev in 1956 produced temporary episodes of ideological liberalization in both Communist China and North Vietnam, episodes that were terminated as soon as those countries' Communist rulers felt their control was threatened. Then in 1959 North Vietnam instigated its war against South Vietnam, using terrorism, surrogate guerrilla forces, and clandestine infiltration of its own troops.

In 1960 Sihanouk, now the elected head of Cambodia, continued to pursue a neutralist policy despite North Vietnam's aggression against South Vietnam. At about the same time Cambodian Communist leaders secretly restructured an underground party apparatus, splitting off from the Indochinese Communist Party and beginning clandestine political activities as the independent Communist Party of Kampuchea (Cambodia). In 1960, as if guided by a signal from Hanoi, the Communist movement in Laos caused the breakdown of its coalition government with neutralists, set up by the 1954 accords, and began combat operations in pursuit of a complete takeover. Only the presence of U.S. troops in Thailand deterred the Communist Pathet Lao from capturing Vientiane, the Laotian capital, in 1962. Although a second Geneva conference, convened in 1962, provided for a neutral government in Laos, by 1963 the Communist Pathet Lao resumed its war for control of the country in violation of those accords also.

In 1964, French-educated members of the secret Communist Party of Kampuchea—now known as the Khmer Rouge—returned to Cambodia and initiated political and guerrilla operations in a bid to seize power. Armed Communist insurgencies were thus making headway in Cambodia, Laos, and South Vietnam.

President Kennedy had earlier sent military advisers to help South Vietnam. In 1965 his successor, Lyndon Johnson, began to send U.S. combat troops to fight alongside South Vietnamese forces against the growing numbers of Viet Cong insurgents and North Vietnamese troops infiltrated through Laos and Cambodia. Sihanouk's one-sided "neutrality" policy permitted the North Vietnamese, backed by the Soviets and Chinese, to transport troops and supplies through Cambodia deep into South Vietnam.

When U.S. military aid to South Vietnam began intensifying, Sihanouk broke diplomatic relations with Washington, in May 1965. Two years later, after an estimated 40,000 North Vietnamese regulars had invaded Laos to support the armed Communist movement there and to guard the movement of their troops and armaments into South Vietnam, Sihanouk publicly blamed Communist insurgents for a peasant uprising in one Cambodian province, and for the first time ordered a massive crackdown on the clandestine Communist Party of Kampuchea. After that, many left-wing elements of his political movement defected and openly joined the Khmer Rouge. In 1968, the Communist insurgency grew as Sihanouk vainly tried to persuade the North Vietnamese army and the Viet Cong to get out of Cambodia.

After nearly five years of Communist guerrilla warfare against his government, Sihanouk finally recognized the extreme danger facing Cambodia. In July 1969, he reestablished diplomatic relations with the United States and asked General Lon Nol to form a new government. In March 1970, Lon Nol staged a coup against Sihanouk and requested U.S. military assistance for Cambodia. Soon thereafter, South Vietnamese and U.S. forces made an incursion into eastern Cambodia in an attempt to disrupt the headquarters and supply systems being used by North Vietnam. One result was to drive the Cambodian Communist guerrillas deeper into Cambodian territory, where they intensified their combat operations.

Sihanouk went into exile in Beijing and joined the Communist Party of Kampuchea (Khmer Rouge) in forming the National United Front of Cambodia (FUNC) in opposition to the U.S.-backed Lon Nol government. Sihanouk's decision to join forces with the Communist movement he had so recently denounced as a major threat to his people was difficult to understand.

In 1971, South Vietnamese forces tried and failed to expel North Vietnamese troops from Laos. At the same time the United States began to withdraw its combat forces as negotiations with North Vietnam proceeded in Paris. Two years later the Paris accords officially ended the war for South Vietnam, and in Laos another cease-fire was signed between the government and the Communist forces. (See chapter appendix.)

In Cambodia the insurgency continued to expand as the Communists immediately began to violate the 1973 Paris accords. These accords, to which South Vietnam had bitterly objected, permitted about 120,000 North Vietnamese troops to remain in northern South Vietnam, but prohibited North Vietnam from any further military reinforcement of any type. North Vietnamese forces were to withdraw completely from Cambodia and Laos. Flouting this provision, North Vietnamese troops remained in both Cambodia and Laos, supporting Communist insurgents there. Within three months of the signing of the Paris accords, North Vietnam had already shipped an additional 30,000 tons of military supplies to its forces inside South Vietnam.[10] Those violations continued unabated, with North Vietnam resupplying both its army units and the few remaining Viet Cong guerrillas inside South Vietnam. In 1974, North Vietnam launched large-scale military offensives against South Vietnam, while in Cambodia control by the Lon Nol government became increasingly limited to the cities and their immediate environs.

In the first months of 1975 North Vietnam and its forces inside South Vietnam launched a series of massive military attacks, which led to the unconditional surrender of the South Vietnamese government at the end of April. Meanwhile in Cambodia, the Khmer Rouge guerrillas had launched a major offensive that culminated in the collapse of the Lon Nol government on April 17, 1975. At that same time in Laos, the Communist Pathet Lao dissolved the National Assembly and took power. All of Indochina, with the exception of Thailand, was now under the control of Communist regimes. In Cambodia, Sihanouk became titular head of state of the new Cambodian government, in which the clandestine Communist Party of Kampuchea (the Khmer Rouge) held the reins of real power.

The Khmer Rouge Regime, 1975–1979

Each of the three new Communist regimes acted swiftly to consolidate its power. Hanoi extended its control into South Vietnam immediately, but did not formally unite the two parts of Vietnam until 1976. Thousands of South Vietnamese government and military officials were executed in the first months of the new regime, while several hundred thousand were put in "new economic zones"—which were little more than forced labor camps located in impoverished, sparsely populated areas.[11]

Hanoi's repression and economic policies sharply reduced the living standards of the people of South Vietnam, although the Soviet Union is estimated to have provided its clients in Hanoi with $2 billion per year in subsidies.[12] By 1977 the regime admitted there were severe food shortages. Meanwhile, hundreds of thousands of ethnic Chinese fled Vietnam, because of systematic persecution while one and a half million South Vietnamese also sought escape by putting out to sea in a desperate flotilla of rickety boats. Of these "boat people" about 500,000 are thought to have died—starved, drowned, or murdered by pirates.

In 1981 Hanoi announced a plan to relocate 10 million Vietnamese by the year 2000, supposedly to reclaim fields abandoned during the war or to open new lands. But many saw in this policy a Communist effort to disperse and punish people suspected of antipathy to the new regime. In 1988, a labor ministry official in Hanoi said that 3.5 million people had been moved under this plan and that by 1990 an additional 1.2 million people were expected to be relocated. But this coercive program failed. Although the government had promised to provide the "settlers" with assistance as well as private land, by 1988 Vietnam with its 63 million people was being described as an economic basket case: "Millions are jobless or underemployed and the country still cannot feed itself."[13]

While the Communist government of a unified Vietnam tightened the screws of oppression and presided over a declining economy, its armed forces with large-scale Soviet assistance dramatically increased in size and capability. In 1977 these forces engaged the new Communist regime in Cambodia in a series of border clashes, which continued and intensified into 1978. The paranoia and extremism of the Khmer Rouge leadership is generally perceived as the reason for its igniting these and subsequent border military attacks.

Meanwhile, in neighboring Laos, the Vietnamese army continued to maintain a presence of 40,000 or more troops. The Communist Laotian government, in tandem with these Vietnamese troops and with full Soviet support, then undertook a series of military actions intended to punish the minority ethnic groups—the Hmong, Meo, and others who had fought the Communists for years. These campaigns reportedly included the widespread use of chemical and toxic weapons during the late 1970s.[14] According to Al Santoli, a longtime observer of Indochina, Communist repression and chemical weapons reduced the population of the Hmong ethnic group from an estimated 400,000 in 1975 to fewer than 100,000 by 1983.[15] After 1975 hundreds of Laotian refugees poured into Thailand each month, and as of 1988 some 380,000 refugees from Laos, Cambodia, and Vietnam were still living in Thai refugee camps.[16] Former Lao prime minister and government adviser Souvanna Phouma told a visiting U.S. reporter in March 1979 that between 10,000 and 15,000 prisoners were being held in Lao "reeducation camps."[17]

But even this repression was overshadowed by that of the Khmer Rouge, which acted against its own people with almost inconceivable brutality.[18] The Khmer Rouge had already demonstrated its cruelty in rural areas under its control. For example, between 1971 and 1975 it had established forced-labor "agricultural collectives" and executed any peasants who opposed them in any way. It also executed Communist cadres returning from training in Vietnam who were suspected of being too close to the Vietnamese Communist authorities.[19] Within the first weeks after its victory in 1975 the Khmer Rouge systematically killed large numbers of former government officials and military personnel. Anyone wearing glasses—hence presumed able to read—was targeted for death. Cambodia became a killing field, exceeding in the proportion of its population even the mass murders of Hitler, Stalin, and Mao.[20]

There were many in the Cambodian capital who had believed a Communist victory would bring peace and some improvement in life. There were even some members of the U.S. Congress who felt and said the same in the spring of 1975. But the following account provides a glimpse of what happened on April 17, 1975, as the victorious Communists occupied Phnom Penh:

> Silent and unsmiling, the Communist soldiers filed through jubilant crowds that quickly fell quiet and fearful. Answering cheers and waves with mask-like indifference, they stopped traffic, ordered drivers out of their vehicles and corralled surrendering soldiers into frightened groups, forcing them to disrobe in the streets. . . . The mood in the capital had changed as if a switch had been thrown. One of those who felt elation turn to dread over the space of a couple of hours was a French priest, Francois Ponchaud. During ten years in Cambodia Father Ponchaud had lived among and come to identify with peasants and the urban poor. . . . He sympathized with the revolution. Though he knew from refugees of acts of cruelty in the liberated zone, he still believed that Cambodia could escape its misery only with a Khmer Rouge victory. But now as he watched the first revolutionary soldiers arrive, doubt became a physical sensation.[21]

For the first two years of its rule, the Communist Party of Kampuchea did not identify itself and initially acted in the name of the "Angka," which in Khmer means "the organization." All twenty leaders of the Angka had been recruited to communism during their studies in France during the 1950s. The two leaders were Saloth Sar (alias Pol Pot) and Ieng Sary. They had married sisters and studied in France together, and were obsessed with the need for secrecy.[22] The first order the Angka issued was to evacuate all cities and towns. Phnom Penh, then swollen to a population of 2 million, many of whom had fled the war in the countryside, was emptied in a matter of days: the old, the sick, infants were driven at bayonet point out of homes, hovels, even hospitals. In his vivid and dramatic account of life under the Khmer Rouge, Dr. Haing Ngor describes the scene:

> A Khmer Rouge shouted, "you have to leave the city for at least three hours. You must leave for three hours. You must leave for your own safety, because we cannot trust the Americans. The Americans will drop bombs on us very soon. . . ." The streets were filled from one side to the

other. . . . We were refugees carrying whatever we could. . . . An exodus of the sick and crippled had begun. All the patients were leaving by order of the Khmer Rouge. . . . [A] man with a bandage over his eyes and amputated legs was being wheeled along the sidewalk on a hospital bed, the IV bag still hanging from the bed rack. . . . The mass of people shuffled forward, but it was difficult to move. Around me on all sides were feet and shoulders and heads. . . . The earlier joy that the war was over had disappeared and its place was taken by the smell of fear.[23]

Much of the extreme radicalism of the Khmer Rouge derived from Mao's Cultural Revolution, which had emphasized persecution of educated people and forced agrarian communalism. The Khmer Rouge divided people into four categories: the party cadre, workers, soldiers, and peasants. In the new order,

not only were there no private plots of land, there was no private property at all. Money was abolished; all exchange was by barter or Party requisition. Children were separated from their parents at the age of six and rarely saw them again after that. Childhood was lost; . . . peasants, workers and soldiers could be assigned to labor anywhere. All religious and social celebrations were prohibited. All travel was banned. . . . Defiance in any form—disobedience or criticism—was punished by death in secret. The dissenters simply disappeared—no one dared ask where they had gone.[24]

Before the Communists began guerrilla operations in 1964, Cambodia was a country renowned for the peacefulness of its people and the gentle nature of its culture. Among the reasons that many Cambodians so misjudged the Communist Party of Kampuchea was their own perception of their country and people as friendly, unwarlike, and given to accommodation. Further, many Cambodians were reassured by Sihanouk's alliance with the Communist Party of Kampuchea and by the fact that so many of them knew people or had relatives fighting with the Khmer Rouge. Dr. Ngor recalls:

Sihanouk was highly respected. Even if Sihanouk was only a figurehead for the Khmer Rouge, it was hard to believe that the cause he represented was cruel or bad. Sihanouk returned to the "liberated" zones in Cambodia in 1973. He still talked to us over the radio from Peking. . . . Every day we heard accounts of government soldiers stealing chickens and livestock from civilians in the countryside . . . but we never heard of the Khmer Rouge stealing anything. . . . It was said that the guerrillas kept to a strict and honorable code of behavior. . . . The Communists seemed like a fresh clean breeze.[25]

Dr. Ngor describes a life of forced labor from dawn to darkness, with political lectures followed by more labor until after midnight—day after day, seven days a week. The Khmer Rouge wielded life-and-death power over the millions of Cambodians torn from their homes and familiar surroundings. He recounts the constant hunger, lack of medicine, and mounting death toll from executions, starvation, and disease. Nearly every day Khmer Rouge soldiers came to take people away, binding their arms behind their backs, dragging them off to the forests, and killing them—with no explanation. Dr. Ngor describes the sense of terror that gripped everyone, knowing each day could well be his last:

> We tried to learn why the Khmer Rouge were killing so many but found no reason. It was just something they did, a craving they could not satisfy. They created enemies to devour, which increased their appetite for enemies. . . . Everything was gone. Society was destroyed and monks and temples destroyed and markets and families and the bonds between humans destroyed. There was no hope.[26]

The U.S. government estimates that Khmer Rouge actions killed between 1.5 million and 3 million Cambodians, out of a population totaling about 7 million in 1975. One U.S. government report states that "hundreds of thousands were probably executed by the regime, often in the most brutal manner. . . . Torture centers were established where detailed records were kept of the thousands murdered there. Few succeeded in fleeing the country or escaped the military patrols."[27]

Even these shocking estimates may understate the depths of suffering. Dr. Ngor points out that among 50,000 Buddhist monks in Cambodia, only 3,000 survived; among 527 medical graduates, only 40 are known to have survived; among 7,000 from his home village, only 550 are known to have survived; and among 41 in his family only 9 survived—this was a death rate of nearly 80 percent.[28]

In September 1975, Sihanouk went before the United Nations to denounce the reports of Khmer Rouge brutality and mass executions as mere rumors, and he argued that the new government should be admitted to membership in the United Nations. Four months later, the Communist Party of Kampuchea dissolved its coalition with Sihanouk and established "Democratic Kampuchea" as a Communist people's republic, which later received UN recognition. A few months later Sihanouk resigned as head of state and was held under virtual house arrest for the next few years. His five children and eleven grandchildren were sent into the countryside, while he lived isolated in the royal palace in the already deserted capital. Many of his

191

children and grandchildren died at the hands of the regime he had helped bring to power.[29]

Vietnamese Occupation and the People's Republic of Kampuchea

When Saloth Sar (Pol Pot) and his Communist associates returned from France to Indochina in the 1950s, they first worked within the Indochinese Communist Party, but came to resent the fact that the Vietnamese were in charge and treated the Cambodians as inferiors. So in 1960 they formed the Communist Party of Kampuchea to be independent of the Vietnamese Communists.[30] By 1973, as their military offensive against the Lon Nol government was increasing in intensity, and despite their need for North Vietnamese military help, they purged and killed large numbers of their own members who had been trained in Vietnam.[31]

In 1977, Pol Pot's military units began a series of battles and border skirmishes with the Vietnamese, who made a drive into Cambodia in May 1978, withdrawing at the start of the rainy season. Possibly Pol Pot's close political and military alliance with Communist China, which bordered Vietnam on the north, emboldened him to believe he could harass Vietnam, a country nine times as large as Cambodia in population. In December 1978, however, Vietnam invaded Cambodia with fourteen battle-hardened divisions, and by January 1979 it had captured the capital and occupied much of the country. As the Vietnamese army closed in on the outskirts of Phnom Penh, a desperate Pol Pot sent for Sihanouk and, according to one account,

> in his soft ingratiating voice . . . apologized to Sihanouk for not being able to receive him sooner. . . . He wanted Sihanouk to help on the diplomatic front. Would he mind going to the United Nations to hold on to Democratic Kampuchea's seat? Sihanouk, astonished, had the presence of mind to agree.[32]

Sihanouk was flown out of Cambodia just before the Vietnamese occupied Phnom Penh, while Pol Pot and many of the Khmer Rouge armed forces retreated to the mountains of western Cambodia along the border with Thailand.

In February 1979, China retaliated for the invasion by attacking the northern provinces of Vietnam. After weeks of heavy fighting and significant casualties on both sides, China withdrew its forces from Vietnamese territory but kept large forces near the border, requiring Vietnam to deploy a larger number of troops and weapons on its northern frontier.[33] The conflict in Cambodia thus pitted the two major Communist powers against each other, with China backing the Khmer Rouge and the Soviet Union backing Vietnam and the Vietnamese puppet government in Cambodia.

Special shipments of Soviet weapons had reportedly built up the Vietnamese forces in 1978 to invasion strength. Over the next decade more than $17 billion in continuing Soviet economic and military aid poured in to help Vietnam maintain its occupation forces in Cambodia and Laos.[34] But to the apparent surprise of both the Vietnamese and the Soviets, who had expected most countries to welcome the removal of the Khmer Rouge, Vietnam's 1978 invasion of Cambodia was denounced by many developing countries as well as by the Western powers.[35] This international opposition continued and was reflected in repeated UN votes in which a large majority of the members called for the withdrawal of Vietnamese occupation forces. In 1985, such a UN resolution passed by a margin of 114 to 21.

A significant proportion of the Vietnamese Communist leadership—civilian and military—is also reported to have opposed the invasion. According to one Vietnamese defector, formerly a senior official in the security system: "Many of us felt [the invasion] was because of Cambodia's alliance with China and our own Party's obedience to Soviet dictates. After 21 years of war, another battle was beginning. I felt it would not be good for the reconstruction of Vietnam."[36]

On January 10, 1979, the Vietnamese set up the People's Republic of Kampuchea (PRK) under Heng Samrin, a former Khmer Rouge official who fled when Pol Pot began to execute members of his regional group in 1978.[37] The new government established another Cambodian Communist party, called the Kampuchea People's Revolutionary Party (KPRP). The Samrin regime pledged to restore freedom of movement, freedom of association, and freedom of religion, and to permit families to be reunited. It also systematically exposed and revealed the execution sites, the torture places, and the human remains of some of the millions of victims of the Pol Pot regime. To establish its own political control, however, the PRK regime itself used secret executions, torture, and other means of repression— although the scale did not approach that of the Khmer Rouge. For example, the U.S. State Department estimated that between 1980 and 1983 several thousand political prisoners were held by the PRK regime.[38] By 1987, however, there were an estimated 200 prisons in PRK-ruled Cambodia, which suggests that the number of political prisoners may have grown.[39]

The Vietnamese occupation regime had arrived with no plan for rebuilding the shattered Cambodian economy and society. On the contrary, the Vietnamese looted factories, warehouses, and homes, while their form of collectivized agriculture resulted in further severe food shortages. In 1979 and 1980 this led to appeals for international aid, and between 1979 and 1981 the United Nations provided emergency relief to the PRK regime of about $213 million. In addition, a number of private volunteer organizations attempted to provide humanitarian assistance.

Throughout its years of occupation, Vietnam reportedly extracted large amounts of fish, agricultural commodities, rubber, and other natural resources from Cambodia. As a densely populated country, Vietnam also systematically attempted to move hundreds of thousands of Vietnamese into Cambodia as permanent settlers. According to an estimate by the chairman of the UN International Conference on Kampuchea in 1984, "a minimum of 500,000 Vietnamese had settled among a Cambodian population of six to seven million." Some estimates, he said, were far higher.[40]

Rice cultivation, which was at about 4 million hectares in 1970, fell to about 1.5 million hectares in 1986 and 1987—a 60 percent decline.[41] The drop in estimated GNP, which had been steady since the Khmer Rouge took power in 1975, continued under the PRK regime. But despite the economic difficulties, the PRK regime imported increasing amounts of weapons during the 1980s, for a cumulative total (from 1980 to 1986) of nearly $1 billion, with more than 95 percent coming from the Soviet Union.[42]

The Armed Resistance Movements

During the years when the Khmer Rouge was turning Cambodia into one vast concentration camp, small groups of an anti-Communist armed resistance managed to operate from the Thai border region. By 1977 rumors of their activity were helping to spark some hope in the victims of the Khmer Rouge regime, as Haing Ngor recalls:

> The cracks began to show. . . . The soldiers didn't like sentry duty anymore and they wouldn't go out on patrol except in groups. . . . Stories had travelled from one cooperative to the next of the freedom fighters based on the border with Thailand, less than a hundred miles away. There [were] so many rumors about the coming of the freedom fighters that people looked up in the sky, wondering when the helicopters were going to land.[43]

In mid-1978, when the Khmer Rouge leadership began warning about invasions from an enemy, for Dr. Ngor and others, "there was only one conclusion"—the freedom fighters "had finally launched their attack." Illustrating the powerful effect of mere word of an armed force opposing an oppressive regime, Ngor recalls: "I could feel the change in my body—a stirring of hope, a strengthening. Now I had something to live for."[44] As it turned out, the enemy the Khmer Rouge feared was Vietnam, not the small anti-Communist resistance.

When the invading Vietnamese ended the Khmer Rouge terror and control in 1979, hundreds of thousands of Cambodians took the opportunity to follow earlier refugees to the Thai border in search of food, shelter, and health services or escape to new countries. At one time nearly 500,000 refugees were living in camps near the Thai-Cambodian border and an additional 100,000 were living inside Thailand.[45] These refugee settlements not only provided sanctuary or escape for individuals and families but now also became the social base for armed resistance movements, not against the Khmer Rouge but against the PRK regime.

Already by mid-1978, the European-based Association of Overseas Cambodians had sent a delegation to the Thai-Cambodian border to establish a formal anti-Communist resistance movement. This ultimately resulted in the establishment of the Khmer People's National Liberation Front (KPNLF), one of three elements of armed resistance to the Vietnamese- and Soviet-backed PRK regime. The second element was the Khmer Rouge itself, which after the Vietnamese invasion had retreated to jungles and forests along the Thai border and, with Chinese support, began organizing for guerrilla warfare. A third element was led by Sihanouk, who established a non-Communist armed resistance group, the Sihanoukist National Army (ANS), in 1981 and later (1989) established a political movement, the National Resistance of Cambodia. Table 6–1 shows the groups thus contending for the future of Cambodia: the PRK regime and, nominally joined in the Coalition Government of Democratic Kampuchea, the Khmer Rouge and the two non-Communist resistance movements.[46]

During the 1980s, armed resistance against the PRK grew steadily. The highest priority of the Soviet- and Vietnamese-backed PRK regime was to establish full control over the territory of Cambodia and to defeat the resistance movements. Beginning in 1980, there was a wet season–dry season alternation in the war between the Vietnamese/PRK and the armed resistance: During the dry season the Vietnamese took the offensive, while the resistance forces attacked during the rainy season.

In 1983, after failing in a major offensive in 1982 against the main Khmer Rouge base in the mountains on the Thai border, the Vietnamese launched a series of massive attacks, backed by tanks and heavy artillery, against refugee camps associated with each of the resistance

195

TABLE 6–1
CAMBODIAN GROUPS AND THEIR INTERNATIONAL ALLIES, 1989

Cambodian Groups	Estimated Forces	Allies
People's Republic of Kampuchea (PRK, 1979) Hun Sen, premier Heng Samrin, leader of the Communist party of the PRK	40,000	Vietnam USSR Soviet allies
Khmer Rouge (Communist party of Kampuchea) Khieu Samphan, nominal head Pol Pot, actual head Son Sen, chief military commander[a]	35,000	People's Republic of China
Khmer People's National Liberation Front (KPNLF, 1979) Son Sann, president	12,000	United States ASEAN countries: Thailand, Malaysia, Indonesia, Singapore, Brunei, Philippines
Sihanoukist National Army (ANS, 1981) Prince Norodom Sihanouk Prince Norodom Ranariddh	18,000	

NOTE: In 1982, the Khmer Rouge, KPNLF, and ANS formed the Coalition Government of Democratic Kampuchea. In 1989 its military command was renamed the National Resistance of Cambodia, with Prince Sihanouk as supreme commander and Khieu Samphan and Son Sann as deputy commanders. The coalition government was endorsed by 115 UN members.
a. My conclusion, based on evidence by Erlanger (see source note below).
SOURCES: Al Santoni, "Cambodia: Freedom's Frontline in Southeast Asia," in Charles Moser, ed., *Combat on Communist Territory* (Lake Bluff, Ill.: Free Congress Foundation, 1985). Steven Erlanger, "The Return of the Khmer Rouge," *New York Times Magazine*, March 5, 1989; for estimated forces, see table 6–2.

groups.[47] These dry-season offensives against the refugee camps along the Cambodian-Thai border recurred in 1984–1985, 1985–1986, and in 1988, but they received very little world attention or condemnation. They have caused thousands of civilian casualties, especially among supporters of the non-Communist resistance groups, since the better armed Khmer Rouge parried the attacks more effectively.

To prevent infiltration of the resistance movements into Cambodia, the PRK regime and the Vietnamese also planted thousands of land mines and attempted to build a massive barrier along the entire border with Thailand. The Vietnamese and PRK reportedly dragooned nearly 1 million Cambodians into building this barrier along the 500-mile border, and tens of thousands are said to have died in terrible conditions during the forced labor.[48] Although the barrier was never completed, it covers close to half the length of the border and has made infiltration by resistance forces more difficult.[49] Nonetheless, by 1987 the Vietnamese and the PRK saw that their efforts to establish complete control in Cambodia were not succeeding; all the elements of the armed resistance continued to grow.

Khmer People's National Liberation Front (KPNLF). Despite the Vietnamese invasion of Cambodia, Western governments were unwilling to provide economic aid to the KPNLF as it was being organized in 1979. Nevertheless, with support from private donations, the KPNLF brought together existing anti-Communist guerrilla organizations and recruited an initial force of about 2,000 by the time it proclaimed its existence and its program in October 1979. At a press conference on the Thai-Cambodian border, the KPNLF called for the following:

- an immediate cease-fire to allow international organizations to bring food and medicine into Cambodia
- withdrawal of Hanoi's troops and their replacement by a UN peace-keeping force
- UN-supervised free elections allowing all Cambodians the right to self-determination
- establishing Cambodia as a neutral country
- cooperation between all Cambodians inside and outside the country in rebuilding the society[50]

Son Sann, a former prime minister of Cambodia, founder of the national bank, and former minister of finance, became president of the KPNLF. He had a reputation for integrity and fairness in his past efforts to bring about a post-Communist settlement. Key military leaders have been General Sak Sutsakhan, a minister of defense during the Republic of Cambodia (1970–1975), who serves as supreme military commander of the KPNLF, and General Dien Del, a senior officer under Lon Nol and commander, then deputy commander, of the KPNLF.

The KPNLF's social base consisted of about 150,000 people in a number of civilian refugee camps on the Thai-Cambodian border.

The U.S. State Department reported that "within the civilian encampments under its control, area and section leaders are elected democratically. They form the civilian leadership in each camp."[51] There has been an enormous difference between life inside these civilian camps, in which the non-Communist resistance groups have authority, and life inside the camps controlled by the Khmer Rouge; each has reflected the political values and perspectives of the resistance group in charge.

The KPNLF not only defended the civilian camps from attack by the Vietnamese and PRK regime (and at times the Khmer Rouge); it also "coordinates food relief from international agencies, housing, medical care, and cultural activities." The KPNLF also reportedly has given serious attention to educating young Cambodians in the refugee camps in reading, writing, and basic skills. In 1983, in one refugee camp there were about 150 teachers, an almost equal number of student teachers, and more than two thousand elementary school students.[52]

But there have also been reports of abuses by some elements of the KPNLF. According to the Lawyers' Committee for Human Rights, in 1985 the KPNLF high command removed two of the most notorious "warlords," Liv Ne and Chhea Chut, from the border as one remedy. Although factional rivalries continued to cause some discipline and morale problems, by mid-1989 Son Sann and General Sak Sutsakhan had instituted a human rights monitoring commission and the KPNLF "was improving its performance and expanding operations inside Cambodia."[53]

To defend the refugee camps, the KPNLF has used military units of battalion size (around 400 men), while guerrilla companies of about 120 men have been the basic units for action inside Cambodia.[54] The total armed strength of the KPNLF grew steadily until the mid-1980s. By one estimate KPNLF forces had reached 15,000–20,000 when the massive 1984–1986 Vietnamese attacks on the civilian refugee camps seriously damaged its units, reportedly reducing the KPNLF to "a few thousand" organized fighters.[55] But another estimate based on U.S. sources put KPNLF strength at about 12,000 in March 1989 (see table 6–2).[56]

Sihanouk Resistance and a Coalition Government. Sihanouk had a history of more than two decades of relations with the Communist leadership of Vietnam before the 1979 invasion. In addition to being asked by Pol Pot to go to the United Nations, he initially tried to engage in negotiations with the Vietnamese invaders.[57] When that

TABLE 6–2
ESTIMATED MILITARY FORCES IN CAMBODIA, 1979–1989

	Resistance (thousands)				Regime (thousands)			Regime Arms Imports (current dollars, millions)
	KPNLF	ANS	KR	Total	PRK	Vietnam	Total	
1979	2	2			NA			10
1980					35	200	235	50
1981	8	4.5	40		20	180	200	70
1982					20			70
1983	11	6	56		20	170	190	140
1984					30	170	200	190
1985			30	50	35	170	205	280
1986								150
1987	7	10	45	62				
1988	5	16	35	56	30	120	150	
1989	12	18	35	65	40	80	120	

NOTE: KPNLF = Khmer People's National Liberation Front; ANS = Sihanoukist National Army; KR = Khmer Rouge; PRK = People's Republic of Kampuchea. Blank spaces indicate no available data.
SOURCES: Al Santoli, "Cambodia: Freedom's Frontline in Southeast Asia," in Charles Moser, ed., *Combat on Communist Territory* (Washington, D.C.: Free Congress Research and Educational Foundation, 1985); Secretary of State George Shultz, "America and the Struggle for Freedom," February 22, 1985, *Department of State Bulletin*, April 1985, p. 17; U.S. Arms Control and Disarmament Agency, *World Military Expenditures and Arms Transfers*, 1987; U.S. Department of State, *Background Notes, Cambodia*, 1984; Address by Charles H. Twining, Director of the Office of Vietnam, Laos, and Cambodia Affairs, September 29, 1988, *Department of State Bulletin*, December 1988, pp. 31–33; U.S. Department of State, *Country Reports on Human Rights Practices for 1987*, p. 649; Cord Meyer, "Cambodia: Challenge and Opportunities," *Washington Times*, January 20, 1989 (based on U.S. government sources); Don Oberdorfer, "Sihanouk's Cambodian Forces Asking U.S. for Arms Aid," *Washington Post*, March 16, 1989; Elaine Sciolino, "U.S. Aims to Buoy Khmer Rouge Rivals," *New York Times*, September 29, 1988 (midpoint of reported "American military estimates"); U.S. Department of State, *Country Reports for 1980*, p. 624; U.S. Department of State, *Country Reports for 1981*, p. 611; U.S. Department of State, *Country Reports for 1983*, p. 795.

failed, and after being flown out of Cambodia as Phnom Penh was about to fall, Sihanouk tried to obtain military assistance from the West and specifically from the United States for a resistance force of

100,000 men, but the Carter administration refused. Secretary of State Cyrus Vance suggested instead that Sihanouk "should direct his efforts toward finding aid for Kampuchean refugees."[58] Sihanouk then withdrew from politics until early 1981, when he announced from Beijing the formation of a new political party: the United Front for an Independent, Neutral, Peaceful and Cooperative Cambodia (FUNCINPEC). As in 1970, Sihanouk had gone to Communist China when he needed an ally.

Al Santoli, one of the most experienced and judicious expert observers of Cambodia, explained China's Cambodia policy of 1981:

> The Chinese realized that the Democratic Kampuchea government of the Khmer Rouge, though still recognized at the United Nations, had a limited political future. . . . [Democratic Kampuchea] needed Sihanouk's adherence to maintain international recognition and to gain respectability among the Cambodian peasant population.[59]

Sihanouk's name still evoked enormous loyalty from the Cambodian peasants, who looked on him as the hereditary leader of their nation. But Sihanouk was not only the king in Cambodian tradition; he was also the first leader of an independent Cambodia and had led the country during the brief years of peace and increasing prosperity— until the Communist guerrilla war accelerated in 1970.

The Khmer Rouge and China had used Sihanouk before, during 1970–1975, as a front man to legitimate the Khmer Rouge and to help bring that regime to power. Would this happen again even though in 1981 Sihanouk did not turn directly to the Khmer Rouge as he had in 1970?

In the summer of 1981, Sihanouk united three different armed resistance groups loyal to him into the Sihanoukist National Army (ANS), with a claimed total of about 2,000 resistance fighters. Its commander was In Tam, a former general of the Republic of Cambodia. The chief of staff was Teap Ben, who had been living in the United States. The background of these leaders and subsequent developments strongly suggested that the ANS resistance movement would be independent and not controlled by the Khmer Rouge.[60] At about the same time the United Nations held an international conference on Cambodia. Its final conclusions, reached in July 1981, essentially supported the goals of the two non-Communist anti-PRK movements, the KPNLF and the Sihanouk group: cease-fire, withdrawal of Vietnamese troops, and U.N.-supervised elections to guarantee Cambodian self-determination.[61] The two movements were supported by the Association of Southeast Asian Nations (ASEAN), the United States, and other free-world countries.

Starting in 1981, China sought the backing of the ASEAN countries—Thailand, Malaysia, Indonesia, Brunei, Singapore, and the Philippines—to try to forge a coalition between all three anti-PRK resistance movements, although both non-Communist movements were totally opposed to any coalition with the Khmer Rouge. At the same time, elements of the KPNLF were deeply distrustful of Sihanouk; they viewed him as a

> self-serving opportunist, remembering that it was he who originally permitted the Vietnamese Communists to stage and operate against South Vietnam and Cambodia and use Cambodia as a port for supplies. Moreover, after 1970 [he] had played a significant role in helping the Khmer Rouge come to power.[62]

To obtain ASEAN agreement to the coalition, China now made important commitments: to stop arming the pro-Chinese Communist insurgencies within the ASEAN countries; to drop its demand for the return of the Khmer Rouge; and to support the results of free elections under UN supervision.[63]

To avoid entering this coalition with the Khmer Rouge, both non-Communist resistance groups sought military help from the free world. But through 1981 and the first part of 1982 no significant amount of military assistance was forthcoming—not even from the Reagan administration. As a result, by June 1982,

> with China promising to aid all three factions if they united, the non-Communists were trapped. The only alternative was to let their organizations in the field die out from lack of aid and concede the future of Cambodia exclusively to the Khmer Rouge or Vietnamese.[64]

This was the political genesis of the three-part Coalition Government of Democratic Kampuchea (CGDK), which was formally proclaimed on June 22, 1982, at a meeting in Malaysia.

Sihanouk became president of this coalition government, Khieu Samphan of the Khmer Rouge became vice president responsible for foreign affairs, and Son Sann became prime minister (see also table 6-1). All three groups agreed that diplomatic posts would be shared—including representation at the United Nations. The program of the KPNLF, including free elections under UN supervision, was accepted by the two other organizations in the coalition.

All three maintained separate armed forces. During the 1980s those of the KPNLF grew, declined, then grew again, while those of the ANS increased steadily and those of the Khmer Rouge averaged about 35,000 (see table 6-1 above). However, these trends strongly suggest that the Chinese did not fulfill their 1981 promise to give military aid in equal amounts to all three groups. The Khmer Rouge received nearly all of China's military aid, which cast doubt on Beijing's other promises. These doubts deepened after the Chinese regime killed hundreds, perhaps thousands, of nonviolent demonstrators and arrested at least ten thousand more in a nationwide repression that began June 4, 1989, in Beijing's Tiananmen Square.[65]

In March 1989, the military command of the coalition government was renamed the National Resistance of Cambodia, with the same three leaders representing the combined organization (see table 6–1). That same month, the military leader of the ANS, Sihanouk's son, Prince Norodom Ranariddh, met with President Bush and other leaders of the new administration in the United States. Reports indicated that Ranariddh was seeking significantly expanded U.S. help for the ANS. He claimed that with American military aid the ANS could increase to about 30,000 by the end of 1989 and thus act as a counterweight to the Khmer Rouge.[66]

As of early 1989, Sihanouk controlled about 60,000 of the 350,000 Cambodian refugees on the Thai-Cambodian border. The U.S. State Department described their camps—in contrast to those under Khmer Rouge control—as "relatively well run" and governed by "looser arrangements that link the civilian and military leadership."[67] Taking into account the estimate of 150,000 persons living in KPNLF refugee camps, this would give the non-Communist resistance an estimated social base of about 210,000 Cambodian refugees.

Communist Party of Kampuchea (Khmer Rouge) Armed Group. In the years since the 1978 Vietnamese invasion the Communist Party of Kampuchea continued to conduct armed operations against the Vietnamese and the PRK regime while attempting to convince the world that it has changed. Although the non-Communist resistance groups continually lacked military and nonmilitary supplies, the Khmer Rouge forces were generously provisioned by China. In early 1989 the Khmer Rouge was thought to have military and other supplies sufficient to meet its needs for two years or more, and it was estimated to control about 100,000 Cambodians living in four known (and an unknown number of secret) military camps along the Thai-Cambodian border. U.S. government estimates reckoned Khmer Rouge armed strength at between 28,000 and 60,000, with "the usual interagency compromise cited officially by diplomats as '30,000 to 40,000.'"[68]

The systematic Khmer Rouge effort to deceive the world about its intentions and political character began in 1980 when it announced that it would no longer seek to create a Communist society in Cambodia.[69] Although the Communist Party of Kampuchea was officially dissolved in 1981, the U.S. State Department observed in 1987 that "most believe that it has continued as the clandestine organization it was before 1975."[70] Although the Khmer Rouge joined in the coalition government with both non-Communist organizations in 1982 and professed its willingness to abide by the outcome of UN-supervised democratic elections, in subsequent years it attacked units of the non-Communist resistance, ambushing them, mining their supply routes and trails, and raiding some of their camps.[71]

Pol Pot announced he was leaving as leader of the Khmer Rouge and would serve only as the military commander. This maneuver replicated the deception the Khmer Rouge played on its ostensible ally Prince Sihanouk during the 1970–1975 period of their alliance with his government in exile. At that time Sihanouk was falsely told that Khieu Samphan was the real leader of the Khmer Rouge and treated him as such when visiting Khmer Rouge areas of Cambodia. After Pol Pot went further and announced his retirement from all military authority and political activity in 1985, a defector from the Khmer Rouge said the Khmer Rouge commanders continue to "obey [Pol Pot] and regard him as the leader."[72]

Only one of the Khmer Rouge's civilian camps is open to Western reporters or any outsiders. One visitor called it a "stage set of devastating cynicism," because religion, money, and private property are allowed; clothing of different colors is permitted; and, instead of executing teachers, since 1986 they have had the motto "education is growth."[73] The testimony of defectors and escapees from the other Khmer Rouge camps shows that this camp is a sham calculated to dupe the outside world.

In summing up an assessment of the Khmer Rouge in 1989, Steven Erlanger writes:

> There is a command elite of party leaders who have access to the best of everything. For the others food and medicine are rationed. Marriage is discouraged. . . . [There are] "women's transportation units" which haul ammunition and mines deep inside Cambodia. Girls as young as twelve are required to be porters. . . . There is as well a sub-class, treated as sub-human virtually as instruments of logistics. They include anyone without a party or military role and they are kept isolated and illiterate.[74]

This description echoes Haing Ngor's view of life when the Khmer Rouge ruled Cambodia:

To the Khmer Rouge we weren't quite people. We were lower forms of life. Because we were enemies, killing us was like swatting flies, a way to get rid of undesirables. We were a disappointment to them. . . . We did not work hard for twenty hours a day, because we were constantly wearing out and getting sick. . . . To us war slaves the old way of life was gone and everything about it half forgotten.[75]

Ten years after Vietnam invaded and ended Khmer Rouge rule, the Communist group's behavior in exile showed that it remained the same. In September 1988, Pol Pot was reported to have told his battalion commanders that they should prepare to occupy half of Cambodia's western provinces once Vietnamese troops were pulled out "and then move in civilians behind them. It [is] important . . . to show the world that it was the Khmer Rouge who had fought hardest against the Vietnamese."[76] Pol Pot was interested only in using the refugees under Khmer Rouge control as pawns to establish political control over Cambodian territory and was heedless of the risk resulting from forcing them within range of Vietnamese firepower. Following that report the Khmer Rouge did in fact force thousands of civilians to move out of the refugee camps into settlements closer to the Cambodian border, where in November 1988 they were shelled and attacked by well-armed Vietnamese troops. In these attacks, the Vietnamese fired "thousands of shells a day" into these settlements, one of which was reportedly "obliterated."[77] In 1989 the Khmer Rouge were not able to occupy any significant amount of Cambodian territory.[78] Nevertheless, Santoli views them as still having the support of about 10 percent of the population.[79]

In 1988 the Khmer Rouge had burned down the hospital in one of its refugee camps in order to prevent any Westerners from having a reason to enter. In 1989 the Khmer Rouge reportedly forced the less able-bodied "to walk through minefields ahead of Khmer Rouge soldiers."[80] Whether this still vicious Marxist-Leninist movement once again takes power in Cambodia is likely to depend on the actions of the many countries that have been involved with Cambodia in recent years, especially China and the United States.

Role of the ASEAN Countries

While much of the focus of the Cambodian conflict has been on Soviet-backed Vietnam and the PRK Cambodian regime it installed on the one side, and the Khmer Rouge, backed by China, on the other, the KPNLF and ANS resistance movements have constituted the "third force," seen as the only real hope for an independent non-Communist future for Cambodia. For a variety of reasons, some of which are discussed in the next section, Thailand and the other ASEAN countries took the lead in providing political and diplomatic support to this third force and worked to bring about the international isolation and condemnation of Vietnam and its PRK regime. The most obvious spur to the ASEAN countries was their own vulnerability to Chinese and Soviet indirect aggression: four of them—Thailand, Malaysia, Indonesia, and the Philippines—had themselves at various times already been the targets of externally supported Communist insurgent movements, a threat that has continued in the Philippines.

At the end of World War II, indigenous Communist groups with strong Soviet and Comintern-type support lauched efforts to take power not only in the newly liberated countries of Europe but also in a number of Asian countries. The Chinese Communists, then heavily backed by Stalin, stepped up their civil war and defeated the Nationalist government in 1949. The Communists of Vietnam launched their war against French colonial rule and won control of northern Vietnam by 1954. The Philippine Communists began an insurgency in the late 1940s which took years to defeat. In the 1970s they reignited a much broader insurgency, which grew into a serious political and military threat to the Aquino government, democratically elected in 1986 to replace the authoritarian Marcos regime.

Malaysia (then Malaya) faced and defeated a Communist insurgency in the 1950s. Indonesia coped with three successive Communist efforts to seize power: a coup attempt in 1948, an attempt to penetrate and subvert the Sukarno government during the 1950s, and the bloody coup attempt of 1965. The 1965 attempt—the work of a large, well-organized Communist party that included elements of the Indonesian armed forces and gained force from a series of mass organizations—nearly succeeded. It had begun taking shape in the early 1960s, just as Hanoi was stepping up its war against South Vietnam and while Communist guerrilla movements in Cambodia and Laos also began their ultimately successful insurgencies.

During the 1960s both the Soviet Union and Communist China were actively providing a wide range of support to these indigenous Communist insurgencies. China was the principal mainstay of the Communist Party of Thailand (CPT), which began military operations aimed at the Thai government in 1964 and grew year by year. In January 1965, in the view of the administration of the newly elected U.S. president, Lyndon B. Johnson, there was no doubt that the Soviet Union and China were providing significant support for indirect aggression against South Vietnam, Cambodia, Laos, Indonesia, and Thailand. It was also believed possible that the Communist insurgencies in Malaysia and the Philippines might flare up again.

By the early 1970s, several factors damped down Beijing's support for these insurgencies. As its dispute with the Soviet Union became more ominous, China sought to normalize relations with the United States, a process that got under way in earnest with the 1972 visit by President Nixon. Also, the Cultural Revolution unleashed by Mao Tse-tung had created so much turmoil in so many Chinese institutions as to reduce Beijing's capacity for external aggression, whether direct or indirect. Nevertheless, both the Soviet Union and China continued their active support for the Communist movements in Vietnam, Cambodia, and Laos that took power in 1975. And by 1978, the mainly pro-Chinese Communist Party of Thailand had 14,000 insurgents active in about fifty-two of Thailand's seventy-two provinces.[81]

With a triumphant, battle-hardened Vietnamese occupation force of 200,000 troops sweeping to the Thai-Cambodian border in 1979, with an internal Chinese-backed Communist insurgency, and with a public declaration by Hanoi that "the liberation of Thailand is a historical necessity,"Thailand and its 55 million people were in danger.[82] As it had for many years, the United States provided Thailand with security and economic assistance, but clearly it would not provide military forces. In consequence the Thai government permitted anti-PRK/Vietnamese resistance movements (including the Chinese-backed Khmer Rouge) to operate from its territory as a means of counterbalancing what it viewed as the immediate and powerful threat from Vietnam.[83]

The experience of Thailand exemplified the position the ASEAN countries were in: In the wake of Communist victories in 1975, which ended any prospect of direct combat support by the United States, the same vulnerability that spurred the ASEAN countries into taking the lead on behalf of the non-Communist Cambodian resistance left them limited in what they could accomplish in this role and under pressure to support the three-part Coalition Government of Democratic Kampuchea. For a fuller understanding of why the backing for Cambodia's "third force" has been far less than the Chinese and Soviet support to their own clients, it is necessary to review U.S. policy and how it evolved.[84]

U.S. Policy since 1978

The United States established diplomatic relations with Cambodia in 1950. From 1955 to 1963, it provided the Sihanouk-led government with about $400 million in economic aid and about $84 million in military aid.[85] The economic aid helped to repair the destruction caused by the first Indochina war and to build an infrastructure that could promote economic development—such as the first all-weather road to the interior from the seaport of Kompong Som (formerly Sihanoukville). Ironically Sihanouk permitted this road to be used by the Vietnamese Communists in the 1960s to supply their troops fighting Americans in South Vietnam.

During 1970–1975, after the relations broken in 1965 were reestablished (in 1969), the United States provided about $1.2 billion in military and about $500 million in economic aid. The war in Cambodia expanded dramatically during these years, as the Lon Nol armed forces grew from about 40,000 to 200,000 to combat the Khmer Rouge, which expanded from an estimated strength of 5,000 in 1970 to 45,000 in 1975.

After the Communist victory in 1975 the United States did not recognize any government in Cambodia and "condemned the brutal character of the Khmer Rouge regime." The United States also condemned the Vietnamese invasion of Cambodia (although it welcomed the end of Khmer Rouge rule) and refused to recognize the PRK regime. It then turned its attention to providing humanitarian relief for the hundreds of thousands of Cambodians who had fled their country. Between 1979 and 1982, about $400 million in UN-coordinated aid was provided for these refugees, of which the United States contributed about one fourth. In succeeding years, as the UN border relief operation coordinated efforts for the more than 300,000 people remaining in camps in Thailand, America's contribution was about one third of the total international assistance budget of some $200 million between 1983 and 1988.[86]

Since 1979, the broad goals of U.S. policy in Cambodia have been the withdrawal of all Vietnamese troops and the establishment of an independent Cambodian government through free elections.[87] But there were some noteworthy shifts in emphasis over the years.

In 1979 and 1980 Washington made a major diplomatic effort to persuade the Soviet Union, Vietnam, and the PRK to allow Western relief supplies to reach the people of Cambodia. In July 1980, Deputy Secretary of State Warren Christopher implored the government of Vietnam and its supporters: "Do not preside over the death of a nation and a people; permit an effective relief effort to go forward."[88]

With the advent of the Reagan administration, a new note was struck about what could be done to bring about the withdrawal of Vietnamese troops. In July 1981, the assistant secretary of state responsible for East Asia said:

> The course of action most likely to result in the removal of Vietnamese troops from Kampuchea [Cambodia] is to make their occupation as costly as possible for Hanoi. We will

continue a process of diplomatic isolation and economic deprivation until Hanoi is prepared to follow the will of the world community . . . and to agree to troop withdrawal, free elections, and an end to outside interference in Kampuchea.[89]

This statement was consonant with the objectives expressed by the 1981 UN conference on Cambodia. In addition, by 1981 two UN General Assembly votes had expressed support for the same objectives as those sought by U.S. policy. Virtually the only countries voting on the side of Vietnam were from the Soviet bloc.

But the stating of objectives left the question of how to achieve them. Policy statements on Cambodia by the U.S. State Department repeatedly emphasized that ASEAN governments should continue to take the lead in pressing for Vietnamese withdrawal and free elections. Following the formation of the Coalition Government of Democratic Kampuchea in 1982 the State Department said: "The formation of the coalition is another significant development in the overall ASEAN strategy of applying political, diplomatic, and economic pressure on Vietnam to negotiate a comprehensive solution to the Kampuchea problem." This would be repeated in 1983, with the added explicit statement that the United States did "not plan to offer military aid to the coalition or any of its members."[90]

U.S. officials have advanced a number of explanations as to why the United States did not provide military aid and why it wanted ASEAN to take the lead. In 1984 Paul Wolfowitz, assistant secretary of state for East Asian and Pacific Affairs, told a conference on the Cambodian crisis that ASEAN should take the lead because "their basic security is at stake" and added that "given our own bitter history in Indochina, no one would want to see this issue become primarily an issue between the United States and Vietnam."[91]

Then, in January 1985, a few days after President Reagan's public affirmation of his commitment to aid anti-Communist resistance movements, Under Secretary of State for Political Affairs Michael Armacost stated that "the sustainability of the [resistance] coalition and its acceptability to the Cambodian people require that the non-Communist factions increase their strength relative to the Khmer Rouge." He added that "failure to address the imbalance within the Cambodian resistance could undermine future possibilities for a political solution."[92]

After these bold statements from the United States, the ASEAN nations made a public appeal in February 1985 for greater international aid to the non-Communist resistance. But neither the U.S.

statements nor this appeal was followed by effective action, and in July 1985, on a visit to Malaysia, Secretary of State Shultz said:

> We do not provide military aid [to the Cambodian resistance groups] and we do not see any special need for it from the United States. . . . I think we are going to have greater success in our program if we keep it the way it now is. Congress is a very changeable operation, they are in favor of something at one time and then some things can happen and they can change their minds and all of a sudden you have got a program that is working that gets derailed.[93]

Although it is true that the administration was then facing strong opposition from many congressional Democrats to its policy of support for the contras in Nicaragua, congressional attitudes toward Cambodia were quite different. Since Cambodia was a victim of overt Communist aggression, liberal Democrats led by Congressman Stephen Solarz of New York were urging the administration to provide assistance for the non-Communist resistance in Cambodia.[94] In fact, only weeks after Shultz's comment Congress took the initiative by appropriating $5 million for the 1986 fiscal year (October 1, 1985, to September 30, 1986). Given the ption by Congress of spending these funds for either economic or military assistance, the State Department spent no funds for military assistance and used only $3.5 million of the $5 million total.[95]

The level of U.S. assistance to the non-Communist resistance remained at $5 million in fiscal year 1987 and 1988, although in fiscal year 1989 (October 1, 1988, to September 30, 1989) the Solarz program of assistance was supplemented by a program, named for Republican Congressman Bill McCollum of Florida, which provided $500,000 for military support from excess Pentagon stocks, including administrative and transport expenses. In fiscal year 1990 the State Department's public request was for an increase to $7 million for the Solarz program and the same $500,000 for the McCollum program.[96]

Thus, although Under Secretary Armacost had been correct that failure to strengthen the non-Communist resistance relative to the Khmer Rouge would undermine efforts for a political settlement, U.S. assistance was both very little and very late; and it had had to be initiated by Congress.

Notwithstanding the minimal commitments of aid, however, in March 1989, the newly elected Bush administration indicated that it would continue to seek the same objectives defined by U.S. policy for the preceding decade: "The verified and complete withdrawal of all Vietnamese forces, effective safeguards against a Khmer Rouge return to power, and the restoration of genuine self-determination to the

Cambodian people." Testifying before the House Foreign Affairs Committee on March 1, David F. Lambertson, deputy assistant secretary for East Asian and Pacific Affairs, called for

> an interim government preceding elections . . . and an international presence established in Cambodia sufficiently strong to be able to monitor effectively the Vietnamese withdrawal, a ceasefire, and other provisions. By whatever title, this should be an armed peacekeeping force, probably under United Nations auspices.[97]

Lambertson added that in the context of an acceptable settlement, the United States was prepared to normalize its relations with Vietnam—which would help its deteriorating economy.

Later in 1989, as an acceptable settlement appeared no closer of attainment, there were reports that the Bush administration would seek additional funding for military aid using the special activities (covert action) funding process.[98] In July, when Secretary of State James Baker met with the foreign ministers of the six ASEAN countries in Brunei, Thailand's Foreign Minister Siddhi publicly stated: "James Baker told me they [the United States] still see it as essential to provide military aid to the non-Communist resistance."[99] Then, on July 21, 1989, the Senate approved by a 59–39 vote legislation that in the words of one senator, "allows the Administration to seek authority from the Intelligence Committee" to provide military aid to the non-Communist resistance. With Congressman Solarz commenting that the weapons should be sent at once since "time is running out,"[100] the favorable Senate vote gave the Bush administration bipartisan political endorsement for taking practical steps to accomplish its stated objectives. It was the eve of a major negotiating conference on Cambodia scheduled to open in Paris at the end of July 1989.

Talks, Meetings, and Negotiations

Since 1945, the Vietnamese Communist movement has had extensive experience in using diplomacy as well as armed force to accomplish its objectives. It violated and broke the Geneva accords of 1954 when this suited its interests. Hanoi manipulated the Laos accords of 1962, the Paris peace accords of 1973, and the 1974 Laos accords on a neutral government. Communist Vietnam's principal patron, the Soviet Union, has a much longer record of making and violating international agreements.[101] "Treaties," Stalin once remarked, "are like pie crusts—made to be broken." The Vietnamese Communist movement and regime summarized its war strategy in the Maoist maxim "Fight and talk, talk and fight," reversing the Clausewitzian dictum that war is the continuation of politics by other means.

During the 1980s the Cambodian conflict produced a number of talks, proposals, meetings, and negotiations. Hanoi made a number of proposals for troop withdrawals, provided that at the *beginning* of such withdrawals all external aid to the armed resistance opposing the PRK regime in Cambodia would be terminated by external powers. They staged a number of well-advertised "withdrawals" which turned out to be nothing more than normal troop rotations. In the spring of 1987, the resistance coalition continued a refusal to talk with the PRK regime alone, saying such an arrangement would imply that the Cambodian conflict was only an internal matter, and insisting that Vietnam be a participant in any negotiations. At the same time Vietnam was refusing to take part in any discussions with the coalition if it continued to include the Khmer Rouge.

During his March 1987 visit to six Southeast Asian countries, including Cambodia, Soviet Foreign Minister Eduard Shevardnadze began to state publicly his desire for a resolution of the conflict in Cambodia. Eight months later a Soviet deputy foreign minister made similar public comments, and a month after that a process of more serious negotiations began when Sihanouk met the premier of the PRK regime in Paris for talks that Sihanouk characterized as "very warm but frank." The talks resulted in an agreement on the outlines of a new negotiating approach.[102] A second round of talks betwen Sihanouk and the PRK was held in January 1988.

In May 1988, Vietnam announced it would withdraw 50,000 troops from Cambodia by the end of the year, and its remaining units would be placed under the command of the PRK regime.[103] The next month, Vietnam announced to the world media that significant numbers of its troops were withdrawing and that its remaining troops were now indeed under the command of the PRK regime and its military forces.[104]

On the Chinese side of the equation, the U.S. administration perceived a "significant evolution," beginning with Beijing's statement on July 1, 1988, that it would accept the agenda of the non-Communist members of the resistance coalition, including the need for a four-party coalition regime with Prince Sihanouk in charge during the Vietnamese withdrawal; imposition of a freeze on all Cambodian forces; and universal mutual acceptance of all factional leaders within the coalition. This last element was taken to mean that Pol Pot and other notorious leaders of the Khmer Rouge would be removed by China from any further role in Cambodia.[105]

This agenda was followed during the first major negotiation among all the participants—the Jakarta Informal Meeting in July 1988, which included the four contending Cambodian groups, Vietnam,

Laos, and all ASEAN members. The U.S. administration interpreted the results of this meeting as producing a consensus on two points: all Vietnamese forces had to withdraw from Cambodia, and the Khmer Rouge had to be prevented from taking power again.[106] Also in July 1988, the U.S. secretary of state met with the leaders of Thailand and China to discuss the need to control the Khmer Rouge. In August the deputy foreign ministers of the Soviet Union and China held their first publicly known talks on Cambodia in Beijing.

Three months later the Cambodian groups and Vietnam held a round of talks in Paris. That same month, November 1988, China's Prime Minister Li Peng stated that China would support a four-group coalition headed by Sihanouk and including the PRK, the KPNLF, the ANS, and the Khmer Rouge. China also affirmed that it was willing to end military aid to the Khmer Rouge not at the end of but during Vietnam's withdrawal process, if the Vietnamese offered an acceptable timetable for troop withdrawal. On the basis of this assurance, the Bush administration's State Department announced in March 1989 its conclusion that China "does not support a return to power of the Khmer Rouge."[107] This was a judgment that remained to be tested. It could also be weighed against the clear evidence that since 1981 China has violated repeated promises to give equal support to the non-Communist resistance. Instead, China has spoken one way while acting to strengthen the Khmer Rouge.

In December 1988 the foreign ministers of the Soviet Union and China met again to discuss Cambodia. That meeting was followed by a Soviet announcement that Moscow sought the earliest possible settlement in Cambodia and was ready to act as a guarantor of any such settlement. In the following month (January 1989) China and Vietnam held their first direct talks on Cambodia. At the same time, the PRK regime conducted its first high-level talks with Thailand since the Vietnamese invasion ten years earlier. Until this point it was China that had made moves in the direction of the Soviet-Vietnamese-PRK position—including accepting the termination of external military aid to resistance forces during the Vietnamese withdrawal, not only at its completion.

When the Soviet and Chinese foreign ministers, Shevardnadze and Quian, met in Beijing in February 1989, it now appeared to be the Soviet Union that was moving a step toward the position of the resistance coalition and China: their joint statement said that both China and the Soviet Union agreed that international supervision was needed to ensure the implementation of a settlement in Cambodia. Although this seemed like a Soviet break with the Vietnam-PRK position, however, there was no need to construe it as such if the international supervision were to be performed by an entity like the former International Control Commission (which Vietnam has wanted) having no real power and with the PRK regime still in control of Cambodia. At the same meeting the two ministers also announced that Gorbachev would visit Beijing in May 1989 for a summit meeting with Deng Xiaoping.

Following the Soviet-Chinese meeting of February 1989, a second Jakarta Informal Meeting (JIM II) was held in Indonesia, on February 19–21, 1989. It was attended by representatives of the four Cambodian groups (with Prince Ranariddh sitting in for his father Prince Sihanouk) and by the foreign ministers of Vietnam, Laos, and the six ASEAN countries. The meeting ended inconclusively, an indication that despite their meetings, the Soviet Union and China had not yet reached a conclusion about how they envisioned the final outcome in Cambodia. Since both Moscow and Beijing had been involved in the violation of international agreements and in the manipulation of "international supervision" arrangements in the past, their tentative agreement in theory would not necessarily mean that either had departed from its ultimate objective of having its client regime in control of Cambodia.

The ongoing situation can best be understood by summarizing the positions of the competing Cambodian groups as given in their formal proposals, offering an interpretation of their aims, and then analyzing the possible differences between the Cambodian competitors and their external supporters which might lead to increased prospects for the success of one or the other of these rival groups.

Proposals and Tactics of the Competing Cambodian Groups

In January 1989 the non-Communist resistance made a five-point proposal. It is consistent with the initial 1982 program of the resistance coalition, the 1985 ASEAN appeal, and Sihanouk's earlier 1986 proposal:

1. Complete Vietnamese withdrawal without any link to the cutting of external assistance to the resistance groups
2. Simultaneous dissolution of the PRK and CGDK regimes
3. Elections under international supervision and control for a new Cambodian government
4. Establishment of an interim four-group government and army
5. An international peace force on Cambodian territory[108]

All these points had been endorsed by the ASEAN countries and the United States over a period of many years and most of them by China and the Khmer Rouge in formal terms. The goal was to establish a

213

neutral, non-Communist government and to prevent either the PRK or the Khmer Rouge from controlling Cambodia. Vietnam and the PRK, however, objected to the dissolution of the PRK regime and to any international peace-keeping or supervisory group that would challenge the control of the PRK regime.

The Khmer Rouge endorsed the five-point Sihanouk proposal and formally stated that it would not take power again in Cambodia. But the clandestine structure of the Khmer Rouge and its aggressive behavior toward its ostensible coalition partners, its oppression of civilians, and the forced relocation of many civilians since 1988 all indicate that the Khmer Rouge intended to use any coalition government in which it participated as a first step toward taking complete control.[109] This was borne out when, in yet another February 1989 meeting, the three elements of the resistance coalition issued from Beijing a plan calling for 2,000 UN personnel to supervise the withdrawal of Vietnamese troops and prevent the Khmer Rouge from taking power; although Khieu Samphan, a close associate of Pol Pot, signed this agreement, he reportedly refused to rule out a future governmental role for Pol Pot.[110]

The formal proposals of the PRK and Vietnam, the third contenders for the future of Cambodia, had the following points:

- Total withdrawal of Vietnamese military forces as of 1990
- External aid to the resistance forces to be ended as the withdrawal begins or during the withdrawal
- Elections to be held with an international presence for monitoring, but under the auspices of the continuing PRK regime as the sovereign government of Cambodia
- No large external peace force[111]

The official Vietnamese idea of international supervision was quite different from that of Sihanouk, the United States, or the ASEAN countries. Hanoi's deputy foreign minister said in January 1989 that any international supervision will

> have to respect Cambodia's sovereignty. In other words it will not have authority over the government. Second, it will not be an occupational force. Third, its only task will be to monitor implementation of the agreement and report violations to the Cambodian authorities [meaning the PRK regime] which alone will decide what must be done.[112]

The PRK regime made similar statements, and continually alleged that "the proposal raised by the opposition factions is only aimed at dissolving the PRK and opening the way for Pol Pot to return to power. . . . We would rather accept the present state of things."[113] In

April 1989 Prime Minister Hun Sen rejected a four-party interim government, rejected a UN peace-keeping force, and implicitly threatened Thailand:

I believe the main key is Thailand, if Thailand would not allow them [the Khmer Rouge] to stay there that would be the end of their resistance. . . . I understand the way they used the Khmer Rouge against us. Therefore we must remove those reasons from them. That is the reason for the withdrawal of the Vietnamese troops. . . . If after the withdrawal, they continue to help the Khmer Rouge, that would be another story.[114]

While Vietnamese and PRK objectives remained the same—to use a peace settlement to stay in power and to cut off external support to the armed opposition—by July 1989 there was more tactical flexibility. Specifically, it was reported that Vietnam and the PRK "would accept a United Nations force in Cambodia to supervise Hanoi's troop withdrawal and monitor any agreement, although weeks later they again rejected UN control.[115]

During 1988 and 1989, as Vietnam and the PRK embarked on a propaganda campaign to create the impression of *perestroika* in a "new" Communist Vietnam that deserves free world economic aid, they also sought to depict the PRK regime as the only alternative to the return of the Khmer Rouge. A *New Republic* editorial in the spring of 1989 concluded that Hun Sen, leader of the PRK regime, had "lately become the darling of Western media visitors. . . . All conclude Hun Sen deserves American political support because he is the only alternative to the return of the Khmer Rouge."[116] Yet, Hun Sen, Chief of State Heng Samrin, armed forces commander Pol Saroeun, National Assembly leader Chea Sim, and many other PRK leaders had been high-ranking Khmer Rouge under Pol Pot during the "killing fields" period.[117]

The Bush administration meanwhile accused the Vietnamese regime of trying to misrepresent the total number of troops it withdrew from Cambodia in 1988. The United States estimated that only about 35,000 rather than 50,000 troops were really withdrawn, and that 60,000 to 70,000 Vietnamese troops remained in Cambodia as of March 1989.[118] Santoli estimated at least 80,000 Vietnamese troops remained in mid-1989.[119]

Further, the Bush administration raised the issue of possible Vietnamese efforts to deceive an international monitoring organization, and warned that "Hanoi must carry out a true and complete withdrawal, without Vietnamese soldiers remaining in Cambodian uniforms or any other subterfuges designed to allow Vietnam to retain control."[120] On April 22, 1989, Thai officials said that "Vietnam did not withdraw 50,000 troops as reported last December but only 20,000 men who were mostly crippled and wounded."[121] And on April 25, 1989, the PRK minister of defense said that "a number of Vietnamese technical experts and instructors would remain in Cambodia after September 1989," the date Vietnam now promised it would have removed all of its troops.[122]

All the actions and words of the Vietnamese and the PRK regime suggest that its real intention during the negotiations has been to use any international agreement as a means to obtain a cutoff of external aid to the resistance groups so that the current PRK regime would remain in power. Prince Ranariddh had cautioned that "everyone seems to be rushing for a settlement, but we do not want a peace like Lebanon. . . . Let's hold out for a good peace."[123] But in late March 1989, the Vietnamese foreign minister admonished the United States not to give additional aid to the Sihanouk-led opposition forces. His warning was blunt:

> If the United States gives more money and arms to Prince Sihanouk it is very bad. But at the same time it cannot help Sihanouk now. Even four or five years ago it could not help. . . . America must take a lesson from the Vietnam war. . . . You know the amount of arms in South Vietnam here during the war and it did not help the former South Vietnamese army to stand.

The Vietnamese foreign minister went on to discuss the possible outcomes his government was prepared for in Cambodia, all of them having the same result—the current PRK regime remaining in effective control of Cambodia.[124]

On July 30, 1989, the foreign ministers of the five permanent members of the UN Security Council (China, France, Great Britain, the United States, and the USSR) met in Paris to participate in a weeks-long, nineteen-nation conference on Cambodia, but the deadlock among the competing views was not broken. Nevertheless, Vietnam announced at the end of September 1989 that it had withdrawn its combat forces from Cambodia, and in the succeeding months the Khmer Rouge as well as the anti-Communist resistance stepped up armed operations inside the country while negotiations continued among all the participants.

Taken together, these developments suggest that each of the three competing elements within Cambodia intends to prevail, and each wants a negotiated settlement that will increase the probability of its doing so. This suggests that the future will depend heavily on the actions of the external supporters of these three groups.

The External Supporters

The PRK depends directly on Vietnam, which in turn depends on the Soviet Union both for military support and as a counter weight to Chinese pressure on its northern border. But the Vietnamese regime is also seeking expanded commercial ties and financial aid from free-world countries, especially the ASEAN countries, Japan, and other prosperous countries in the region. There have been reports that Japan promised $1 billion in economic aid if Vietnam would withdraw its forces and compromise.[125]

The Soviet Union for its part wants to normalize relations with China, which may help explain its apparent agreement to international supervision of a Cambodian settlement. Reduced Soviet military support for Vietnam and the PRK would be welcomed by China, although Soviet aid to Vietnam reportedly increased from $2 billion in 1987 to $3 billion in 1988.[126] One possible Soviet demand of China in return could be a Chinese commitment to terminate its assistance to the Afghan resistance, and perhaps even future Chinese pressure on Pakistan to reduce or terminate its support to the anti-Soviet resistance in Afghanistan. (Pakistan would have a difficult time resisting such pressure if it were jointly applied by the Soviet Union, India, and China.) Perhaps the Soviet Union might trade a pro-Chinese Cambodia—one governed again by the Khmer Rouge—for a cutoff or sharp reduction of Chinese military aid to the Afghan resistance, leaving a pro-Soviet regime in Afghanistan.

The Khmer Rouge drive to take power depends both on its clandestine operations against the Sihanouk-led coalition, of which it is ostensibly a member, and on continued Chinese support. A new Khmer Rouge takeover could occur through the kind of Soviet-Chinese arrangement just described, or through some other trade-off between those two countries in which the Soviet Union would press Vietnam to withdraw its troops and to permit the Khmer Rouge to take over through an intermediary process of power sharing in a four-party coalition regime established by a negotiated settlement.

But to date events seem to be moving toward victory for the PRK regime. China had made formal concessions—especially in promising to cut off weapons to the Khmer Rouge before a complete Vietnamese withdrawal and in accepting the resistance coalition's demand that the Khmer Rouge not be allowed to take power again. China might enter into a secret agreement with the Soviet Union to cut the Khmer Rouge off militarily and resettle its leaders and key cadres far from Cambodia. This, of course, would likely be in return for Soviet concessions on other issues between them, of which there are many. For Beijing this could improve its relations with Moscow and perhaps

217

even with Washington, which has clearly expressed its view that a return of the Khmer Rouge is the worst possible outcome for Cambodia.[127]

The chances for the non-Communist resistance groups to prevail manifestly depend in great measure on actions taken by the ASEAN countries and by the United States. In January 1989 veteran foreign policy observer Cord Meyer enunciated a positive view of both ASEAN and U.S. policy and concluded that "Mr. Bush has a good chance of presiding over a peaceful settlement in Southeast Asia in the first year of his presidency," meaning one in which the non-Communist resistance would prevail.[128] Much of the reason for that hopeful conclusion rested upon Meyer's judgment that the Soviet Union was no longer willing to subsidize the Vietnamese government's occupation of Cambodia, and that Vietnam would therefore be compelled to make a reasonable agreement because of its severe economic difficulties. On the negative side, in 1988 another analyst concluded that "strong U.S. friends such as Thailand and Singapore are now less willing to support the Cambodian [non-Communist] resistance because of its lack of progress, for which Washington is partly to blame."[129]

Santoli notes that in January 1989 the foreign minister of Thailand led a delegation of diplomats and businessmen to Vietnam "to facilitate the new policy of [the] Prime Minister . . . to change Indochina from a 'battlefield to a marketplace.' "[130] A series of agreements between Thailand and Vietnam were signed while the Vietnamese and PRK governments still adamantly refused to accept the resistance coalition's demand that the PRK government be dissolved under the terms of a peace agreement before any elections could be held. In Santoli's view, this was de facto acceptance by one key ASEAN country of a pivotal Vietnamese and PRK requirement—one that would guarantee that the PRK regime would remain in power under the terms of a settlement.

Subsequent to these Vietnamese-Thai conversations and signed agreements on commercial matters, Santoli concluded that the PRK regime "has seduced the Thais with offers of trade and to take back the 300,000 Cambodian refugees who are currently in Thailand." Finally, to secure its position should a coalition government with Sihanouk or other elements of the resistance emerge, the PRK regime reportedly assembled the military attachés of Vietnam, Laos, and the Soviet Union on January 3, 1989, and required all military and police officials in the Cambodian regime to promise to be "resolutely loyal to the Kampuchean People's Revolutionary Party [not to the government of Cambodia] and always implement the line and policy of the party."

At the same time, the Bush administration continued the program of minimal aid to the non-Communist Cambodian resistance groups. On May 11, 1989, however, it was reported that the Bush administration, "drawing a parallel between pro-U.S. rebels in Afghanistan and those in war-torn Cambodia, plans to begin shipping arms to Cambodian opposition forces led by Prince Norodom Sihanouk by September [1989]." This report was followed by an announcement from Democratic Senator Claiborne Pell of Rhode Island that he would introduce legislation banning any military aid to the non-Communist resistance while it remained "associated" with the Khmer Rouge. Vice President Daniel Quayle sharply criticized the Pell proposal: "This would prevent us, in effect, from providing any further support to Prince Sihanouk and the non-communist resistance forces and would decrease the prospects for a peaceful settlement in Cambodia."[131] Santoli shared this view: "The effect of the Pell amendment," he warned, "would be to *increase* [italics added] the likelihood of Khmer Rouge predominance. . . . [It] would condemn Cambodia to a future comprised of further political repression, economic stagnation, and bloodshed."[132]

On May 14, 1989, Sihanouk's representative to the United Nations published an article calling for President Bush to "save suffering Cambodia by endorsing the initiative . . . to provide lethal assistance to the non-Communist resistance." He added: "If the United States does not help the Cambodian people in this critical period, it will sacrifice them to the Communist monsters."[133]

On the same day, all six ambassadors to the United States of the ASEAN countries signed and published in the *Washington Post* a joint statement opposing the Pell prohibition. It would, they said,

> represent a reversal of U.S. policy on Cambodia, an attempt to prematurely break up the U.N.-recognized Coalition Government of Democratic Kampuchea, and force Prince Sihanouk . . . into the arms of Hun Sen [leader of the PRK]. It now seems to be in vogue to favorably contrast the PRK regime with the . . . Khmer Rouge. . . . However, it also should be remembered that Hun Sen was himself a former commander of the Khmer Rouge. . . . The PRK is not a legitimate government.[134]

Then, in June 1989, the Bush administration reportedly made a policy decision which—unless reversed by pressure from Congress—made it highly likely that the PRK regime would ultimately prevail. The Bush administration

> decided it would accept a compromise solution for a new government . . . including shared power between Prince

219

Norodom Sihanouk and the present Vietnamese-backed [PRK] regime. . . . [This] probably reflects the deterioration in U.S.-China relations following China's brutal repression . . . [and] may also indicate the U.S. no longer trusts China to prevent the Khmer Rouge from taking control.[135]

Although July brought the 59–39 Senate vote rejecting Pell's prohibition on military aid to the non-Communist resistance, the publicly available information suggests that as of 1989 none had been provided by the Bush administration. Therefore in the 1990s, it was likely that decisions by the Soviet Union and China would have the greatest impact in determining the future of Cambodia.[136] Therefore, even the prospect for a non-Communist Cambodia seemed to rest on a possible—but unlikely—decision by both Moscow and Beijing that each would rather settle for a neutral, nonaligned, and demilitarized Cambodia under a non-Communist government than risk the permanent entrenchment of a regime subservient to its rival.

In actuality, prospects seemed greatest that the PRK regime would remain in power following the declared Vietnamese troop withdrawal—with perhaps some figurehead involvement by Sihanouk and non-Communist elements in a "coalition." This view was bolstered by a report in May 1989 that "Moscow has strengthened the Phnom Penh government by shipping tanks and heavy artillery and by training Cambodian pilots for MiG-21 aircraft."[137] Those Soviet actions suggested that the journalist Lally Weymouth was correct in describing Hun Sen after meeting him as "a Southeast Asian version of Afghanistan's Najibullah."[138]

The Future of Cambodia

The Paris conference on Cambodia convened in late July 1989. The participants included Sihanouk of the Coalition Government of Democratic Kampuchea, Hun Sen of the PRK, the five permanent members of the UN Security Council, the six ASEAN countries, India, Japan, Canada, Australia, a delegation from the Non-aligned Movement, and the UN secretary general.[139] Hun Sen was reported as saying that "an international conference does not have the right . . . to impose a coalition on the Cambodian people."[140] Sihanouk told a news conference that the first four hours of talks with Hun Sen had been "painful," while Hun Sen accused Sihanouk of reversing "a consensus" reached in previous talks that the Khmer Rouge would be excluded from any coalition.[141]

The U.S. State Department described its own negotiating objective as "a comprehensive settlement [which] has three elements: The verified withdrawal of Vietnamese forces, prevention of a Khmer

Rouge return to power, and self-determination for the Cambodian people."[142] "Self-determination for the Cambodian people," although positive, was a less explicit goal than past U.S. statements that the PRK regime must be replaced by a government chosen in free elections. As such, it created an opening for granting the PRK regime control over the process intended to accomplish that self-determination.

But if U.S. policy is to help the people of Cambodia achieve freedom, its first objective must be to help them attain an independent non-Communist government—and that means neither the PRK nor the Khmer Rouge. The newly elected Bush administration, however, was advised by a "bipartisan group of the country's leading experts on Cambodia, Vietnam and Laos" to accept the continuation of the PRK regime.[143] And a former member of the Lon Nol cabinet, living in the United States, wrote in May 1989 that "U.S. military aid should not be given to any Cambodian group" and concluded that "there are seven million people living in relative security under the Hun Sen government" and this "fact of life" should be accepted.[144]

While less brutal than the Khmer Rouge regime, the Soviet- and Vietnamese-backed PRK has been and remains a repressive Communist dictatorship. If an international settlement were to leave that regime in place, it is unlikely that the hundreds of thousands of refugees would want to return; and once the regime had fully consolidated its power and ended armed resistance, it would be free to intensify an aggressive campaign against its non-Communist neighbors. The Bush administration should therefore not take part in any international arrangement that legitimates the current PRK regime, no matter what cosmetic coalition might be used to disguise this fact.

Instead, the United States should use its full influence with the ASEAN countries and their free-world trading partners such as Japan to maintain a unified free-world coalition in support of the goal of an independent, non-Communist government for Cambodia. This means in turn that all these countries should continue to withhold economic aid or any financial subsidies or credits from the Vietnamese and PRK regimes, as well as from China, until Vietnam and China end their support for the two Communist contenders for power. With U.S. leadership, the combined political and economic weight of the free-world coalition could over time produce positive results, since in fact neither the Soviet Union, China, nor Vietnam needs a Communist Cambodia.

The United States should also make the end of Soviet support for the Vietnam-PRK axis a major issue of bilateral relations. Further, the United States should conduct a vigorous public diplomacy campaign in all the industrial democracies to make the case that the PRK regime is not the only alternative to the Khmer Rouge—which is the Soviet-Vietnamese propaganda line—and that economic benefits for the Soviet Union should be withheld until there are independent, non-Communist governments in Cambodia, Afghanistan, and Angola, at the very least.

At the same time, the United States and other friendly nations should increase their political, economic, and military support to the non-Communist resistance forces. As the Center for Security Policy suggested in June 1989, "The United States should join French efforts in training Sihanouk supporters at the national, grassroots, and regional levels in administrative and political organization skills, and should extend such training to Son Sann's forces, which are not currently beneficiaries of this assistance."

Military assistance is essential. The Center for Security Policy recommends the following:

• The United States should provide military assistance such as uniforms, radios, rifles, mine detectors, ammunition and transport vehicles as a matter of utmost urgency.

• The United States should collaborate with France in providing training outside of Cambodia for military personnel loyal to Sihanouk and Son Sann in guerrilla warfare and logistics.

• The United States should work with the British in supporting ASEAN's efforts to keep the noncommunist resistance supplied with arms and other materials.[145]

With a realistic level of military assistance, the non-Communist resistance forces could expand within six months from their current estimated 30,000 (compared with 35,000 for the Khmer Rouge) to between 60,000 and 70,000. That would provide the people of Cambodia their first practical opportunity to rally to the cause of non-Communist forces that have some reasonable prospect of success. The political and military effect could be a rapid growth in the popular base as well as the military forces of the non-Communist resistance, with a concomitant weakening of the Khmer Rouge and of the Hun Sen PRK forces. Vietnam would then face the decision whether to conduct another massive invasion of Cambodia.

With such sustained political, diplomatic, and military actions by the United States and other free-world countries, it is possible that the people of Cambodia could recover their freedom—an impossibility should the Khmer Rouge or the PRK regime prevail.

Appendix: Indochina Chronology, 1945–1979

	VIETNAM	CAMBODIA	LAOS
1945	Imperial Japan grants independence to the puppet government under Emperor Bao Dai; after Japan is defeated, Vietnamese Communists declare a new Democratic Republic of Vietnam.		
1946	France uses force to retake control and the Communist-led insurgency begins.	France recognizes autonomy within French Union of Indochina.	
1949	Chinese Communists take power on mainland China and join the Soviet Union in helping the Vietminh.		France recognizes autonomy within French Union of Indochina.
1953		Cambodia becomes fully independent.	
1954	Geneva accords partition Vietnam into Communist North Vietnam and non-Communist South Vietnam.		Geneva accords provide full independence, with the Communist Pathet Lao occupying two northern provinces.
1955	Ho Chi Minh visits and signs aid agreements with the USSR and Communist China.	King Sihanouk declares neutrality, abdicates in favor of his father, founds a political movement, wins elections in 1955 (and 1958, 1962, and 1966).	

	VIETNAM	CAMBODIA	LAOS
1959	North Vietnam initiates terrorist and guerrilla war for control of South Vietnam, using the Viet Cong/NLF in the South.		
1960		Sihanouk, elected head of state, pursues a neutralist policy; Communist leaders secretly restructure an underground party apparatus.	Neutralist-Communist coalition government breaks down.
1962			Communist Pathet Lao are deterred from taking power by U.S. troops in Thailand.
			Second Geneva conference produces a new accord on a neutralist government.
1963	President Diem is overthrown by a military coup.	Government closes United States diplomatic mission.	Communist Pathet Lao resume war for control of Laos.
1964		French-educated leaders of the secret Communist Party of Kampuchea initiate war for control of Cambodia.	
1965	U.S. combat troops are sent to aid South Vietnam; U.S. begins bombing North Vietnam.	Sihanouk breaks relations with United States.	
1967		Sihanouk blames Communist insurgents for peasant uprising.	Premier says 40,000 North Vietnamese have invaded Laos.

VIETNAM	CAMBODIA	LAOS
1969		Diplomatic relations with U.S. are reestablished; Sihanouk asks General Lon Nol to head a government.	U.S. begins bombing North Vietnamese infiltration routes through Laos.
1970		Lon Nol coup deposes Sihanouk. South Vietnamese and U.S. forces attempt to disrupt headquarters and supply lines of the Communist forces inside Cambodia; the monarchy is abolished.	
1971	U.S. begins to withdraw combat troops.		South Vietnamese unsuccessfully attack North Vietnamese troops inside Laos.
1973	Paris accords officially end war; key provisions of the accords are violated by the North Vietnamese.	The Communist insurgency expands.	Cease-fire signed between the government and the Pathet Lao.
1974	North Vietnam launches major offensive against South Vietnam.	Lon Nol government controls only the cities.	
1975	North Vietnam and South Vietnamese Communists lead major offensive and take power.	Communist insurgents launch major offensive and take power.	Communist Pathet Lao dissolve the National Assembly and assume power; an estimated 40,000 North Vietnamese troops remain in Laos.
1976	North and South Vietnam are united.		

	VIETNAM	CAMBODIA	LAOS
1977	UN Security Council admits Vietnam's border fighting with Cambodia; Vietnam has severe food shortages.		
1978	In December, Vietnam attacks, conquers, and occupies Cambodia.		
1979	In February, China attacks Vietnam, penetrates 20 miles, and withdraws.	The People's Republic of Kampuchea (PRK) is established by the Vietnamese.	

7
Nicaragua

In 1959 Castro took power in Cuba, and in 1979 the Sandinistas began their rule in Nicaragua. These two related events marked an epoch in the history of Latin America—a region of thirty-two countries and more than 440 million people—and in its relationship with the United States. After the Sandinista regime began, both a civic, unarmed opposition and an armed resistance emerged within Nicaragua. That struggle has significant implications for the 100 million people living in the area from Panama to the southern border of the United States.

Background

European colonization of the Western Hemisphere began nearly five hundred years ago. Spain ruled nearly all the current nations of Latin America until they revolted in the early nineteenth century, with most attaining independence in the 1820s. Cuba was an exception; it became independent in 1902 as a result of the Spanish-American War. Brazil gained independence from Portugal in 1889. The final major movement toward independence occurred during the past three decades, when the former colonies of the United Kingdom and the Netherlands in the Caribbean and its rimland became self-governing and sovereign.

During the early part of the nineteenth century, the United States gave its moral and political support to the movement for independence from Spain and proclaimed the Monroe Doctrine in 1823 to discourage European powers from seeking to supplant Spain as new colonial rulers. The first efforts at cooperation among the newly independent states began during this period. In 1824 Simon Bolívar sought "the establishment of certain fixed principles for securing the preservation of peace between the nations of America, and the concurrence of all those nations to defend their common cause each contributing thereto on the basis of population."[1] In Central America there were also various unsuccessful attempts to unify its five small republics. Beginning in 1888 the United States took the lead in fostering inter-American cooperation; this resulted in the establishment of the Pan American Union (1910) and ultimately to the Organization of American States (1948).

For the first three decades of this century, the United States intervened frequently in the Caribbean region. In 1904 President Theodore Roosevelt proclaimed his corollary to the Monroe Doctrine asserting the right of the United States to prevent European intervention by taking action in Western Hemisphere countries that "chronically" failed to meet their international obligations. This led to interventions of varying duration in the Dominican Republic, Haiti, Cuba, and Nicaragua, with the United States seeking to establish internal order and financial stability and then withdrawing. Events in Nicaragua during those years had a direct bearing on later developments.

Early U.S. Involvement. The military ruler of Nicaragua from 1893 to 1909, a member of the Liberal party, had kept the neighboring countries of Central America in turmoil by attempts to forge a Central American union under his domination. Members of the opposition Conservative party revolted, and in 1910 the United States mediated an agreement for an electoral process to choose new leaders. In 1911, this led to the choice of Conservative Adolfo Díaz as president, who was then recognized by the United States. In 1912 U.S. President Woodrow Wilson, agreeing to the request of President Díaz, sent a contingent of about two hundred U.S. Marines to help end a Liberal party effort to take power in violation of the 1910 agreement. After the Liberal party's armed opposition ended some months later, a detatchment of one hundred American Marines remained in Managua as a safeguard.

This initiated two decades of U.S. efforts to help establish a process of regular, fair national elections in Nicaragua. There were successful elections in 1916 and 1920, but in 1923 the death, through natural causes, of President Diego Chamorro led to internal conflict. The election in 1924 gave the presidency to a Conservative, whom the United States initially refused to recognize because of "patent electoral fraud"; after he promised to conduct fair elections in 1928, however, U.S. recognition was granted.

In August 1925 the one hundred U.S. Marines were withdrawn, and a month later a revolt led by a rival Conservative broke out. The president resigned and Vice President Sacasa, a Liberal, claimed succession. But the Nicaraguan congress appointed former Conservative President Díaz to fill the remainder of the term. In December 1925, Sacasa, with diplomatic and military support from Mexico, proclaimed himself the constitutional president and began an armed revolt. President Díaz again called on the United States for military help, and by March 1927 about two thousand Marines had arrived in Nicaragua.

By May 1927, with the United States as a mediator, Díaz and Sacasa reached a truce. President Díaz would complete his term, Liberals would enter his government, and there would be amnesty for all; a nonpartisan National Guard would be established; and once again a small contingent of Marines would remain.

Only one Liberal general rejected this settlement. In the spring of 1927, General Augusto Cesar Sandino took his troops into the interior and began guerrilla warfare. As agreed, however, national elections were held in November 1928, with the Liberal war hero General Moncada winning an overwhelming victory. Looking ahead, Liberal and Conservative leaders agreed to U.S. supervision of the congressional vote in 1930 and of the next presidential election in 1932. Nevertheless, General Sandino continued his insurgency—even against the president from his own Liberal party.

In 1932, another Liberal, former Vice President Sacasa, was elected president in what would be the last free election in Nicaragua. (The 1990 election was partially free and unsuccessfully rigged by the Sandinistas.) On January 2, 1933, the day after the elected president was inaugurated, the last group of U.S. Marines was withdrawn. President Sacasa then initiated negotiations with General Sandino (who had rejected aid offered by the Salvadoran Communist leader, Farabundo Martí), and a preliminary truce agreement was reached. But despite General Sandino's promise to end his revolt, some guerrilla activity continued. In February 1934, President Sacasa and General Sandino met at the presidential palace to discuss the continuing insurgency; upon departing, Sandino and his aides were murdered by palace guardsmen.[2]

Although the Hoover administration had begun a process of ending three decades of U.S. intervention in the Caribbean region, it was President Franklin Delano Roosevelt, inaugurated in 1933, who proclaimed and implemented the Good Neighbor policy in conformity with the Democratic party platform of 1932, which called for noninterference in the internal affairs of other nations. The Roosevelt administration carried out this policy by signing the 1933 inter-American convention renouncing intervention (keeping, however, an explicit reservation permitting action "by the law of nations as generally recognized"); by withdrawing troops from Nicaragua (1933) and Haiti (1934); and by signing new treaties with Cuba (1934) and Panama (1936), in which the United States voluntarily rescinded earlier treaty provisions giving it broad rights of intervention.[3]

In 1936, the U.S. policy of nonintervention firmly in place,

General Anastasio Somoza Garcia, commander of the small National Guard established to preserve the constitutional electoral system, forced himself into the presidency. The representative of the United States in Nicaragua urgently recommended to the Roosevelt administration that it intervene against Somoza and on behalf of fair elections. But President Roosevelt took no action. As a result, General Somoza virtually remained in power until his assassination in 1956.

Beginnings of Communist Subversion. The Soviet Union, meanwhile, was giving little attention to Latin America. Nevertheless, in 1920, at the Second World Congress of the Comintern in Moscow, Lenin had met two of the Mexican delegates and expressed strong interest in "Mexico's strategic relationship with the United States" and in "whether there was a strong opposition movement to the United States, and if there was a strong peasant base for a Communist movement." The Latin American office of the Comintern was established in Mexico, staffed first by a Russian and then by founders of the Japanese and Indian Communist parties. It was the Mexican Communist party—founded in 1919, nine years before Mexico's current ruling party—that organized Cuba's and Guatemala's Communist parties, which then helped establish El Salvador's.[4]

Concerning Nicaragua, the Sixth World Congress of the Comintern in 1929 formally called on the working classes to support General Sandino's guerrilla forces. The Comintern later condemned Sandino, however, after he signed his preliminary truce with Sacasa in 1933. In 1929 the Comintern had also ordered the Mexican Communist party to stage an armed rebellion, an attempt that failed and led Mexico temporarily to suspend relations with Moscow in 1930. Later Argentina and Uruguay did the same—also to protest Soviet intervention through subversion.

In 1932, when El Salvador's Communist party claimed its candidates had won the Salvadoran elections and the government refused to recount the votes, an uprising organized by Communist leaders among sympathetic units of the armed forces was crushed. Despite this failure and the call by the 1935 Comintern congress for peaceful popular front tactics in Europe, the Comintern sought to ignite popular insurrections in Latin America. Later in 1935, a Brazilian Communist, a solider, attempted an armed revolt, which was also defeated. In the late 1930s, however, Soviet strategy shifted to counter the threat from fascism, leading the Communist parties of Mexico, Cuba, Venezuela, Canada, and the United States to issue a joint appeal to "strengthen Pan-American democracy."

OAS Resistance to Aggression. The U.S. adoption in the 1930s of noninterventionism, combined with the threat from Fascist and Communist subversion, increased the willingness of the Latin American countries to strengthen inter-American security cooperation. As World War II was ending, most Latin American governments did not want the emerging United Nations collective security system to supplant or prohibit the regional arrangements that had evolved to date.[5] This was one consideration behind the inclusion of Article 51 in the UN Charter, which would be cited by the Reagan administration in arguing the legitimacy of external aid to the Nicaraguan resistance during the 1980s:

> Nothing in the present Charter shall impair the inherent right of individual or collective self-defense if an armed attack occurs against a member of the United Nations until the Security Council has taken the measures necessary to maintain international peace and security.

As the cold war intensified in 1947, Western Hemisphere nations moved to establish their own formal collective security system apart from the United Nations. The Inter-American Treaty of Reciprocal Assistance (signed in Rio de Janeiro and called the Rio Treaty) was the first treaty of collective self-defense to be concluded under Article 51 of the United Nations Charter. The scholar J. Lloyd Mecham notes, "In reconciling defensive alliance with obligations of U.N. membership, [it] was destined to serve as a model for the North Atlantic Treaty (NATO) and similar pacts." In 1948 this treaty entered into force, and the Organization of American States was created. The first application of the new institutions was to help democratic Costa Rica repel an armed attack from the dictatorship in Nicaragua. The OAS succeeded in halting that open military attack and did so in subsequent disputes; but it became less effective against indirect aggression in the 1970s.

The aggressor in 1948 had been the regime of Anastasio Somoza Garcia, who in 1947 had installed a hand-picked successor, President Arguello. When he refused to be a rubber stamp, however, Somoza seized power again. The United States initially withheld diplomatic recognition from this regime because it had been established by a military coup. This stance reflected a prodemocratic policy the United States attempted to follow from 1945 to 1949, when it sought to support diplomatic initiatives from democratic Uruguay and Guatemala for inter-American collective actions to prevent the establishment of antidemocratic regimes. The intention of the United States was to avoid repeating the mistake of "intervention by inaction," which had permitted the original Somoza regime to be established. This was expressed in a thesis proposed by Uruguay in 1945 and

231

revived by President Reagan in the 1980s: that parallelism between democracy and peace must constitute a strict rule of action in inter-American policy.[6]

The United States also withheld diplomatic recognition from the military regimes established by coup in Venezuela in 1948 and Panama in 1949. But few Latin American countries followed this approach, apparently finding dictatorship a lesser evil than compromising the nonintervention principle. The Truman administration then returned to a de facto recognition policy, dealing with governments that were in control.

Meanwhile, in April 1948, when the Ninth Conference of Inter-American States convened in Bogotá, Colombia, U.S. Secretary of State George C. Marshall opened the meeting by condemning Soviet violations of the Yalta agreements promising free elections for Eastern Europe, and Stalin's blockade of West Berlin, among other hostile Communist actions. The secretary of state called for inter-American cooperation to meet the Communist threat. The next day, April 9, 1948, a Colombian political leader was assassinated (by persons still unknown, as would occur in Nicaragua thirty years later), sparking a riot by his followers. This disturbance became a massive, violent upheaval when "Communists rushed to the scene to fan the flames, [since] many Communists from other countries, including Fidel Castro, . . . foregathered to discredit or disrupt the conference." These events led to a unanimous inter-American resolution opposing communism.

A Lesson for Castro. The OAS repeated their resolution opposing communism in 1951, after North Korea's attack on South Korea in 1950. But except for the Soviet placement of missiles in Cuba in 1962, the threat from communism in Latin America took the form of indirect aggression and subversion, as was occurring inside Guatemala in the early 1950s. There, a reformist military coup had ended a thirty-year military dictatorship in 1944 and produced the elected government of Dr. Juan José Arevalo in 1945. The small Guatemalan Communist party soon began infiltrating that government. By the 1950 presidential elections,

> Colonel Jacobo Arbenz Guzman, candidate of the pro-Communist wing of the National Renovation party, was an easy victor in the 1950 presidential campaign—thanks greatly to the elimination by assassination of his principal rival. . . . Soon after the inauguration of President Arbenz, in March, 1951, . . . the energetic Communist minority influenced the new president and rapidly took over, . . . [using] the principle of indirect control. . . . [B]y the time the Arbenz govern-

ment was three years old, the Communists were in a position to shape government policies.[7]

The evidence shows that during the Arbenz government, "Guatemalan Communist leaders made frequent trips to the USSR and satellite countries for training and instruction. Fundamental tasks to be undertaken by the Communist party in Guatemala were assigned to it by Moscow. [One of these was] to penetrate and subvert the neighboring Central American states. This resulted in the movement into Nicaragua, El Salvador, and Honduras of propagandists, organizers, and agitators who used Guatemala as a base. These events led the United States to propose at the Tenth Conference of Inter-American States in March 1954 a "Declaration of Solidarity . . . against the intervention of international Communism," which stated that "domination or control of the political institutions of an American state by the international Communist movement . . . endangers the peace and calls for appropriate action." This resolution passed by 17 to 1 (Guatemala opposing), an immediate result of which was that the "Guatemalan government reacted rather violently to consolidate its power. . . . The secret police . . . instituted a reign of terror. . . . There were mass arrests, suspension of constitutional guarantees, and opposition party leaders were killed."[8]

In May 1954, it was disclosed that a ship with Soviet-bloc weapons was en route to Guatemala. Then, in June 1954, with help from the United States "a small rebel force of only a few hundred men invaded Guatemala. . . . Virtually no opposition was encountered. When [it] had penetrated scarcely twenty miles, the Arbenz government toppled because of army defection."[9]

This Communist failure in Guatemala was observed by Fidel Castro, then in exile in Mexico, having failed in his first attempt to launch an armed rebellion in Cuba. A key lesson both Castro and the Sandinistas would take from these events in Guatemala was the need to eliminate the threat of a military coup or defection by establishing their own new, totally controlled armed forces. Castro also decided he must initially not be explicit about his Communist political beliefs and hostility to the United States.

Castro Takes Power in Cuba and Becomes a Soviet Ally

In 1952 General Fulgencio Batista overthrew the elected president of Cuba and was soon faced with increasing political opposition and armed rebellion from Cuban groups seeking the restoration of constitutional government. One exception was the Communist party of Cuba, which had long had an alliance of convenience with Batista. After having been imprisoned and then released under amnesty,

Fidel Castro and his brother, Raul Castro, went to Mexico, obtained weapons and funds, and then returned to Cuba with eighty-two guerrillas in December 1956. Only eighteen survived immediate attacks by the Batista armed forces.[10]

During the next two years Castro proclaimed his goal to be the restoration of constitutional democracy with free and fair elections. He gave special emphasis to courting public opinion in Cuba and the United States, at the same time continuing to recruit new guerrilla fighters. In early 1958 the United States embargoed further military sales to Batista (as would occur twenty years later in Nicaragua), and this was interpreted within Cuba as a sign that the Batista regime could not hold out much longer. In the summer of 1958 the Cuban Communist party made a secret alliance with Castro while he continued to proclaim his democratic goals.[11] In early January 1959, under pressure from mounting armed and unarmed resistance, Batista fled; Castro, supported by 2,000 to 4,000 guerrillas, entered the capital as the victorious liberator who would restore constitutional democracy.[12]

The United States provided immediate diplomatic recognition, and during Castro's visit to the United States in the spring of 1959 offered economic aid, which Castro rejected. In fact, from his first weeks in power in 1959 Castro took actions totally contrary to his professed political objectives, surprising the overwhelming majority of the Cuban people and many in the U.S. government and media who had believed him. These actions constituted a program of repression, militarization, and indirect aggression.

The initial focus of Castro's repression was the leadership of Batista's roughly 35,000-member armed forces. On January 8, 1959, on a Cuban rifle range,

> hundreds of soldiers from the defeated army . . . had been lined up in a trench, knee deep. . . . Their hands were tied behind their backs, and they were machinegunned where they stood. Then with bulldozers the trenches were turned into mass graves. . . . Nor was it an isolated instance.[13]

Additional hundreds were executed, while thousands were imprisoned in newly built concentration camps, during Castro's first months.

Initially Castro established a dual system of governance—one set of organizations with nominal authority, in which his democratic former allies would work; and another inner circle of organizations through which Castro and his associates would really control Cuba. (The Sandinistas repeated this in 1979.) Some months after this, Castro began to turn on many of his former allies in the anti-Batista movement: "A Soviet-style secret police was established. . . . Thousands were arrested . . . [and] held for years. . . . Prison camps were established [with] starvation, beating, torture . . . [and] hard labor."[14] The regime also established its control through "Committees for the Defense of the Revolution," a neighborhood spying system. Over the next thirty years, thousands would be executed, tens of thousands imprisoned—many for ten, twenty, or more years. In 1989, Cuba was second only to Nicaragua in the number of political prisoners in Latin America.

Soviet Military Aid. Perhaps to avoid the fate of Arbenz in Guatemala, Castro eagerly sought relations with the Soviet Union. In July 1959 he sent his chief of intelligence to Mexico for meetings with the Soviet ambassador.[15] In November 1959, Castro sent two officials to meet with visiting Soviet Deputy Premier Anastas Mikoyan in Mexico, and soon thereafter "nearly a hundred Soviet technicians arrived in Havana. . . . Many of these . . . were actually Spaniards taken by their communist parents to the USSR after the Spanish Civil War and subsequently trained as Soviet military and intelligence operatives."[16]

Soviet military cooperation, initially covert, began in late 1959.[17] In the summer of 1960, "seven hundred Soviet bloc 'technicians' arrived accompanied by huge crates and boxes. Cuban stevedores were forbidden to handle other suspicious cargoes that were unloaded at . . . northern Cuban ports."[18] These Soviet-supplied weapons included tanks, artillery, and anti-aircraft guns amounting to about 28,000 tons in 1960 and reaching 250,000 tons in 1962. After the Cuban missile crisis and the Soviet dismantling of its missile bases in Cuba in October 1962, the supply of weapons declined to an average of about 20,000 tons per year during the rest of the 1960s. During the 1970s the average was about 10,000 tons annually until the African interventions with Cuban troops began in 1975, when it returned to about 20,000 tons. This flow of weapons stayed roughly constant until it sharply increased to about 58,000 tons annually after the Sandinista takeover in 1979. (See figure 7–1.)

The quick and massive Soviet military help was decisive in defeating the Cuban exile force at the Bay of Pigs in April 1961.[19] Reported disputes with the Soviet Union about tactics for spreading revolution may have caused the reduction in Soviet military supplies from 1963 to 1967.[20] By the spring of 1968, Soviet pressures had persuaded Castro to sign a secret agreement promising no public criticism of the Soviet Union or of the established Communist parties of Latin America, and accepting virtual Soviet management of the Cuban intelligence service. After the Soviet invasion of Czechoslovakia in August 1968 removed the liberalizing Communist regime there, Castro explicitly endorsed the Brezhnev Doctrine.[21]

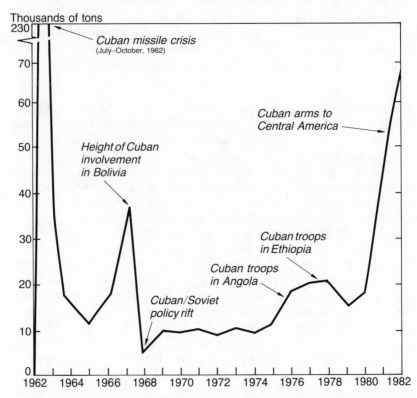

FIGURE 7–1
Soviet Military Deliveries to Cuba, 1962–1982

Thousands of tons

Cuban missile crisis
(July–October, 1962)

Cuban arms to
Central America

Height of Cuban
involvement
in Bolivia

Cuban troops
in Ethiopia

Cuban troops
in Angola

Cuban/Soviet
policy rift

Source: White House Office of Media Relations and Planning, *White House Digest*, July 6, 1983.

As a result of this Soviet military aid, Cuba, with a population remaining at about 10 million, built the largest armed forces in Latin America. By 1986, Castro's forces had a total strength of about 297,000 (162,000 active duty, 135,000 reserves), with another 500,000 in a "territorial militia." These forces had nearly 1,000 tanks, more than 200 jet combat aircraft, helicopter gunships, large quantities of other weapons, and naval and amphibious landing ships.[22] The Soviet military presence in Cuba in 1962, protecting and supporting the attempted missile emplacements, is estimated to have been about 40,000 troops.[23] In 1986, that presence was estimated to be about 7,700 (2,800 military advisers, 2,800 combat brigade, and 2,100 intelligence). The Soviet Union has conducted numerous military reconnaissance and other operations against the United States from Cuba (twenty-five Soviet naval visits between 1969 and 1986), as well as extensive electronic intelligence gathering from regional government and civilian communications, using its large facility in Cuba.[24]

Cuban Armed Subversion. Using repression and Soviet-armed Cuban troops to keep his regime in power, Castro launched or supported a series of aggressive attacks against peaceful states through armed subversion. In 1958, before taking power, Castro had already written to a relative about his plans for a "war against the United States." As early as April 1959, three months after Castro took control, plans for aggression through armed subversion became reality—lasting thirty years and still continuing—when guerrillas provided with weapons, money, and training in Cuba landed on the coast of Panama. In June 1959 Castro provided similar support to Nicaraguan guerrillas seeking to bring down the government in Nicaragua. In addition, in 1959 he began supplying radical groups from Haiti and the Dominican Republic with weapons and training. But authoritarian regimes were not the only targets. In the summer of 1959, Castro began what would be a bloody ten-year war against the newly elected democratic government of Venezuela, fragile because it had just succeeded a military dictatorship.[25]

The Soviet Union established full diplomatic relations with Cuba in May 1960 and markedly increased its military support to Castro after Soviet Premier Nikita Khrushchev had walked out of the four-power summit. In July 1960, Khrushchev declaimed:

> We shall do everything to help Cuba and her struggle. . . . Figuratively speaking, in case of need, Soviet artillery men can support the Cuban people with their rocket fire should aggressive forces in the Pentagon dare to start an intervention against Cuba. And let them not forget that, as the latest tests have shown, we have rockets capable of landing precisely on a given square at a distance of 13,000 kilometers [8,000 miles].[26]

Terrorism, kidnapping, violence, and guerrilla warfare instigated by Cuban-backed groups in a number of Latin American countries led to the downfall of constitutional governments as the military seized power in response to the international violence brought on by Castro's outside intervention. The OAS on a number of occasions condemned Cuban aggression through armed subversion (see table 7–1). In 1964 OAS foreign ministers passed this particularly significant resolution against Havana:

> The Republic of Venezuela has been the target of a series of actions sponsored and directed by the government of Cuba

TABLE 7–1
CUBAN INDIRECT AGGRESSION IN LATIN AMERICA AND OAS RESPONSE,
1959–1967

	Cuban Action	OAS Response
1959	80–100 guerrillas invade Panama from Cuba.	OAS aircraft and patrol boats force surrender.
1961	Intervention and subversion alleged by Peru.	OAS Council confirms Cuban subversion.
1961	Threat to hemispheric peace and security alleged by Colombia owing to Cuban army of guerrillas.	OAS excludes Castro government from participation.
1962	Installation of Soviet nuclear weapons and missiles.	OAS authorizes individual and collective measures, including force.
1963–64	Arms shipments to pro-Castro guerrillas in Venezuela.	OAS verifies facts, votes sanctions against Cuba.
1967	Intervention alleged by Venezuela and Bolivia.	OAS condemns Cuba, extends sanctions, including cutoff of government sales and credits.

SOURCE: Author, from information provided by the OAS.

openly intended to subvert Venezuelan institutions and to overthrow the democratic government of Venezuela through terrorism, sabotage, assault and guerrilla warfare. . . . The aforementioned acts, like all acts of intervention and aggression, conflict with the principles and aims of the inter-American system. . . . The acts verified . . . are considered an aggression and an intervention on the part of the government of Cuba in the internal affairs of Venezuela, which affect all the member states.

Cuba had already been excluded from participating in the OAS in 1961 as a result of its armed subversion against Colombia, and in the 1960s many governments broke diplomatic relations with Castro. The finding in the case of Venezuela in 1964 codified the fact that the initiation of armed subversion is tantamount to aggression. This would become an important issue in the 1980s, when the Reagan administration charged the Sandinista regime in Nicaragua with initiating armed subversion against its neighbors beginning in 1979. In President Reagan's view, this Sandinista aggression justified the United States in providing military aid to the Nicaraguan armed resistance in defense of OAS and Rio Treaty allies, such as El Salvador, which were the objects of Sandinista-aided aggression.[27]

In 1966 Castro convened the Tri-continental Congress to bring together anti-Western terrorist and guerrilla movements from Latin America, Africa, and the Middle East. At this time Cuba and the Latin American armed groups it supported began establishing close links with the Palestine Liberation Organization and other Palestinian terrorist groups. Latin American terrorists would subsequently participate in many joint operations with Palestinian terrorist groups.[28]

In 1967 Castro established the Organization of Latin American Solidarity to tie together more closely the far-left terrorist movements throughout the Latin American region. The theme at the founding conference was clearly stated: "The first duty of all revolutionaries is to make revolution." After the conference Radio Havana, speaking for the Castro regime, proclaimed: "After Cuba in Latin America, Nicaragua could be the first liberated country."[29] By 1967, at least twelve training camps for terrorists had been set up in Cuba, reportedly under the direction of the Soviet KGB.[30]

Despite his reported differences with the Soviet Union about tactics during the 1960s, Castro continued aggressive operations not only in Latin America but also in Africa. Following Castro's secret 1968 agreement with the Soviet Union and his reported submission to Soviet strategic guidance, Castro continued these subversive activities but at the same time moved to reestablish diplomatic relations with a number of Latin American governments during the early 1970s. So far, none of the Cuban-supported terrorist groups had succeeded in taking power. The increasingly unpopular Allende regime in Chile, which was heavily penetrated by Communist elements, had been overthrown in a military coup in 1973.

The Soviet-encouraged surprise attack by Egypt on Israel, the Yom Kippur War, also occurred in 1973. Castro broke diplomatic relations with Israel and, apparently at Soviet request, sent thousands of Cuban tank troops to help Syria during the War of Attrition in 1974. This marked the first deployment of regular Cuban combat troops abroad, an action that writer Carlos Montaner has called "Cuban military imperialism."[31] Prime Minister Golda Meir of Israel later revealed in an autobiography that the United States asked Israel not to publicly expose or condemn this Cuban involvement in the Middle East.

President Nixon had begun discussions to normalize relations with the Castro regime in 1973, when no Cuban troops were in combat abroad. By the time President Carter broke off the talks in 1979, Castro had deployed more than 70,000 military and secret police personnel to support the taking of power by new Communist regimes in Angola, Mozambique, Ethiopia, Nicaragua, and Grenada. Except for Grenada, where a U.S.-led collective security force of Caribbean democracies routed the Soviet- and Cuban-supported regime in 1983, Cuban intelligence, military, and other personnel continue to prop up pro-Soviet regimes in each of those countries. As the scholar Mark Falcoff has written: "The Castro dictatorship aligned itself voluntarily with the Soviet Union. In this sense it could be said that Cuba . . . is a genuinely dependable Soviet ally."[32]

The Soviet Union rewarded this Cuban cooperation by providing ever-higher levels of economic support and military supplies to Castro during the 1970s and the 1980s. During most of this time Soviet economic subvention amounted to about 25 percent of Cuba's annual gross national product, about $3 billion a year during the 1970s and about $5 billion a year during the 1980s. As a result Cuban economic dependence on the Soviet Union became far greater than its dependence on the United States had been in Batista's day.[33]

Castro's years of failed subversive efforts in Latin America only led him to redouble his efforts in the late 1970s. This included establishing the Americas Department as an agency designed, according to a 1981 State Department report, to

> centralize operational control of Cuba's covert activities . . . [bringing] together the . . . military [and] the General Directorate of Intelligence into a far flung operation that includes secret training camps in Cuba, networks for covert movement of personnel and material between Cuba and abroad and sophisticated propaganda support.[34]

The same report points up the importance of Mexico as "a principal base for Cuban contacts with representatives of several armed Latin American groups on guerrilla strategy, logistical support, and international activities. . . . Cuba's embassy in Mexico City is its largest diplomatic mission in the hemisphere."[35] One close student of Castro has written that his secret and open wars "monopolize most of the indefatigable Cuban leader's interest and efforts. . . . Castro is the embodiment of an endless war."[36]

In late 1977 the Cuban dictator began to provide increased support for armed Communist groups in Central America. Nearly twenty years of revolutionary warfare, the lessons learned from earlier failures, and dramatically increased Soviet support had all added to the resources and tactical options now at his disposal. Castro may also have been emboldened by the apparent passivity of the United States in the face of the establishment of Communist regimes in Vietnam, Cambodia, Laos, Angola, Mozambique, Ethiopia, and Afghanistan within a period of four years (1975–1978) spanning administrations of both political parties.

Castro's Four-Part Strategy. The evidence suggests that in 1977 Castro decided that Nicaragua and perhaps all of Central America were ripe for expanded revolutionary warfare. Drawing on his own success in taking power, he developed a careful four-part strategy, which would have its first test in Nicaragua. Castro decided the extreme left must do the following:

1. It must unify all major Marxist-Leninist groups and put an end to the sectarianism that had split them into rival factions.

2. For the purposes of deception and tactical advantage, the groups must establish a "broad coalition" with non-Communist elements of the opposition and make promises of fair elections and democracy leading to a "broad-based government."

3. This Communist-guided "broad coalition," backed by systematic propaganda and political action, must work to obtain international support from free-world sources. At the same time the target regimes had to be discredited and cut off from political and military help from the free world.

4. Cuba and the Soviet bloc must provide sharply increased covert military, political, and propaganda support along with manpower to be supplied by various Marxist-Leninist terrorist and guerrilla groups that were currently in exile.

Sandinistas Take Power

The regime of General Anastasio Somoza Garcia began with a military coup in 1936 and ended with his assassination in 1956. One of his sons, Luis Somoza, then took over the presidency and began a process of internal political liberalization and tolerance.

In 1961, with help from Castro, three members of the pro-Moscow Nicaraguan Socialist (Communist) party—Carlos Fonseca, Silvio Mayorga, and Tomas Borge—founded the Frente Sandinista de Liberación Nacional (FSLN, the Sandinista National Liberation Front, or Sandinistas).[37] Of these three founders, only Borge is still living. After their victory he gained control of the secret police as minister of interior.

The Sandinistas began armed attacks inside Nicaragua in 1963 but suffered a serious military setback in 1967. The movement remained very small for many years. There were an estimated 150 Sandinista guerrillas during most of the 1960s and about 300 during 1971–1977 (see table 7–2, in the next section). By 1975, they had split

241

into three factions. The Ortega brothers led the ostensibly more moderate *Tercerista* faction, which called for cloaking the Marxist-Leninist beliefs of the Sandinistas and seeking aid from non-Communist sources.[38]

Elections were held in 1967 and 1974, but most democratic opposition groups believed Anastasio Somoza Debayle (the second son of Somoza Garcia) had won through electoral fraud. In 1972 a massive earthquake destroyed most of the capital, Managua, and in the wake of this catastrophe Somoza was accused of diverting International Relief supplies and funds for his and his cronies' personal use. The earthquake and its aftermath combined with the growing armed operations of the Sandinistas to intensify widespread opposition to the Somoza regime.

In 1977 with Castro apparently convinced that Nicaragua was ripe for destabilization, a high-ranking official of Castro's Americas Department began making numerous secret visits to Nicaragua, urging reunification of the Sandinista factions. At the same time, this Cuban agent "concentrated on building a supply network for channeling arms and other supplies" to the Sandinistas.[39]

In the spring of 1977, business, religious, professional, and civic leaders who were ostensibly independent of the Sandinistas established the Group of Twelve, who declared that peace inside Nicaragua was impossible unless the Sandinistas were brought in as part of a new government. Most members of the Group of Twelve later admitted that they were secret Sandinistas.[40] In January 1978 a popular newspaper publisher and former opposition presidential candidate, Pedro Joaquin Chamorro, was assassinated by persons still unknown. The Chamorro and Somoza families had had a long political rivalry, and *La Prensa*, the Chamorro paper, was a persistent critic of Somoza. The assassination was immediately blamed on the Somoza regime and sparked a massive increase in popular disaffection with it.[41]

In 1977, the Carter administration suspended military and economic assistance to Somoza on grounds of human rights abuses. On February 8, 1979, the United States formally terminated military aid; and, as in the case of Cuba twenty years earlier, this was perceived as a sign of strong U.S. disapproval of the government in power.

At Havana's World Youth Festival in July 1978, the Cuban efforts to unite the three Sandinista groups were pronounced successful. The Castro regime called on Latin American Marxist-Leninist groups attending that meeting to demonstrate solidarity with the Sandinistas by staging terrorist operations in their own countries. In the autumn of 1978,

> arms were flown from Cuba to Panama, transhipped to Costa Rica on smaller planes and supplied to [Sandinista]

guerrillas based in northern Costa Rica. To monitor and assist the flow, the Americas Department established a secret operations center in San Jose [Costa Rica]. By the end of 1978, Cuban advisors were dispatched to northern Costa Rica to train and equip the FSLN forces with arms which began to arrive direct from Cuba. FSLN [guerrillas] trained in Cuba . . . continued to return to Nicaragua via Panama.[42]

The pace of Cuban armed subversion against the Somoza regime increased in early 1979, when

Cuba helped organize, arm and transport an "internationalist brigade" to fight alongside FSLN guerrillas. Members were drawn from several Central and South American extremist groups, many of them experienced in terrorist activities. Castro also dispatched Cuban military specialists to the field to help coordinate the war efforts.[43]

In March 1979, Castro summoned leaders of the three Sandinista factions to a meeting in Havana to work out a unity pact. At this meeting three representatives from each of the factions became the nine-person directorate that ruled Nicaragua for ten years. Castro also required the Sandinistas to follow his tactic of promising democracy and establishing a coalition with the opposition group of non-Communists that by then had emerged as a leading democratic opponent of the Somoza regime.[44]

A series of events that had begun in August 1978 contributed to Castro's confidence in March 1979 that the Somoza regime was ripe for overthrow if the Sandinistas were tactically cunning enough. In August 1978 the non-Communist democratic opposition to Somoza, the Broad Opposition Front (FAO), issued a call for Somoza's departure and presented a plan for the democratization of Nicaragua. In September 1978, the OAS (with the encouragement of the U.S. government) began to consider the situation in Nicaragua. In October, the OAS began a two-month effort to bring about a transition from the Somoza regime. This involved the United States, Guatemala, and the Dominican Republic as the negotiating group. In January 1979, this OAS mediation effort ended when Somoza rejected the demand that he step aside so an interim government could supervise an election for a successor regime. In February 1979 the United States responded to that refusal by formally terminating military aid to Nicaragua and withdrawing its military assistance group and all Peace Corps volunteers. The size of the embassy staff was also cut in half.

It was in the context of the U.S. withdrawal from Nicaragua and the greatly stepped-up Cuban covert support for the Sandinistas that the final months of the drama were played out. In April 1979, the

Sandinistas, taking Castro's advice, formed a coalition with the non-Communist democratic opposition, professing that they shared the common goal of constitutional democracy. In May, Castro visited the president of Mexico, who shortly thereafter called publicly for the overthrow of the Somoza regime—thereby violating the Mexican doctrine of nonintervention.

During May and June 1979, while Cuban covert operations were helping the Sandinistas grow into an armed force that would reach about 5,000, the governments of Mexico, Venezuela (under the Social Democratic president, Carlos Andres Perez, who returned to office in 1989), Panama, and Costa Rica joined together in a political coalition opposing Somoza and calling for his removal. In June, a provisional Government of National Reconstruction (GRN) was formed in Costa Rica, consisting of three Sandinistas and two leaders of the non-Communist opposition. Meanwhile, the Carter administration had secretly given Somoza an ultimatum: only if he resigned and left Nicaragua when requested would the United States grant him and his family political asylum. After Somoza accepted this ultimatum, the U.S. ambassador advised him that a number of political steps remained to be taken before he should publicly announce his resignation.[45]

On June 21, 1979, the foreign ministers of the OAS reconvened to continue the earlier discussion (held in September and October 1978) of the conflict in Nicaragua. On June 23, the OAS for the first time in its history approved a resolution calling for the removal of a government still in substantial control of its territory. This resolution, introduced by the Venezuelan government, called for "the immediate and definitive replacement of the Somoza regime" and

> the installation in Nicaraguan territory of a democratic government . . . [with a] guarantee of the respect for human rights of all Nicaraguans without exception . . . [and] the holding of free elections as soon as possible that will lead to the establishment of a truly democratic government that guarantees peace, freedom and justice.[46]

This OAS resolution was clearly an endorsement of a successor government in Nicaragua contingent on its firm commitment to all the elements of genuine democracy and free, fair elections "as soon as possible." Over the next weeks this became the subject of intense negotiations involving the Carter administration, the Sandinistas, and the coalition of governments led by Mexico, Venezuela, Costa Rica, and Panama that during the preceding months had been actively involved in the effort to bring down Somoza.

Belatedly the Carter administration had come to understand that while the internal democratic opposition to Somoza had good intentions, it lacked any military capability to counterbalance the armed Sandinistas. In May 1979 President Carter had received a summary report on the massive Cuban covert operation supporting the Sandinistas, and in late June the administration sought to have an OAS peace force established to guarantee that the democratic conditions of the June 23, 1979, OAS resolution would be enforced. This belated proposal was blocked by Mexico and subsequently dropped by the Carter administration.

After long negotiations, which included senior officials of the U.S. State Department, the Government of National Reconstruction (GRN) junta, and the Sandinistas as a political movement, the GRN and the Sandinistas sent written commitments to the OAS that they would abide by the OAS conditions of free elections and full respect for human rights leading to the establishment of a "truly democratic government." Following those written commitments to the Organization of American States, on July 12, 1979, the United States took the remaining step of calling on Somoza to resign so that the GRN could be announced as the interim government pending democratic elections.

Somoza resigned on July 17, 1979. Two days later Sandinista military forces arrived in Managua and the GRN ostensibly assumed power. In fact, from that date, July 19, the nine-person directorate of the Sandinista movement ruled Nicaragua with total disregard for the democratic commitments it had made to the OAS. Emulating Castro, the Sandinistas moved almost immediately to institute a regime characterized by repression, militarization, and aggression through armed subversion against its neighbors. While doing this it continued its propaganda efforts to deceive free world public opinion and win the support of free world governments.[47]

From the start the Sandinista regime gave special attention to obtaining material and political support not only from the usual Soviet-bloc sources and such far-left allies as Cuba, Vietnam, North Korea, the PLO, and Libya but also from free-world countries. Castro had recognized by the late 1970s that he had made a mistake in being too visibly brutal in consolidating his regime. He advised the Sandinistas to maintain a façade of political pluralism in order to deceive free-world countries in Latin America and Europe that could supply important political and economic support. Strong support was given the Sandinista revolution by Mexico and the social democratic governments in Venezuela and Costa Rica. They in turn served to deceive and mislead social democrats in many European democracies into believing that the Sandinistas were committed to a new type of democratic revolution—not another Communist revolution.

In April 1979, the Socialist International (the international organization of democratic socialist parties) gave its official endorsement to the coalition of Sandinistas and non-Communists that had just been formed at Castro's secret urging. Endorsements of the Sandinista movement by Mexico and by social democratic movements in Latin America and in NATO nations in Europe contributed to the misunderstanding of it in the free world. It also resulted in hundreds of millions of dollars in economic assistance to the Sandinista regime from West European countries—assistance that continued long after it was obvious that this was a pro-Soviet dictatorship rather than some new form of revolution. After Nicaragua set the precedent, Mexico, the Socialist International, and many social democratic parties endorsed each of the new "revolutionary coalitions" that were established in Central America according to Castro's new tactical approach (see table 7–3 below). The Kremlin also endorsed this tactic: "The Sandinista victory in 1979 prompted the Soviets to anticipate a chain reaction of leftist upheavals and revolutions throughout Central America."[48]

Sandinista Aggression in Central America

On July 21, 1979, two days after the Sandinistas took power, leaders of the Communist guerrilla movement from El Salvador met with Sandinista leaders in Nicaragua to discuss future Sandinista support for an expanded Salvadoran Communist insurgency. At the same time many Cuban military and intelligence personnel along with civilian advisers began arriving in Nicaragua.[49] The Sandinistas and their Cuban allies were eager to build on the momentum of successful revolutionary warfare and political deception. In the next months and years a clear pattern of sharply expanded revolutionary violence against the other countries of Central America emerged in accordance with Castro's new tactical plan (see table 7–3 below). These other countries, while capable of democratic reform, were also vulnerable to armed subversion by growing numbers of externally guided guerrillas, as shown in table 7–2.

Within weeks of taking power, the Sandinista party leadership held a three-day conference in which it outlined a strategy for the revolution *sin fronteras* (without borders). It emphasized use of deception domestically and internationally while establishing the organizations needed to control Nicaragua and build up a new and powerful military under tight party control. The decision to act immediately to spread Communist revolution was recorded in a September 1979 Sandinista party document: "The foreign policy of the Sandinista People's Revolution is based on the full exercise of national sover-

TABLE 7–2
NUMBERS OF ARMED GUERRILLAS OF THE EXTREME LEFT IN CENTRAL
AMERICA, 1960–1982

	1960–70	1971–77	1978	1979	1980	1981	1982
Nicaragua	150	300	2,000	4,500	—	—	—
El Salvador	0	300	850	2,000	3,500	4,500	9,000
Guatemala	600	600	600	1,000	2,000	3,000	3,000
Honduras	0	0	some	some	some	100	200
Costa Rica	some	some	some	some	some	some	some
Total	750	1,200	3,450	7,500	5,500	7,600	12,200

SOURCE: U.S. government unpublished, declassified estimates, 1983.

eignty and independence and on the principle of revolutionary inter-nationalism."[50] Speaking more plainly in 1981, Tomas Borge, head of the secret police, said, "This revolution goes beyond our borders. Our revolution was always internationalist."[51]

From a Marxist-Leninist perspective, the countries of Central America were highly vulnerable because (except for Costa Rica) they were governed by military regimes, many of their people lived in poverty, and the Carter administration seemed to have turned away from these countries, including suspending military aid. Ironically, this decision by Castro and the Sandinistas to increase pressure on the Central American countries coincided with nearly two decades of exceptional economic growth and improving living conditions. The combined populations of the countries of Central America increased from about 12 million in 1960 to about 23 million in 1980. During those years the gross national product of these countries increased from $282 per capita to $1,205. From 1960 until 1977 the average annual rates of economic growth in Central America were among the highest in the world; the regional average was nearly 7 percent. Life expectancy at birth increased from about 52 years in 1960 to 63 in 1980, while the proportion of school-age children enrolled in second-ary schools increased from 14 percent to about 34 percent and the adult literacy rate increased from 43 percent to 64 percent.[52] Once the Soviet–Cuban-supported network targeted Central America for in-creased violence after the Sandinista victory in 1979, however, years of economic growth were followed by years of economic decline, as the expanding far-left guerrilla groups used violence against people, destroyed economic infrastructure, and frightened away both domes-tic and foreign investment capital.

El Salvador. The four-step pattern of expanded armed subversion was clearly followed by Cuba and its regional allies. El Salvador was the next target (see table 7–3). This densely populated Central American country of about 4.5 million people had been the scene of a bloody, unsuccessful Communist-led insurrection in 1932. Military regimes had ruled since then, except for periods beginning in 1948 and 1961 when reform-oriented military officers led two important attempts at establishing constitutional government. These efforts opened up the political system during the 1960s for elections in which the conservative Christian Democratic and Social Democratic parties competed.

In 1970 the more radical elements of the clandestine Communist party broke away and began a gradually increasing campaign of terrorist violence. This created a climate of fear and counteraction leading to military intervention in the 1972 election to prevent the victory of the center-left Christian Democratic presidential candidate, José Napoleon Duarte. A series of military-led regimes followed until a 1979 coup by reformist officers led to the establishment of a civil-military coalition government intended as a transition to democracy. It implemented major land reforms in 1980, which provided land to about 1 million peasants and provided that the former owners were to be compensated partly in cash and partly in government bonds.[53] The Communist insurgency grew in the early 1980s but fair and open elections were successfully held in 1982, 1984, and 1989, institutionalizing a still fragile democracy.

At a meeting in Havana in December 1979, Castro had sought to unify the various armed and unarmed Marxist-Leninist groups and the Communist party of El Salvador into an effective coalition. This resulted in formation of a unified guerrilla command and a broad "Revolutionary Democratic Front," which included the small Social Democratic party and a splinter group of Christian Democrats. In May 1980 another unity meeting was held, this time in Managua. This led later in 1980 to the establishment of the Farabundo Martí National Liberation Front (FMLN), which would function as the command and leadership structure for the Communist guerrillas. Their forces expanded from about 850 in 1978 to 2,000 in 1979 and about 3,500 in 1980, peaking at some 9,000 in 1982 (see table 7–2).

During this concerted effort to take power in El Salvador, the Communist guerrillas had the full political, diplomatic, military, and covert backing of the Soviet Union, Cuba, and Nicaragua. One U.S. government report notes:

> The FMLN headquarters in Nicaragua evolved into an extremely sophisticated command and control center. . . . Guerrilla planning and operations are guided from this

headquarters where Cuban and Nicaraguan officers are involved in command and control. . . . The FMLN headquarters in Nicaragua also coordinates propaganda and logistical support for the insurgents, including food, medicine, clothing, money . . ., weapons, and ammunition.[54]

Figure 7–2 shows the supply routes from Cuba to Nicaragua and from Nicaragua to Honduras and El Salvador.

Guatemala. As in El Salvador, various armed Marxist-Leninist guerrilla groups broke away from the Guatemalan Communist party during the 1960s when it was reluctant to use violence. Castro had supported these breakaway organizations from the time they were established, and increased his military and covert aid to them after the Sandinista victory. In 1980, four such Guatemalan organizations met in Nicaragua at the invitation of the Sandinista leaders and Cuba

FIGURE 7–2
MAJOR CENTRAL AMERICAN ARMS ROUTES

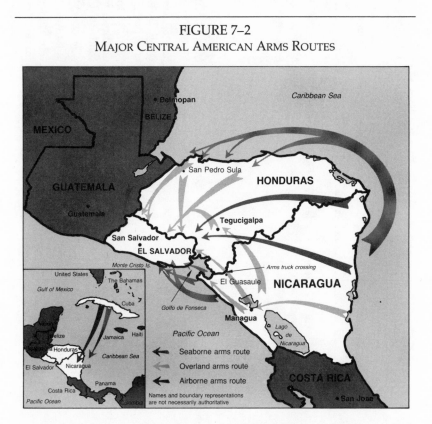

SOURCE: U.S. Department of State and U.S. Department of Defense, *Background Paper: Central America,* May 27, 1983, following p. 6.

249

TABLE 7-3
Four-Step Pattern of Extreme-Left Action in Central America, 1978–1983

Targets	Cuban-Encouraged Unification of the Extreme Left	Coalition with Non-Marxist–Leninist Groups	Efforts to Obtain Non-Communist International Support	Expanded Cuban/Soviet-Bloc Military and Propaganda Support
Nicaragua	July '78: Cuba announces unification of three Sandinista factions at World Youth Festival. Mar. '79: Unity pact renewed in Havana.	Jan. '79: FAO formed.	Early '79: Meeting in Mexico. May '79: Meeting in Costa Rica.	Fall '78: Arms sent by Cuba via Panama and Costa Rica. May–July '79: 500 tons of Cuban arms for the final offensive, which succeeded July 15.
El Salvador	Dec. '79: Havana meeting creates unity agreement with FARN, FPL, and PCES. Jan. '80: CRM created to unify extreme left. May '80: ERP joins and DRU is created. Nov. '80: FMLN created; unites all Marxist-Leninist groups.	Apr. '80: Democratic Front formed. May '80: Revolutionary Democratic Front (FDR) established to include the Democratic Front under the command of the extreme left (CRM).	Mar. '80: Handel[a] trip to Mexico. July '80: Handel[a] trip USSR, Bulgaria, Vietnam, Ethiopia. Nov. '80: International meeting for Salvadoran solidarity in Mexico. Aug. '81: Mexican/French initiative. Feb. '82: Mexican "power-sharing" negotiating proposals.	Jan. '81: Unsuccessful "final offensive." Jan.–Mar. '82: Preelectoral offensive. Mid-'82: Unsuccessful major guerrilla offensive to halt elections. Oct. '82: Beginning of expanded military attacks, terrorism, and economic sabotage.

Guatemala	June '80: Unification effort.	May '80: Democratic Front (FDCR) created.
	Feb. '82: URNG formed after Havana meeting (but PGT-O not included).	Feb. '82: Creation of Guatemalan Committee for Patriotic Unity (CGUP) announced in Mexico.
Honduras	April '83: Top four Honduran insurgent groups announce creation of unified group (DNU); Communist party at first not member but has since joined.	

NOTE: FARN = Armed Forces of the National Revolution; FPL = Popular Liberation Forces; PCES = Communist party of El Salvador; CRM = Revolutionary Coordinator of the Masses; ERP = Popular Revolutionary Army; DRU = Unified Revolutionary Directorate; FMLN = Farabundó Marti National Liberation Front; URNG = Union of the National Revolution of Guatemala; FAO = Broad Opposition Front of Nicaragua; PGT-O = Guatemalan Party of Labor-Orthodox.
a. Leader of the Communist party of El Salvador.
SOURCE: Author.

to discuss unity. In November 1980, the Guerrilla Army of the Poor (EGP), the Rebel Armed Forces (FAR), the Organization of the People in Arms (ORPA), and the dissident faction of the Guatemalan Communist party (PGT/D), with representatives of Castro present, signed a unity agreement in Nicaragua. After this unity agreement, Castro substantially increased the flow of weapons to the Guatemalan Communist guerrilla groups and their numbers increased.

That same year, as part of the effort to deceive and obtain endorsement and aid from non-Communist groups, the Guatemalan guerrilla groups also established the Democratic Front against Repression (FDCR). The final step in unification took place in February 1982 when all the Guatemalan Marxist-Leninist guerrilla organizations met in Cuba and established the National Revolutionary Union of Guatemala (URNG) as the central command organization. The URNG in turn established the Guatemalan Committee for Patriotic Unity (CGUP) in Mexico as its propaganda front. As in the case of the Sandinistas and the FMLN, the Socialist International and some other non-Communist groups endorsed this new Communist-led coalition.

A widespread perception that the 1982 elections in Guatemala were not fair led to a military coup by General Efrain Ríos Montt. He pledged to bring about a transition to constitutional democracy and to improve the government's counterinsurgency tactics. After some months, General Oscar Humberto Mejía Victores took over and promised to continue the transition to constitutional democracy. By 1984, elections for a constituent assembly were held, a new constitution was drawn up, and fair presidential elections in 1985 resulted in the election of Marco Vinicio Cerezo, a Christian Democrat who was inaugurated as president in January 1986. Meanwhile, the far-left guerrilla groups had declined in numbers. This was due in part to the positive political changes within Guatemala and in part to the containment of Cuban and Sandinista-aided armed subversion, caused by their need to direct more effort against the growing and increasingly effective anti-Sandinista armed resistance inside Nicaragua.

Honduras. After a series of military regimes, Honduras attempted to return to a constitutional government with elections in 1965. In 1971 that nation held its first direct election of a president since 1932. A series of coups, however, returned the military to power until 1982, when Honduras made a peaceful transition to constitutional democracy.

Although Honduras is the poorest country in Central America, bad blood between Castro and small groups of Honduran radicals, along with the strength of its prodemocratic labor unions, had helped spare Honduras the far-left violence experienced elsewhere in the region. By the late 1970s, however, Castro resumed military training for members of the Honduran Communist party, integrating them into an "Internationalist Brigade" fighting in Nicaragua.

In 1979 Castro had decided that El Salvador and Guatemala would be next after Nicaragua to come under Communist control. In the meantime, Honduras would be used as a transit point for moving supplies and insurgents into those countries.[55] In 1979 and 1980 Castro successfully intimidated the military regime in Honduras into acquiescing in this movement of military supplies and guerrillas from Nicaragua to El Salvador through its territory. He also wanted Honduras to remain neutral and to reject cooperation with the Reagan administration.

Sandinista aggression against Honduras, meanwhile, started in late 1979 when Sandinista military units crossed into Honduras on several occasions, saying they were in hot pursuit of former members of the Somoza National Guard. In 1980, armed Honduran Marxist-Leninist groups with close ties to the Sandinistas staged a number of terrorist incidents, including the kidnapping of a Honduran banker.[56] In January 1981, Honduran police caught Salvadoran FMLN guerrillas unloading weapons from a truck that had just come from Nicaragua; it contained more than one hundred automatic rifles and about 100,000 rounds of ammunition along with other military equipment.[57] A few months later, Honduran authorities intercepted another large truck from Nicaragua concealing large quantities of weapons, ammunition, and propaganda materials for the Salvadoran guerrillas.

In November 1981 Honduran police raided the safe house of a Marxist-Leninist group, capturing terrorists including Hondurans, Uruguayans, and several Nicaraguans, who told the authorities that the Nicaraguan government had supplied them with funds and explosives. The captured evidence indicated that this terrorist group "was formed in Nicaragua at the instigation of high level Sandinista leaders. The group's chief of operations resided in Managua. Members of the group received military training in Nicaragua and Cuba. The documents included classroom notebooks from a one year training course held in Cuba in 1980."[58] Over a year later, in December 1982, a Guatemalan Marxist-Leninist guerrilla faction kidnapped the daughter of Honduran President Roberto Suazo Cordova as another means of exerting pressure and intimidating the government of Honduras. (After this failed to break the president's will, she was released.) In the spring of 1983 four far-left Honduran insurgent groups and the Communist party of Honduras established a unified organization—again following Castro's tactical advice.

But the democratic government of Honduras that took office in January 1982 rejected all Cuban and Sandinista attempts to pressure or persuade it into neutralism. Quite the contrary, it increased its cooperation with the United States and the other Central American countries. After 1985, when Honduras held a second round of democratic elections and freely chose a new president, and until 1989, various efforts to infiltrate guerrillas into Honduras from Nicaragua and begin expanded terrorist and insurgent operations continued to fail.

Costa Rica. Costa Rica has had a functioning democratic political system since 1948 and has the highest standard of living in Central America. In 1978 and 1979, Costa Rica participated directly in helping the Sandinistas defeat the Somoza regime. Nevertheless, the Sandinistas initiated aggression against Costa Rica in 1980. This included armed attacks on Costa Rican vessels on the San Juan River in October 1980. The following year, the Costa Rican Communist party established its own armed unit, having sent cadres to fight with the Sandinistas. Evidence exists that the Sandinistas provided training, logistical support, and weapons to this armed Costa Rican Communist unit. The Sandinistas have also been implicated in a number of assassinations and attempted assassinations of anti-Communist Nicaraguan exiles living in Costa Rica. In early 1982, the Costa Rican government uncovered in the capital, San Jose, a terrorist cell with two Nicaraguan members who confirmed that they were acting on the orders of the Nicaraguan embassy in Costa Rica. This terrorist cell had thirteen vehicles designed for arms smuggling and more than 170 weapons including "machine guns, TNT fragmentation grenades . . . ammunition . . . and five hundred combat uniforms."[59]

All these acts of armed subversion by Cuba and Nicaragua against peaceful and friendly neighboring countries in Central America occurred months or years before the rise of the armed resistance in Nicaragua. Nor has Central America alone been the target of Sandinista aggression. Secretary of State Shultz noted in a February 1986 policy statement that the Sandinistas' "messianic impulse to violence" has "touched virtually the whole hemisphere," citing arms they have sent to guerrilla groups in Central America and in Colombia, and military training they provided for terrorists in Ecuador, Venezuela, Brazil, Uruguay, and Chile.[60]

Sandinista Repression

The Sandinistas and the Castro regime sought to conceal their material support to and collaboration with other Marxist-Leninist armed groups throughout Central America. Following Castro's tactical advice, the Nicaraguans promised democracy and formed an alliance with non-Communist groups; they muted their Marxist-Leninist beliefs and masked their true purposes, both to consolidate power within Nicaragua and to benefit from the economic aid that only free-world countries could provide.

These tactics succeeded. The United States warmly welcomed the new Government of National Reconstruction (GRN) by providing immediate diplomatic recognition and, within the first four weeks, nearly $25 million in economic assistance. During the first two months, despite a concurrent series of hostile and dictatorial actions by the Sandinistas, the United States and the Inter-American Development Bank (with U.S. encouragement) together gave the Sandinistas more than $100 million in economic aid (see table 7–4). During the first two years of the Sandinista regime, direct U.S. economic aid reached $118 million; an additional $240 million came from multilateral sources. Between July 1979 and December 1982 the Sandinistas received a grand total of $1.6 billion in economic assistance from non-Communist countries.[61]

In September 1979, President Carter received Daniel Ortega and Alfonso Robelo of the GRN in the White House. Only days earlier the Sandinista leadership had formulated explicit, written plans for their rule, according to which the GRN was "an alliance of convenience organized . . . to thwart Yankee intervention." The FSLN was to set up a wide variety of organizations to include "an army politicized without precedent, organized within the state," even though, as the Sandinistas acknowledged, there was no real danger from a resurgent National Guard—which had fled or been imprisoned—or from any of the neighboring countries. The plans included maintaining the appearance of an alliance with non-Communist elements in "the expectation of financial help from the Western bloc," although the "need to appear reasonable during the 'intermediate' phase was beginning to cause dangerous problems such as an independent labor movement." Non-Communist political parties were also to be maintained for the time being "because of international opinion." But, the Sandinistas made clear, as "an organization whose greatest aspiration is to retain revolutionary power," they supported "world revolution."[62]

While eager for economic aid from free world sources, the Sandinistas immediately turned to their long-term Communist ally in Cuba for the means to consolidate their power. Within a week after the Sandinistas took power there were about one hundred Cuban military and secret police personnel in Nicaragua. By October 1979,

TABLE 7-4
ECONOMIC AID TO NICARAGUA AND SANDINISTA ACTIONS,
AUGUST–SEPTEMBER 1979

	Source of Aid	Amount (in millions)	Purpose	Sandinista Actions
August	USAID	1.9	Food	Newspaper *El Pueblo* shut down. Sandinistas begin military buildup, construct new bases and airfields. Sandinistas move to consolidate labor unions under two Sandinista organizations. 606 Nicaraguan students go to Cuba.
	USAID	6.9	Loan commodities for distribution	
	USAID	17.6	Loan to finance sale of agricultural commodities	
September	IADB	20	Multipurpose loan	New militia organized. Sandinistas facilitate shipment of arms, supplies, to Salvadoran insurgents, provide training facilities. Pham Van Dong, premier of Socialist Republic of Vietnam, arrives. Daniel Ortega and Alfonso Robelo meet with President Carter at White House.
	IADB	36.5	Agriculture/ industrial loan	
	IADB	25	Industrial loan	
Total		107.9		

SOURCE: U.S. government data, 1981.

this had increased to two hundred and by July 1980 to several hundred. The number reached about 9,000 Cubans by 1984, of which about 3,000 were military or secret police operatives (see figure 7–3). These Cubans, together with other Soviet-bloc personnel, immediately began helping the Sandinistas establish a new secret police, a greatly expanded prison system, a new military, and the neighborhood "Committees for the Defense of the Revolution" modeled on Castro's block committees, all of which would be instruments for control of the population and the concentration of power in the hands of the nine-person ruling directorate.

In the government sector, the Sandinistas maintained a dual structure much as Castro had initially done. While including non-Communists for the sake of attracting further economic help from non-Communist countries, the Sandinista directorate, like the Soviet Politburo, essentially monopolized all power. By 1987, one analysis would show that the 9 members of the directorate, along with the 103

FIGURE 7–3
CUBAN PRESENCE IN NICARAGUA, 1979–1984

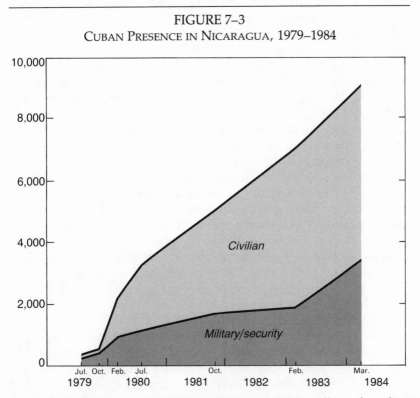

SOURCE: Adapted from White House Office of Public Affairs, fact sheet accompanying speech of President Reagan on Central America, May 9, 1984.

Sandinistas in the National Assembly, who together in effect constituted the FSLN's Central Committee, held 237 of the top formal
positions in the Nicaraguan government.[63]

The Sandinistas also immediately established typical totalitarian
mass organizations to control civil society, including political parties,
students, labor, youth, women, the professions, and of course the
trade unions. Persuasion, pressure, and coercion were used to bring
Nicaraguans into these Sandinista-controlled organizations.

Initially the majority of Nicaraguans hoped and believed that
genuine democracy was being ushered in with the Sandinista-led
revolution. The traditional democratic political parties reestablished
themselves and sought to expand their activities in a normal fashion.
The Sandinistas did not want to prohibit or destroy these parties, but
they used every means available to a dictatorship to harass, hamper,
and intimidate them. This was true in 1979 and remained true in
1989. Among the instruments used by the Sandinistas were the *turbas
divinas*—mobs controlled by the secret police—which would be used
to attack the headquarters and candidates of the democratic political
parties. Such intimidation was frequent in the Sandinista-adminis-
tered national elections of 1984 and 1990.

From the very start of the regime the Sandinistas attempted to
consolidate organized labor into two Sandinista-controlled group-
ings, one for rural workers and one for industrial workers. The
traditional Social Democratic and Christian Democratic trade unions
and their national federations were persecuted and harassed. This
included blacklisting those who joined the non-Sandinista trade
unions; removing such individuals from jobs, using secret police
mobs to attack them; and the harassment, arrest, secret imprisonment, and at times execution of democratic trade union leaders.[64]

Sandinista repression of religion was carried out in a number of
distinct, carefully calculated phases. Long allied with Palestinian
terrorist groups, the Sandinistas had a record of declared opposition
to Israel; in 1978 they had burned the only synagogue in the capital
of Nicaragua. Shortly after taking power the Sandinistas made the
leaders of the small Jewish community of Nicaragua some of the first
victims of their policy of repression and confiscations. Within months
the entire Jewish community of Nicaragua had fled.[65]

The Catholic church and its leadership had taken a strong stand
against the Somoza dictatorship. The archbishop of Nicaragua, Mi-
guel Obando y Bravo, had explicitly stated that the Somoza regime
had become intolerable and that the Nicaraguan people were justified
in taking up arms to remove it. The Sandinistas recognized that in a
predominantly Catholic country like Nicaragua they had to be ex-

tremely cautious in dealing with the Catholic church. Their first step was to establish a secretly Sandinista-controlled "popular church" using a small number of Catholic priests who had joined their movement.

During the visit of Pope John Paul II in 1983, the Sandinista regime staged hostile political demonstrations during the huge outdoor mass celebrated by the pope. In March 1984 the *Catholic Standard* (of Washington, D.C.) quoted the president of the Conference of Catholic Bishops of Nicaragua as stating clearly that "the Sandinista government through its ideology and method is a Marxist-Leninist government." In April 1984 the Nicaraguan bishops issued a pastoral letter calling for peaceful dialogue among all groups—including the Sandinista regime and the contras, the armed resistance. In a June 4 interview published in *Excelsior* (Mexico City), the head of the Sandinista secret police, Tomas Borge, responded with contempt: "Those bishops belong to a race of traitors, to the sector that has turned itself over to imperialism."

In the summer of 1981 the Sandinistas began reducing the access of the church leadership to the media; by Easter 1982 church leaders were required to provide the Ministry of Interior with copies of their sermons in advance of any broadcasting. The Sandinista secret police harassed and intimidated leaders of the religious organizations. Monsignor Bismarck Carballo, communications director for the Archdiocese of Managua and a key aide to the archbishop, was called to the home of a female parishioner where "he was forced to disrobe by security force personnel and then forced [naked] into the street in front of TV cameras and Sandinista mobs planted in advance."[66]

The small Protestant communities and churches in Nicaragua were put under even more severe and direct pressure by the Sandinista secret police. In July 1982 the head of the secret police publicly accused a number of Protestant churches of

> being funded by the CIA. . . . Some of them have mother churches in the United States. . . . It is evident we have to make a serious study to counteract their diversionist activity financed by the CIA . . . and take measures of a police nature . . . in order to control and neutralize certain activities.[67]

Not long after, *turbas divinas* attacked Protestant churches throughout Nicaragua and by August 1982 more than twenty Protestant churches in Managua had been seized. Many Protestant leaders were then forced to leave Nicaragua.

The Sandinista directorate also strictly controlled the rights of speech, assembly, and organization. Whenever it suited the directorate's purposes, the leaders of the democratic opposition groups within Nicaragua were allowed to function visibly and publicly. But they were often restricted and faced continuing harassment, arrest, and coercion.

Within days of taking power the Sandinistas seized the television stations and then the radio stations, except for one owned by the Catholic church. But the church station has been subject to strict censorship and intermittent shutdowns for many years. Only one non-Communist newspaper was published during the Sandinista years, La Prensa, the paper founded by Pedro Joaquin Chamorro. His widow, Violeta Barrios de Chamorro, the opposition's presidential candidate in the February 1990 elections, had been a member of the original Government of National Reconstruction, but in April 1980 she resigned in protest against Sandinista repression, remaining in Nicaragua as editor of La Prensa. This one non-Communist newspaper was subjected to continuing pressure by the Sandinista regime, including prepublication censorship.[68]

The victims of Sandinista repression include an estimated 2,000 to 4,000 persons secretly executed by the regime, and 35,000 imprisoned between 1979 and early 1987. As of 1987 there were forty-eight local police prisons and twenty-three Sandinista prisons, including nine secret police detention facilities and a number of clandestine houses that held five to ten prisoners in total secrecy.[69] A 1986 U.S. government report shows photographs of ten new political prisons built by the Sandinista regime. In 1989 an estimated 7,000 to 8,200 political prisoners were held in such facilities.[70] These political prisoners included about 2,000 former Somoza National Guard soldiers held since 1979, as well as Nicaraguans accused by the regime of collaborating with elements of the democratic opposition. Virtually all of these political prisoners were tried and sentenced by "special tribunals" without benefit of any real defense. The independent Permanent Commission on Human Rights (CPDH), established during the Somoza years and critical of both the Somoza and the Sandinista regimes, reported that "many prisoners [in Sandinista prisons] are kept in isolation, some are kept hanging by their hands, and beatings and torture are everyday occurrences."[71]

The Sandinistas also forcibly relocated more than 250,000 Nicaraguans, coercing families into moving out of zones where they might have provided help to the contras and placing them under government control in makeshift living quarters.[72] The first such mass resettlement occurred in December 1981 after the Protestant, English-speaking Miskito Indians resisted the Marxist-Leninist indoctrination being forced upon them and their children, and demonstrated in the wake of expropriation of tribal landholdings. The Sandinistas responded to this resistance with persecution: In January and February 1982 virtually all of the forty-three villages of these Protestant Indian communities were destroyed. About 15,000 of these Indians living on the east coast were removed to detention camps in the interior of Nicaragua, while about 30,000 escaped to Honduras, where they became a focal point of armed resistance against the Sandinista regime. (In March 1982 the U.S. government provided before and after photographs of the destroyed Indian towns and of the detention camps.)

The Sandinistas admitted to relocating about 250,000 people, but the U.S. government estimated that the number forcibly relocated may have reached 300,000 by 1986. Sandinista repression also caused an exodus of Nicaraguans, on a scale similar to that of the relocations. According to most estimates, by 1987 more than 300,000 Nicaraguans—or about 10 percent of the country's population—had fled. About 60,000 were estimated to have gone to Honduras, more than 100,000 to Costa Rica, and about 150,000 to the United States. Some U.S. State Department officials estimated that about 500,000 Nicaraguans fled the Sandinista regime.[73] On September 9, 1987, the *New York Times* quoted U.S. officials as saying that 110,000 Nicaraguan refugees were living in Honduras, about 25,000 of them in UN refugee camps.

The Sandinistas sought to conceal the extent of their repression through an international propaganda campaign. This included inviting citizens from the United States and other free world countries to visit and experience "the real Nicaragua." In this the Sandinistas emulated the Castro regime (which in turn learned from the Soviets). They deceived many visitors by giving them access to "typical" political, labor, peasant, and other groups—including religious organizations affiliated with the "popular church"—all designed to create a façade of normality and pluralism inside Nicaragua in order to consolidate their power and to achieve their international revolutionary objectives.[74]

In 1980 the Sandinista leadership announced it would not hold elections until 1985. But after the United States rescued its own citizens and helped restore democracy in Grenada in October 1983, the Sandinistas scheduled elections for November 1984. In a secret May 1984 speech, one of the Sandinista directorate members said candidly: "We see the elections as one more weapon of the revolution to bring its historical objectives gradually into reality. Therefore, we intend to take advantage of them."[75] Using carefully concealed pressure, the Sandinistas in 1984 denied the coalition of democratic

261

opposition groups fair access to the media and the opportunity to organize and campaign effectively.

The democratic opposition consisted of the leaders of four democratic political parties (the Democratic Conservative party, the Social Christian party, the Social Democratic party, and the Liberal Constitutional party), along with two democratic trade union confederations internationally affiliated with the Christian Democratic and Social Democratic movements, and a federation of cooperatives and business groups. But the Sandinistas created a climate in which free elections were impossible. In the weeks preceding the 1984 election secret police mobs physically attacked Arturo J. Cruz, Sr., the presidential candidate of the democratic coordinating group, and broke up opposition political rallies. As a result, the major democratic opposition coalition withdrew from the election. Nevertheless, the Sandinistas went ahead with their bogus election, arranging for several minuscule Marxist-Leninist parties to the "left" of the FSLN along with two small factions of non-Communist parties to participate; when the final votes were counted it could thus appear to international observers that the Sandinistas had won out among six competing parties.[76]

Besides using coercion during the campaign, the Sandinistas also used the Sandinista defense committees to intimidate the population into voting "correctly" by threatening the loss of ration cards for food and other essentials. Most important, the Sandinistas maintained total control of the vote-counting process.

In early 1989, as part of international negotiations concerning Central America, the Sandinistas promised to hold another round of elections for national office in February 1990. Their political goal was to have these elections legitimated by the United Nations, which in July 1989 agreed to monitor them, the first time the UN had undertaken such a role.[77] In April 1989, leaders of the democratic civic opposition groups had already stated publicly that rules and procedures for the 1990 election would not guarantee fairness and openness, and in June 1989 the Bush administration protested the steps taken by the Sandinistas to tilt the 1990 election.[78]

Only days before the February 25, 1990, election the AFL-CIO and other organizations issued reports documenting the systematic efforts of the Sandinistas to harass the democratic opposition throughout the campaign, deny it equal access to the media, and use government and military resources on behalf of the regime candidates. Furthermore, more than one hundred on-site observers from the United Nations, the OAS, and the Carter Presidential Center in Atlanta, Georgia (presumably including former President Jimmy

Carter, who was the official head of the OAS observer group) were cited as supporting these concerns. The AFL-CIO report also noted that the Sandinista "party apparatus is virtually inseparable from the government and the army . . . [and] the State Security police [has] some 20,000 agents . . . [with] a well documented ten-year record of infiltration of opposition groups, nighttime home visits, threats and violence. . . . Why . . . should [this] election campaign be any different?"[79]

Despite the unfairness of the campaign, the presence of many hundreds of foreign observers and the courage of the Nicaraguan people resulted in a vote in which the democratic opposition candidate, Violeta Barrios de Chamorro, obtained a reported 55 percent of the vote and Daniel Ortega received 41 percent.[80] This defeat stunned the Sandinistas, who had been confident that they could, as in 1984, ensure their own victory. Ortega conceded defeat and made a gesture of cooperation by visiting Mrs. Chamorro in her home. But the next day, after a five-hour meeting of one hundred top Sandinistas, Ortega demanded the immediate demobilization of the Nicaraguan armed resistance as a condition for a "peaceful transition" and indicated the Sandinistas would "continue governing from below" by maintaining their hold on key institutions such as the army, the security forces, and many parts of the government.[81] The inauguration of a democratic government presided over by the newly elected leadership seemed likely to be followed by a complex, often invisible, struggle, with the Sandinistas seeking to maintain their dominance over Nicaragua.

Following their founding in 1961, and in their 1967 program, the Sandinistas had been explicit about their commitment to Marxism-Leninism. It was only during the time of Castro-inspired deception starting in 1977 that they became more guarded and ambiguous. Once in power, the Sandinistas continued to be deceptive but from time to time expressed their beliefs and objectives with candor. A 1978 Sandinista communiqué declared, "Marxism-Leninism [is] a sure guide for the transformation of society." In June 1980, while receiving extensive economic aid from the Carter administration, Tomas Borge put it bluntly: "The Nicaraguan revolutionaries will not be content until the imperialists have been overthrown in all parts of the world."[82]

That same year the Sandinista foreign minister said that while the United States may look at Central America as five countries, "we regard ourselves as six different states [including Panama] of a single nation in the process of reunification."[83] The following year the minister of defense, Humberto Ortega, said plainly: "Marxism-Len-

263

inism is a scientific doctrine that guides our revolution. . . . Without Sandinismo we cannot be Marxist-Leninist and Sandinismo without Marxism-Leninism cannot be revolutionary.[84]

Militarization and Economic Failure

The Sandinista regime celebrated its first anniversary in July 1980 with a huge military parade. It was attended by a large group of visiting well-wishers, including officials from the Soviet Union and other Communist countries, the PLO, Libya, and a representative of President Carter. Fidel Castro attended, and when he returned to Cuba for his annual July 26 celebration he told the world:

> Now we are not two in the hemisphere, we are three [Cuba, Nicaragua, and Grenada]. . . . There will be no *coup d'etat* in Nicaragua because the people have the power. The people have the arms. What happened in Chile cannot happen here. . . . The experiences of Guatemala [1954], El Salvador [1932], Chile [1973] and Bolivia [1967] teach us.[85]

As noted earlier, what those earlier failures had taught Castro, and what he in turn had taught the Sandinista leaders, is that the revolutionary elite must establish its own, totally controlled armed forces, and these must be large enough to control the population and deter intervention. In Nicaragua the army is not in fact controlled by the formal government but by the Sandinista party.

The Sandinistas moved to expand their armed forces rapidly, building the largest and best-equipped military machine ever seen in Central America. Starting with about 6,000 guerrilla fighters in July 1979, the Sandinistas already had active-duty armed forces of about 24,000 by January 1980, 39,000 by January 1981, and 41,000 by January 1982. This rapid buildup *preceded* the gradual rise of the armed resistance, which did not begin combat operations receiving U.S. aid until 1982.

Nor was this military buildup a response to the size of neighboring armed forces. Costa Rica to the south had disbanded its armed forces in 1948, maintaining a civil guard of about 8,000 which has not increased in numbers during the 1980s. Honduras to the north had an armed force of about 16,000 in 1979, which it increased gradually to about 22,000 by 1984. By that time Nicaragua already had 67,000 on active duty (see table 7–5) and total trained forces of about 102,000.

The buildup of the Nicaraguan armed forces continued after 1984, reaching 75,000 on active duty in 1985 and 80,000 as of January 1989 (with an estimated total of 120,000 including reserves and all other trained forces).[86] Somoza's small National Guard had numbered

TABLE 7-5
MILITARIZATION AND ECONOMIC DECLINE IN NICARAGUA, 1977–1987

	Population (millions)	Armed Forces (thousands)	Resistance (thousands)	Military Expenditures ($ millions, 1987)	Arms Imports ($ millions, 1987)	Economic Aid from Non-Communist Countries	Per Capita GNP ($, current)[a]	Exchange Rate[b]
1977	2.6	6	—	1,131	17	45	750	1
1978	2.6	6	—	1,397	16	—	840	1
1979	2.7	6	—	1,000	7	120	660	—
1980	2.8	24	—	1,986 (E)	14	224	740	14
1981	2.9	39	.4	2,528 (E)	200	176	860	24
1982	3.0	41	4	3,830 (E)	177	123	920	40
1983	3.0	46	7	4,024 (E)	317	123	880	72
1984	3.1	67	14	4,935 (E)	382	117	860	230
1985	3.2	74	20	5,541 (E)	330	105	790	675
1986	3.2	75	20 (E)	NA	600	NA	730	2,000
1987	3.3	80	24 (E)	NA	540	NA	830	8,000 +

NOTE: E = estimate; NA = not available.

a. GNP per capita in current U.S. dollars from World Book, *World Tables, 1975–89* (Baltimore: Johns Hopkins University Press, 1989), pp. 430–31. (The change from a per capita GNP of $740 in 1980 to $830 in 1987 *current dollars* implies at least a 30 percent decline given U.S. inflation rates; Norman Baily has estimated that by 1989 per capita GNP had fallen to $300 in current dollars. See Norman Baily, "The Economic Recovery of Nicaragua," in *Building Democracy and Free Enterprise in Nicaragua* (Washington, D.C.: International Freedom Foundation, 1990), pp. 5–13.

b. Market exchange rate of Nicaraguan *cordoba* with one U.S. dollar, *Diario Las Americas*, November 28, 1987; by November 1987 it had fallen to 23,000.

SOURCES: U.S. Arms Control and Disarmament Agency, *World Military Expenditures and Arms Transfers, 1988*, p. 55; U.S. Department of State, *The Challenge to Democracy in Central America*, June 1986, p. 38; Organization for Economic Cooperation and Development, *Geographic Distribution of Financial Flows to Developing Countries.*

about 6,000, with an expansion to 10,000 during the last stages of the civil war in 1979. It never had more than 3 antiquated tanks and some 31 armored vehicles. By January 1982, the Sandinistas had a total of 30 Soviet tanks and 45 armored vehicles. They were also greatly expanding their helicopter and antiaircraft forces. By 1985, they had 350 tanks and armored vehicles, a force of about 45 military aircraft, and more than 30 attack helicopters, including the Soviet MI-24 "flying tank."

This unprecedented military buildup not only threatened Nicaragua's neighbors; it caused resentment among those whose sons and brothers had been conscripted for military service. It also strained Nicaragua's fragile economy. For the years 1979 to 1985, estimated total military expenditures were about $2.8 billion, the cost of Soviet-bloc weapons imports alone amounting to about $1.8 billion. During those same years, the Sandinista regime received economic aid totaling more than $1 billion from non-Communist countries (see table 7–5). The *New Republic* of September 28, 1987, said that the regime also received nearly $8 billion in additional credits from non-Communist countries from 1979 to 1987, when its external debt rose to $10 billion.

During the Sandinistas' first eight years, despite the enormous inflow of aid and credits from the non-Communist world, the per capita income in Nicaragua declined steadily, dropping about 30 percent by 1987. The market value of the Nicaraguan *cordoba* declined sharply year by year. From parity with the dollar in 1978 it fell to about 675 to the dollar in 1985, 8,000 per dollar in early 1987, and to 23,000 to the dollar by November 1987.

The U.S. government estimated that from 1986 to the first quarter of 1989 Soviet-bloc weapons shipments to Nicaragua increased sharply, totaling $1.7 billion.[87] Added to the $1.84 billion in 1979–1985 expenditures for Soviet-bloc weapons, it made a total of $3.1 billion in Soviet-bloc weapons imports by the Sandinistas. In March 1989 the White House issued a formal statement noting "that the deliveries of military equipment have been sustained at a high level for several years" and that there was no evidence of a Soviet cut-off. In May 1989, Soviet President Gorbachev assured President Bush that Moscow had stopped arms shipments to Nicaragua; but in October 1989, the United States again stated that Soviet weapons shipments continued at a high level—but through Cuba.

Moscow may have required the Sandinistas to pay in hard currency or commodities such as gold or food products for a large proportion of these weapons, since that has been a frequent Soviet practice. There have been reports that the Sandinistas used gold from Nicaraguan mines in partial payment. In any case, the depressed

Nicaraguan economy, marked by severe shortages of food, medicines, and other essentials, showed that Western economic aid did not help the poor and needy of Nicaragua, but probably constituted an indirect subsidy of the military buildup.

The Sandinista regime and its sympathizers blamed the actions of the contras and the U.S. economic sanctions imposed in 1985 for Nicaragua's sharp economic decline. In fact, before the armed resistance began to function in 1982, and several years before U.S. economic sanctions (May 1985), the combination of Nicaragua's military buildup, its massive expansion of the government sector in order to establish its dictatorial control, and its partial nationalization of industry and agriculture all probably contributed to a severe economic decline.[88] Moreover, after the spring of 1988, when contra combat operations diminished with the cutoff of military aid by the U.S. Congress, the economic problems of the Sandinista regime grew worse.

The Nicaraguan Resistance

Emergence of the Contras. The overwhelming majority of the Nicaraguan people supported the revolution against the Somoza dictatorship. They believed the promises of the democratic opposition, the Sandinistas, and the exile Government of National Reconstruction that the purposes of the revolution were to establish democracy, a mixed economy, and internal peace. But as more and more of the Nicaraguan people experienced Sandinista repression, militarization, and Communist indoctrination, popular opposition grew more widespread. Many Nicaraguans resisted passively; some resisted through civic, political, and religious institutions; and some decided that only *armed* resistance could bring about the democratic Nicaragua they had hoped for in 1979. Three centers of armed resistance emerged, whose leaders and adherents became collectively known as the contras (a term intended by the Sandinistas to be pejorative—*contra*-revolutionary—but that the resistance viewed as *contra*-tyranny).

The Nicaraguan Democratic Force. By November 1979, Sandinista strong-arm methods and economic demands had caused a number of the independent farmers, cattlemen, and tradesmen of the central and northern region to turn against the regime. In 1978, the Sandinistas had organized the "Anti-Somocista Popular Militia" (Milpas) against Somoza. Now some former members of those anti-Somoza militias reestablished their armed groups, this time to fight the Sandinistas. By July 1980 these small groups of farmers had captured one town, but the Sandinista armed forces quickly regained control.[89]

These peasants, small farmers, and ranchers of central and northern Nicaragua would become the nucleus of the largest component of the Nicaraguan armed resistance, the Nicaraguan Democratic Force (FDN), after its formation in 1982.

Indian resistance. A second focus of armed resistance derived from the Protestant, English-speaking Indian communities of the Atlantic coast. As early as the fall of 1979, these Indian peoples (Miskito, Suma, Ramo) protested the Sandinistas' use of Cuban teachers for indoctrinating their children in Marxism-Leninism. In the fall of 1980 they began mass protests after the Sandinistas expropriated tribal landholdings as a prelude to collectivizing them. In response, the Sandinistas used arrests, "disappearances," intimidation, and other secret police tactics against the Miskito Indians and then in December 1981 began the systematic burning of more than forty Indian villages. About 15,000 Indians were forcibly transported to forced labor camps far away from their ancestral lands. The thousands of Indian families who fled into Honduras later became another center of armed resistance.[90]

The Armed Force of Nicaraguan Resistance. The third focal point of armed resistance was in the south. There, in November 1980, the Armed Force of Nicaraguan Resistance (FARN, Fuerza Armada de la Resistencia Nicaragüense) was established by Nicaraguan political leaders who had grown disillusioned with the Sandinistas. It became an active focus of anti-Sandinista operations in 1982 when a flamboyant former Sandinista military commander, Eden Pastora, established the Democratic Revolutionary Alliance (ARDE), based in Costa Rica.

According to an analysis by the U.S. Department of State, the overwhelming majority of the members of the resistance movement were young men in their teens or early twenties, of whom only about 200 among 20,000—or less than 1 percent—ever served in Somoza's National Guard. Among the 147 top military leaders, extensive documentation and analysis indicates that 50 percent were drawn from civilian life and had no previous military experience, 33 percent (forty-nine persons) had served in the Sandinista armed forces, and 17 percent (twenty-five persons) had been with the National Guard.[91]

Over the years the resistance forces generally conducted their operations in accordance with the recognized rules of warfare. For some years they had a manual produced in accordance with International Red Cross standards outlining the code of conduct they were expected to follow. Although in all warfare some innocent civilians are unintended victims of combat and of improper and brutal actions, the evidence shows that the resistance conducted trials and punished individuals convicted of abuses. The Sandinista regime and its allies, however, in an effort to deny the Nicaraguan resistance external aid, mounted a propaganda campaign of staged incidents and false allegations of human rights abuses. A defector from the Nicaraguan secret police "reported that Borge [who controls the secret police] has formed units that wear FDN uniforms and carry out atrocities to discredit the resistance movement."[92]

U.S. Aid to the Contras. In January 1981, the Carter administration suspended U.S. economic aid to the Sandinistas on the basis of evidence that the Sandinistas had provided military support to the Salvadoran Communist guerrillas for their January 1981 offensive. Soon after his inauguration, President Reagan resumed this economic aid and said it would continue only if the Sandinistas ceased all military support to Communist guerrillas. By April 1981 it was clear that the Sandinistas were continuing to give military aid to guerrillas attacking neighboring governments, so President Reagan suspended U.S. economic aid also.

In November 1981, as the Sandinistas continued to give support from their territory to Marxist-Leninist guerrilla and terrorist groups attacking the governments of other countries, the Reagan administration decided as a defensive measure to provide military support to the armed resistance movements in Nicaragua. The administration viewed this aid as entirely consistent with the inherent rights of self-defense under international law. The Sandinista regime had initiated aggression through armed subversion in 1979 and had continued this aggression despite warnings from both the Carter and Reagan administrations over many months.[93] Aid to the Nicaraguan armed resistance was seen as a means of countering Nicaraguan aggression, tying down Sandinista armed forces, thereby making it far more difficult for the Sandinistas to operate air, land, and sea guerrilla supply systems from their territory.

The political-military effectiveness of supporting the Nicaraguan armed resistance was based on the historical experience of insurgency. As the armed resistance expanded, the Sandinistas would have to grow ten times as fast to contain it (according to the classic 10-1 ratio needed against guerrilla forces), placing greater strains on the economy and accelerating the internal collapse of the regime.[94] If the United States were firm in its support of the resistance, and if it announced that it would prevent foreign troops from supporting Nicaraguan combat forces, massive defections might occur, triggering either a Sandinista decision to hold free and fair elections or the emergence of a more moderate faction willing to end armed subver-

269

sion and hold fair elections. Over the next eight years the issue of U.S. military aid to the Nicaraguan armed resistance, or contras, would become one of the most controversial in U.S. foreign policy. While an overwhelming majority of Republican members of Congress (usually 90 percent) supported President Reagan, a majority of Democratic members (usually more than 80 percent) opposed military aid to the resistance. While only a small number of the congressional Democrats disagreed with the Reagan administration on the facts about Nicaragua, most believed that other nonmilitary means should be used to deal with Sandinista actions.

During fiscal years 1982–1984 the United States reportedly provided an estimated $72 million in military aid. During this time the resistance expanded from a few hundred to about 4,000 in 1982 and 14,000 by 1984 (see table 7–6). The rapid growth of the armed resistance was fueled not only by Sandinista repression but also by the Sandinistas' decision in 1983 to begin massive conscription into the Nicaraguan army. The Catholic church explicitly opposed this conscription, arguing that Nicaraguan citizens had no moral obligation to serve in an army under the control of the Sandinista party rather than of the government.

In 1984 the U.S. Congress terminated military aid after press reports of a CIA effort to mine Nicaraguan harbors. But for fiscal years 1985 and 1986 they continued to vote for modest amounts of nonmilitary assistance. With some aid from other countries, the

TABLE 7–6
U.S. AID TO THE NICARAGUAN RESISTANCE, 1982–1989

FY	Estimated Resistance Forces (thousands)	U.S. Funding (millions of dollars)		
		Military	Nonmilitary	Total
1982	4	19		19
1983	7	29		29
1984	14	24		24
1985	20	0	27	27
1986	20	0	14	14
1987	24	70	30	100
1988	20	0	32	32
1989	13	0	48	48
Total		142	151	293

SOURCES: U.S. Department of Defense, U.S. Department of State, *The Challenge to Democracy in Central America*, June 1986, p. 38; *New York Times*, March 25, 1989.

resistance continued expanding, reaching about 20,000 in 1985 and 1986.[95] In June 1986, President Reagan won a key vote in Congress and obtained $100 million for the resistance—$70 million for military and $30 million for nonmilitary aid. This enabled the armed resistance to mount an extensive challenge to the Sandinista regime in 1987, but no further military aid followed. Over the eight years (FY 1982–89), a total of about $293 million is reported to have been provided by the United States, of which $142 million was in military aid.

Organizational Developments. The strongest of the three components of the Nicaraguan resistance had always been the northern forces of the Nicaraguan Democratic Force (FDN). As with all the resistance organizations, the FDN adopted a political program like the one originally promised by the Government of National Reconstruction to the Organization of American States—implementing genuine democracy, maintaining a mixed economy, and conducting a nonaligned foreign policy. This program has always included the explicit willingness of the FDN to participate in and facilitate genuinely democratic elections if the Sandinista regime would provide the necessary conditions: freedom of speech, assembly, and organization.[96] (This is in sharp contrast to the Communist FMLN of El Salvador, which refused to participate in democratic elections and in fact used military attacks and terrorism in efforts to disrupt them.)

In 1985, the United Nicaraguan Opposition (UNO) was established in an effort to unify the FDN and the Miskito Indian resistance movement while also attracting elements of the southern armed resistance (FARN and ARDE) into a broad coalition. The UNO had a military command which was under Colonel Enrique Bermúdez and a political directorate led by Adolfo Calero. All the members of the UNO directorate had been prodemocratic opponents of the Somoza regime who later became opponents of the Sandinista dictatorship.

Later in 1985, however, Eden Pastora and about five hundred of his followers surrendered to the Costa Rican authorities, ending their participation in the armed struggle against the Sandinistas. The next year the newly elected president of Costa Rica, Oscar Arias, began preventing armed resistance operations from Costa Rican territory. He removed from the Costa Rican government those officials who had been helping the contras and closed the contras' support facilities.

Meanwhile, the contras' efforts at unification met only partial success as differences remained among the leaders of the three resistance groups, especially regarding the allocation of outside support. Adolfo Calero resigned temporarily from the UNO directorate in February 1987, and Arturo Cruz, Sr., resigned in March complaining that the FDN military leadership was exerting disproportionate influence.

Then, in May 1987, the UNO and the Southern Opposition Bloc (the successor to FARN) agreed to form the Resistencia Nicaragüense (RN), a multiparty coalition to be led by a seven-man civilian directorate. A Nicaraguan Resistance Assembly was established, composed of representatives in exile of the major democratic political parties, of democratic trade unions, business and agriculture, and community organizations in the south and the Indian region. This assembly chose the Nicaraguan Resistance Directorate, which had authority over the political and military components of the Nicaraguan resistance (see figure 7-4).

At the same time, the Yatama Assembly was established consisting of village, religious, and military leaders from the Indian and black communities in the Atlantic coast region (see figure 7-4). The Yatama Assembly and the Council of Elders of the Indian communities chose the directorate of the Yatama resistance movement. By the spring of 1987, these two resistance coalitions together accounted for about 24,000 armed insurgents, of which about 15,000 were under the Nicaraguan Resistance Directorate, many having been part of the FDN over several years. These new institutions were to establish civilian contol over resistance military operations and to provide a broad array of prodemocratic Nicaraguan leaders with experience in pluralist decision making and governance.

The resistance movement continually faced threats from the large Nicaraguan secret police, intelligence, and military forces. They also faced the challenge of surviving in a complex international political environment, in which the Democratic majority in the U.S. Congress was increasingly unwilling to provide military assistance.

Military Developments, 1982–1988

Military operations of the resistance forces expanded in 1982 and 1983 and then ebbed in 1984 and 1985 as a result of the 1984 cutoff of military aid by Congress. During this time, the contras reduced the Sandinistas' ability to help the Communist guerrillas in El Salvador and Guatemala, and those insurgencies began to contract.

In 1985 Congress refused for the second year in a row to provide military aid to the Nicaraguan resistance but did provide $27 million in nonmilitary assistance. President Reagan, however, was opposed to termination of military aid to the Nicaraguan resistance on the basis of mere promises by the Sandinistas to democratize and take

272

other actions in the future, and in remarks at the White House on April 4, 1985, he reaffirmed his four-part policy toward Central America (democratization, economic improvement, defense against both violent states, and diplomacy) and called upon Congress to provide monthly aid to the contras. This was not done in 1985, and President Reagan tried again to obtain this aid in early 1986. But on March 20, 1986, in a 222-210 vote the Democratic majority in the U.S. Congress again rejected President Reagan's request for military aid to the resistance forces.

Only days later the Sandinistas massed an estimated 20,000 troops and launched an invasion of Honduras, seeking to destroy the resistance forces in their border camps. The United States was quick to provide the Honduran government with increased military aid, including a helicopter airlift that enabled it to move its defense forces to the border region. In the meantime, the contras inflicted heavy casualties on the invading Sandinista army and then moved more of their combat forces back into Nicaragua. By May 1986, there were an estimated 8,000 to 10,000 contras fighting inside Nicaragua on the northern front.

In June 1986, after President Reagan made a second effort to persuade the legislators, Congress approved $100 million in aid ($70 million for military purposes, $30 million for nonmilitary) for the Nicaraguan resistance, as noted earlier. The tide had turned; the president won a major political victory. This success was followed by a flow of additional supplies to the contras, but it did not begin until late 1986.

Starting in September 1986, after a two-year lull, Indian resistance fighters became more active. But in October the Sandinistas shot down a resupply plane that was part of a privately established network. In November the Iran-contra issue surfaced, leading to the removal of two U.S. National Security Council officials who without presidential authority had diverted funds from an authorized military sale to Iran into the private contra supply network. This revelation put President Reagan on the political defensive for two reasons: first, he had to investigate to determine what had occurred while Congress itself conducted two investigations; second, many in Congress contended that the diverted funds amounted to a circumvention of congressional prohibitions on military aid to the contras by the Department of Defense or the Central Intelligence Agency.[97]

These events and the unfriendly attitude of the new Arias government in Costa Rica meant that toward the end of 1986, resistance military operations virtually ceased in the southern part of Nicaragua, as the Sandinistas launched strong attacks there. By the end of 1986,

FIGURE 7-4
Organization of Nicaraguan Resistance, 1987

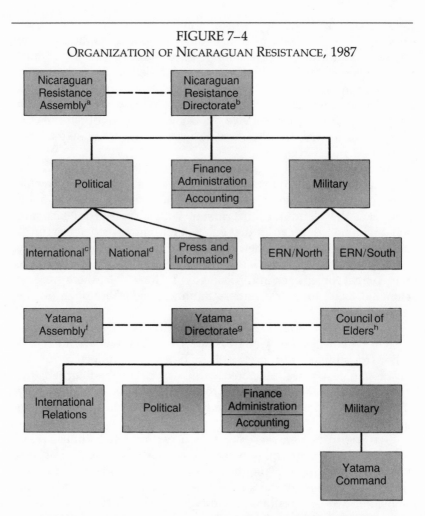

Note: ERN-National Resistance Army; BOS-Opposition Block of the South.

a. The Resistance Assembly, an advisory body to the Resistance Directorate, is composed of 54 representatives-in-exile of the Social Democratic, Liberal, Conservative, and Social Christian Parties; representatives from labor, business, and agricultural sectors of society; as well as BOS and the Atlantic Coast.

b. In May 1987, the Nicaraguan Resistance (RN) Directorate was formed. It comprises six civilians of equal ranking: Aristides Sanchez, Alfonso Robelo, Azucena Ferrey, Pedro Joaquin Chamorro, Alfredo Cesar, and Adolfo Calero. A seventh seat is reserved for a member of the Yatama Directorate.

c. The International Relations Committee, headed by Donald Castillo, represents the Nicaraguan Resistance in such countries as Costa Rica, Guatemala, Panama, Colombia, Argentina, Canada, Venezuela, Italy, Spain, France, and the Federal Republic of Germany.

274

there were about 12,000 resistance troops in the north of Nicaragua (and several thousand in Honduras) but only about 1,000 remaining in the south.

But in 1987 the resumption of U.S. military assistance helped the contras attain steadily increasing success. Contra strategy called for thousands of resistance troops beginning to reinfiltrate Nicaragua to establish a presence throughout the country, prevent government troops from dislodging them, challenge Sandinista authority and control, and capture the popular imagination in preparation for larger offensives. Starting in February 1987, the contras sharply accelerated their hit-and-run attacks on military vehicles, garrisons, electrical and communications facilities, and the much larger Sandinista army units sent to prevent their reinfiltration. They reported 119 such actions in February, which equaled the number mounted at the peak of their activity in 1985.[98] As reported in the *New Republic* of April 6, 1987, Enrique Bermúdez claimed his troops initiated sixty clashes per week with the Sandinistas in the first two months of that year. The article also reported that James LeMoyne of the *New York Times* and Peter Collins of ABC found the contras well trained and enthusiastic during a two-day stay with them in late March 1987. According to the same article, Gen. Paul F. Gorman, former chief of the Panama-based U.S. Southern Command, stated on February 24, 1987, that "the Nicaraguan rebels of the FDN have a fighting chance to present to the Nicaraguan people an alternative to the oppression and militarism of the government in Managua."

Some 500 U.S.-made Redeye missiles, purchased with part of the $100 million allocated by Congress, reportedly began to arrive in late

---

d. The National Committee is responsible for domestic and exile political affairs.

e. Press and information is responsible for media liaison, press, and public affairs, as well as the production and broadcasting of *Radio Liberacion*, and the production of the monthly journal, *Resistencia*.

f. The Yatama Assembly consists of village, military, and religious leaders throughout the Atlantic Coast region. The June 1987 Assembly had more than 1,500 participants, with some 49 towns and villages represented.

g. The Yatama Directorate is composed of six Atlantic Coast leaders in exile: Brooklyn Rivera, Stedman Fagoth, and Wycliffe Diego (all Miskito Indians), Morlan Charley Lopez (Sumo Indian), and Walter Ortiz (Rama Indian). The sixth seat is reserved for a representative of the Creole (black) population.

h. The Council of Elders, composed of recognized tribal leaders, is to perform judicial functions and advise the Yatama Directorate.

SOURCE: U.S. Department of State, *Nicaraguan Biographies: A Resource Book*, Special Report no. 174, January 1988, p. 41.

May 1987, enabling contra troops to shoot down numerous Sandinista aircraft. By late July 1987 the resistance claimed to have shot down at least ten helicopters, about 20 percent of Nicaragua's air force. According to diplomats in Managua, in early July 1987 Nicaragua's air force included some fifty-two helicopters—forty MI-17s or MI-8s, and some twelve MI-24 and MI-25 helicopter gunships. In addition, six Soviet MI-17 replacement helicopters had arrived at the port of Corinto in late June 1987. In all, the Soviets delivered close to 15,900 tons of military supplies to the Sandinistas in the first half of 1987, compared with 12,500 tons during the same period in 1986 (23,000 tons for all of 1986).[99]

Air resupply flights to the contras increased dramatically in the spring of 1987, allowing their units to range widely. More than 200 tons of supplies were reportedly dropped between April and late June. According to Major Adolfo Chamorro of the Sandinista Defense Ministry, CIA supply flights averaged at least one per day since late March. Western diplomats estimated thirty to forty flights per month since April. As contra attacks increased throughout northwest and southwest Nicaragua, including Managua, U.S. officials were reported as stating that the resistance could soon pose a major threat to Sandinista rule.[100]

By mid-1987 the resistance reported 1,360 armed clashes in the first half of 1987, estimating nearly 3,000 government troops killed and a similar number wounded. This casualty rate indicated a large increase in military activity over 1986 (when 866 clashes had left a reported 2,247 Sandinistas dead and 3,159 injured). For the period of January to July 1987 the contras were reported to have shot down thirteen Sandinista helicopters, destroyed fifty-five army barracks and bases, and captured large amounts of weaponry and ammunition. At a July 1987 State Department briefing, a U.S. military official stated that some 14,000 contra combatants were operating inside Nicaragua and that 355 tons of supplies had been successfully airdropped to them.[101]

Resistance forces in the north of Nicaragua launched an offensive in late August 1987 that netted them sharp gains. According to the resistance, their forces fought the Sandinistas in 276 separate clashes in August, an almost 50 percent increase over the 186 reported in July. Ninety-one battles took place during the first half of September, fifty-four of them in central Nicaragua (Jinotega and Matagalpa provinces).

By early September the resistance had gained an unprecedented foothold in central Nicaragua. According to local residents, contra forces appeared to operate from bases in the mountains northeast of the town of Muy Muy in Matagalpa province. By early October the contras could move about freely and were close to establishing a semipermanent presence in three eastern provinces—Matagalpa, Boaco, and Chontales. Fighting in this region often closed nearby roads for days at a time.

By their own account, the Sandinistas came under increasing contra pressure in September 1987, reporting 300–400 battles per month in more than two-thirds of Nicaragua. Early in the month, contra forces regained their stronghold in the northern Bocay region of Jinotega province, which they had evacuated the previous year. On September 8 contras attacked the military garrison at La Patriota; on September 11 they raided Sandinista military bases at El Achiote and Walawa near Rio Blanco; and on September 14 they launched an ambush that destroyed four Soviet-made jeeps. On September 25, contras with Redeye missiles shot down two Soviet-made MI-25 helicopters in Matagalpa and another in Zelaya Sur, near Nueva Guinea. According to contra spokesmen, the resistance fought 297 battles with the Sandinistas in September, most of which took place in Jinotega, inflicting 1,751 casualties on the regime.[102] Indian resistance activity in the northeast also increased.

On October 1, 1987, fiscal year 1987 military funding from the United States ended—although supplies remained "in the pipeline." Congress then began stopgap funding for the resistance, which included $20 million in nonmilitary aid. Contra forces increased resistance activity in October 1987, impressing Western diplomatic observers by successfully carrying out coordinated assaults in several parts of the country. Citing the military effectiveness of the attacks and related diversionary moves, European and Latin American diplomats in Managua reportedly praised the resistance as a serious fighting force. According to these reports, contra commanders prefaced one major assault with an elaborate feint several miles north to divert Sandinista attention. Nearly one thousand contra troops stationed across a sixty-mile region in two central provinces succeeded in drawing at least two elite government battalions northward away from the target region three days before the main attack. These diversionary actions also resulted in the shooting down of a Sandinista MI-17 transport helicopter.

In October 1987, Bermúdez said his forces had achieved a capacity to attack Sandinista forces with "relative freedom." The contras claimed to be fighting about ten engagements daily against the Sandinistas, almost double the rate of summer 1987. In early October they launched a large offensive along the Rama road, shutting down the Sandinistas' most important supply line. Figure 7–5 provides an

277

FIGURE 7-5
RESISTANCE ACTIVITIES AND FORCED REMOVAL OF POPULATION BY THE SANDINISTA REGIME, 1987

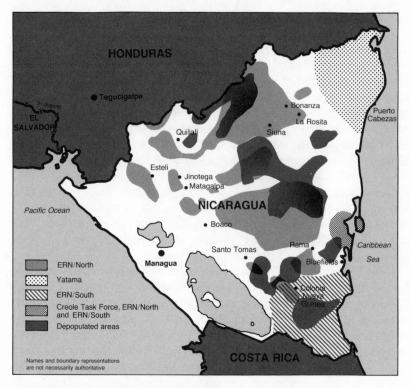

NOTE: ERN-National Resistance Army.
SOURCE: U.S. Department of State, *Nicaraguan Biographies: A Resource Book*, Special Report no. 174, January 1988, p. 49.

overview of resistance activities and forced removals of the population by the Sandinista regime in the autumn of 1987.

By November 1987 the Sandinistas were putting heavy pressure on the contras, including sweeps through the northern hills, but in a tactical shift they did not use planes. The contras' U.S.-supplied Redeyes, it was clear, had begun to neutralize the enormous Sandinista air advantage. Mounting Sandinista casualty figures reflected the increased pace of resistance actions in late 1987.

By the end of 1987 the Nicaraguan resistance had reached its military high point, operating continually and effectively in half of Nicaragua. It had countered the Sandinista air force and was attacking government positions in the northern, central, and southern

278

parts of the country. In December, more than seven thousand resistance troops launched a massive, coordinated operation in which they captured and briefly held the northeastern towns of Siuna, Bonanza, and La Rosita. The armed resistance was also active in the southern zone in December 1987.[103]

Contra forces kept up this heavy military pressure on the Sandinistas during the first two months of 1988. In February 1988 southern front forces clashed with Sandinista troops in twelve engagements in the provinces of Rio San Juan, central Zelaya, and southern Zelaya, inflicting eighty-one casualties. That same month, the U.S. House of Representatives rejected President Reagan's request for $36 million in contra aid, including $3.6 million in military aid. Congress also rejected a Democratic alternative of $30 million in nonmilitary aid because the Republicans wanted another vote on military aid. Meanwhile, as has been noted, in 1986 the Soviet Union increased its military support to the Sandinistas, supplying them with over $500 million in military aid during 1987 and $100 million during the first three months of 1988.

As in 1985, once the U.S. congress delayed and then cut off military aid, the military position of the contras steadily declined. In mid-March 1988 some two thousand Sandinistas again attacked across the border into Honduras in a pincer movement aimed at the contras' supply facilities and headquarters complex. Three thousand U.S. troops were quickly airlifted to Honduras to back up the Honduran forces that met the Sandinista attack. With the help of a Honduran air strike against the invaders, the resistance held its ground and launched a successful counterattack.

At the end of March 1988, Sandinista and contra negotiators agreed to a sixty-day truce beginning April 1 in order to facilitate negotiations. Two resistance leaders have indicated that some Democratic members of the U.S. Congress told them Congress would cut off even nonmilitary aid unless they agreed to this truce.[104] Nevertheless, in the months following the cutoff of U.S. military aid, thousands of resistance soldiers were forced by shortages and Sandinista attacks in violation of the truce to return to Honduras. By mid-1988 about 11,000 had taken refuge in the border zone, with the number increasing to twelve thousand late in the year.

In April 1988, Congress approved $48 million in nonmilitary aid for the resistance. The food, medicine, and other nonmilitary supplies bought with this money arrived slowly, and the resulting shortages contributed to dissension within the resistance. Some contra commanders complained that their fighters were on the brink of starvation as they prepared to withdraw from Nicaragua to Honduras. These tensions over supply shortages came to a head in April and May 1988, when several important field commanders rebelled against Enrique Bermúdez and unsuccessfully tried to force his removal as military commander.

At the end of 1988 Republican Congressman David Drier of California visited contra camps along the Nicaraguan border. His delegation reported that contra morale was high, that the forces were ready, and that the resistance leaders and soldiers were convinced that the United States would not let them down by denying them military assistance.[105] American officials overseeing distribution of nonmilitary aid also reported that contra morale continued to be high.

By the winter of 1988, however, only about 2,000 to 3,000 contras remained inside Nicaragua, and only small numbers could move in and out of the country, engaging in sporadic conflict throughout the year. Military activity remained minimal after March 1988; the military success of 1987 had effects on Sandinista diplomacy, and the focus shifted from late 1987 to the international negotiations.

International Dimensions of the Conflict

The balance of forces in the conflict between the Sandinistas and the resistance has been directly affected since 1981 by the evolution of U.S. Central America policy and by international political events.

From its first days in office, the Reagan administration recognized that it faced two major foreign policy challenges in Central America: the need to help friendly Central American countries institutionalize democracy and resist the expanding Marxist-Leninist threat from insurgency and political subversion and the need to find ways of persuading the Sandinista regime in Nicaragua to implement its democratic promises to the Organization of American States and to end its armed subversion against peaceful neighboring countries. These two imperatives of U.S. foreign policy would become the focal point of highly partisan political controversy within Congress during both Reagan terms.

As we have seen, during four of its eight years, the Reagan administration was not able to obtain support from a majority in Congress for continuing military aid to the Nicaraguan armed resistance. After it did succeed in obtaining support for its policies toward the four friendly Central American countries, promising results were visible there by 1989, when democratic transitions were firmly under way. This progress remained fragile and reversible, however, as the Communist regime in Nicaragua continued to work with the Soviet

Union and Cuba in helping Marxist-Leninist guerrillas attack El Salvador, Guatemala, Honduras, and other countries.

Reagan's Central America Policy. In March 1981, President Reagan stated that he opposed the violent right in El Salvador as well as the violent left and supported reforms, begun in 1980, that provided land for hundreds of thousands of formerly landless peasants, with compensation to be paid the former owners. In January 1981 and again in August 1981 the Reagan administration also made overtures to normalize relations with Nicaragua on condition that the Sandinistas cease their aggression through armed subversion.

For the friendly countries of Central America, President Reagan defined a strategy with four elements: (1) the encouragement of democracy; (2) substantially increased economic aid for development and improved living conditions; (3) increased military assistance to help them defend themselves against both the violent left and the violent right; and (4) active diplomacy to bring about genuine political settlements. Speaking to a joint session of Congress on April 27, 1983, the president formally enunciated these four basic aspects of U.S. policy for Central America:

> First . . . we will support democracy, reform and human freedom. This means using our assistance, our powers of persuasion and our legitimate internal "leverage" to bolster humane democratic systems where they already exist and help countries on their way to that goal complete the process as quickly as new institutions can be changed. . . . Second, we will support economic development. By a margin of two to one our aid is economic. . . . Third, in response to the military challenge from Cuba and Nicaragua—to their deliberate use of force to spread tyranny—we will support the security of the region's threatened nations. We do not view security assistance as an end in itself but as a shield for democratization, economic development and diplomacy. No amount of reform will bring peace so long as guerrillas believe they will win by force. . . . Fourth, we will support dialogue and negotiations—both among the countries in the region and within each country.[106]

During the early 1980s, a significant number of Democratic members of Congress opposed President Reagan's policy on El Salvador. They believed that instead of relying on democratic elections and military aid to encourage democracy and combat insurgency, the United States should press for a negotiated internal settlement involving power sharing between the government and the Marxist-Leninist guerrilla groups, a point of view shared by Mexico. The newly elected

281

Socialist government of France also endorsed it when in August 1981 it issued a statement jointly with Mexico calling for recognition of the Marxist-Leninist guerrillas and negotiations between them and the Salvadoran government to establish a new government through power sharing. This approach was immediately rejected in a joint statement by El Salvador and fifteen Latin American countries.

In a meeting in December 1981, by an overwhelming vote of nineteen to one, the OAS called on its members to support the process of democratic elections in El Salvador. At the OAS meeting, Secretary of State Alexander Haig explained the policy of the United States as follows: "President Reagan has made clear that we have no plans to send combat troops to Central America. But we will provide needed economic and military assistance. Small countries must be able to call for help when help is needed."[107]

In March 1982, the people of El Salvador voted in overwhelming numbers despite a countrywide terrorist campaign by the Communist guerrillas seeking to prevent the elections. These elections marked the beginning of the transition to democracy in El Salvador, demonstrating the soundness of the administration's prodemocratic policy. Nevertheless, a majority of Democratic members of the U.S. Congress voted to provide only half the military assistance for El Salvador requested by the administration, because they continued to favor a political coalition with the Salvadoran guerrillas rather than a military solution—that is, the defeat of the Communist guerrillas.

In October 1982, Costa Rica convened a meeting of seven Caribbean Basin democracies, including the United States. They issued the Declaration of San Jose, calling for the encouragement of democratic institutions and opposing the hostile activities of the Sandinista regime, including its aggression and massive military buildup.[108] At about the same time, the United States announced the Caribbean Basin Initiative, which provided one-way, free trade access to the U.S. market, the world's largest. This offer was made to countries of the Caribbean Basin, including Central America, that met certain criteria, including the observance of human rights and movement toward political democracy. This initiative was part of the tangible commitment of the Reagan administration to provide increased economic help for Central America, as demonstrated by the increase in economic assistance from the very modest amount of $61.8 million in 1978 to $369 million in fiscal year 1982, $631 million in fiscal year 1983, $830 million in fiscal year 1984, and $1.1 billion in fiscal year 1985 (in constant 1983 dollars).[109]

A Bipartisan Commission. In 1983, in an effort to achieve a domestic political consensus on Central America, President Reagan announced the formation of a bipartisan commission. It would have a staff and access to U.S. officials and information, and would produce in six months a comprehensive, in-depth analysis of the issues accompanied by policy recommendations for the administration. Henry Jackson, the highly respected Democratic senator from Washington, had suggested the bipartisan commission to President Reagan, and UN Ambassador Jeane Kirkpatrick endorsed it. Jackson had become extremely concerned about the trend of events in Central America, fearing that the continued success of Soviet- and Cuban-backed Marxist-Leninist guerrilla movements posed a direct threat of a Communist takeover in Central America and Mexico. In 1982 he had warned: "Leftist revolts in Nicaragua, El Salvador, and Guatemala are the preliminary stage for the ultimate assault on Mexico, the true Soviet objective in the Western Hemisphere."[110] Former Secretary of State Henry Kissinger chaired the bipartisan commission, which included Nicholas Brady (appointed secretary of the treasury in 1989), Henry Cisneros (mayor of San Antonio, Texas), Lane Kirkland (president of the AFL-CIO), Richard Scammon (scholar), John Silber (president of Boston University), Potter Stewart (former associate justice of the Supreme Court), and Robert Strauss (former chairman of the Democratic National Committee).

In its January 1984 report to President Reagan, the Kissinger Commission, as it was called in the media, concluded that the balanced approach of President Reagan to the crisis in Central America was correct, but the level of both economic and security aid should be substantially increased. It also concluded that "as Nicaragua was already doing, additional Marxist-Leninist regimes in Central America could be expected to expand their armed forces . . . bring in large numbers of Cuban and other Soviet-bloc advisers, [and] develop sophisticated agencies of internal repression and external subversion."[111] The consequences, the commission said, would include a permanently increased U.S. defense burden, far greater limitations on America's ability to defend its commitments in other parts of the world, and "almost surely" a stream of refugees, perhaps millions of them, seeking entry into the United States.

Acting on the commission's recommendations, in February 1984 President Reagan sent Congress a proposal for a five-year program of expanded economic and military assistance to include about $7.9 billion in economic aid and guarantees for fiscal years 1985–1989 and about $515 million in military assistance for Central America for the next two fiscal years.[112]

But despite the bipartisan composition of the commission and the overwhelming emphasis of President Reagan's program on democratic institution building and economic improvement, many Democrats in Congress remained in opposition, especially to the proposal to provide increased levels of military aid to El Salvador. In fiscal years 1981–1984, the administration had requested a total of $532 million in military aid for El Salvador, but Congress approved $263 million.

Reagan's Appeal to the Nation. In May 1984, after another round of genuinely democratic national elections in El Salvador, in which the voters chose center-left Christian Democrat Duarte as president, Reagan confronted the Democratic majority in the U.S. Congress on his Central America policy. In a nationally televised speech to the nation on May 9, he warned that the ultimate consequences of failure to help the friendly countries of Central America to defend themselves could be

> a communist Central America with additional communist military bases on the mainland of this hemisphere and communist subversion spreading southward and northward. This communist subversion poses a threat that one hundred million people from Panama to the open border on our south could come under the control of pro-Soviet regimes.

This was the first of many warnings by President Reagan that both Mexico and Panama could come under the control of pro-Soviet Communist dictatorships unless Congress provided the resources needed to support democracy and defeat communism.

Further, President Reagan pointed out that in 1983, while the Soviet bloc had provided Cuba and Nicaragua with $4.9 billion in economic and military support, total U.S. assistance to all of Central America was about $800 million. He put the stakes clearly: "The simple questions are, will we support freedom in this hemisphere or not? Will we defend our vital interests in this hemisphere or not? Will we stop the spread of communism in this hemisphere or not?" Summarizing the progress made toward democracy in the region, he noted that in El Salvador land reform was moving forward, benefiting more than 550,000 peasants since March 1980. Progress in land reform, however, was not tantamount to the elimination of the Communist threat, as the president pointed out: "Many can't farm their land; they'd be killed by the [Communist] guerrillas if they do." The president then declared:

> If the communists can start war against the people of El Salvador, then El Salvador and its friends are surely justified

in defending themselves by blocking the flow of arms. If the Soviet Union can aid and abet subversion in our hemisphere, then the United States has a legal right and a moral duty to help resist it.

At the close of this speech the president repeated the words of President Harry Truman when he proposed the Truman Doctrine in 1947 before a joint session of Congress: " 'The free peoples of the world look to us for support in maintaining their freedoms. If we falter . . . we may endanger the peace of the world, and we shall surely endanger the welfare of this nation.' " President Reagan concluded: "Communist subversion is not an irreversible tide. We've seen it rolled back . . . the tide of the future can be a freedom tide. All it takes is the will and resouces to get the job done."[113]

The day following this dramatic appeal to the nation the president won the vote in Congress on economic and military aid for Central America by the narrow margin of 212 to 208. As had been the pattern over the years, about 85 percent of the Democratic members of the House voted against Reagan's funding request, while virtually all the Republicans voted with him. From that point through 1989, the administration continued to find just enough Democratic support to maintain economic and security assistance for the friendly Central American countries.

The trend of events showed that the Reagan administration's prodemocratic policy for Central America was working. Honduras had made a peaceful transition to democracy, and in 1985 there was a new round of presidential elections and a peaceful transfer of power to the newly elected president. El Salvador's reformist President Duarte served through the end of his term in June 1989, when the successful presidential candidate of the democratic right succeeded him in another peaceful transfer of authority. Guatemala held constituent assembly elections in 1984 and open elections for the presidency in 1985; a reformist Christian Democrat, Vinicio Cerezo, was inaugurated in January 1986. Costa Rica maintained its democracy with free elections in 1982 and 1986, with the next scheduled for 1990.

As these positive changes were occurring in Central America, the net strength of the Communist guerrilla groups declined in El Salvador and Guatemala, as did their levels of popular support. As already noted in the case of Guatemala, an important factor in permitting and preserving democratic gains was the growing strength of the armed democratic resistance inside Nicaragua, because coping with this challenge forced Managua to divert resources from its support for subversion in the region. But on this issue President

Reagan did not receive continued support from enough Democrats in Congress.

Opposition to U.S. Military Aid. Ironically, 1984, the same year that marked a positive turning point in congressional support for President Reagan's policy toward the friendly countries in Central America, marked a negative turning point for the military aid to the Nicaraguan resistance undertaken by the administration in late 1981. Press reports in April 1984 that the United States had been directly involved in the mining of a Nicaraguan harbor added fuel to arguments building against further military aid. In 1983, a Democratic majority in the House had voted against such aid, but it had been approved by the Republican-controlled Senate and subsequently by the full Congress.[114] In dealing with the mining controversy, in which some members of the Senate Select Committee on Intelligence claimed they had not been adequately briefed, the White House released an unprecedented joint statement by the secretaries of state and defense, the national security adviser, and the director of central intelligence, which said in part:

> We state emphatically that we have not considered, nor have we developed plans to use U.S. military forces to invade Nicaragua. . . . It has been alleged by critics of the administration that certain activities in the Central American region have not been adequately briefed to appropriate committees of the Congress. To the contrary, all U.S. activities in the Central America region have been fully briefed in detail to the committees of the Congress which exercise jurisdiction.

Another source of congressional opposition to U.S. aid to the Nicaraguan resistance stemmed from reports that the contras were involved in narcotics smuggling. Senator John Kerry, a Democrat from Massachusetts, pursued these allegations over several years in a subcommittee investigation. On April 13, 1989, a U.S. Senate subcommittee headed by Senator Kerry issued a report, which concluded that "there was no evidence that Contra leaders were smuggling drugs, but individual Contras and mercenaries were [involved]." The report essentially absolved the Nicaraguan resistance movement as an organization of allegations of drug smuggling but said the Reagan administration had been lax in "failing to provide law enforcement . . . with the support information they needed to make arrests or otherwise enforce the law." The ranking Republican on the subcommittee, Senator Mitch McConnell of Kentucky, criticized the report for inaccuracies and misleading conclusions.[115]

Some in the administration had urged President Reagan to move immediately to follow up on his May 1984 success in getting military aid to El Salvador. That was the time, they argued, for him to seek a vote on military aid to the contras. Others contended he should wait until the end of the fiscal year in September 1984 to make this request. By that time, however, the Democratic majority in Congress had an additional argument to use against further aid to the Nicaraguan resistance.

The Contadora Process. A multilateral diplomatic process had been set in motion in January 1983 in the hope of arriving at a comprehensive political settlement of the conflicts in Central America. It was known as the Contadora process because it originated with a meeting of the foreign ministers of Colombia, Mexico, Venezuela, and Panama on the Panamanian resort island of Contadora. By September 1983, these four countries, acting as mediators, had held meetings with the five Central American countries and produced a statement of twenty-one objectives, which included the implementation of genuine democracy in Nicaragua and an end to its aggression through armed subversion. The United States had supported this diplomatic initiative—sending special presidential envoys to travel between the participating countries in an effort to facilitate the negotiations—and endorsed the twenty-one objectives.[116]

Mexico had taken the lead in the Contadora process from the start. After the visit of Castro in 1979, Mexico had pursued an unabashedly pro-Sandinista diplomacy in Central America, often in close coordination with the leadership in Managua and Havana. When the Carter administration sought in June and July 1979 to establish an OAS peace force to ensure that the Sandinista-led interim government would abide by its democratic commitments to the OAS, Mexico blocked the proposal. In early 1981, following condemnation by the Carter administration of Managua's military support to the Salvadoran Communist guerrillas, the head of Mexico's governing party flew to Managua, where he offered the Sandinistas full solidarity and made threats against the United States. And it was the president of Mexico who in 1982 had proposed a "peace plan" for Central America that would have involved cutting off all U.S. military aid to the Central American countries, leaving the Sandinista regime in place and the Nicaraguan armed resistance without any aid.

In September 1984, the first draft of the Contadora treaty was produced; it essentially followed the formula proposed by Mexico in 1982. It was immediately accepted by Nicaragua's ruling directorate, *provided that there would be no changes of any kind.* Many Communist governments and their supporters promptly launched a massive propaganda and political action campaign aimed at pressuring the governments of Central America to sign this draft treaty. At the same time, Democrats in the U.S. Congress who strongly opposed military aid to the Nicaraguan resistance used this proposed treaty to demand that the United States "give the peace process a chance" by cutting off additional military funding for the contras.

In late September 1984, the four friendly Central American countries rejected this first draft. They contended that it served Managua's overriding objective of prohibiting aid to the contras upon signature, while leaving the issue of their aggressive behavior to later negotiations. Another objection was that not only were the verification provisions weak, but there were no provisions for enforcement. Despite this rejection by the four friendly Central American countries, Congress refused to continue military aid to the contras, leaving President Reagan with the choice of going along or of vetoing a massive end-of-year appropriation bill. Such a veto would have temporarily suspended the operations of the U.S. government on the eve of the U.S. presidential election, and the president was forced to accept the cutoff.

Meanwhile, in June 1984 U.S. Secretary of State Shultz had initiated a series of bilateral U.S.–Nicaraguan negotiations. Although nine sessions were held, they produced no results and the initiative was suspended in early 1985. The Contadora negotiations were also derailed during 1985 by Sandinistan armed incursions into Costa Rica, sparking strong Costa Rican protests to the OAS.

In August 1985, Mexico and the other three Contadora mediating countries brought in an additional four Latin American countries—Argentina, Brazil, Peru, and Uruguay—as the "Contadora support group." But Mexico continued to play the dominant role and took the lead in drafting successive versions of a Contadora treaty. When a third draft was presented to the Central American countries in September 1985, Costa Rica, Honduras, El Salvador, and Guatemala once again rejected it as not meeting the original twenty-one objectives. At the end of 1985, the Sandinista regime formally proposed to the OAS that Contadora negotiations be suspended until May 1986, when a new president of Costa Rica would take office.

In March 1986 the Sandinistas attacked the resistance in Honduras, stiffening the resolve of the Central American countries to win realization of the 1983 objectives. Nevertheless, the Contadora mediating and support group countries under Mexico's leadership went on to produce yet another treaty draft in June 1986—perhaps with the aim, as in 1984, of undercutting President Reagan's prospects for winning an impending congressional vote on military aid for the contras. Once again the proposed treaty would have required an immediate halt to U.S. funding of the Nicaraguan resistance while allowing the Sandinistas to delay negotiating reductions in weapons and troop levels. And once again the four friendly Central American countries rejected the defective Contadora draft.

Iran-Contra and the Arias Plan. In November 1986 the series of revelations that came to be known as the Iran-contra affair changed the political vectors, first in the United States and then in Central America. The presidentially authorized sale of weapons to supposed moderate factions in Iran undercut the Reagan administration's strong stand against terrorism. Although the president insisted it was not an "arms for hostages" deal, it had that appearance. Moreover, the administration had been urging U.S. allies not to provide arms to Iran, and this revelation made it look hypocritical.

The evidence concerning unauthorized diversions by administration officials of profits from those weapons sales to the Nicaraguan armed resistance prompted investigations, first by President Reagan (the Tower Commission) and then by both houses of Congress from December 1986 through August 1987. With a cloud of scandal thus settling over the Reagan presidency and gravely weakening it, President Oscar Arias of Costa Rica offered in February 1987 an alternative to the failed Contadora negotiating process in the form of his own plan for a Central American peace agreement.

Over several years Mexico had tilted the political dynamics of the Contadora negotiating process toward Nicaragua. Initially, among the nine countries (five Central American and four mediating countries), there had been essential agreement among four Central American and three mediating countries against the views of Mexico and Nicaragua. As Mexico vigorously pushed its position, however, and the United States failed to counter it effectively in bilateral conversations with the other mediating countries, the balance shifted. All four mediating countries joined Nicaragua against the four other Central American states, resulting in a five to four split in 1984 and early 1985. Then, with the addition of the four Contadora support group countries, the balance became nine to four in the autumn of 1985. Mexican pressures gradually moved Guatemala to the Mexican side in 1986, making the lineup ten to three, with only Costa Rica, El Salvador, and Honduras holding out against the Mexican (and Sandinista-Cuban) viewpoint.

With the Contadora process at an impasse, President Arias in February 1987 proposed his peace plan. Like the Contadora draft treaty, it required an immediate end to aid to the contras, but also required a process of democratization leading to free elections within each country, including Nicaragua (as President Reagan had called for since 1981). But despite positive rhetorical goals, the Arias plan retained most of the serious deficiencies of implementation from the previously rejected Contadora treaty drafts. Nevertheless, since Mexico and the other Contadora countries endorsed it, the effect was a further shift in the political equation—to eleven to two, with El Salvador and Honduras refusing to accept the Arias plan. As with the draft Contadora treaties, they viewed its key deficiency as the prior dismantling of the contras without any guarantee of genuine democracy in Nicaragua.

The resistance of El Salvador and Honduras to pressures from Mexico and other Contadora states to accept the earlier draft treaties and the 1987 Arias plan was rooted in their understanding of the Sandinista regime. They also believed that President Reagan would persist—and ultimately succeed—in his efforts to obtain military support from Congress for the Nicaraguan armed resistance. The Iran-contra affair, however, began to undermine their confidence.

Congressional opponents of aid to the contras had confidently expected the Iran-contra hearings to reinforce their coalition within the U.S. Congress. Instead, the nationally televised testimony of administration witnesses at the congressional investigation gave millions of Americans their first opportunity to learn what the Sandinistas had been doing in Central America. As the hearings ended in August 1987, many Republican members of Congress believed the tide of public opinion had turned in support of aid to the contras. Republican Congressmen Jack Kemp of New York and Henry Hyde of Illinois urged Reagan to seek full military support of more than $200 million before the end of the fiscal year on September 30, 1987. But aides to House Speaker Jim Wright, White House Chief of Staff Howard Baker, and Secretary of State Shultz worked out a statement to be signed by both President Reagan and Speaker Wright. This compromise formula involved a reiteration of the Sandinistas' obligations to implement democracy and cease aggression through armed subversion but delayed any vote on further military aid to the Nicaraguan resistance pending the outcome of negotiations with the Sandinistas, which would continue at least through the end of September 1987. Against the advice of Secretary of Defense Caspar Weinberger and Congressman Kemp, who warned Reagan of the effects of such an agreement on the Central American summit that was about to consider the Arias plan, the president signed this joint declaration with Speaker Wright on August 5, 1987.

This "Reagan-Wright plan" was interpreted in Central America as the end of President Reagan's insistence that military support should be given to the contras until a democratic government was established in Nicaragua through free and fair elections and its armed subversion of its neighbors ended. Since 1984, President Reagan had rejected a number of State Department initiatives for a political settlement that would have permitted ending aid to the Nicaraguan resistance first in return for Sandinista promises to move toward democracy in the future. Time and again, the president had turned down such proposals coming from within his administration. Time and again he had reiterated his policy objectives as he sought to persuade Congress to approve military aid.[117]

This insistence on the correct sequence—genuine democracy in Nicaragua first, then a cutoff of aid to the contras—had been at the core of opposition by all four friendly Central American countries to Contadora treaty drafts. In rejecting the drafts, these four countries had relied on President Reagan's repeated statements that the contras would receive support until genuine democracy and peace had been attained in Nicaragua.

The impact of the Reagan-Wright plan on the Central American leaders was unintended but predictable. As they now saw it, President Reagan was prevented by the Iran-contra affair from continuing to seek military support for the Nicaraguan resistance. President Duarte of El Salvador confided to the visiting Republican Congressman Jack Kemp that he could not sleep the night he heard about the Reagan-Wright plan, since it seemed to imply Reagan's abandonment of the Nicaraguan resistance.[118]

The Reagan-Wright plan thus became the catalyst that ended years of resistance by El Salvador and Honduras to the pressures from Cuba, Nicaragua, and the eight Contadora countries. On August 7, 1987, the five Central American countries agreed upon a modified version of the Arias plan calling for a cease-fire, negotiations between existing governments and their unarmed opposition, the end of external aid to irregular forces, amnesty with the release of political prisoners, and steps toward the democratization of Nicaragua. Within ninety days after reaching agreement on the plan, the five Central American foreign ministers were to meet again to assess progress on the cease-fire, amnesty, and internal democratization. An international verification commission, decided upon some days after the plan was announced, was to consist of representatives appointed by the eight mediating and support group countries, the five Central American countries, and the secretaries general of the OAS and the United Nations.

This verification commission would, in effect, bring the Contadora countries into the Arias plan in an important operational role and thereby provide Nicaragua with likely support, given Mexico's influence over those countries on this issue and the years of close Mexican, Nicaraguan, and Cuban cooperation. The verification group was to meet in 120 days and then report to the Central American presidents shortly before the presidents' final assessment of compliance with the Arias plan, 150 days from the signing (January 1988).

The Arias plan as agreed upon was widely and warmly hailed by opinion leaders in the United States, Latin America, and Europe. Symbolic of this euphoria was the award to President Arias of the Nobel Peace Prize in October 1987. Yet some analysts were skeptical. Dr. Susan Kaufman Purcell wrote in *Foreign Affairs* (Fall 1987) that the Arias plan

> seems more favorable to the Sandinistas than the rebels. At the beginning of the process the rebels [are to] give up all leverage, cease firing and stop receiving aid and take their chances in the political arena, but full democratization is deferred and no sanctions are mandatory unless the process collapses later.

In the words of resistance leader Enrique Bermúdez, "The Arias Plan . . . asked for our immediate surrender in exchange for promises of future democratization of Nicaragua."[119]

The practical effect of the Arias plan was to provide the Sandinista regime a means of continually prolonging discussions about a political settlement and its own democratization and to give the Democratic majority in the U.S. Congress a basis for opposing any further military aid to the Nicaraguan resistance. House Speaker Wright unilaterally abrogated his August 5 agreement with President Reagan. The original Reagan-Wright plan provided for a suspension of administration requests for military aid to the contras. The Sandinistas would be asked again to (1) cease aggression through armed subversion, and (2) establish a timetable and political process leading to free and fair elections. The action of Speaker Wright implied his presumption that whether or not the Sandinistas took these two significant actions, the Democratic majority in Congress would vote no further military aid as long as some type of peace process continued. As Speaker Wright endorsed the even weaker Arias plan he said: "I can't conceive of providing any military aid [to the Nicaraguan resistance] in a time of peace."[120] Speaker Wright and his allies in Congress were now taking the "peace process" of the Arias plan as the equivalent of peace.

The "Peace Process." The Sandinista regime immediately set about attempting to appear in partial compliance with the Arias plan. As the democratization terms of the accord required full freedom of speech, assembly, and political organization, the Sandinistas at once responded by permitting the banned *La Prensa* newspaper to begin publishing and the silenced Catholic radio station to resume broadcasting. But in both cases these independent media were warned not to publish or broadcast items unfavorable to the regime.

Shortly after he signed the Arias plan, Daniel Ortega told a news conference, "We are already practicing democracy." On returning to Nicaragua from the Central American summit, he added: "The document speaks about democratization and free elections. . . . We are not speaking about anything new. . . . We have had free elections here." This hardly suggests Ortega thought any real improvements were required.

On August 15, 1987, however, Sandinista police used violence to break up a peaceful protest by opposition parties. They also beat and jailed Lino Hernández, head of the independent Permanent Commission on Human Rights of Nicaragua, and Alberto Saborio, head of the Nicaraguan Bar Association. A few weeks later, the Sandinistas released these individuals to a visiting U.S. senator, Democrat Tom Harkin of Iowa, an active opponent of contra aid, who expressed "deep appreciation" in a news conference. Congressman Peter Kostmayer, Democrat of Pennsylvania, had publicly assured Ortega in Managua that all he had to do to stop contra aid was open the Catholic radio station, let *La Prensa* publish, and free Lino Hernandez.[121]

On September 9, 1987, El Salvador's President Duarte publicly accused the Sandinista regime of continuing to provide weapons and other support to Salvadoran Communist guerrillas in violation of the Arias plan. These charges were repeated by President Duarte on December 1 and on January 6, 1988, he presented detailed evidence.[122]

In the fall of 1987 the Sandinistas received a great deal of favorable press attention when they released almost 1,000 political prisoners; but about nine thousand were still being held in violation of the provisions of the Arias plan. The Sandinistas also refused to hold direct negotiations with the Nicaraguan resistance from August through October 1987. But the mounting contra military activity finally prompted the Sandinistas to agree to indirect negotiations beginning in November 1987. These broke down the following month when the Sandinistas, in violation of a cease-fire, launched military operations against the resistance.

After the five Central American presidents met on January 16,

1988, to assess compliance with the Arias plan, the four democratic Central American presidents issued a joint statement saying that Nicaragua had failed to comply. They demanded "total compliance, without excuses" with all aspects of the Arias plan. Moreover, the four presidents accepted Duarte's proposal to reject any extension of the Arias deadlines and to terminate the verification commission. Duarte called the commission's final report to the presidents "disrespectful" and biased against the four democracies and in favor of Nicaragua.[123]

The Sandinistas responded with a new set of promises: to suspend the state of emergency; to "convoke direct talks" immediately with the Nicaraguan resistance; and to implement a partial amnesty once a cease-fire was agreed upon and the resistance had been "incorporated into the civil sector." The regime in fact announced an end to the state of emergency, but at the same time arrested five more opposition leaders. Toward the end of January 1988, Managua announced it would allow thirteen independent radio and print news organizations to begin operating; at the same time, Sandinista-controlled mobs (the *turbas divinas*) attacked the headquarters of the democratic coordinating group while police looked on passively.

Despite such repeated contradictions between the actions and the words of the Sandinista regime, neither the four Central American governments nor the Reagan administration acknowledged that by the end of January 1988 the Arias plan had failed. Instead, Senator Christopher Dodd (Democrat of Connecticut), chairman of the U.S. Senate committee monitoring compliance, and a longtime opponent of aid to the contras, spoke about "flexible" standards of compliance.

As direct cease-fire negotiations between the Sandinistas with the contras began in early 1988, House Speaker Wright proposed a program of $48 million in nonmilitary aid for the contras, with the proviso that previously authorized but unsent military equipment not be shipped. As mentioned earlier, some Democratic congressmen reportedly told the resistance leaders that unless they signed a truce agreement with the Sandinista regime, this nonmilitary aid package would not pass the Congress.

On March 24, 1988, the Sandinista regime and the resistance signed an agreement at the border town of Sapoa, Nicaragua. It provided for a sixty-day cease-fire, from April 1 to May 30, 1988, and for resistance troops to enter designated truce zones while the Sandinistas permitted nonmilitary supplies to be delivered to the resistance forces inside Nicaragua. Managua also agreed to release one hundred political prisoners within a matter of two weeks, half of the remaining political prisoners when all resistance forces had entered the truce zones, and the remaining political prisoners when a permanent truce had been established.

Once again, the Sandinista regime was promising to do what it had already promised and failed to do in the Arias plan—to release all political prisoners—and the Sandinistas once again promised full freedom of expression inside Nicaragua. Speaker Wright, however, said the truce agreement would lead to passage of nonmilitary aid within a week; Secretary of State Shultz publicly praised it. The one hundred political prisoners were released on March 27, 1988, and the Sandinistas took other steps to create the impression of compliance with the truce.

But simultaneously the Sandinistas prevented the delivery of most of the nonmilitary supplies to resistance forces inside Nicaragua and initiated a campaign of propaganda and intimidation to persuade resistance forces to surrender. In violation of the cease-fire they staged a number of military attacks on the resistance. Adolfo Calero of the resistance directorate accused the Sandinistas of carrying out an artillery bombardment of resistance forces in truce zone positions in two provinces on April 4, 1988. On April 13, 1988, Sandinista troops again attacked into Honduras in violation of the truce.

The Sandinistas also continued their internal repression. They prevented the shipment of newsprint to *La Prensa* by a private humanitarian organization, and they continued to harass members of the unarmed democratic opposition, for example, arresting five striking workers on April 27, 1988.

For the Sandinistas the "peace process"—the cease-fire and ongoing talks with the resistance—was ideal. It provided them with an opportunity to increase their military strength, refurbish and redeploy their forces, locate contra units, and make use of the more than $500 million in Soviet-bloc military aid they had received during 1987 and the estimated $100 million delivered by the Soviet bloc during the first three months of 1988. Meanwhile, the contras were cut off from further military aid and found their store of food, ammunition, and weapons rapidly diminishing.

In mid-May 1988, Ortega threatened that if the resistance did not accept Sandinista peace terms soon, the Nicaraguan army would carry out "actions on a scale never before seen in this war."[124] This threat led President Reagan to state on May 24:

> During the 60-day truce established under the Sapoa agreement signed March 23, the Sandinistas have continued, and, indeed, intensified, their repression of the Nicaraguan people. They have not carried out their commitments under the Guatemala accord of August 7, 1987 [the Arias plan], or

under the Sapoa agreement. . . . If the current stalemate in the peace process persists and the Sandinistas continue their policies of repression, then we will call upon the Congress to reconsider its . . . decision to curtail assistance to the Nicaraguan freedom fighters.[125]

At the end of May, Ortega declared that the Sandinista regime would unilaterally extend the cease-fire another month, until July 1, 1988. Essentially the Sandinista regime recognized that its interest was best served by a strategy of "running out the clock"—using up the final months of the Reagan administration, extending the "peace process" month by month into the fall 1988 U.S. presidential election campaign, hoping that the question of further military aid would be delayed until after the election or into the Bush administration. This is exactly what occurred: the Reagan administration deferred action on the issue and by public announcement in October left it to the next administration.

By the autumn of 1988, only an estimated 2,000 to 3,000 resistance fighters remained inside Nicaragua. Small numbers were able to move in and out of the country, and military activity remained at the minimal level it had reached as of the March 1988 Sapoa truce. By the end of 1988, it was estimated that about 12,000 resistance fighters were outside of Nicaragua along the border region, where they continued their training and prepared for future combat.

New Agreements. In November the government of Honduras gave the United Nations a proposal for a multinational effort to oversee the dismantling of Nicaraguan resistance forces based on its territory. This action provided an important indicator to President-elect Bush of the direction in which the friendly Central American countries were likely to move unless they received a clear message that the next U.S. president would vigorously attempt to obtain full military funding for the Nicaraguan resistance.

To Republican congressional supporters of military aid to the resistance, the arguments were clear: The Democratic majority's belief that cutting military aid to the resistance would bring about a more reasonable Sandinista regime had been discredited by the events of 1987 and 1988. In fact, with the end of military aid to the resistance and the phasing out of their combat operations, the regime became more repressive internally and more aggressive internationally, as its military support to the Salvadoran Communist guerrillas expanded.

Moreover, the Sandinista regime and its far-left guerrilla allies resumed a campaign of assassinating its present and past opponents in Honduras and elsewhere in Central America. On January 7, 1989, contra military commander Manuel Antonio Rugama was assassinated in Tegucigalpa, Honduras; on January 25, 1989, General Gustavo Alvarez Martinez, former chief of the Honduran Armed Forces, who had been helpful to the contras and retired some years earlier, was also assassinated in Honduras.

President-elect George Bush had issued a strong statement of support for the Nicaraguan resistance on the day following his election. But as the weeks went by with no further word from him about military aid to the resistance, the Sandinistas and their political allies, including Mexico and other Contadora countries, began seeking yet another settlement favorable to the Sandinista regime. At the February 1989 inauguration of Carlos Andres Perez, once again president of Venezuela, Daniel Ortega proposed a plan to disarm resistance fighters and settle their families inside Nicaragua.

The El Salvador accord. On February 8 and 9, 1989, the Central American foreign ministers met at the United Nations to prepare for a summit of Central American presidents on February 15 in El Salvador. At their meeting the foreign ministers agreed in principle to UN verification of the security provisions of the 1987 Arias plan, including the prohibition on aid to irregular armed forces operating against any of the five governments. At the summit meeting the five Central American presidents announced their agreement to develop within ninety days a plan to dismantle Nicaraguan resistance bases in Honduras and to relocate the contras and their families to Nicaragua or some third country. These actions would be examined by a border verification force under UN auspices.

In return, the Sandinistas agreed to hold their national elections in February rather than November 1990 and to allow monitoring by foreign observers; again they promised to ensure full freedom of speech, assembly, and political organization, and to release an unspecified number of political prisoners. Honduran military commanders were soon reported willing to cooperate in dismantling contra base camps and relocating the contras.

Unlike the 1987 Arias plan the February 1989 plan omitted a requirement for the relocation of Salvadoran and other Communist guerrilla groups based on Nicaraguan territory. It also transferred responsibility for verification from Latin American countries to the United Nations.

A bipartisan U.S. agreement. The El Salvador accord of February 1989 reportedly took the Bush administration by surprise. The president's initial response was to announce, on February 23, 1989, that he would seek continuation of "humanitarian support" for the con-

297

tras. After weeks of secret negotiations with Republican and Democratic congressional leaders, on March 24 Bush announced a bipartisan accord. The administration agreed not to seek further military aid for the contras before the February 1990 Nicaraguan elections.

The Democratic congressional leadership agreed to continue nonmilitary funding for the Nicaraguan resistance through February 1990 at the prevailing monthly rate of about $4.4 million. The joint statement also endorsed the August 1987 Arias plan and the February 1989 El Salvador accord, and the administration pledged to increase its support for regional diplomatic efforts. A side agreement required the Bush administration to obtain the written approval of four congressional subcommittees to continue the nonmilitary funding beyond November 30, 1989.

The text of the bipartisan agreement asserted that the executive and the Congress were united on a policy to achieve these U.S. goals: the democratization of Nicaragua; an end to Sandinista subversion and destabilization of Nicaragua's neighbors; and an end to Soviet-bloc military ties that threaten U.S. and regional security. And to be successful, the agreement stated, as reported in the *New York Times*, March 25, 1989:

> the Central American peace process cannot be based on promises alone. It must be based on credible standards of compliance, strict timetables for enforcement, and effective ongoing means to verify both the democratic and security requirements of those agreements. We support the use of incentives and disincentives to achieve U.S. policy objectives.

But after the bipartisan agreement was announced the Republican and Democratic participants seemed to have different interpretations of it. The Bush administration expected to keep the Nicaraguan resistance in reserve as a fighting force in case the Sandinistas did not hold genuinely democratic elections. The Democratic congressional leadership said, however, that it had not agreed to any such contingency. Further, since the agreement specified that the nonmilitary funds to the Nicaraguan resistance "shall also be available to support voluntary re-integration or voluntary regional relocation by the Nicaraguan resistance," some Democratic members of Congress contended that Nicaraguan resistance was intended to be dismantled through relocation.

The bipartisan accord was also explicit in stating that

> while the Soviet Union and Cuba both publicly endorsed the [Arias plan], their continued aid and support of violence and subversion in Central America is in direct violation of that regional agreement. The United States believes that

President Gorbachev's impending visit to Cuba represents an important opportunity for both the Soviet Union and Cuba to end all aid that supports subversion and destabilization in Central America.

But during Gorbachev's visit to Cuba in April 1989, he and Castro signed a new twenty-five-year treaty of cooperation and friendship. Neither ruler agreed to end military assistance to Nicaragua or to the Communist insurgent forces in Latin America. In fact, the Soviet Union reiterated the position it took at the December 1987 U.S.-Soviet summit: it would stop supplying military aid to Nicaragua only when the United States ended its military support to the democratic governments of Central America.

After the tide of contra pressure on the Sandinista military regime reached its height at the end of 1987 and then began to recede, Soviet military support for Cuba and Nicaragua remained massive. Communist guerrillas in El Salvador continued to receive more and better weapons, enabling them to intensify their combat operations.

Freedom for the Nicaraguan People

Days before another Central American summit, in August 1989, President Bush reportedly began a campaign to dissuade Central American leaders from seeking the dismantling of the contras as a fighting force before the February 1990 Nicaraguan presidential election. But on July 27, 1989, as President Bush was reported delivering this message to the presidents of Costa Rica and Honduras, the United States voted in favor of a UN Security Council resolution calling for the dismantling of all guerrilla forces and the establishment of a UN monitoring force on the Nicaraguan (but not the Salvadoran) border. That resolution encouraged those seeking the dismantling of the contras, among them Senator Dodd, a longtime contra critic. In early August Dodd accused the administration of trying to coerce Honduras into allowing contra camps to remain in its territory by withholding some $70 million in economic aid, which the administration contended was linked to economic reforms in Honduras. Dodd also threatened to end the bipartisan agreement on continued nonmilitary aid for the resistance if the Bush administration persuaded the Central American leaders not to dismantle the contras.[126]

Resistance commander Enrique Bermúdez was blunt in his assessment:

The Sandinistas have played the United States for a fool. Without doubt, Nicaragua's freedom movement is today in the most dangerous position since its founding, and the United States—part-time ally of freedom—can take most of

299

the blame. As the result of Washington's appeasement, the Nicaraguan people are forced to live under a totalitarian regime that Jim Wright and his liberal Congressional colleagues would not tolerate . . . if it were inflicted on them.[127]

In fact, during 1989 most contras were outside Nicaragua, and the few inside were virtually inactive. Thus, in the months leading to the February 1990 election, the Sandinistas did not have the pretext of contra threats to justify their actions. Under greatly intensified foreign scrutiny as the election approached, the repressive nature of the Sandinista regime was exposed. The Arias and El Salvador accords had provided timetables for the democratization of Nicaragua, but many Sandinista actions violated them. Commenting on the election laws enacted in April 1989, Jeane J. Kirkpatrick wrote in the *Washington Post*, on May 1, 1989:

> First, the new law guarantees definite [Sandinista] domination of the supreme electoral council which will oversee the elections. . . . Second, it sharply limits the opposition's access to television. Third, it gives the government an overwhelming financial advantage and provides that the electoral council will receive one-half of any foreign funds provided to the opposition parties. Fourth, it prohibits absentee voting by the nearly 1,000,000 Nicaraguans who are temporarily living outside their country.

The victory of the democratic opposition in the February 1990 election showed, however, that despite their efforts the Sandinistas had not been able to defeat the democratic hopes of the Nicaraguan people.

The inauguration of Mrs. Violeta Chamorro on April 25, 1990, offered the hope for the long-delayed genuine democracy promised in 1979. The Bush administration lifted economic sanctions and asked $300 million in economic aid for the people of Nicaragua. But the Sandinistas retained control of the 80,000-strong army and threatened to "govern from below." The danger persisted that once the contras were disarmed and dismantled, the Sandinistas would use one means or another to deny the Nicaraguan people the freedom they have long fought for.

But if democracy is successful in Nicaragua, it would demoralize and isolate the Communist insurgencies in El Salvador and Guatemala. In this way the prospects for peace, democracy, and economic progress would be enhanced for all the people of Central America.

8
Comparative Analysis and
Alternative Futures

History has proved President John F. Kennedy correct in his 1961 prediction that the free world faced "a long twilight struggle" against tyranny and other scourges of humanity. He spoke shortly after Nikita S. Khrushchev, then perceived as a "reformist Soviet leader," announced that Moscow would intensify its efforts to help pro-Soviet groups take power with special emphasis on armed "liberation movements" in developing countries. But could President Kennedy have imagined that eleven new pro-Soviet dictatorships would be established during the 1970s while U.S.-Soviet détente was in full flower? While the spotlight of international attention had focused on the hopes and expectations of U.S.-Soviet détente—reflected in a procession of five summit meetings starting in 1972 between the Soviet ruler, Brezhnev, and Presidents Nixon, Ford, and Carter—in the shadows Moscow persisted in the indirect aggression that helped bring those eleven pro-Soviet dictatorships to power.

This concluding discussion establishes the context for the analysis by providing an overview of U.S.-Soviet relations and the situation in each of the five wars. Next, there is an interpretative and comparative analysis of the five Communist regimes, the resistance movements, the foreign policies of the Soviet Union and the United States in these conflicts, and the possible human, regional, and geopolitical consequences of the success or defeat of the resistance movements. How can the United States and other free-world countries still help these resistance movements—despite their current very unpromising condition—liberate their people from pro-Soviet dictatorships?

Overview of U.S.-Soviet Relations and the Five Wars

As we have seen, for most of the 1980s in five of these eleven countries armed resistance movements fought to bring an end to Communist dictatorships established in the 1970s. The Communist regimes caused immense human suffering, first as they imposed communism, then as they fought to defeat the anti-Communist movements. By

1989 among the 46 million living in these five countries in 1979, more than 3 million had been killed, more than 200,000 imprisoned, about 7 million displaced from their homes to other locations within their countries, and 8 million became refugees living in camps or otherwise resettled outside their countries, while additional hundreds of thousands had also fled but were not living in refugee camps (see table 8–1).

Despite this immense human suffering, despite the fact that these were the first post World War II cases of sustained armed resistance to Soviet-backed Communist regimes, and despite the intrinsic drama of this David and Goliath combat, these wars for the most part took place in the twilight of Western media attention and public interest. Exceptions to this lack of sustained media coverage and public attention mostly occurred when major political settlements were close to being signed or when opponents sought to end U.S. aid to the Nicaraguan or Angolan resistance.

By the start of his second term in early 1985, President Reagan had obtained congressional support for an improvement in U.S. military forces, launched the Strategic Defense Initiative, and proclaimed his intention to support the anti-Communist resistance movements, which had stalemated the Communist regimes in all five

TABLE 8-1
HUMAN CONSEQUENCES OF THE FIVE PRO-SOVIET REGIMES, 1975–1989

	Population (millions, 1979)	Deaths	Political/ Prisoners	Internally Displaced	In Refugee Camps Abroad[a]
Afghanistan	15	1,300,000	50,000+	2,000,000	6,000,000
Cambodia	6	1,500,000	unknown	2,000,000	346,000
Angola	8	50,000[b]	10,000	700,000	400,000
Mozambique	14	175,000	5,000–200,000	2,000,000	1,200,000
Nicaragua	3	9,000	43,000	250,000–300,000	46,000
Total	46	3,034,000	108,000–303,000+	6,950,000	7,992,000

a. UN *World Refugee Report,* reproduced in the *Washington Post,* October 6, 1989, p. A41; these numbers include only those in refugee camps; hundreds of thousands of others have become residents of other countries after fleeing.
b. Author's estimate.
SOURCES: As noted in individual country chapters. See also notes a and b.

countries despite massive Soviet-bloc military support which by then included about 325,000 Soviet, Vietnamese, and Cuban combat troops and thousands of additional foreign personnel. After becoming the new Soviet ruler in 1985, Mikhail Gorbachev moved to establish a new era of U.S.-Soviet détente. Moscow returned to the arms control negotiations it had suspended and the spotlight of world attention was again focused on a procession of U.S.-Soviet summits (Reagan-Gorbachev 1985, 1986, 1987, 1988; Bush-Gorbachev 1989). A new mood of optimism about East-West relations contributed to expectations of an end to the cold war and to a cumulative decline in U.S. defense budgets totaling about 11 percent from 1986 to 1989— even though Soviet military budgets increased by about 15 percent in those years.[1]

In May 1989, President Bush declared that in its relations with the Soviet Union the United States had moved "beyond containment" and that the new task was to help integrate Moscow into the world economy. This hopeful perspective was followed in an October 1989 speech by Secretary of State James Baker, who declared that there was "a historic opportunity with the Soviet Union" to "leave behind the postwar period with the ups and downs of the Cold War." Almost paraphrasing Henry Kissinger's expressed hopes during the détente of the 1970s that Western trade, aid, and credits to Moscow would establish a web of mutually beneficial relationships leading to a more peaceful Soviet foreign policy, Baker offered "technical assistance in certain areas of Soviet economic reform." "We want *perestroika* to succeed at home and abroad," he said, "because we believe it will bring about a less aggressive Soviet Union, restrained in the use of force and less hostile to democracy."[2] In November 1989, in response to the dramatic process of political liberalization in Eastern Europe and the Soviet decision not to use military force to maintain Communist power there, President Bush proposed a U.S.-Soviet "partnership for freedom."[3]

The hopes expressed by Secretary of State Baker in October 1989 were counterbalanced to some extent by a number of concerns raised in the same speech. "While President Gorbachev has promised cuts in the Soviet defense budget," Baker said, "we are still looking for concrete results." Further, Soviet espionage operations against the United States and its allies were reported to have increased steadily during the Gorbachev years as well. With respect to "regional conflicts," Baker pointed to a "very mixed" record of Soviet actions; he explicitly criticized "a surge" of military deliveries to the pro-Soviet regimes in Afghanistan, Cambodia, and Ethiopia and described this surge as indicating "a seeming preference [for] military solutions."[4]

As the preceding chapters have shown, this criticism of Soviet actions during the Gorbachev years was warranted. Despite the renewal of U.S.-Soviet summit meetings, the signing of agreements, withdrawals of many foreign combat troops from Afghanistan, Cambodia, and Angola, and Soviet acquiescence in the massive demonstrations in Eastern Europe that, in the fall of 1989, began a hopeful process of political liberalization, Gorbachev had maintained or increased Soviet military, diplomatic, and other support for the five pro-Soviet regimes against the anti-Communist resistance movements.[5]

At the end of 1989, there were visible but still reversible outcomes of this complex political-military-international duel between the Soviet Union, its allies, and the five dictatorships on the one hand and the United States, its allies, and the anti-Communist armed resistance movements on the other. In every case except Nicaragua the pro-Soviet regimes remained in power, had gained in legitimacy within the non-Communist world, and seemed likely to win. Almost as a corollary, the anti-Communist resistance movements, while not defeated or significantly weakened in any military sense (except in Nicaragua), were nevertheless facing a future that seemed far more uncertain than it had four years earlier when President Reagan proclaimed his intention of helping them win. The effect of expanded Soviet military supplies to the five regimes, coupled with announced troop withdrawals of the visible foreign Communist combat forces, three political settlements, continuing negotiations, and incessant propaganda had left the anti-Communist resistance movements more vulnerable than when Gorbachev came to power in 1985. In Nicaragua the vote for the democratic opposition in the February 1990 election and the inauguration of its leader as president in April 1990 offered the possibility that the still significant military and clandestine power of the Sandinistas might be overcome by the new democratic government.

Afghanistan. In May 1988, after Soviet troops began their withdrawal, Deputy Assistant Secretary of State Robert A. Peck told Congress that despite a "surge" of Soviet military deliveries, a "process of defeat, defection and retreat" was "likely to gain momentum." The Communist regime's "tenure will not be prolonged," he said, "and the way will soon be opened for freedom and self-determination."[6] But the Najibulla regime remained in control of all the major cities, and the Soviet Union maintained a massive flow of weapons and other supplies to the regime. An estimated 4,600 military supply flights were made from February to October 1989, along with the supply of 900 heavy Scud surface-to-surface missiles and hundreds of tanks and armored vehicles. The total value of Soviet aid to Kabul was put at $250 million to $300 million per month.[7] Further, the Soviet-Iranian entente of June 1989 seemed to have shifted Iran toward support of the Najibulla regime, with the Soviet foreign minister in August 1989 complimenting "the wholly positive attitude" of Iran and praising the "growth of realism and a constructive Afghan policy in Teheran."[8]

At the same time the Afghan resistance faced a shortage of weapons due to a reported sharp reduction during 1989 in U.S. deliveries and problems with the U.S. supply process. In the late summer of 1989, Senator Gordon Humphrey and other members of Congress reportedly took these facts directly to senior Bush administration officials.[9] After a visit to the region, Senator Claiborne Pell, chairman of the Senate Foreign Relations Committee, reported to the Senate in October 1989: "At exactly the time the Soviets were increasing their military support . . . supplies to the mujahideen were dramatically reduced. Tragically for the resistance, this also coincided with the heaviest and most equipment-intensive fighting of the war."[10]

When the United States revealed that some Soviet troops remained in Afghanistan, Senator Pell criticized "too much emphasis on an elusive military victory and too little on finding a political formula to end the fighting," a sign of potentially reduced political support among Democratic members of Congress.[11] At the same time, the divisiveness within the resistance and the political difficulties posed within Pakistan by the Afghan war, as well as other problems facing the Bhutto government, raised questions about how long the resistance could count on Pakistan's support of its objective of an independent non-Communist Afghanistan.[12] Prime Minister Bhutto was reported to have concluded that the resistance should "stop looking for a military victory and seek a speedy political settlement."[13]

Cambodia. The Soviet- and Vietnamese-backed Hun Sen regime in Cambodia failed to obtain the international legitimation it sought during the August 1989 international conference in Paris. To reinforce its client, Moscow was reported to have doubled its military support to the Cambodian regime during 1989 to an annual level of about $500 million, with deliveries including 100 tanks and sixteen jet fighters. The Vietnamese claimed in the United Nations that "from September 27, 1989 there does not remain a single volunteer soldier in Cambodia—either army-man, adviser or military employee." But the Cambodian resistance groups and "many southeast Asian nations challenge this assertion, accusing Vietnam of leaving thousands of soldiers disguised as militiamen and settlers."[14]

In January 1990, the five permanent members of the UN Security Council (China, France, the United Kingdom, the United States, and the USSR) agreed on a new plan for Cambodia, which included UN verification of the withdrawal of all foreign troops; an effective UN presence inside Cambodia during a transition period leading to free and fair elections conducted under direct UN administration; and a new National Council to serve as the entity of Cambodian sovereignty (instead of the PRK regime or the UN-recognized armed opposition coalition, CGDK). But negotiations among all the parties continued because the PRK regime (still backed by Vietnamese military power) sought to structure the implementation of this plan to guarantee its continuation in power.[15] Therefore, the prospects remained that the three-sided war would continue between the Chinese-backed Khmer Rouge, the Soviet–Vietnamese-aided regime, and the non-Communist resistance, with the latter receiving too little military aid to challenge the two Communist groups.

Angola. During an October 1989 meeting with President Bush in Washington, D.C., the leader of UNITA heard the United States reiterate its "long-standing support for a cease-fire and face-to-face negotiations and ultimately free and fair elections,"[16] a welcome affirmation of Savimbi's own goals and proposals. But little else went well for UNITA after the signing of the Angola-Namibia accords in December 1988.

South African military support ended, leaving UNITA dependent on neighboring Zaire for the receipt of military and other external supplies. In June 1989, after threats and blandishments from the Communist side, the ruler of Zaire turned toward political and diplomatic cooperation with the MPLA regime. President Mobutu of Zaire publicly agreed with the MPLA allegation that Savimbi had agreed to go into exile and have UNITA "integrate" with the MPLA— a statement Savimbi and UNITA deny. Mobutu then indicated no more weapons for UNITA would transit Zaire. Nevertheless, in their October 1989 meeting President Bush urged Savimbi to "work with President Mobutu and others in the region to foster the peace-process."[17] While about 20,000 of the 50,000–60,000 Cuban troops were reported to have left Angola by November 1989, UNITA Vice-President Chitunda said in February 1990 that 37,000 still remained— far more than the level permitted by the accords until July 1991. Further, Castro had laid the foundation for slowing or reversing the complete withdrawal of Cuban troops by writing to the UN secretary general in August 1989 that this might become necessary because of "violations" of the accords by others. And in the winter of 1989 Castro proclaimed a unilateral suspension of the Cuban withdrawal for some weeks.

After winning 57 percent of the vote in the November 1989 UN-supervised election, the pro-Soviet SWAPO movement was on the way to power in Namibia; indeed, its leader, Sam Nujoma, became president on March 21, 1990. UNITA became increasingly isolated politically. From December 1989 it faced an offensive by some 10,000 MPLA troops aided directly, according to Chitunda, by 900 Soviet military personnel. UNITA was hampered by a severe shortage of essential supplies such as antitank weapons, ammunition, and fuel.[18]

Mozambique. The Frelimo Communist regime continued to control most cities and some rural areas while the anti-Communist guerrillas continued to control most of the countryside and much of the population. More than seven thousand foreign troops sent by Mugabe in Zimbabwe continued to aid the Frelimo regime despite repeated reports that these would be withdrawn.[19] These troops ambushed Dhlakama, the Renamo leader, as he went to an ostensibly safe airfield meeting en route to truce negotiations with Frelimo. That attack failed to kill or effect the capture of Dhlakama. On October 16, 1989, Dhlakama began a new round of negotiations with Frelimo in Kenya under the mediation of foreign ministry officials from Kenya and Zimbabwe. These produced no result.

It was then reported that the Frelimo regime "will hold direct negotiations with Renamo only after the rebels recognize the government as legitimate" and that "the government has offered to guarantee the insurgents full participation . . . [in] general elections scheduled in 1991 as individuals . . . [but] Renamo must disappear as a movement."[20] In other words, just as in Angola, the Communist regime in Mozambique was refusing to compete in free elections but instead offered the anti-Communist resistance movements a form of surrender to be followed by their integration into the existing one-party political system.

The regime continued to have the support of the Soviet bloc and some important non-Communist countries, while the resistance movement became more isolated politically. Even further isolation of Renamo occurred when at the end of 1989 the Bush administration—despite the formal treaties of alliance between Frelimo and the Soviet Union—removed Mozambique from the list of countries designated as Marxist-Leninist. This made Mozambique eligible for loans from

307

the U.S. Export-Import Bank and other economic benefits.[21] Such action would be consistent with the report that a senior U.S. embassy official met with Dhlakama in Kenya and "sought to express the Bush administration's support for the Frelimo government proposals."[22]

Nicaragua. While the Sandinistas repeatedly promised to abide fully by the terms of the August 1987 Arias plan for Central America at some future date, the Democratic majority in the U.S. Congress refused to provide additional military assistance to the contras, who in turn became more politically isolated. In July 1989, the Sandinistas celebrated their tenth anniversary in power. Soon after, the United States voted for a UN Security Council resolution calling for the disbanding of all "irregular forces" in Central America (including the contras and Communist guerrilla groups but operationally focused on the contras).

President Bush sought to persuade the presidents of the four democratic Central American countries not to carry out the dismantling of the contras until after the February 1990 national election in Nicaragua. But at their August 6–7, 1989, summit meeting the four allied Central American presidents agreed with the Sandinista position that the contras should be dismantled by early December 1989. The presidents also decided that the dismantling should be supervised by a combined UN-OAS commission.[23] This was a potentially enormous setback for the contras and occurred through a combination of pressures from the Communist side, mistakes and inattention by the Bush administration,[24] and reported threats by leading Democratic members of the U.S. Congress, who used continued U.S. economic aid to Honduras and El Salvador to win acquiescence. "Senator Christopher Dodd . . . undertook a personal diplomatic mission through Central America to promote the early disbanding of the rebels [contras]" shortly before this was agreed upon at the August 1989 summit meeting.[25]

From 1979 to the autumn of 1989, the Soviet Union and its allies had provided the Sandinistas with an estimated $3.1 billion in weapons—$2.2 billion of this during the Gorbachev years, when the annual rate of supply nearly doubled.[26] This was three times as much in military supplies as the United States sent to all the Central American countries and the contras during the 1980s. Although Moscow had promised in May 1989 to halt unilaterally the delivery of weapons to Nicaragua, the State Department announced in October 1989 that Soviet weapons continued to be shipped to Cuba and that "Cuban arms supplies to Nicaragua . . . increased" during 1989, with the result that weapons deliveries to Nicaragua showed a "modest increase" over the already high levels of 1988.[27]

The Soviet foreign minister followed extensive consultations with the U.S. secretary of state in late September 1989 with a visit to Nicaragua and then to Havana. In Nicaragua, Soviet Foreign Minister Shevardnadze proposed to continue the alleged cutoff of Soviet weapons to Nicaragua if the United States would cease providing weapons to all the other Central American countries. Further he proposed that the USSR and the United States "jointly preside over deep cuts in arms stockpiles and armed forces throughout the region."[28] This Soviet proposal was seen by some observers as a sign that "the Bush Administration was seeking an accommodation with the Soviets in Central America" and by others as bringing the Soviet role in the region "practically to a par with that of the United States."[29]

Speaking to 2,500 contras in October 1989, a UN official told them they should disband: "You are Nicaraguans . . . not the object of a [U.S.] policy that is anachronistic and has been abandoned by the country that helped you." Following a written protest by U.S. Secretary of State James Baker that "it is imperative that the UN be and be seen to be impartial," the UN secretary general repudiated his employee's remark to the contras.[30]

Meanwhile, the Sandinistas continued shipping weapons secretly and providing other military support to Communist guerrillas in neighboring countries in violation of repeated promises made in the various Central American agreements. In October 1989 concealed weapons seized from a truck that had just crossed from Nicaragua into Honduras en route to El Salvador included rocket-propelled grenades, automatic rifles, ammunition, explosive detonators, and urban guerrilla training manuals.[31] Nevertheless, in late October 1989, the Sandinistas were given further legitimation by being invited to attend a summit meeting in Costa Rica of Western Hemisphere democracies, also attended by President Bush. At that meeting the Sandinistas announced they were ending the formal cease-fire and resuming full-scale military operations against the contras.

Then, on November 11, 1989, the Salvadoran Communist guerrillas launched a simultaneous, surprise attack inside thirty Salvadoran cities and towns, tried to assassinate the entire civilian and military leadership of El Salvador in the capital, and in more than three weeks of combat caused more than 4,000 to be killed and wounded. Speaking to the Organization of American States, the U.S. Secretary of State Baker condemned the Salvadoran Communist guerrilla attacks on civilian homes in the cities and towns as "terror pure and simple" and went on to state: "The Soviet Union, if I may say so, bears a special responsibility because its arms and money moving through Cuba and Nicaragua continue to support violence, destruction and war."[32]

The contras remained intact through the February 25, 1990, election, which was won by the democratic opposition. The Sandinista leadership was stunned by the election results, promised to respect them, but then insisted that the contras must disband at once and that the Sandinistas would retain control of the 80,000-strong army, the estimated 20,000-member secret police, and other government agencies. At the same time the Sandinistas strengthened their neighborhood committees of activists and issued threats, such as the statement of Luis Carrión Cruz, a member of the ruling directorate: "The security of the country depends entirely on the integrity of the Sandinista People's Army and the Ministry of the Interior [secret police]. If they [the government-elect] do not accept this they will be responsible for throwing the country into total chaos. The keys to peace or war are in their hands."[33] The inauguration of the democratically elected president in April 1990 offered hope for freedom in Nicaragua. But since the Sandinistas were permitted to retain control of the military forces, disbanding the contras before the elected Chamorro government took effective authority inside Nicaragua and before the Sandinista army and secret police were dismantled posed the threat of continued Sandinista dominance.

The Pro-Soviet Regimes

After the Soviet Union decided in the late 1950s to expand activities in the developing countries, and especially after deciding in 1961 to support armed pro-Soviet movements, it gave continuous support to all of the movements that evolved into the Communist regimes of the 1970s. It is noteworthy that all five Communist movements began their operations in the early 1960s; the Sandinistas were the first, in 1961, and the Communist party of Afghanistan the last, in 1965. Soviet bloc support increased markedly as the movements came closer to taking power. The most dramatic instance was the Soviet movement of Cuban combat troops into Angola in 1975 to ensure an MPLA takeover.

The impact of Communist ideology, Soviet training, and the will to power of these national Communist elites is visible in the similarities between these five regimes on three different continents. Each began as a very small Communist movement of highly ideological and determined, mainly urban persons living in societies that were predominantly agricultural and rural. All five movements showed a dualism in their projection of ideology: On the one hand they were explicit about their commitment to Marxism-Leninism. This could be seen in their programmatic statements, in their internal doctrinal disputes and feuds and purges, and in their repeated professions of loyalty to the Soviet Union and the international goals of communism, along with their participation in many international Communist celebrations and activities over the years. At the same time, these movements tried to create the impression among non-Communists that they represented a broader coalition and a commitment to pluralism. This masked their core ideology.

As these five movements came closer to taking power, the need to deceive citizens of their own countries and leaders of the non-Communist countries about their Communist ideology became greater. The blurring of their ideology became more pronounced as the movements came to power. The Afghanistan Communist regime initially declared its intention to maintain "positive neutrality," and the Sandinistas described themselves as committed to democracy and pluralism, as did the SWAPO movement in the fall of 1989 when approaching power in Namibia.

With the exception of the Sandinistas—where the degree of repression was less severe than in the other countries—the movements in power seemed to repeat partially the historical tragedies of Soviet communism. While proclaiming reformist and nationalist goals and attempting to allay the growing suspicion and fears of non-Communist leaders and the broad population, these pro-Soviet regimes undertook repression on a scale never before seen in their societies. In four of the five countries, thousands of leaders in public affairs, education, the professions, communications, and religious institutions were executed, tortured, or imprisoned by the Communist elites. Then when this repression prompted spontaneous and unorganized resistance, it was met with even harsher repression in a cycle that deepened the human suffering. The exception, the Sandinista regime, was under the tutelage of Castro, who realized his own mistake in publicly executing those he branded counterrevolutionaries and thereby losing for many years the economic support of non-Communist countries. Castro probably advised the Sandinistas to maintain the façade and tone of political pluralism to deceive both their own population and their large neighbor to the north. Even so, the Sandinistas, while meeting virtually no resistance, immediately imprisoned several thousand former soldiers of the Somoza regime, who had been promised amnesty if they surrendered, and are believed to have secretly executed hundreds of people in their first months.

The internal repression, which grew with time, was matched by a dogmatic application of Marxist-Leninist economic approaches of the mid- and late 1970s. But the seizure of private institutions, including industries, financial institutions, and social service and welfare organizations, now seems to have been motivated as much by the new regimes' efforts to control society as by Marxist economics.

In all five countries, the new regimes gave greatest attention to building new military organizations and internal institutions of social control. Here the corps of Soviet and allied advisers were of crucial importance. As economic conditions worsened under the repression, mismanagement, and corruption, the size, power, and effectiveness of the internal security and military organizations steadily grew.

With the exception of the Sandinistas, each of these regimes was rent by blood purges among competing Communist factions. These varied in intensity, with the toll of victims in Angola and Mozambique reaching the hundreds and in Afghanistan and Cambodia perhaps the thousands. An eyewitness described the intraregime purges in Cambodia: "The leaders and their subordinates were not simply executed. First they were tortured and made to confess to 'crimes' they had never committed. Nobody was safe from the purges."[34] Thus the Stalin era found an echo in Communist Cambodia, Afghanistan, and Mozambique.

The Sandinistas may have avoided these purges in part because thousands of Cubans, sent by Castro, played such a significant part in the regime. These outside cadres may well have served as a glue holding the Sandinista regime together and reducing internal rivalries. In addition, the Sandinistas and Castro both understood that any internal purges could seriously weaken the regime in the face of a threat they perceived from the United States. This lesson was undoubtedly reinforced by the example of Grenada in 1983. An internal dispute there between two Communist factions led to the killing of former Prime Minister Bishop and some of his cabinet by one faction and then to the removal of the Communist regime by an international military action led by the United States.

There is no evidence that any Soviet bloc country attempted to reduce internal terror or take any action against the mass repression launched by these new Communist regimes. The evidence suggests that the Soviet Union and its allies concentrated on building the internal security apparatus and the military and on extracting economic benefits from these countries, while leaving the treatment of the people to the local Communist elites.

After the armed resistance movements began to grow in Afghanistan, Angola, Mozambique, and Cambodia, however, the Soviet Union encouraged new internal and international political strategies of "national reconciliation." The more powerful the anti-Communist

312

resistance movements grew, the more the regimes backpedaled rhetorically from their triumphant assertion of Communist symbols and goals. All five regimes made transparent attempts to project moderation, reasonableness, and willingness to recognize past political and economic mistakes. To win greater support from non-Communist countries, the Soviet Union advised them to do three things:

• broaden their political base and adopt a more conciliatory posture toward important groups and symbols in their society
• take some steps back from economic collectivization
• point to these positive tendencies and use diplomacy to seek increased Western economic aid and legitimation

In Afghanistan efforts at national reconciliation regimes began in 1982. The red flag was removed and Islamic colors restored; adherence to Islam was professed; the name was changed from the People's Republic of Afghanistan to the Republic of Afghanistan; and another new constitution was promulgated in 1987. The new Afghan political order provided for a new "Islamic party" and a "new parliamentary front" and ostensibly established a coalition government that was not under Communist control. Communist movements in Eastern Europe had taken power in the late 1940s as the "Socialist Unity party" (East Germany) or the "Polish Workers party," and in "coalition" with ostensibly independent but in fact subservient "opposition parties." That era has much to teach about the methods used by the five Communist regimes under discussion here.

As an important part of the continuing "reconciliation" phase, the regimes made new international approaches and called for negotiations. Seeking to isolate the United States and other countries supporting the contras, the Sandinistas worked closely with Mexico to build a sympathetic coalition of Latin American countries. Angola and Mozambique began negotiations with South Africa in 1984; their aim was to end South Africa's support for the armed resistance movements opposing their regimes. The PRK regime in Cambodia and the Afghan regime used negotiations during most of the 1980s to win international legitimacy and make a display of benign political intentions for the future. At the same time, the regimes eventually all professed a new-found economic pragmatism and desire for improved commercial relations with non-Communist countries.

While the five regimes thus used symbols and diplomacy to alter the opinion of non-Communist governments about them and, more important, to obtain economic aid, they used executions, imprisonment, torture, and forcible displacement or exile to control their own citizenry. As these tragic events went on month after month, year

313

after year, with victims piled upon victims, because the media of the non-Communist world had and sought very little knowledge and sources about the internal actions of the regimes, little notice was taken of them.

For the most part, the West gave little attention to the cooperation these regimes extended to other pro-Soviet groups operating against neighboring countries. The Sandinistas have actively aided Communist guerrillas attacking El Salvador, Guatemala, and other countries since 1979. The other regimes provided similar military and political support from their territories, although in the case of Mozambique, Afghanistan, and Cambodia this appeared to shrink as internal armed resistance grew.

All the regimes showed over the years that they placed the maintenance of power, their Soviet links, and their support for revolutionary violence abroad above their direct economic interests. The Mozambique regime, for example, sacrificed hundreds of millions of dollars in annual revenue from tourism and trade as a result of its support for armed action against South Africa and against the white minority government in Rhodesia, even though it desperately needed that revenue. From 1985 the Sandinista regime was subject to economic sanctions by the United States, formerly its major trading partner, because of its aggression through armed subversion. In every case, however, the regimes used diplomacy, propaganda, and the Soviet bloc and its supporters in non-Communist countries to win support, which included substantial sums of Western economic and financial assistance.

The methods of these regimes can be summarized as a progression of recruitment, deception, consolidation, repression, and pseudoreconciliation in the face of sustained resistance. From their beginnings as Communist political movements, through their periods of expanding armed coalition, to their seizure of power and beyond, these five Communist regimes have shown tenacity, ruthlessness, tactical flexibility, and skill in deceiving and manipulating some elements in the non-Communist world. This record is likely to continue.

The Resistance Movements

The resistance movements were far more diverse in their origins, actions, and beliefs than the Soviet-guided regimes they fought against. In four of the five cases—Mozambique was the exception—the resistance movements began not under the guidance of external powers, but as an indigenous reaction to the repression of the Communist regimes. In every case, however, it was the violence of the regime, its coercive measures, its persecution of traditional political, civic, social, and religious leaders and institutions, and its failed economic policies that caused individuals to risk their lives in armed opposition rather than submit.

Many of the leaders and fighters in the resistance movements initially came from the earlier anticolonial movements and from those who had opposed absolutism before the Communist takeovers. A common element among the ideologies espoused by these movements was freedom. Their experience with the repression and controls of Marxism-Leninism had totally discredited it. The resistance leaders expressed their intention to establish governments that would emphasize human freedom and individual dignity and that would be established by individuals making choices. The major area of similarity among the resistance movements was this commitment to freedom and constitutional government, which went far beyond the rejection of communism. It implied a rejection of all dictatorship, including any that might be established by a triumphant resistance organization.

The aim of the contras was to implement the democratic promises made to the Organization of American States in 1979. For Savimbi of UNITA it was to carry out the 1975 Alvor accords, permitting the people of Angola to choose their government through free elections. In Mozambique Renamo also committed itself to open elections, as did the Afghan and Cambodian resistance movements. Afghan resistance members disagreed about the form of a post-Communist parliamentary government—whether the king might return, for example, and the degree of participation of the Moslem clergy—but there was a consensus that the government should be based on popular consent as traditionally expressed through the local and tribal assemblies, the pattern adopted by the Afghan interim government.

In contrast to the Communist movements, the anti-Communist resistance leaders and groups have resolved differences without assassinations and blood purges. Exceptions were the Hekmatyar faction of the Afghan resistance, which was held responsible for violence against other resistance commanders, and of course the Khmer Rouge in Cambodia, which demonstrated by its attacks on the non-Communist resistance and by its other violence that it remained an extremist organization, seeking to replace one Communist dictatorship with another.

The general pattern of internal nonviolence reflected the rejection by the resistance movements of coercive governance and is all the more remarkable given the length of these wars, given the numbers of occasions when the Communist regimes must have tried

315

to penetrate and disrupt them, given the life-and-death nature of their struggles year after year, and, most important, given the many opportunities for recriminations following political and military setbacks.

While rejecting Marxism-Leninism, the resistance movements accepted the importance of a social welfare role for the state. At the same time, failure of Communist agricultural policies in all five countries convinced the resistance leaders of the virtues of free markets. Looking to the example of the social-market democracies in Western Europe and elsewhere, they emphasized in their programmatic statements some national responsibility for health, education, and welfare, but at the same time made clear that farmers and other producers must be free to participate in the economy through the market mechanism.

Seeking to co-opt elements of the resistance, the five Communist regimes tried to create the appearance of accommodation and reconciliation. But firsthand experience with communism made the resistance immune to the proffered "broad-based coalitions," "integration with guarantees of amnesty," and similar Communist formulas.

The growth of all five resistance movements was steady until a combination of international, rather than internal, events reversed it. External support became an important factor in helping the resistance movements survive and expand. This external support included not only political and financial aid from major powers such as the United States but also the help of contiguous countries from which the resistance could operate with some security from military and paramilitary attack. Contrary to widespread belief, Communist insurgencies in the post World War II era did not win simply on the basis of their activities within the target countries. External sanctuary was usually a major component of success. Their external support included not only weapons but also intelligence, communications, and diplomatic efforts to isolate and discredit target regimes.

The five resistance movements have also relied on one or more contiguous countries for political and logistic support. In the case of the Afghan resistance it was Pakistan and China; for the contras it was Honduras and for some years Costa Rica. The Cambodian resistance could not have sustained itself without its bases in Thailand and political and material support from the ASEAN countries and others. The UNITA resistance was helped by a number of non-Communist countries and received direct support (until August 1988) from South Africa through Namibia and from Zaire. The Renamo resistance was helped by a few African countries and had relied for some years on support from and through South Africa and Malawi.

The Communist regimes and their allies, especially the Soviet Union, devoted important political and diplomatic efforts to terminating or reducing support from contiguous countries. These efforts were supplemented by coercive terrorism and by severe military attacks across borders—from Nicaragua into Honduras, from Cambodia and Vietnam into Thailand, and from Afghanistan into Pakistan. But in no case did the regimes and their Soviet and Cuban allies make a sustained open military assault that led to a conventional war.

Countries in the regions maintained support for the resistance movements because they feared that the new Communist regimes would conduct armed subversion against them. Persuading them otherwise has been a focus of diplomatic efforts of the five Communist regimes and their allies. One such effort was aimed at President Arias of Costa Rica, who took office in 1986.

The resistance movements showed their greatest vulnerability on this point: understanding and countering the international political tactics of the Communist regimes and their allies. It is quite understandable that their leaders, caught up in conflict, would have difficulty devising strategies to counter the process of political and diplomatic isolation undertaken by the Communist regimes and their international supporters (see table 8–2). The United States and other major non-Communist countries could have played a major constructive role here but failed. The record suggests that the United States itself was often deceived by the words and promises of Communist diplomacy.

The resistance movement that functioned least effectively in the international political arena was Renamo, understandably so because it was also the most isolated politically from the start and possessed the fewest resources. The non-Communist resistance in Cambodia also suffered from a lack of resources, apparently also from a lack of encouragement and effective political guidance and was unable to build effective non-Communist support outside the region. Within the region, the ASEAN countries continued to support the non-Communist resistance in Cambodia, despite the ambiguity of Thailand (see table 8–2). This is testimony to the political representation and communication by the resistance within the region.

The Afghan resistance was instantly understood and widely supported in the non-Communist world, especially in the industrial democracies. But over the years, the resistance did too little to communicate its purposes, progress, and program outside. Although support in the industrial democracies continued, the Afghan cause failed to gain depth either in understanding or in the involvement of

317

TABLE 8–2
CHANGES IN INTERNATIONAL SUPPORT FOR THE COMMUNIST REGIMES
AND THE RESISTANCE MOVEMENTS, 1985 AND 1989

	Regime Supporters		Resistance Supporters	
	Autumn 1985	1989	Autumn 1985	1989
Nicaragua	USSR/Allies Cuba Mexico Some UN members Some NATO/EC Libya/PLO members	USSR/Allies Cuba Mexico More UN members Some OAS members Some NATO/EC Libya/PLO	United States *Honduras* Costa Rica Guatemala El Salvador	United States
Angola	USSR/Allies Cuba Some OAU Some NATO/EC	USSR/Allies Cuba Many OAU Many NATO/EC *Zaire*	United States Eight OAU members *Zaire* South Africa	United States Some OAU members Some countries
Afghanistan	USSR/Allies Cuba Libya/PLO India	USSR/Allies Cuba Libya/PLO India Iran	United States *Pakistan* Saudi Arabia PRC Iran	United States *Pakistan* Saudi Arabia PRC (?)
Cambodia[a]	USSR/Allies Vietnam	USSR/Allies Vietnam *Thailand* UN[b, c] France	United States *Thailand* Malaysia Singapore Indonesia Philippines France UN[b] PRC[b] South Africa A few OAU members	United States Malaysia Singapore Indonesia Philippines *Thailand* A few countries
Mozambique	USSR/Allies Cuba Many OAU A few NATO/EC	USSR/Allies Cuba Many OAU Many NATO/EC South Africa United States	Malawi Some OAU South Africa	

NOTE: Italics indicate the contiguous country providing essential support. OAU is the Organization of African Unity, including virtually all fifty-three African countries.
a. Except for that marked b, resistance support is for non-Communist movements.
b. Supporter of resistance coalition, including Khmer Rouge.
c. Tilting toward acceptance of PRK regime de facto.
SOURCE: Author.

politically relevant groups that could sustain a free-world policy until the success of the resistance. In the U.S. Congress, for example, there was enormous bipartisan support during 1987 and 1988 as congressmen from both political parties sought to ensure that U.S. diplomacy would support the attainment of an independent non-Communist Afghanistan. Despite this bipartisan support, however, the executive branch agreed to a settlement that failed to remove the Communist regime.

Angola offers perhaps the only example of a resistance movement that became increasingly effective in the international political arena. By the mid-1980s UNITA had come to understand that it needed a more active political presence in western Europe and the United States, and in 1986 it began receiving U.S. military aid. When later faced with the need to fend off cuts in this aid, UNITA also had to learn the intricacies of the political differences within Congress and the executive branch. By contrast, Renamo in Mozambique— never was able to organize any systematic campaign to overcome the deep-seated resistance of the U.S. State Department to providing it any aid.

Like the Angolan resistance, the Nicaraguan resistance was comfortable in the mainstream of Western political institutions. Throughout the 1980s in the United States, Europe, and Latin America, it tried to communicate its purposes and obtain increased political support. The uncertainties of its continued U.S. funding caused by the opposition of the Democratic majority in Congress, however, in combination with its lack of resources and the active counterdiplomacy of Mexico and the non-Communist countries, undercut its international political efforts. The Nicaraguan resistance faced a triple international challenge: first maintaining a coalition of regional supporting countries, all of which were being pressured by Communist and other countries such as Mexico to abandon the resistance; second, understanding the political dynamics within the U.S. Congress and between the elements of the executive branch and making an impact in time; third, coping with the repetitive efforts by the Communist side to use international organizations such as the United Nations, the OAS, and the Socialist International to criticize, discredit, and delegitimate the resistance.

All of the resistance movements faced the responsibility of providing food, clothing, medicine, and basic social facilities for tens of thousands, cumulatively millions, of family members of their supporters. It is little remarked that over the many years of struggle the resistance movements have carried out these responsibilities reasonably well. Although the free-world countries helped feed and clothe

the millions of refugees who fled the pro-Soviet regimes, the resistance movements for the most part organized life among the refugees and provided governance in both the liberated and refugee areas. Although no comprehensive study has been made, the success of the governance of resistance movements is evident from the thousands of people who fled the regimes to live in the resistance zones or to go into exile where the resistance had influence. Had any of these resistance movements governed in a repressive, brutal, or economically devastating way, the Communist side would have made much of such evidence in its international propaganda.

The conduct of the resistance movements has been reasonably consistent with civilized norms of warfare, although some individual commanders in all five movements undoubtedly acted in brutal or irresponsible ways. In Afghanistan rocket attacks against strongholds in defended cities, according to the regime, killed civilians. But there are virtually no confirmed reports that any of the resistance movements has waged a campaign of violence against unarmed civilians. In contrast to the brutality of the Communist regimes against ordinary men, women, and children, the resistance movements focused on military or economic targets.

Soviet Foreign Policy

Soviet policy in all five of the conflicts was marked by the clear determination to help the pro-Soviet regimes remain in power and to defeat, neutralize, or isolate the resistance forces. As CIA Director William Casey said in 1986, a "hallmark [of the Gorbachev era] is an intensified effort to nail down and cement these Soviet bridgeheads."[35] These clear strategic goals of Soviet policy under Gorbachev marked a continuation of those set by Brezhnev, Andropov, and Chernenko.

There are a number of reasons why the Soviet Union has been determined to maintain the pro-Soviet regimes in power. First, the original geopolitical goals cited by Brezhnev—control of the energy resources of the Persian Gulf and the mineral "treasure house" of southern Africa—along with the strategic prize of a pro-Soviet Mexico provided enormous incentives for the Soviet Union. This is true whether looked at from the perspective of political power or of economic needs. The Soviet Union could obtain enormous economic resources from the three geopolitical zones in which its efforts have been concentrated for the past twenty years. The economic resources of southern Africa, the Persian Gulf, and Mexico could in turn be used to exert enormous influence to extract economic benefits from Europe and Japan—and to some degree the United States—through the manipulation of supplies and prices for energy and other mineral commodities needed by the industrial democracies. But the defeat of the resistance movements became a prior condition for further progress toward those goals.

A second reason for Soviet determination to maintain these regimes in power is the legitimation they give to the Soviet Union itself. This argument seems to be undercut by the apparent willingness of the Soviet leadership to permit Poland, Hungary, East Germany, Czechoslovakia, and perhaps, Bulgaria and Romania to evolve from past forms of the one-party Marxist-Leninist states. Although the full extent of this willingness remains to be tested by future events, it has led many to believe that the Soviet leadership would tolerate the end of Communist rule in those countries, that is, to repeal the Brezhnev Doctrine in fact if not in word.

But the Communist structure of power may not have been irreversibly changed. The secret police, the national armed forces, and the Soviet military forces in Eastern Europe may continue to provide the hard core elements of the Communist parties with instruments for maintaining or regaining some important control over political life. In contrast, the victory of a resistance movement in any of the five countries would mean the complete defeat and removal of a Soviet-backed regime and a Marxist-Leninist political movement. There is an important difference between political evolution in Eastern Europe, which the Soviet regime explicitly tolerates, and the total removal of a Communist governing apparatus against the clear wishes and efforts of the Soviet Union over many years. Therefore, Soviet determination to prevent the regimes from being defeated in these conflicts could continue irrespective of events in Eastern Europe.

A third reason is the likely Soviet perception of a cumulative unraveling of pro-Soviet regimes should these anti-Communist resistance movements succeed. The full removal of the Sandinista regime and power, entrenched for ten years, might lead to the removal of the thirty-year-long Castro regime, potentially weakened through its failures, the age of the leadership, and the execution, imprisonment, and dismissal of military leaders in Castro's purges of 1989. The victory of UNITA in Angola could increase the prospects for Renamo's victory against the Frelimo regime in Mozambique, and perhaps even endanger the Mugabe regime in Zimbabwe (which in December 1989 proclaimed its establishment of a Marxist-Leninist state), and thereby reduce the likelihood of a pro-Soviet South Africa. A resistance victory in Afghanistan might be perceived by the Soviets as setting the stage—irrespective of any actions of a post-Communist regime—for armed insurgency among the tens of millions of disaffected Moslem peoples in Soviet Central Asia. This concern would be even greater in the context of *glasnost*-inspired unrest within the Soviet Union. The same might be said for the establishment of a non-Communist Cambodia and its possible impact on the people of Vietnam. In short, the Soviet leadership and the leaders of the pro-Soviet regimes could see precisely what became evident in Eastern Europe in 1989: the broad majority of the people reject Communist regimes because of what they have done and what they are. Therefore, the Soviet Union could perceive more at issue in the outcome of these regional wars than the potential for gains in economic resources and political power. Their allies' defeat might initiate additional reversals of past gains and perhaps spark more unrest on Soviet territory itself.

Although the Soviet Union has been willing to use a broad array of political, diplomatic, military, and other means of indirect aggression to support these regimes, it has set strict limits on its own direct military confrontation with neighboring states and with the United States or other supporters of the resistance movements.

While remaining constant in its strategic purposes, the Soviet Union displayed a great deal of tactical dualism and flexibility at two levels. First, in the U.S.-Soviet relationship, the Soviet Union under Gorbachev moved to reestablish a détente by reopening negotiations on major arms control issues, conducting dialogues about the "regional conflicts," and using diplomacy to create a sense of its willingness to be reasonable concerning the regional conflicts. All the while, it continued and even expanded its military support to the pro-Soviet regimes. Second, in the maneuvering and diplomacy surrounding each of these five wars, the Soviet Union pursued the tactical approach, long established in Communist tradition, summarized by the Vietnamese Communists as "talk and fight."

In all five conflicts the Soviet Union worked closely with its key regional allies and the pro-Soviet regimes to coordinate political, propaganda, diplomatic, clandestine, and military actions aimed at legitimating the pro-Soviet regimes, strengthening them militarily, and isolating the anti-Communist resistance movements. Among many examples were the Contadora talks and draft treaties followed by the 1987 Arias plan as a means of ending U.S. military aid to the Nicaraguan resistance while simultaneously the Soviet Union doubled military aid to the Nicaraguan Communist regime. When the Mexican sponsorship of regional political agreements (1982–1986) repeatedly failed to bring about the desired result, the new president of Costa Rica was persuaded to come forward with essentially the same approach and found himself strongly supported by the entire Soviet propaganda and political action apparatus.

The Afghanistan negotiations under UN auspices that began in 1982 were coordinated with a series of cosmetic internal political changes and maneuvers made under Soviet guidance. Starting in 1985 those processes were used to persuade the U.S. State Department to agree to cut off all external military aid to the resistance once Soviet troops *began* to leave. This agreement, made without the knowledge of President Reagan, set the stage for the final process of negotiation in 1987 and 1988, when the Soviet Union achieved its aim: credit for having withdrawn its troops coupled with the preservation of the pro-Soviet Kabul regime. When President Zia of Pakistan complicated the postagreement prospects for the Kabul regime by ignoring Soviet warnings to stop supplies to the resistance, he was assassinated—most likely by the Soviet Union acting in concert with the Kabul regime.

In Angola, the Soviet Union encouraged both the MPLA regime and the Frelimo regime to initiate negotiations with South Africa in 1983 and 1984. At the same time, the Soviet Union began a series of overtures and threats toward the South African leadership. Soon after, the pro-Soviet African National Congress (ANC) began a campaign combining violence with calls for free-world economic sanctions against South Africa, fulfilling a Soviet prediction of what South Africa could expect if it continued to provide military aid to UNITA and Renamo. Agreements in 1984 meant to turn South Africa away from the anti-Communist resistance movements broke down, but in 1987 and especially in 1988 the Soviet Union again took the lead in structuring a political and diplomatic process meant to end South Africa's aid to the anti-Communist resistance movements. Although the Soviet Union was not a direct participant in the final series of Angolan negotiations in 1988, it had high-ranking personnel present at all the talks. Simultaneously in the spring of 1988, it provided logistical support for Cuba to increase sharply its military presence in Angola, just as Gorbachev and Reagan were meeting in Moscow and agreeing on an intensive series of talks that would produce an agreement on Angola and Namibia—another classic example of the "talk and fight" strategy in which the Communist side increased both its military pressure and its diplomatic activities to spur its opponents to be more conciliatory in the negotiating process.

Perhaps most remarkable in this process, which extended over some years, was the ability of the Soviet Union and its key allies to create almost overnight a mood of expectation among non-Communist diplomats and media observers about its willingness to be reasonable: A point of view that served Soviet interests would be disseminated through customary propaganda techniques and soon would be taken up by some media commentators and analysts who seemed to believe the misinformation cues predicting a "genuine settlement."

The Soviet Union also seemed able to use its propaganda resources to change perceptions of the five pro-Soviet regimes. For example, in a matter of months in 1988 the Soviet-disseminated view of the Afghan Communist regime switched from weak, on the brink of collapse (before the signing of the April 14, 1988, agreement), to strong and resilient (after Soviet troop withdrawal was reported completed in February 1989). At one stage of negotiations, when the Soviet Union wanted to create a sense that it was desperate for an agreement and that it was prepared to see the Afghan regime crumble, the Western media reported that Soviet safe-conduct passes were being distributed to the Afghan Communist regime so that they could flee at any moment—as if such a piece of paper would be needed for crossing into the Soviet Union if that suited Soviet interests. This perception of a fragile Afghan regime on the point of collapse was widely shared by official U.S. and other observers. But once the Soviet Union had the agreement it wanted, there was no more talk of safe-conduct passes or the imminent collapse of the Kabul regime. To the contrary, the Soviets were then perceived as determined to continue the Kabul regime, while the resistance movements were portrayed as fragile, divided, and weak. These shifting perceptions could be observed in the comments of officials from free-world governments, including the United States, and in the general media reporting on Afghanistan, and similar shifts occurred in each of the major regional conflicts.

A number of examples illustrate the pattern of close Soviet cooperation with its regional allies. The Soviet Union was a direct participant in the Afghanistan talks and saw to it that a Kabul regime delegation was always present for the Soviet delegation to consult and brief. In the Angolan talks when the USSR was not a formal direct participant, it was nevertheless permitted to have observers present in all the talks, who were in close consultation with the MPLA regime and Cuba. In the many Central American negotiations involving Nicaragua, Cuban officials were either an informal part of the Nicaraguan delegation or were close at hand. Behind the Cuban officials working with the Nicaraguan officials, Soviet personnel probably provided up-to-the-minute information and, perhaps, suggestions to guide Sandinista diplomacy.

In the four cases where extensive negotiations occurred during the 1980s, the pro-Soviet regimes achieved far more legitimacy and acceptance in the non-Communist world than they had enjoyed at the beginning of the process. The Soviet Union understood that the very process of involving the regimes in negotiations under UN or regional auspices would work to legitimate those regimes, making them appear to be the "government," not just the current regimes, and would reduce their isolation from the non-Communist world. In contrast, the United States made a double mistake: first, in failing to realize that this was the likely result of such a process; and second, in failing to ensure the involvement of the anti-Communist resistance movements at all times as equals in the negotiations enjoying the same advantages as the pro-Soviet regimes.

The Soviet Union and its regional allies seem to have invented a new and successful political approach during the 1980s: the use of an ostensibly neutral non-Communist country in the region as a stalking horse for the political result preferred by the Communist side. Mexico played this role in the case of Nicaragua. Once the contras became a threat, the Mexican foreign ministry evolved a "peace plan," with Cuban encouragement, that was to have the effect of leaving the Sandinista regime in place and dissolving the anti-Communist resistance movement. First proposed in 1982 by the president of Mexico, this approach became the essence of the regional negotiating process. It involved Mexico and three, then seven other Latin American countries, all seeking to pressure four Central American countries into acceding to a settlement they had repeatedly rejected. From 1979 the successive foreign ministers of Mexico coordinated with Cuba and Nicaragua before proposing new draft treaties and then mobilized the other Latin American countries to put pressure on the non-Communist Central American countries to sign those treaties.

The same approach was applied in Angola, with South Africa being persuaded and pressured to turn away from the resistance movements opposing the Angolan and Mozambican Communist regimes. Once the Angola-Namibia accords were signed in December 1988, coercion and deception were used to make the president of Zaire less willing to cooperate with UNITA. In the case of Cambodia, Soviet-backed Vietnam reached out to the new Thai leadership in 1988 with the promise of Southeast Asia as a "market" for Thailand if the Vietnamese-backed regime would retain control of Cambodia. In the Afghan case, India played the role of the non-Communist country supporting Communist objectives in the United Nations and other international arenas. If both Iran and India worked for a "political solution" in Afghanistan, involving a coalition between the Kabul regime and elements of the resistance, the Kabul regime could remain dominant. The usefulness of these non-Communist regimes as a de facto partner of the Soviet Union and its regional allies is that it misleads the leaders and the public in non-Communist countries. Those regimes also provide a valuable patina of respectability for the agreements reached.

Soviet actions in these five wars suggested that Moscow was applying the lessons of past negotiations with non-Communist regimes. One lesson was that the Communist side could break signed agreements with impunity. After Vietnam broke the international agreements of 1954, 1962, and 1973, the same Communist regime was taken as a valid negotiating partner during the 1980s—and Vietnam even proposed a revival of the same type of agreement for Cambodia that it had broken before. Although the MPLA broke the Alvor accord in 1975, virtually no mention was made of it in the 1980s except by UNITA. Nor did the December 1988 accords on Angola and Namibia take account of this past conduct of the MPLA regime and Cuba and provide for effective measures to guarantee verification and compliance. The lesson the Soviet Union no doubt communicated to its regional allies is that once agreements are signed there is little need to be concerned about monitoring, verification, or adverse consequences in the event of nonimplementation.

At the same time, the Soviet Union understands that the signing of such political agreements—which are always greeted with great hopes in the non-Communist countries—creates a sense of "peace in our time" with respect to that particular conflict. The non-Communist governments seldom observe ensuing events closely but typically reduce their support for the anti-Communist resistance movements. Beyond that, the agreements themselves, as reached in Central America, Afghanistan, Angola, and Namibia, have legitimated the pro-Soviet regimes by assuming they are legitimate and may well continue in power. These three agreements testify to the skill of the Communist side and the incompetence of their negotiating partners, including the United States.

The Soviet Union also gained confidence from these conflicts about its influence over UN organizations. In the 1950s and 1960s, the Soviet Union depended upon the participation of allied Communist regimes in international control commissions to neutralize effective monitoring of the Communist violations of agreements.[36] But in 1986 Moscow announced it would pay its dues for the peace-keeping operations of the United Nations, and in 1987 Gorbachev called for greatly expanding the role of these organizations. By the late 1980s the Soviet Union assumed it could rely on the United Nations itself to advance Soviet purposes or at least not too adversely affect them in Afghanistan, Angola, and Nicaragua. The lack of effective response by the UN monitoring organizations in the face of Soviet bombing of Afghan resistance forces from Soviet territory and Sandinista aggression against El Salvador through armed subversion suggests this Soviet confidence is partly warranted (although UN observers were mildly critical of some Sandinista abuses during the campaign for the February 1990 presidential election).

The strategy of national reconciliation is another example of the advice Moscow gave these regimes, drawing upon Soviet experience. Concerned about their capacity to overcome the internal armed resistance movements, Moscow advised all of the regimes to appear moderate in order to obtain greater support from non-Communist countries. The recommended approaches were adopted by all five pro-Soviet regimes and were reinforced by the international "peace negotiations." As one longtime observer of the Soviet Union put it: "The centerpiece of Soviet strategy in the Third World under Gorbachev has been public calls for governments of national reconciliation [in which] the basic idea was to appear conciliatory but to increase the military pressure."[37]

Another aspect of contemporary Soviet foreign policy that emerges from an analysis of these five wars is the intention to exploit the economic resources controlled by these regimes. After World War II Stalin's regime used its political success in Eastern Europe to strip industrial and economic resources from East Germany, Czechoslovakia, and the other satellite countries. In the 1980s Moscow in effect tried to do the same in these five countries. Cuba and Vietnam had already demonstrated that economic and military supplies from the Soviet Union had to be repaid in some practical way. Cuba has repaid its support from Moscow (estimated in 1988 at 25 percent of Cuban GNP or $4–5 billion) with the tens of thousands of combat and secret police personnel it sent to Africa and elsewhere to help other pro-Soviet regimes. Communist Vietnam and Mozambique have paid for their Soviet military supplies with the labor of tens of thousands sent to work in harsh climates in the Soviet Union and throughout the Soviet bloc countries. As with the five regimes discussed here, a precise accounting of these payments is not possible because the Soviet Union and its allies have made great efforts to keep these transactions secret.

In the case of Afghanistan, a high Soviet official has claimed that everything the Soviet Union has had to spend on its military occupation and weapons supplies has been paid for with Afghan natural resources extracted from the mineral-rich regions on the Soviet border. In the case of Angola, most of its oil earnings (nearly $12 billion during the first ten years) probably went to pay Cuba for the troops and the Soviet Union for its weapons. (Quite possibly Cuba, in turn, was required to pay Moscow a share of those dollar earnings as part of the large Cuban-financial debt to the USSR.) In addition there are many reports about the Soviet extraction of natural resources like minerals and timber from Angola and Mozambique, as well as large scale depletion of fish and other sea resources by Soviet commercial fleets off the coast of Angola and Mozambique.

In its fight against Renamo, Mozambique did not receive the tens of thousands of Cuban troops that Angola did, perhaps because the Frelimo regime could not pay for them in hard currency. The estimated amount of Soviet weapons ($2 billion) provided to Mozambique roughly kept pace with the hard-currency Western economic aid ($2.7 billion) provided over the years. The data suggest that part of the free-world economic help to Mozambique and Angola was diverted to Moscow to pay for weapons it shipped the regime.

Cambodia paid Vietnam, and indirectly the Soviet Union (which charged Vietnam for its military supplies) for its occupation forces with land used by an estimated 500,000 Vietnamese settlers over a period of ten years. In the case of Nicaragua, which Moscow supplied with about $3.1 billion worth of weapons, much of the hundreds of millions of dollars' worth of free-world economic assistance may have gone to pay for those weapons. According to frequent reports, gold from Nicaraguan mines has filled Soviet and Cuban coffers. At the same time, in this small country of about 3 million persons, a billion or more dollars in assistance from non-Communist sources produced little evidence of projects in health, education, or economic development. Soviet relations with these additions to its empire in general have the economically exploitative character described by Lenin in his critique of imperialism.

Authoritative U.S. government sources have estimated the value of weapons supplied by the Soviet Union to these five countries during the 1980s at $6 billion to $10 billion per year (and totals for the decade at $60 billion to $100 billion).[38] The delivered weapons are costed on the basis of assumed production costs (perhaps discounted if used) and converted into dollars. As a means of measuring the extent of Soviet military exports, this approach does provide a consistent method for all the different countries to which weapons are sent. But do these estimates measure net costs or gains for the Soviet Union? The actual current value of the second- and third-hand weapons usually sent to these regimes may be virtually nothing to Moscow, since such weapons have been eliminated from the Soviet armed forces as part of its massive military production and modernization that has gone on for many years. Further, if the Soviet Union charges the receiving countries the initial cost of these weapons in hard currency or commodities such as gold or oil, the weapons are a major export, earning Moscow tens of billions in foreign exchange or commodities, which the regimes cannot easily refuse to pay. Therefore, these enormous shipments may serve the Soviet Union as an aid to its intensive military modernization, as a source of needed hard-currency income and commodities, and as a means for keeping pro-Soviet regimes in power and dependent on Moscow.

U.S. Foreign Policy

The fiftieth anniversary of the Munich agreements in 1988 was an occasion for recalling that well-intentioned but poorly conceived international political settlements can increase the risks of wider conflict rather than promote genuine peace. One commentator noted that, in reaching agreements with Hitler, British Prime Minister Chamberlain "without the slightest doubt . . . believed he had performed an act of great nobility."[39] So too, as the Reagan administration came to an end, the president and his State Department probably felt they had done their best in the negotiations concerning these five wars and performed "an act of great nobility" when agreements were signed. Except in Mozambique these conflicts received an enormous amount of attention from the executive branch during the Reagan years, with the State Department leading the negotiating process.

A major problem, however, was the difference between the policy objectives of the president and the operational goals set by the Department of State. In four of the five wars, President Reagan was clear about his objectives: the restoration of independent non-Communist governments (Mozambique was the exception). These objectives of the president were made explicit not only in his written decision directives to the leadership of the executive branch but also in public speeches, including major speeches to the U.S. Congress and to the American people on television. The public process of affirming these objectives—"helping freedom fighters not just fight and die for freedom, but win freedom"—had been given an added dimension in the president's state of the union addresses of 1985 and 1986. In early 1985, CIA Director William Casey also gave public speeches clearly enunciating the objective of helping the anti-Communist resistance forces win. Once President Reagan had declared this as policy, Secretary of State Shultz also spoke eloquently on behalf of the cause of the anti-Communist resistance movements.

U.S. assistance to the Afghan resistance had begun in the Carter years and retained strong bipartisan support throughout the 1980s. The initial objectives of this aid included both the withdrawal of Soviet forces and the liberation of Afghanistan from the Communist regime, and during the Reagan administration both objectives were clearly expressed by the president and became the basis of policy in the executive branch, with full support from the Congress. Next came U.S. aid to the anti-Communist resistance in Nicaragua. A strong faction among Democratic members of Congress adamantly opposed this military assistance; they did not see the Sandinista regime as a threat to neighboring states or to its own people, or to the interests of the United States warranting this type of international action. Although this congressional opposition did not yet command a majority in 1983, the Department of State—while providing rhetorical support to President Reagan's objective of a democratic, free government in Nicaragua established through fair elections as had been promised the OAS in 1979—formulated as an operational objective a political settlement that would leave the Sandinista regime in place and dismantle the contras in return for an end to Nicaraguan armed subversion against neighboring countries.[40] From the time Secretary Shultz agreed to this objective in 1983, the State Department worked toward this end.

In the case of Angola the Republican leadership in Congress failed in its first attempt to remove restrictions on military aid to the UNITA anti-Communist resistance in 1981. Following declaration of the Reagan Doctrine in 1985, however, the Republican leadership was successful—the prohibitions were repealed in the summer of 1985. Then, despite Secretary Shultz's earlier stated support for aid to the anti-Communist fighters, the Department of State strongly opposed action within the executive branch to bring the issue to President Reagan for decision and opposed proposals in Congress to provide funding for the anti-Communist resistance.[41] Nevertheless, CIA Director Casey brought the issue to President Reagan, who told the people of the United States, after his first summit meeting with Gorbachev, that military aid would be provided to UNITA.

In the case of Cambodia, the Reagan administration and Secretary Shultz endorsed the goals of the resistance and the establishment of an independent non-Communist Cambodia as the objective of U.S. policy, but chose not to provide any direct military support. In the case of Mozambique, the Department of State opposed any aid to the resistance forces, preventing this issue from reaching President Reagan for decision in the the early 1980s; the State Department subsequently persuaded the president to endorse its policy of normalization with the Frelimo regime, which was publicly signaled by the president's meeting at the White House with the Frelimo leader in September 1985.

Mozambique has always been a special case. The record suggests that the U.S. government seems never to have understood that the Frelimo movement was Marxist-Leninist and would be a Soviet ally. In 1974–1975, when Portugal negotiated the Frelimo takeover without consulting the people of Mozambique, the United States made no objection. After the newly installed Frelimo president hailed the Communist conquest of South Vietnam, Cambodia, and Laos in the spring of 1975 as a "victory over the most criminal and bloodthirsty aggressors of our time, American imperialism," President Ford sent a warm letter congratulating him on taking office. The Reagan State Department and ultimately the Reagan administration has tried for years to "wean away" the Mozambique regime from its Soviet ties with political and economic cooperation. NATO countries were encouraged to become involved with the regime. The Department of State warmly greeted the Frelimo regime's plans for economic reforms and liberalization in 1983 and welcomed each new announced reform as a sign that the regime was becoming neutral, rather than remaining a Soviet ally. In 1985, Republican senators wrote Secretary Shultz to urge a "pro-Western strategy" in southern Africa to include expanded support for UNITA in Angola and for Renamo in Mozambique, as well as for political action to encourage a peaceful transition to multiracial democracy in South Africa. After the Department of State opposed aid to the anti-Communist resistance in Mozambique, however, the majority in Congress acquiesced.

In four of the five countries, then, the State Department took as its operational objective the removal of Communist troops from foreign territories, the end of armed subversion, or both, rather than victory for the anti-Communist resistance movements, the goal of the president. This difference was illustrated by a battle over the president's major proposal to the United Nations in October 1985 for a "regional peace process." The text the Department of State provided for President Reagan would have had him welcoming the Communist regimes back into the world of free nations once foreign Communist troops were withdrawn. Because of last-minute objections by CIA Director Casey, President Reagan changed the State Department text to conform to his own policy objectives, which sought to bring about governments transformed by "democratic revolutions" and fully respectful of human rights. But this did not change the State Department's approach.[42]

Until the end of 1989 the Democratic majority in Congress had exerted a highly negative influence on the president's objectives only in the case of Nicaragua. In Afghanistan, Angola (after 1985), and Cambodia, a majority in Congress was prepared to support President Reagan's objectives. Repeated efforts to restrict or cut off military aid to Angola were defeated during 1986–1989. Congress acted in 1988 to oppose the State Department's willingness to cut off virtually all military aid to the resistance in Afghanistan at the start of a Soviet troop withdrawal. Even in the case of Nicaragua, had the State Department fully supported his objectives, President Reagan could have built on his June 1986 success in obtaining $70 million in military aid for the resistance. Despite the Iran-contra congressional investigations, he could probably have won additional military aid to the contras. But the State Department's support for the Reagan-Wright plan in turn led to the Arias political settlement of August 1987; that settlement gave the Democratic majority in Congress a political basis for deferring and ultimately defeating President Reagan's request for military aid for the Nicaraguan resistance in 1987 and 1988.[43]

The differences between elements of the Congress and the president on military support of the Nicaraguan resistance reflected constitutionally proper disagreements. But actions *within* the executive branch against the policy decisions of the president, or actions not authorized by the president that undermine his policy decisions (as a number of State Department negotiating initiatives did), pose serious challenges to the president's authority over the executive branch in foreign policy. That lack of unity behind President Reagan's policy within the executive branch itself hindered the effort to help the anti-Communist resistance movements win.

A second major problem of American foreign policy has been a lack of understanding of the wars being waged. The Soviet Union understood that defeating the resistance movements required activities in three arenas: the individual countries, where the Communist regimes were to be supported with political and military means; the regional political context, where the resistance movements were to be isolated from contiguous countries that gave them support; and the international arena, where the pro-Soviet regimes were to seek political and economic support from non-Communist sources while resistance movements were to be isolated. Most important, the resistance movements had to be defeated in the U.S. Congress. With some important exceptions, many U.S. State Department officials did not fully grasp the three arenas in which this political-military warfare was being simultaneously fought and often seemed surprised and outmaneuvered when events in one arena had consequences in another. For example, the U.S. secretary of state urged President Reagan to sign the Reagan-Wright plan in August 1987, apparently not realizing that this would likely be followed by the regional presidents' signing the Arias plan.

The fundamental flaw was the State Department's assumption in all regional conflicts after 1985 that withdrawal of foreign troops would lead to internal political liberalization, transition away from one-party dictatorships, and a cessation of aggression against their neighbors. This misunderstanding of the pro-Soviet regimes and their most important allies, Moscow and Havana, reflected an inability to learn from the post–World War II agreements with Communist regimes and movements. In the 1962 Laos agreement the United States had failed to learn from the mistakes of the 1954 Indochina agreement; nor were the lessons of Communist violations of both those agreements reflected in the negotiations of the 1973 Vietnam agreements. A synthesis of that historical experience was prepared for the Reagan administration leadership in 1984 and later published by the Department of Defense. It showed that the Communist signatories to four major regional political settlements (including the Korean settlement) conducted massive violations of the agreements; that international monitoring processes were totally ineffective in preventing these violations; and that the end result was the breakdown of the agreements and three Communist victories.[44]

This experience might have taught that a pro-Soviet regime must give up its monopoly of power and compete in free and fair elections; that rigorous terms of settlement are needed; that verification and compliance monitoring mechanisms must be created that cannot be sabotaged by the Communist side; and that the agreements themselves must provide specific sanctions against either side in the event of major violations. None of the political settlements under review had any of these features. They were all loosely drawn, the monitoring mechanisms were inadequate, and the agreements had no provisions for sanctions against violators.

Throughout the 1980s the United States was largely unable to achieve the president's purposes in these wars. Because of the lack of systematic coordination of diplomacy, international information activities, political action activities, military support, and special operations, the initiative almost always seemed to be taken by the Communist side. In Angola, for example, the United States made too little effort to isolate the MPLA from free-world economic aid, even though it had broken the 1975 Alvor agreement for free elections and was therefore illegitimate. There was hardly any mention of the guerrilla training bases Angola provided on its territory for aggression against neighboring countries. Similarly, too little was done to demonstrate to friendly countries in Latin America and NATO that the Sandinista regime had broken its 1979 democratic promises to the OAS and initiated aggression through armed subversion against neighboring countries. Although President Reagan frequently drew attention to these legitimate causes of action underlying the U.S. military support for the contras, the United States failed to take the issue to international organizations (such as the OAS) where Nicaraguan aggression could and should have been condemned. This happened even though the CIA declassified a great deal of information proving Sandinista aggression. In contrast, five years after its founding the Sandinista regime sought to have the International Court of Justice find against the United States and its allies for aiding the contras. This successful effort enhanced the Sandinistas' legitimacy in the eyes of some countries.

In the case of Afghanistan and Cambodia, the United States and other free-world countries were effective in obtaining annual UN votes of condemnation against the illegitimate regimes established by Soviet or Vietnamese invasion. But this was not buttressed by an international campaign to obtain legitimacy and at least political and economic support for the anti-Communist resistance forces.

Over a nine-year period there is no evidence that the U.S. president and his senior advisers ever examined the strategic implications and opportunities of these five conflicts or considered together and explored the common aspects of Soviet tactics on behalf of the Communist regimes. Nor does there seem to have been any systematic effort after the signing of the three agreements (Central America, March 1987; Afghanistan, April 1988; Angola, December 1988) to establish a careful U.S. monitoring process to ensure that the agreements being implemented were having the results intended. And there is no sign of any contingency plans dealing with violations of these agreements by the Communist side.

Another major shortcoming has been the failure of the United States to work closely with the resistance movements in the political and diplomatic process. The United States did not insist that the resistance movements in one way or another be represented in the negotiations. As a result, many resistance leaders have felt more like objects of U.S. policy than participants in an effort to achieve common objectives. In great measure that was true because the State Department's objectives have differed from those of the resistance movements. This distance between the resistance movements and the United States weakened the anti-Communist effort more with each succeeding phase of the years-long diplomacy. While the Communist side used the negotiating process as a means of legitimating the pro-Soviet regimes—bringing them into contact with international organizations and other governments, consulting them, and having them treated as the de facto governments of their countries—the United States failed to take actions that could have enhanced the international standing of the resistance movements. Nor did the State Department show that it understood that diplomacy in itself could affect the resistance-regime balance of power—depending on the skill of each side.

In signing the Afghan agreement as a guarantor, the U.S. government stated that this in no way implied recognition of the Kabul regime. But the act of guaranteeing a political agreement between the Kabul regime and the government of Pakistan put the United States on record as in fact recognizing the Soviet-backed regime as the "government" of Afghanistan. From that point, more countries began giving diplomatic recognition to the Kabul regime as the government of Afghanistan. The same result followed U.S. participation in the Angola-Namibia settlement. The effect has been to give legitimacy and diplomatic recognition to the MPLA regime, which has helped it attain a key objective: access to World Bank and IMF economic resources.

In the same way, the Arias agreement on Central America was followed by further international acceptance of the Sandinista regime—well in advance of any evidence that it would hold and genuinely abide by the results of democratic elections in February 1990. The legitimation of the Sandinista regime persisted even in the face of evidence made public by the governments of El Salvador and Honduras that the Sandinistas continued to ship weapons to Communist guerrillas in neighboring countries. In another example of legitimation, President Bush participated on October 27-28, 1989, in a meeting in Costa Rica of Latin American democracies that excluded Cuba, the Noriega regime in Panama, Chile, and Haiti, but included the Sandinista regime.[45]

These issues of legitimacy are important in themselves, but they also have great tactical importance for the outcome of the wars. As Ambassador Kirkpatrick has written, these wars are won "by eroding the will of the stronger."[46] Isolating the regimes and building support for the resistance through effective communications, diplomacy, and political actions should have been an integral part of U.S. strategy. Too little was done for the resistance movements by the United States while the Soviet Union campaigned to reduce support for the resistance movements in the non-Communist world.

All of these observations point to one dominant characteristic of U.S. foreign policy with respect to these five conflicts: it was too often conducted on a day-to-day basis, looking at each conflict and negotiation in isolation with the typical negotiator's perspective of seeking some kind of an agreement within a given period of time. For example, the assassination of President Zia on August 17, 1988, was not carefully examined by the U.S. government; nor were its implications considered for the Afghan agreement, for judgments about Soviet intentions in all these wars, not even for the on-going Angolan negotiations. This is known in part because in 1989 the U.S. Congress began investigating whether the State Department avoided gathering information that might have pointed to Soviet responsibility for that assassination.[47]

Nevertheless, despite these U.S. shortcomings in its policies in these five conflicts, the Reagan Doctrine may well have made a major contribution to the defense of freedom, whatever the final outcomes. Without it the United States might have taken no interest in these struggles; it might have remained neutral. Or worse, if the prescriptions of those Democrats in Congress who opposed military aid to the anti-Communist resistance movements had been followed, the United States might have helped bring about "power sharing" government, as, for example, in El Salvador as France and Mexico proposed in 1981. This might have unintentionally hastened Communist victories in Central America and southern Africa and helped those who believed that the Soviet- and Vietnamese-backed regime in Cambodia should be given international recognition.

Either set of alternative U.S. policies—neutrality or misguided support for coalitions with Communist movements and regimes— would likely have seen the defeat of the resistance movements years ago. None of the countries contiguous to the war zones whose help has been critical to the anti-Communist resistance movements could have withstood the coercion of the Soviet Union and its regional allies had they not been backed by the United States. Furthermore, the combination of the Reagan Doctrine and the courage of the resistance fighters and their supporters inside these countries probably helped prevent Soviet-backed takeovers during the 1980s. The resistance movements were, in effect, the line of first defense for neighboring countries, which would have been subjected to more intense armed subversion by each of these five regimes if they had not had to give first priority to staying in power. The Soviet leadership also came to realize that additional conquests through indirect aggression might also meet sustained armed resistance and that even with hundreds of thousands of combat troops and unlimited brutality, this form of warfare could prevent the consolidation of Communist power for years. These factors, in turn, may have contributed to the change in strategy that made the USSR unwilling to use military threats or armed force in 1989 to prevent the gathering momentum of political liberalization in Eastern Europe.

Comparing the United States and the USSR

While the Soviet Union remained steadfast in seeking victories of the pro-Soviet regimes over the resistance movements, the United States has been divided internally in its strategic objectives. The Soviet Union worked closely with the regimes and other allies to coordinate its political-diplomatic, propaganda, clandestine, and military activities. The United States did not fully involve the resistance in the major negotiations, did not seek to legitimate the resistance movements through the negotiating process, and often failed to coordinate effectively its political, diplomatic, covert, and military activities—though there were exceptions. The Soviet Union clearly learned from past negotiations with the United States and taught the lessons to its partners. By contrast, the most elementary precautions for effective political settlements were virtually ignored in the proposals by the U.S. side.

Finally, throughout the 1980s the Soviet Union maintained a double-track relationship with the United States: negotiations and normalization combined with efforts to strengthen pro-Soviet regimes and undertake indirect aggression and other activities inimical to U.S. interests. During the Gorbachev years the Soviet Union has used the rhetoric of cooperation in a highly effective way to persuade many U.S. officials that the Soviet Union intended to be reasonable in these regional political settlements. It was careful to see, however, that the settlements agreed to by its allies would not result in their losing power.

The United States should have maintained an effective dual strategy but did not: negotiations and dialogue combined with adequate levels of continued help to ensure that the anti-Communist resistance movements succeed. In these five conflicts, the two superpowers have pursued different objectives for many years. The classic definition of power in international relations is "the capacity to achieve intended effects." The evidence from these five wars is that the Soviet Union is achieving its "intended effects" and that Tocqueville's observation—discussed in the introduction—has applied to this dimension of U.S. foreign policy. Because of the contrast in the competence of the Soviet Union and the United States, the pro-Soviet regimes are likely to remain in effective control (Nicaragua may be an exception)—unless the Soviet Union changes its current policy and withdraws its political and military support.

337

Geopolitical, Regional, and Human Consequences of Victory or Defeat for the Resistance Movements

In 1956 Nikita Khrushchev was reported to have told the Twentieth Congress of the Communist Party of the Soviet Union that, until then, Moscow had tried to avoid capitalistic encirclement, but from that time the emphasis would be on encircling the capitalists.[48] In the late 1950s the Soviet leadership gave markedly increased attention to developing countries.[49] The announcement in 1961 that the Soviet Union would support "wars of national liberation" provided the rationale for what Moscow was already doing. In effect a more than thirty years' war has been waged by the Soviet Union using the techniques of indirect aggression to bring pro-Soviet regimes to power. This indirect aggression continued during the détente of the 1970s and, as pointed out earlier, led to the establishment of eleven new pro-Soviet regimes. President Jimmy Carter began his term of office in 1977 with the confident declaration that the United States had "lost its inordinate fear of communism"; after the Soviet invasion of Afghanistan in 1979, he said that for the first time he understood the hostile character of Soviet foreign policy.

As the Reagan administration was preparing to take office in November 1980, I prepared an overview of the key strategic targets of this Soviet indirect aggression and the coalition of pro-Soviet regimes and entities that was helping indigenous pro-Soviet groups take power in target countries. This overview of three geographic regions suggested that Mexico, South Africa, and Saudi Arabia and other Persian Gulf countries were the focal points of Soviet intentions (see table 2–2).

The more assertive foreign policy and military modernization of President Reagan's first years in office, the growing effectiveness of the anti-Communist armed resistance movements, the tragic consequences of conquest by pro-Soviet elites in killing fields from Cambodia to Afghanistan all combined with the changes of Soviet leadership from Brezhnev to Andropov to Chernenko to Gorbachev to stem further Soviet advances through indirect aggression. Although some observers would add that Gorbachev's "new thinking" in foreign policy was also a major factor in reducing Soviet hostile actions, this has not been the case in the developing world. In addition to the massive political, military, clandestine, diplomatic, and propaganda efforts during the Gorbachev years against anti-Communist armed resistance movements, the Soviet Union continued trying to bring pro-Soviet regimes to power in virtually all the developing countries that were major targets at the start of the 1980s. Although the rhetoric and methods changed with the expansion of the negotiating and

338

diplomatic components, the threat of additional pro-Soviet regimes coming to power in developing countries has remained. But any new commitment of Soviet combat forces in visible units and any open use of allied regime forces in the context of invasion seemed unlikely—though they might be used to respond to "invitations" to keep pro-Soviet regimes in power.

Steps toward political liberalization in Eastern Europe do not contradict the facts of Soviet actions in the developing regions. As history has demonstrated, the Soviet Union is capable of conducting a differentiated foreign policy. It can offer elements of genuine normalization and zones of reduced threat, as it seems to be undertaking toward the major economic and military powers of the world, while continuing indirect aggression to bring additional pro-Soviet regimes to power. Should the need arise the Soviet Union is likely to use whatever coercion is necessary to halt or reverse liberalization in Eastern Europe. The events of 1953, 1956, 1968, and 1981 demonstrated that the NATO alliance would not pose a military challenge to the Soviet use of coercion or military force against any East European regime or population. (As personal relationships are reaffirmed between the people of East and West Germany with the disappearance of the Berlin Wall, however, West Germany might seek to use its economic resources and perhaps its own or NATO military forces to deter the use of Soviet force in East Germany.)

Continuing political liberalization in Eastern Europe is likely to make the hard-line elements of the Soviet Communist leadership uneasy, from fear of an uncontrollable process that would spread into the Soviet Union itself and require enormous coercion to repress. The Soviet leadership might, however, have confidence in its ultimate capacity to use its own secret police and military instruments to keep power. Significant liberalization in Eastern Europe could be permitted for the sake of helping Moscow obtain economic resources from the West, obtaining the neutralization of Germany and the de facto end of NATO, and creating a mood of Western confidence that communism is no longer a threat. That could be the perfect background for helping additional pro-Soviet groups take power in key vulnerable countries (especially South Africa and the Persian Gulf), which could add enormously to the economic, political, and military power of the Soviet Union. In my view, this is far more likely if the resistance movements are defeated, and for that reason it is important to explore the broader consequences of the outcomes of these five wars in the 1990s.

Success for the anti-Communist resistance movements would rapidly improve the lives of the people living in those countries. It

339

would bring about the voluntary repatriation of large proportions of the more than 8 million who are now refugees, and it would likely be followed by improved living standards as elements of a market economy returned with substantial foreign aid. Victory for the anti-Communist movements would also sharply increase the prospects for peace in each of the regions. Such a major setback for world communism could be especially significant in the context of current efforts at political liberalization in Eastern Europe and in the Soviet Union itself. Revelations of the enormous suffering imposed by these pro-Soviet regimes on their peoples would further convince the world that the Communist system as such—not only particular leaders like Stalin or Pol Pot—produces repression and failure, despite differences in national histories, cultural and religious traditions, and Communist leadership groups.

In contrast, defeat for the anti-Communist resistance movements is likely to mean increased suffering for the people within the countries, with the likelihood that tens of thousands, perhaps hundreds of thousands, would be killed by the victorious regimes to ensure that armed resistance would never rise again. Taking as an estimate approximately 300,000 resistance fighters in all five countries, and assuming an average family size of about six per resistance fighter, 1.8 million people would be in danger of execution, incarceration in concentration camps, or other severe punishment. In addition, entire groups of people who showed their hostility to the regimes, such as the Ovambo in Angola, who constituted 40 percent of the population, might be subjected to systematic repression and deprivation, which could cause additional tens of thousands of deaths.

Further, these victorious pro-Soviet regimes would probably join again with Moscow in concealed aggression against neighboring countries. This surge of indirect aggression could result in death and suffering for millions of people and bring additional pro-Soviet regimes to power, together with a new level of human suffering and significant setbacks for the free world. The principal targets are likely to be the Persian Gulf oil states, South Africa after the establishment of the pro-Soviet regime in Namibia, and Mexico should there be additional Communist victories in Central America. The victories and defeats of the five anti-Communist resistance movements are not necessarily linked to one another, with the possible exception of Angola and Mozambique, where the fate of Renamo and UNITA could have an important mutual effect. Since some anti-Communist resistance movements might succeed while others are defeated, the consequences of victory or defeat in the case of each country will be briefly examined.

Afghanistan—the Persian Gulf

In Afghanistan victory for the resistance would likely be followed by the reestablishment of a moderate regime governed by representation through the tribal assemblies on the principle of either the *shura* or the *Loya Jirga* and expressed through parliamentary institutions. After a period of debate and trial and error concerning the extent of the Moslem clergy's involvement in governance, five of the seven Sunni, Pakistan-based resistance groups are likely to reach a consensus on a system that would have the support of the overwhelming majority of the Afghan people. The remaining two resistance organizations might represent the 15 percent of the Afghan population that is Shiite and press for a more fundamentalist form of government. Some form of devolution of authority to regional or community groups over governmental functions having especially significant religious connotations, such as education, would be a means of solving this problem.

Although the majority of the resistance organizations might conflict with the more fundamentalist minority, the return of moderate government to Afghanistan probably would not be disrupted for long, unless armed support for the minority came from the fundamentalist regime in Iran. In any case, a majority Sunni parliamentary government in Afghanistan would bring a far better life to the people of Afghanistan; it would permit the restoration of both the modern and the traditional institutions and of civil society and would end the massive repression and warfare on a nationwide scale; it would also set the stage for the return of the 6 million Afghan refugees.

There is little question that Afghanistan would pursue a foreign policy of neutrality. It would not seek to stir up the predominantly Sunni Moslems in the Soviet Union, because such actions would invite a massive Soviet counteraction. A moderate, independent Afghanistan would be a force for peace and stability in the entire region, an especially important factor for Pakistan and the Persian Gulf countries. And a moderate, independent Afghanistan with close economic relations with the industrial democracies through aid, investment, and commerce could be a positive model for Iran. It could show the Iranian leadership that a devoutly Islamic nation can maintain good relations with the non-Communist world.

Understanding the possible consequences of the defeat or neutralization of the anti-Communist resistance in Afghanistan requires a look at Soviet foreign policy in the Middle East. For seven decades the Soviet Union has attempted to bring pro-Soviet regimes to power on its southern border, in the Persian Gulf region. Its forces invaded and occupied northern Iran and withdrew in 1921 under British pressure. A treaty conferred the right of Soviet intervention, however, should any hostile activities emanate from Iran. The Iranian government has announced its abrogation of this treaty on numerous occasions, but the Soviet Union has refused to recognize that fact.[50] The 1939 Hitler-Stalin pact provided the clearest statement of Soviet strategic interests in the region by defining the Persian Gulf as "the center of aspirations of the Soviet Union."[51] Even before World War II ended, the Soviet Union began a campaign of clandestine operations and political action to take control of northern Iran. It left its military forces in place in contravention of promises to Great Britain and the United States at the 1943 Tehran summit. In 1946, after it staged a secession of two northern provinces from Iran, [52] President Truman quietly threatened Stalin with nuclear attack. With the withdrawal of Soviet military forces, the newly established republics collapsed. The Soviet Union then turned to political and clandestine action.

The gains sought by the Soviet Union in the Middle East can be seen in an overview of world oil production and reserves (see table 8–3). In 1988 Saudi Arabia, Kuwait, and the United Arab Emirates produced about 9 million barrels of oil a day and accounted for 355 billion barrels of oil reserves. This compares with the U.S. oil reserve estimated at 27 billion barrels, and a total oil reserve for the rest of the non-Communist world estimated at about 142 billion barrels. A major purpose of Soviet foreign policy in the post–World War II era has been to bring pro-Soviet regimes, which would eventually be controlled by Moscow, to power in oil-producing countries. This would increase the resources available to the Soviet Union as well as provide a means for using oil prices and supplies to pressure and neutralize Europe and Japan, which depend on the Persian Gulf suppliers for nearly all their oil imports.

Since the mid-1950s there seems to be a pattern in the Soviet actions focused on countries contiguous to oil-producing countries as well as the oil-producing countries themselves.

First, Soviet military aid and sales have been used to establish relationships with factions in the military, creating a network of pro-Soviet officers. Next, the targeted country then tends to shift its foreign policy toward the Soviet Union and away from the West. Friendship or cooperation treaties are often followed by military and political linkages to the Soviet Union. In some cases, pro-Soviet regimes have been established, and in others, coups have been attempted. Table 8–4 shows this pattern during the past forty years. Among the countries contiguous to the Persian Gulf oil states, Syria, South Yemen, Afghanistan, and Ethiopia moved toward alignment with the Soviet Union. In Egypt the Sadat regime ended its Soviet

TABLE 8–3
GEOPOLITICS OF OIL, 1988

	Production *(millions of barrels per day)*	Reserves *(billions of barrels)*
Pro-Soviet or Soviet-leaning Oil Regimes		
USSR	13	59
Iraq	3	100
Libya	1	22
Iran	3	93
Total	20	274
Oil Regimes at Risk		
Saudi Arabia	5	170
UAE	2	92
Kuwait	2	62
Subtotal	9	324
Mexico	3	54
Total	12	378
Other Major Oil Producers		
Venezuela	2	58
United States	9	27
Nigeria	2	16
Norway	1	11
Algeria	1	8
Indonesia	1	8
Canada	2	8
India	1	6
Subtotal	19	142
China	3	24
Total	22	166

SOURCE: U.S. Energy Information Administration, 1989, on oil production and reserves; author's conceptualization of the international situation of the various countries.

alignment after the 1971 pro-Soviet coup failed and the Soviet-aided surprise attack against Israel on Yom Kippur in 1973 was defeated. Among the oil-producing countries, Libya and in some measure Iraq moved closer to Moscow after military factions replaced the pro-Western monarchies. Emboldened by its success through indirect aggression in the 1970s, Moscow attempted to speed up the pace; it backed unsuccessful attempts to bring pro-Soviet elements to power

343

TABLE 8-4
PATTERN OF EVENTS AND SOVIET ACTIONS IN THE MIDDLE EAST, 1950–1989

	Pro-Western Regime Removed	Soviet Military Sales or Aid Begun	Political Shift toward USSR	Friendship or Cooperation Agreements with USSR	Pro-Soviet Coup[a]
Countries Contiguous to Oil Producers					
Egypt	1952	1955	1956[b]		(1971)
Syria	1954	1956		1980	
Yemen					
			1967 (civil war		
South	1958/67	1970s	1962–1979)	1979	1978, 1986
North		1980s			
Ethiopia	1974	1956	1975	Many after 1977	1977
Afghanistan	1973	1956	1973–75	Many after 1978	1978
Oil Producers					
Iraq	1958	1958	1969	1972/79	(1978)
Libya	1969	1969	1970s		
Iran	1979	1984	1987–89	1989	
Saudi Arabia					(1979)
Bahrain					(1981)
Kuwait					(1983)
United Arab Emirates					

a. Unsuccessful attempts are in parentheses.
b. Reversed, 1972–1973.
SOURCE: Author.

in Iraq (1978), Saudi Arabia (1979), Bahrain (1981), and Kuwait (1983). These were unsuccessful.

During the Iran-Iraq war, from 1980 to 1988, the Soviet Union supplied weapons to both sides and managed to maintain relations with both regimes. After the removal of the pro-Western regime in Iran, the USSR made an intense effort in the late 1980s to establish a close relationship with Iran's Islamic fundamentalist regime and fan hostility against the United States and the pro-Western oil regimes in the Persian Gulf, especially Saudi Arabia. In 1987 the Soviet Union vetoed UN sanctions against Iran for refusing to accept the UN

Security Council resolution calling for a cease-fire in the Iran-Iraq war. In addition, Iran and the Soviet Union were reported to have "negotiated contingency plans for transporting Iranian oil through Soviet territory to the Black Sea for export" in the event of a U.S. naval blockade of Iran's coast.[53] The Soviet Union and Iran signed an economic agreement in August 1987, and an accord in June 1989 that "commits Moscow to participate in a $15 billion economic reconstruction program in Iran." The June 1989 accords also included a Soviet agreement to sell Iran weapons estimated to be worth $3 billion.

This Soviet-Iranian rapprochement significantly added to the threat of internal destabilization against the Persian Gulf oil states. They would have to resist both the Islamic fundamentalists and the far-left secular organizations, such as the Popular Front for the Liberation of Palestine and the pro-Soviet regime in South Yemen that had worked closely with the Soviet Union. This could be seen as the type of two-sided threat from radical Islamic fundamentalists and pro-Soviet extremists I warned about in 1979.[54]

Although these potential threats might exist regardless of the outcome of the war in Aghanistan, the Soviet Union would hesitate to use its full means of indirect aggression against the Persian Gulf oil states as long as the Afghan resistance posed a real threat. That caution during the past few years partly accounts for the Gorbachev peace and diplomatic offensive in the Persian Gulf and the Middle East. A Sunni Moslem movement that had defeated a Soviet-backed Communist regime in Afghanistan could set a dangerous example and exercise strong appeal to the 50 million to 70 million predominantly Sunni Moslems of Soviet Central Asia, especially with the increased assertiveness of ethnic and religious groups made possible by *glasnost*. Even if a non-Communist Afghan government did nothing to stir up Soviet Moslems, such a regime would constitute a powerful symbolic rejection of Moscow, all the more so if the Soviet Union were perceived as destabilizing Moslem countries in the Middle East.

Some will contend that victory for the pro-Soviet regime in Kabul need not necessarily unleash more assertive Soviet indirect aggression in the Persian Gulf. That may be true, but the record suggests otherwise. At the end of World War II the USSR tried to annex northern Iran; in 1978 a Communist coup was successful in Afghanistan; and in 1979 the pro-Western regime came to an end in Iran. Although South Yemen had tilted toward the Soviet Union since 1967, Soviet-guided Cuban forces in 1978 solidified the control of a pro-Soviet faction, which then declared South Yemen the only Marxist-Leninist state in the Arab world. In November 1979, pro-Soviet Libya incited mobs to burn the U.S. embassy and anti-American radicals seized hostages in the U.S. embassy in Iran, while a lightning coup directed from South Yemen was attempted against the pro-Western regime in Saudi Arabia. In the view of James Phillips, a seasoned analyst of Soviet actions in the Middle East, the 1979 coup attempt in Saudi Arabia illustrated actual and potential threat:

> Approximately 5,000 Soviet-bloc advisors control the Yemeni armed forces and civil service bureaucracies. These run South Yemen's secret police while the Cubans provide the backbone for a praetorian guard that shields the regime from its own people. . . . The Popular Front for the Liberation of Palestine (PFLP), a Marxist-Palestinian splinter group, operates terrorist training bases [in South Yemen] in which Soviet-bloc advisors as well as Palestinians train a wide variety of terrorists from around the world. [South Yemen hosts] leaders of the Communist party of Saudi Arabia, Palestinian groups hostile to Riyadh's traditional leadership and Saudi dissidents. According to western European intelligence sources, seventy of the five hundred men who seized the Grand Mosque in Mecca [Saudi Arabia] in 1979 were trained by Cubans with Soviet supervision at a PFLP camp in South Yemen. During the uprising, the South Yemeni army was mobilized along the Saudi border "apparently poised to intervene on the pretext of defending the Holy Places if the revolt showed signs of success."[55]

In this bold effort to seize the oil of the Persian Gulf, the Soviet Union sought to conceal its involvement by working with regional allies.

Similar coalitions attempted coups to bring a radical group to power in Bahrain in 1981 and in Kuwait in 1983. According to one report, the Bahrain coup "was believed to have been master-minded by an Iranian revolutionary thought to have connections with the KGB."[56] The National Liberation Front of Bahrain was "reluctant to proclaim itself a Communist party [but] it is treated as one in Soviet sponsored international conferences."[57]

The failure to bring pro-Soviet factions to power in the Persian Gulf has resulted in a return to the more methodical approach followed elsewhere. The Gorbachev regime has been seeking to open diplomatic relations with Saudi Arabia, which terminated them with Moscow in 1938. It has succeeded in opening relations with the United Arab Emirates (1985) and Oman (1985) and has undertaken extensive military sales and other assistance in North Yemen. Saudi Arabian officers serving with the peace-keeping force in Lebanon in the mid-1970s were reported to have been "approached by Syrian agents of the KGB seeking to build a 'Nasserist' faction in the Saudi army."[58] Over many years, the Soviet Union has supported efforts by its ally in South Yemen to bring a pro-Soviet faction to power in North Yemen and in the neighboring sultanate of Oman. In 1976, the Popular Front for the Liberation of Oman (PFLO), supported by the Soviet Union and South Yemen, was defeated "with the assistance of seconded British officers, Iranian troops (from the then pro-Western regime), and Jordanian advisers. The remnants of the PFLO fled to South Yemen and still enjoy the 'support of the Soviet people.' "[59]

If the Soviets maintain a cooperative relationship with Iran, they can be less concerned about Iranian fundamentalism or a hostile Iranian regime. In early 1990 the Soviet-Iranian relationship was tested when Soviet Azerbaijani dissidents seized weapons and took an anti-Communist stand. They are ethnically the same as Iranian Azerbaijanis and asked Iran for help. But Iran gave no help of any kind and made no protest as Soviet troops sent by Gorbachev quickly suppressed the Azerbaijani armed movement. Moscow fears that a non-Communist Afghanistan would not be as compliant as Iran. Therefore if the pro-Soviet regime remains in power in Kabul, Moscow will have a greater sense of security about its southern border in the 1990s. That could increase Soviet willingness to intensify its efforts to bring Persian Gulf oil states into its orbit.

Moscow could take several tactical approaches against the Persian Gulf oil states in the coming years. It could use its dual strategy of normalizing state-to-state relations while expanding clandestine networks hostile to the regimes. It could secretly help Iran bring down the regime in Kuwait, Saudi Arabia, or some other oil state. That could increase Iran's power, however, and the appeal of Islamic fundamentalism, making it more difficult for the Soviet Union to use clandestine means to bring its own faction to power in Iran.

Another approach might be to use Baluch separatism to accomplish two Soviet goals: dismembering Pakistan and bringing a pro-Soviet faction directly to the Persian Gulf area (see figure 8–1). The Baluch peoples live in Afghanistan, Pakistan, and Iran. They account for only 3 percent of the population of Pakistan, but they occupy 60 percent of the territory. It would serve the interests of both the Soviet Union and India to use Baluch separatism to bring about the dismantling of Pakistan. Using a pro-Soviet regime in Afghanistan as a base, the Soviet Union could help pro-Soviet Baluch elements secede from Pakistan. Then both Moscow and Kabul could recognize and protect this "new country." If Iran were cooperating with the Soviet Union, this new Baluchistan could be carved out of the territory of Pakistan alone. If not, it might include some Iranian territory. Iranian military reprisal could be deterred by Soviet threats across its border with

FIGURE 8–1
POTENTIAL SEPARATIST STATES CARVED OUT OF PAKISTAN

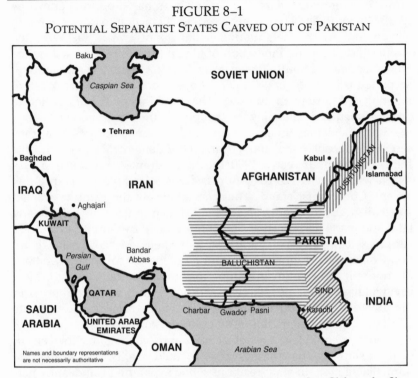

SOURCE: Adapted with permission from Robert Morris, *Our Globe under Siege III* (Mantoloking, N.J.: J & W Enterprises, 1988), p. 77.

Iran. A defector from the Soviet-led Afghan army was reported to say that Moscow is training 8,000 Baluchi dissidents. According to another source, 7,500 Soviet-led guerrillas are in Baluchistan, who could "field 15,000–20,000 additional ones in a matter of weeks." And, according to another report, Ataulla Mengal, a leftist Baluchi leader, declared in 1983 that Pakistan "must cease in its present form" and announced the formation of a "Baluchistan Liberation Organization to lead the armed struggle."[60]

If India and the Soviet Union joined with the Kabul regime to bring about an independent Baluchistan, Pakistan probably could not resist, especially if the process occurred in stages that looked like a domestic upheaval within Pakistan. It is quite possible that Soviet and Indian political warfare against Pakistan would include the revival of the Pushtunistan issue, a separatist movement covertly supported by the Soviet Union since the 1920s, and destabilization activities in the heavily populated Sind region of Pakistan (see figure 8–1). The continued existence of Pakistan as a pro-Western state might therefore be threatened by the victory of the pro-Soviet regime in Kabul. A pro-Soviet Baluch regime on the Persian Gulf would in itself be a major strategic breakthrough for the Soviet Union and would add momentum to pro-Soviet groups in the Persian Gulf oil states. In 1982, the Communist defense minister of Afghanistan said that in advancing international communism he hoped the Afghan army would play a "significant role . . . like that played by the Cuban and Vietnamese armies."[61] If the pro-Soviet regime in Kabul defeated the resistance, might Afghan military and commando forces be used to prop up new pro-Soviet regimes in the Persian Gulf states, as Cuban troops were used in Angola and Ethiopia?

The Soviet Union also could secretly aid indigenous pro-Soviet organizations, such as the Iraqi and Iranian Communist parties, and pro-Soviet separatist or armed groups such as the Kurdish Democratic party, the Peoples Mujihadeen Organization, and the Azerbaijan Democratic party. But as long as an independent non-Communist regime seems possible in Afghanistan, many Soviet maneuvers against the oil states of the Middle East would be risky. While the precise nature of future Soviet moves cannot be known, what can be said, given the historical pattern of these conflicts, is that should the Afghan resistance be defeated or neutralized the Soviet threat to the Persian Gulf oil nations and Pakistan would increase significantly.

Angola and Mozambique—South Africa

The anti-Communist resistance movements in Angola and Mozambique have defined success as free and fair elections that permit the 14 million people in those two countries to choose their governments. If such elections were held, the Communist regimes would probably be turned out of power. Some coalition of non-Communist groups, including the anti-Communist resistance movements, would become the new governments in Angola and Mozambique.

The repression that has characterized both countries under the Communist regimes installed in 1975 would end, and living conditions would be improved. Both countries had flourishing rural economies which were severely damaged by the Marxist-Leninist economic policies. In Mozambique, people were forced to relocate on a massive scale into regimented production communes. In Angola, a non-Communist government could use the sizable annual oil revenues to improve living conditions and the economy, rather than pay for Soviet-bloc weapons and Cuban troops. The end of Communist rule would enable Mozambique to use its natural assets as a transportation corridor and center for tourism to restore earnings in foreign exchange that also could help to improve living conditions. The

349

victory of non-Communist movements in Angola and Mozambique would probably be followed by a significant increase in free-world economic assistance, expanded commercial relations, and at some point investment. Freed of the repression and dogmatism of the Marxist-Leninist regimes, both Angola and Mozambique would make efforts to bring these results about.

Prospects for peace in southern Africa would also improve. Non-Communist governments led by black citizens of Angola and Mozambique would not permit the pro-Soviet African National Congress or other pro-Soviet armed groups to operate from its territory. The positive example of these changes in Angola and Mozambique in combination with the revelations of the full extent of Communist oppression since 1975 might also have a moderating effect on neighboring regimes, including Zimbabwe and Zambia. Concerns about Communist encirclement have been a part of political discourse in South Africa since the MPLA and Frelimo took power in 1975; they could be put aside. The potential example of non-Communist constitutional governments with pro-Western black leaders in Mozambique and Angola would encourage those significant elements of the white and black communities in South Africa who seek a peaceful transition to genuine multiracial democracy.

Finally, revelations of the human suffering caused by Communist rule in Angola and Mozambique would surely follow in the wake of non-Communist governance in both countries. They would have an important effect throughout Africa in showing the mistake of pursuing the Marxist-Leninist path. In combination with the revelations already coming from the Soviet Union and Eastern Europe, the facts of MPLA and Frelimo oppression might reduce the appeal of pro-Soviet organizations, such as the African National Congress in South Africa, and of Marxist-Leninist elements within all organizations.

Unfortunately, these prospects are not the most likely ones. The consequences of UNITA and Renamo defeats must therefore be examined.

The South West Africa Peoples Organization (SWAPO) was determined to take power in a newly independent Namibia using the April 1989–April 1990 transition process. It is a sign of the effectiveness of SWAPO's propaganda (and of its Soviet and Cuban supporters) that the Organization of African Unity endorsed, in advance of the November 1989 elections, the use of armed force by SWAPO should it not receive the two-thirds of the votes that would enable it to control the writing of the new constitution, under which the final elections would be held in 1990.[62] SWAPO received 57 percent of the November

1989 vote, and its leader, Samuel Nujoma, became president of independent Namibia on March 21, 1990. As SWAPO consolidates its power in Namibia, UNITA will probably be ever more isolated on its southern border and cut off from supplies from that direction. In discreet ways SWAPO is likely to collaborate with MPLA regime efforts to encircle Savimbi, in both a political and a military sense. The SWAPO movement is unlikely to risk open military action against UNITA unless it receives thousands of Cuban or other Soviet-allied military forces to serve as a "defensive barrier" against incursions or threats by UNITA or South Africa.

The December 1988 Angola-Namibia accords provided that by November 1, 1989, some 25,000 of the more than 50,000 Cuban troops would be withdrawn from Angola. There was virtually no public discussion whether this occurred, although UNITA seemed to agree that close to that number of troops had withdrawn. But UNITA contended in early 1990 that instead of the permitted 17,000 Cuban troops there were 37,000 Cuban troops left. Further, as discussed earlier, UNITA contended that these Cubans were backing up the large MPLA military attack begun in December 1989 with the direct involvement of an estimated 900 Soviet military personnel. The U.S. State Department publicly criticized this MPLA offensive and Soviet support, stating: "We are very concerned about the . . . offensive military action by the MPLA. [It] is receiving close support from a substantial number of Soviet military advisers at the front line."[63]

In late 1989 hundreds of Cuban troops were reported arriving inside Mozambique to reinforce the thousands of Zimbabwean troops helping the Frelimo regime against Renamo, and there were reports of an increase in Soviet military aid to the Frelimo regime.[64] The addition of Soviet-allied troops, Cubans or North Koreans, would be a logical extension of the reported visit of Cuban Defense Minister Raul Castro and a large delegation of Cuban officers to Mozambique in 1988. In the autumn of 1989 chemical weapons for large-scale use against Renamo were included in reports of increased Soviet-bloc aid. Renamo would lack the experience, resources, and support to defend against such weapons.

The disinformation campaign to delegitimate Savimbi and UNITA in the non-Communist world continued, along with efforts to persuade President Mobutu of Zaire to reduce sharply or totally cut off the transporting of military supplies to Savimbi. At the same time, increased military deliveries from the Soviet bloc to the MPLA increased the likelihood of offensives aimed at the military defeat of UNITA. The accords stated that 17,000 Cuban troops could remain in Angola until July 1991 and established virtually no mechanism to verify their withdrawal reliably. Cuban troops, perhaps with additional Soviet or allied troops, could in the future participate in or back up MPLA military offensives. The 1988 Angola-Namibia accords permitted the Communist regimes in Cuba and Angola unilaterally to change (even reverse) the withdrawal schedule of Cuban troops if either should decide that South Africa or any other country has violated the agreements. Castro did this for some weeks in late 1989 and could again.

To deter South African military intervention on behalf of UNITA or of prodemocratic elements inside Namibia should it become clear that SWAPO is seeking to establish a pro-Soviet dictatorship, the Soviet international propaganda and political action network would probably call for massive Western economic sanctions against South Africa. Since South Africa decided in 1988 to go along with the Namibia-Angola settlements endorsed by the U.S. Department of State, the U.S. Congress reduced pressure for additional sanctions against South Africa. Although important steps toward ending apartheid were taken by the South African government elected in September 1989, the Soviet Union's international propaganda network could still step up the campaign for sanctions. South Africa would then be less likely to provide military assistance to UNITA.

If SWAPO does establish a pro-Soviet regime in Namibia and if Renamo in Mozambique and UNITA in Angola are substantially weakened, neutralized, or defeated, the consequences would affect South Africa directly. The Soviet Union and its regional allies would seek to bring the pro-Soviet African National Congress (ANC) to power. Although the ANC began in 1912 as an organization of black South Africans committed to equal rights for all, its leadership was taken over by the late 1940s by the South African Communist party, commited to the establishment of a Marxist-Leninist regime. In the nearly fifty years since then, the ANC included many non-Communist elements in its broader membership ranks and in some of its affiliated organizations and fronts, such as the United Democratic Front. Nevertheless it remained a Marxist-Leninist controlled organization with extensive links to the Soviet Union, to pro-Soviet regimes in the region, and to international sources of Communist support.[65]

The African National Congress seemed to be following the Namibia model, using the resources of the Soviet Union and its allies to legitimate it as the sole authentic representative of the black people of South Africa. Just as SWAPO used the designation given by the General Assembly, the ANC could use the endorsement of the Organization of African Unity to seek undeserved UN legitimation. This method of international political action and propaganda was also used effectively in the case of the PLO.

While the ANC becomes perceived by most of the governments and the media of the non-Communist world as the sole authentic representative of the black people of South Africa, the Soviet Union and its allies could secretly build up its military cadres. The pro-Soviet regimes of Namibia, Angola, Zimbabwe, and Mozambique would virtually surround South Africa, with Botswana the only exception on its border. Those regimes could provide bases and support facilities for the ANC to train thousands of South Africans for infiltration as agitators, terrorists, guerrillas, and participants in a wide array of organizations, including labor unions, church groups, and media organizations. Some would probably join the South African police and military forces to spy on their operations and undermine morale from within.

As an American expert on the Soviet Union in Africa, Peter Vanneman, commented in 1988, "There are few parts of the world where Communist theories about the inevitability of revolution seem more applicable than the Republic of South Africa."[66] For decades, the USSR has supported the South African Communist party and the ANC, and in the late 1980s, its embassy presence in southern Africa was reported to have increased by a factor of three. A pro-Soviet regime in South Africa would ensure the continuity of Communist rule in the other southern African countries, as well as Soviet access to the mineral riches of all southern Africa, including South Africa.

As Paul Johnson reminded us, the Soviet Union and South Africa together control 99 percent of the world's platinum, 97 percent of its vanadium, 93 percent of its manganese, 84 percent of its chromium, and 69 percent of its gold.[67] All the industrial democracies need these metals, especially the platinum group metals, for essential industrial processes, including the production of advanced weapons. In the early 1980s the United States imported from South Africa 61 percent of its cobalt, 55 percent of its chromium, 49 percent of its platinum, 44 percent of its vanadium, and 39 percent of its manganese.[68] South Africa, Zaire, Zambia, and Zimbabwe compose one of the "two great treasure houses on which the West depends" that Brezhnev referred to in his statement during the détente of the 1970s. The Soviet aim, he said, was to "gain control" of it and the energy of the Persian Gulf.[69] With a pro-Soviet regime in power in South Africa, Moscow could extract billions of dollars annually from the industrial democracies by establishing a much higher cartel price for these essential minerals. The influence that the Soviet Union could obtain through the control of these mineral riches could pose a sharply increased threat to the United States and the entire non-Communist world. The Soviet Union might condition access to these resources on ending support to Israel, for example, or cutting military spending, or withdrawal from NATO, or ending SDI research. Moscow would seek to use control over the minerals of southern Africa to divide Europe and Japan from the United States—an outcome even more likely if the USSR also controlled one or more Persian Gulf oil states.

Is South Africa vulnerable to such a process of planned political destabilization? Three groups have competed for the future of South Africa: a pro-apartheid minority of whites; an antidemocratic and anti-apartheid sector led by the African National Congress; and a prodemocratic, anti-apartheid coalition of white and black organizations and leaders, which includes a cross-section of political, civic, religious, and labor groups. Unfortunately, the third group receives least attention in the non-Communist world. The strategy of the Soviet Union would be to have the ostensibly non-Communist ANC— like the PLO and SWAPO—perceived in the free world as the only legitimate alternative to the existing apartheid system. Projecting an image of its new thinking and international moderation, the Soviet Union would try to persuade many in the South African government and the white leadership that it wanted normal relations with South Africa, especially business relations. South African resentment of condemnations and sanctions by the major industrial democracies— especially the United States—would help the Soviet effort. Simultaneously, the ANC would seek to project an image of moderation and willingness to work with white South Africans. In time, South Africa and the non-Communist world would prefer an ANC-led regime to a modestly reformed but still unacceptable apartheid system.

As reforms were carried out by the white government and ANC influence would increase, the pro-apartheid white minority organizations could well use more violence. Violence from the Right and Left extremes could require the government to use force to maintain civil order. That in turn might increase South Africa's isolation as deeper and additional economic sanctions might be enacted by industrial democracies. The Soviet Union is experienced in exploiting this form of political warfare. Working through its allies in the region to conceal its hand, it could encourage violence, polarization, and breakdown, while working for the legitimation of the ANC not only by African countries but in much of the non-Communist world.

Although some in South Africa assume that their military forces can always rescue them, this form of indirect aggression takes its toll in gradual stages that rarely present the opportunity for conventional military defense. The internal breakdown of institutions occurs in a manner that rarely permits the clear identification of the causal factors. Should this process of political and economic destabilization accelerate, South African leaders might realize they should not have agreed to the political settlements of 1987–1988 for Namibia, Angola, and Mozambique. They should instead have focused on making a peaceful transition to genuine multiracial democracy within South Africa and Namibia, while supporting the anti-Communist resistance movements in Angola and Mozambique.

Between the pro-Soviet ANC extremists on one side and the pro-apartheid whites on the other, a broad coalition of black and white leaders and organizations could work with the government of President de Klerk to bring about a peaceful transition to multiracial democracy. The new South African government system could include a bicameral legislature like that in the United States, with one house representing all the people on the basis of one person, one vote, and the other representing communities whose interests need to be safeguarded (as the U.S. Senate provides two seats for each state, giving equal weight to California, with a population of 28 million, and Wyoming, with 300,000). All persons should have equal protection under the law through a constitutional system that guarantees civil liberties, as in the U.S. Bill of Rights. Such a multiracial democracy could establish the consensus within South Africa and strong public support from free-world countries, which might enable it to withstand Communist destabilization efforts even if UNITA and Renamo were defeated. The likelihood of such a peaceful transition, however, would be far less if UNITA and Renamo were neutralized or defeated and a ring of pro-Soviet dictatorships provided bases for pro-Soviet extremists to be trained, armed, and infiltrated into South Africa.

Nicaragua—Central America and Mexico

The objectives of the civic, unarmed opposition and the armed resistance to the Sandinistas have always been the same. Both have sought the free and fair elections promised by the anti-Somoza coalition to the Organization of American States in 1979. Both the civic and the armed opposition have believed that the overwhelming majority of Nicaraguan people would reject the Communist regime and elect a coalition of genuine democrats. In various Central American summit agreements of 1988 and 1989, the Sandinistas promised elections at the end of February 1990. The armed resistance supported the participation of all the Nicaraguan people if elections were truly free and fair, in contrast to the rigged electoral process the Sandinistas staged in 1984.

The dramatic rejection of the Sandinistas in the election held on February 25, 1990, was followed by Mrs. Violeta Chamorro's assumption of the presidency in April 1990. But the Sandinistas retained control of the secret police, the army, and much of the civil service. An elected democratic leadership that really could govern Nicaragua would end the disguised but pervasive repression the Sandinistas instituted. The secret police apparatus would probably be dismantled, together with the Sandinista block committees and the military draft. All political prisoners would be freed. And Sandinista economic mismanagement, which accounts for most of the economic hardship, would be replaced by a more sensible mixed government-market approach. Even before the transition to the elected government, the Bush administration announced the lifting of the U.S. economic sanctions imposed in 1985 and a proposed $300 million program of economic aid. Total free world economic assistance might even exceed the many hundreds of millions of dollars provided by non-Communist countries to the Sandinista regime, which was mostly diverted to the apparatus of repression and militarization. The economic situation in Nicaragua could therefore begin to improve after a non-Communist government took full and effective control of all Nicaraguan national institutions—including the military.

Once that had occurred, the armed Communist insurgencies in El Salvador and Guatemala and the small armed and unarmed Communist movements in the other Central American countries would probably weaken and become demoralized. The removal from Nicaragua of the radio command and control facilities, the terrorist and guerrilla training facilities, and the logistical network running from Cuba through Nicaragua to other countries would cause serious problems for the Communist guerrillas. Although the Castro regime would probably use other routes to provide weapons, money, intelligence, and training to the Communist guerrillas, a non-Communist regime fully in control in Nicaragua would greatly increase the chances to end the insurgencies. It would strengthen the genuinely democratic elements in the region and weaken both the far left and the far right, which though small remains a potentially destabilizing threat in El Salvador and Guatemala. In all the Central American countries as well as in Panama and Mexico, the prospects for peace and for the continuation of democratic evolution in the entire region would be greatly increased.

Revelations of internal repression and external aggression of the Sandinista dictatorship, as well as of its links to the Soviet Union and Cuba, could sharply reduce the appeal of communism throughout Latin America. These might add to the silent crisis of legitimacy faced by the Castro dictatorship in Cuba. Castro has therefore been determined that the Communist revolution not be irreversibly undone in

Nicaragua or in any other country. Should the anti-Communist resistance movements also succeed in Angola and perhaps Mozambique, revelations of repression by Castro's secret police and military forces would further serve to discredit Castro. In my judgment, Castro's public trial and execution of four leading Cuban military officers in June 1989 was intended to deter the Cuban military from considering any action to end the rule of the Castro brothers.

If the Sandinista apparatus continued to exercise significant power in Nicaragua and the democratic leaders and opposition were neutralized, or only able to exercise real authority on some economic and symbolic issues, there could be a return of the threat about which President Reagan warned in May 1984: a Communist Central America and Mexico.

Some Democratic and most Republican leaders shared this concern. Early in 1984 the Bipartisan Commission, established at Sen. Henry Jackson's suggestion and led by Henry Kissinger, reported: "As Nicaragua is already doing, additional Marxist-Leninist regimes in Central America could be expected to expand their armed forces, bring in large numbers of Cuban and Soviet advisors, and develop sophisticated agencies of internal repression and external subversion."[70]

The Sandinista regime became the aggressor in the region in 1979 when it initiated armed subversion against its peaceful neighbors. This aggression continued despite the August 1987 Arias plan, as President Duarte of El Salvador stated in 1988 and as was demonstrated by the flow of weapons from Nicaragua for the Salvadoran guerrilla attacks on cities in late 1989.

After President Carter, President Reagan, and the Central American leaders tried diplomacy and economic aid to persuade the Sandinistas to become democratic and stop armed subversion, aid was given to the contras beginning in 1982. This aid was viewed as consistent with the right of states to defend themselves and their allies. In 1986 Secretary of Defense Caspar Weinberger told Congress that if it cut off aid to the contras, the Sandinistas would expand their military support to the Communist insurgencies in El Salvador and Guatemala, with full Cuban and Soviet backing. Events proved him correct. Weinberger also said that thousands of Sandinista soldiers might be disguised as guerrillas and infiltrated into neighboring countries. According to reports, in August 1989 Nicaraguan strongman Daniel Ortega boasted to the leaders of El Salvador about his supply of weapons to guerrillas in El Salvador and Honduras, alluding to his sending Nicaraguan combat troops in disguise.[71]

If, for example, Nicaragua could send armed forces to fight

disguised as guerrillas at the rate of 100 per day, in seven months the Salvadoran Communist guerrillas could have an additional 20,000 troops. Since about ten soldiers are required to contain one insurgent, the Salvadoran government would be faced with the virtually impossible task of adding about 200,000 soldiers to its forces—a fourfold increase costing an additional $2 billion a year.

A Communist Central America might be achieved in two stages. The first would include increased Communist terrorism and guerrilla attacks leading to panic, turmoil, and internal polarization; perhaps one or more military coups and the return of the violent right; and the consequent cutting off by Congress of vital U.S. military and perhaps economic aid to some friendly Central American countries. In the second stage, the emboldened Communist groups would step up terrorist, military, and political action using their "united front" approach to deceive non-Communist elements into helping them take power.

History suggests that such Communist victories in Central America would be followed by a strategy aimed at bringing the pro-Communist elements in Mexico (and perhaps Panama) to power. The small but well-developed Communist movement within Mexico, with the support of the Soviet Union and Cuba, could use the Communist countries of Central America as a base area.

Mexico's plight during the 1980s is well known: deep poverty unalleviated by the oil boom; the belief of many Mexicans that economic mismanagement and corruption within the ruling Institutional Revolutionary party (PRI) led to the economic crisis of 1982 and subsequent economic decline; and the failure of the governing party to fulfill its promises of political liberalization.

Yet the strength of the Mexican political system may be seen in its six decades of political stability, its forty years of steady economic growth (1941–1981), and its adaptation to the effects of the 1982 economic crisis and its gradual recovery under the leadership of President Salinas, inaugurated in late 1988. Mexico would be likely to remain stable, changing through evolution, unless a Communist victory in Central America led to a Communist attempt to gain control in Mexico.

Except for the governing party, only the Communist movement in Mexico is organized in every area of political life. It has a political party with tens of thousands of members, millions of voters, and a clandestine apparatus. Some key labor unions are Communist, and Communists have penetrated government-controlled unions. After the economic crisis in 1982, additional Communist peasant organizations were formed throughout the country, together with a wide array of Soviet-supported front groups and two large Communist-controlled coalitions of disaffected poor. In addition Mexican Communists have cooperated closely for decades with the Soviet bloc, which has maintained an unusually large diplomatic presence in Mexico City. The PLO and many Cuban-aided Latin American and other terrorist organizations have also maintained facilities in Mexico.

A Communist strategy would employ deception to prevent the people of Mexico and the United States from understanding that a seizure of power was taking place. Undercover groups could deepen the crisis through strikes, demonstrations, attacks on tourists, and sabotage of oil production facilities, sharpening the downward economic spiral and deepening the misery of the poor.

In this hypothetical strategy, the tactics might be derived from one or more of the approaches that have been tried in other countries. For example, clandestine pro-Communist elements within the Mexican governing party might cooperate with the Communist party and gradually gain full control—this was the approach in Czechoslovakia in 1948. Communist cadres within the military might stage a coup to "reform the Revolution"—this method was used in Ethiopia in 1977 and in Afghanistan in 1978 (why did Castro confer a medal on two senior Mexican military officials in 1987?). Elements of the governing party might openly join with Communist-controlled fronts in a coalition defined as the authentic or the reformed governing party. All of this could be accompanied by terrorism directed at moderate Mexican leaders by groups claiming to represent various regional, economic, or ultra-rightist interests but in fact operating under covert Communist control.

Since most U.S. leaders lack knowledge of Mexican politics, a carefully disguised Communist government could be in power before any consensus formed in the United States to help the people of Mexico defend themselves. Communist victory in Central America and Mexico would confront the United States with an entirely new geopolitical threat, which could worsen as and if the Castro-Sandinista pattern of repression, militarization, and aggression through armed subversion was repeated on a far larger scale.

Even a liberal observer of U.S. foreign policy understood in 1983 that this negative consequence was a real possibility:

> What happens if . . . Mexico has acquired a leadership, political system and degree of militarization . . . along the lines of what Castro has achieved in Cuba? . . . The sequential triumphs of leftist revolutions . . . could increase the chances for upheaval in Mexico. . . . The security problem for the United States would be second only to the one posed by the USSR itself.[72]

Some might contend that such negative consequences could be avoided if the United States would commit troops to the defense of friendly governments on its southern border that were threatened. The Reagan administration opposed the use of U.S. combat forces because the countries of Central America and Mexico have the people and the skills to defend themselves—if Congress would provide the economic and military aid needed to offset the massive Soviet and Cuban intervention.

Moreover, should a visible crisis raise the question of sending U.S. military forces, the governments would probably appear repressive and unrepresentative of their people during the political polarization and breakdown likely to precede Communist victories, so the United States would have another reason not to send troops to help. Congress is also likely to have cut or refused economic or military aid, and, quite correctly, neither political party would favor committing U.S. troops to the defense of the Central American countries—even if the threat to Mexico began to be perceived. In the nature of indirect aggression, the crisis appears to most outside observers to be primarily due to internal factors. If the Congress has cut or terminated military aid, and if internal political breakdown has begun, then foreign Communist troops are unlikely to invade across borders in a way that would encourage the United States to send combat forces.

If Mexico changed its present ambiguous relationship with the United States to one that was hostile and pro-Soviet or pro-Castro, it would be likely to do so in a gradual and deceptive way. The Mexican far-Left groups and leaders would profess to be seeking only to reform the internal political and economic system and to want constructive and positive relations with the United States. The danger might never be clear enough either to the political or civic leadership of Mexico or to the United States to bring about timely cooperative action that could prevent a takeover. Since the vulnerabilities of Mexico derive from the internal practices of the governing system, it would be argued in the United States that avoiding a takeover would depend not on U.S. policy but on reforms within Mexico. And the takeover could be so gradual that no clear occasion would arise when U.S. assistance would be perceived as decisive.

If the result of such indirect aggression were successful in the 1990s, millions of refugees from the region between Panama and the U.S. border would try to enter the United States. Experience suggests that from 10 to 20 percent of the population of countries that come under Communist control flee; that could mean that 10 million to 20 million people might try to enter the United States as refugees. The costs for those who fled Cuba in 1980 suggest that the annual U.S. costs for refugee resettlement would be on the order of $100 billion to $200 billion.[73] There would also be costs of defending the southern border of the United States—land, sea, and air—against the threats of hostile infiltration and military attack across our southern border. Cuba has a military force of 280,000 in a population of 10 million, and Sandinista Nicaragua has had 120,000 in 3 million. At that proportion, armed forces in all these countries might total 3 million troops within a period of several years. Even without Mexico, if the 25 million people of Central America militarized to the level of Nicaragua in 1989, they would have armed forces of about 1 million (since their combined population is about nine times that of Nicaragua).

In 1984, the Bipartisan Commission led by former Secretary of State Henry Kissinger estimated that approximately $200 billion a year would be needed in added defense costs to provide for the security of the southern border in the face of a Communist Central America and Mexico.[74]

The geopolitical position of the United States could also be entirely changed by a Communist Central America and Mexico. As the Bipartisan Commission predicted in 1984, such a development would make U.S. defense commitments in the Middle East, Europe, Japan, and other key parts of the world difficult if not impossible to meet. The military buildup and the armed subversion hostile Communist neighbors would likely launch against other countries would preoccupy the United States. The Atlantic alliance might be jeopardized, especially if the direct Soviet military threat were perceived to be reduced by the political liberalization in Eastern Europe.

All these potential costs and burdens for the United States—or even a significant proportion of them—would serve Soviet objectives. Additional economic and political strains on the United States render it less capable of maintaining a high-technology defense and a presence in Europe, the Middle East, and Asia. Such setbacks to the United States could occur without risk to the Soviet Union of direct conflict with the United States, since the strains could be imposed through indigenous pro-Soviet regimes. But the ability of the elected democratic government in Nicaragua actually to govern there and the continuation of the democratic progress being made in the rest of Central America, Panama (after the December 1989 removal of the Noriega dictatorship), together with the pragmatism of the Salinas regime in Mexico, could render this negative scenario highly unlikely.

Cambodia—Southeast Asia

If the non-Communist resistance forces in Cambodia received adequate help and if the Soviet Union and Communist China were thereby persuaded that neither of their proxies would dominate Cambodia, then an independent non-Communist government could be established there. In addition to increasing the personal freedom of the surviving 6 million Cambodians, such a government would be one to which hundreds of thousands of Cambodian refugees would return. Since Cambodians have probably suffered more under Communist rule than any other people, a new non-Communist government would receive a generous outpouring of humanitarian and development assistance from democratic countries.

In the region, an independent and increasingly prosperous Cambodia could sharply reduce the threat of future Communist indirect aggression against Thailand and Malaysia. As a point of contrast and symbolic attraction for the people of Vietnam and Laos, it might contribute to the liberalization of those countries.

But a less hopeful future is also possible. The non-Communist resistance could lose either through the victory of the Soviet- and Vietnamese-backed PRK regime currently in power or through a Khmer Rouge victory over that regime. The record of suffering from 1975 to 1978 imposed by the Khmer Rouge regime makes clear that its victory would be the greater evil for the people of Cambodia. Khmer Rouge actions in the refugee camps it has controlled since 1979 also show that it is likely to reestablish its brutal system. A Khmer Rouge victory would probably result in additional hundreds of thousands and perhaps even millions of deaths in the coming years. Should the Communist Chinese regime reestablish the Communist insurgency in Thailand, which it began supporting in 1964 (but ceased in 1982), a Khmer Rouge regime—beholden to Communist China—would probably also support it, which could bring violence to the 52 million Thai people. Despite the hardening of Chinese Communist internal control since its repression of the democracy movement in June 1989, however, China might be reluctant to risk its broader interests by resuming its indirect aggression in Southeast Asia.

In the event of a PRK victory and subsequent consolidation of its control over Cambodia, the hard-line Communist regime in Vietnam might return to its original plans. Hundreds of thousands of Vietnamese might be resettled in the rich lands of Cambodia. And at some future time both the Vietnamese and the Cambodian Communist regimes might support Communist guerrillas seeking to destabilize Thailand, Malaysia, and other countries in the region. Unlike the Sandinista regime in Nicaragua, however, where the ten-year pattern of its indirect aggression against neighboring countries makes its continuation highly likely if the Marxist-Leninist groups there keep much of the power, neither the Communist regime in Vietnam nor a future PRK regime in Cambodia would necessarily follow an aggressive pattern that might jeopardize their economic objectives in the next decade. It is also not evident that the Soviet Union would have any strategic interest in supporting such aggression in the next years. Moscow would, however, probably be given formal naval access rights to the Cambodian port of Kampugsom.

The defeat of the anti-Communist resistance in Cambodia should not, however, be measured primarily in terms of geopolitical effects. Rather, such a defeat would symbolize the inability and unwillingness of the free world, including the United States, to help even a small, once peaceful country, that is willing to take up arms to liberate itself. In proportion to population, totalitarianism has inflicted the greatest human suffering in recorded history in Cambodia. Although witnesses to this suffering have proven the facts to the free world, Cambodian people would in the end still have been denied the support they needed to liberate themselves from yet another failed Communist system.

Global Impact of the Resistance Movements

The millions of persons executed, killed, imprisoned, and displaced from their homes and the millions of exiles from these five countries show that the repression, economic failure, and external aggression initiated by the new pro-Soviet dictatorships have lost them the support of the people. The armed anti-Communist resistance movements are an expression of this rejection. Those movements have held to their goals of establishing independent non-Communist constitutional governments and have continued to battle year after year for them. As CIA Director William J. Casey predicted in 1986, the Soviet Union and its allies have invested enormous resources—political, diplomatic, covert, paramilitary, and military—to strengthen these pro-Soviet regimes and to help them neutralize and ultimately defeat the anti-Communist resistance movements. In fact, as analyst Charles Waterman put it, "the Soviet response . . . has markedly intensified" during the Gorbachev era.[75]

In fact, as Professor Richard Pipes of Harvard University noted: "One paradoxical effect of the Gorbachev peace offensive has been to promote Soviet interests in regional conflicts. . . . Its clients in Cambodia, Angola, Nicaragua, and Afghanistan have been growing stronger at the expense of U.S. interests."[76]

Vladimir Bukovsky, a former citizen of the Soviet Union, has written, "The only tangible measure of success the Soviet system could provide has been the Soviet empire abroad."[77] And Charles

Waterman noted that "the tenacity of dictatorial Communist regimes has historically proven greater than the somewhat fickle cycles inherent in the democratic process."[78]

The third-ranking official of President Reagan's State Department, Under Secretary of State Michael Armacost, said in 1988 that the "Afghan model" should serve as a prototype for the settlement of "regional conflicts." In an important policy speech Armacost underscored President Reagan's view that the "urgent goal of U.S. policy" in Afghanistan was "the complete and total withdrawal of Soviet troops and the restoration of Afghan national independence."[79] But in 1989, facing the failure of the Afghan agreement to accomplish the objective of ending Communist rule in Afghanistan, some senior State Department officials began pretending that U.S. objectives in signing the Afghan accords of 1988 had been merely the withdrawal of Soviet combat forces.

The Soviet Union agreed that the "Afghan model" should be applied in the Angola war, and it was. As this analysis has demonstrated, in the political settlements in Central America, Afghanistan, and Angola, and in that proposed for Cambodia by the Soviet- and Vietnamese-backed Communist regime, the formula would be the same: promises about the withdrawal of foreign Communist troops and the future actions of the existing pro-Soviet regional regime would be exchanged for political commitments by the non-Communist side. In the end the Soviet Union expected that anti-Communist resistance movements would be increasingly isolated from free-world military and diplomatic support and that the pro-Soviet dictatorships, established during the détente of the 1970s, would remain in power. In Nicaragua this formula partially failed when the democratic opposition won the February 1990 elections. As long as the Sandinista party remains intact and in control of the powerful military, however, the threat of continuing Communist dominance or return to full power remains.

This analysis of these five wars in the twilight has raised the question of the comparative effectiveness of the United States and the Soviet Union in the achievement of their foreign policy purposes. Except perhaps in Nicaragua, none of these movements has yet succeeded in bringing about independent non-Communist governments to replace the pro-Soviet dictatorships. Unfortunately, the record from these five wars on three continents raises serious questions about the U.S. capacity to sustain a strategy to cope with the negative as well as the positive aspects of contemporary Soviet foreign policy. If these anti-Communist resistance movements are defeated, tragic consequences will follow for the people in those countries, along with significant gains for Moscow and setbacks for freedom in the world. And, if the human, economic, and geopolitical consequences of the defeat of the anti-Communist resistance movements include even some of the negative possibilities described earlier, this failure may later be seen as an important setback in U.S. foreign policy. Despite the enormous courage and suffering of those involved in the anti-Communist resistance movements, the USSR has been more effective than the United States in achieving its foreign policy objectives in these five wars.

Although Alexis de Tocqueville's doubts about the capacity of democracies to pursue strategic objectives have been and may continue to be proved correct in most of these five conflicts, in the larger sweep of history the Reagan Doctrine may have made an important contribution to the beginning of the unraveling of the Soviet empire visible in Eastern Europe at the end of 1989.

In 1979, after the Soviet invasion of Afghanistan shattered illusions about Soviet international conduct, President Carter took the important decision of providing military support to the armed anti-Communist Afghan resistance. Expanding that support, President Reagan decided to provide military support to the anti-Communist resistance movements in Nicaragua and Angola. Other free-world countries helped the anti-Communist resistance movements in Cambodia and Mozambique. This outside support not only has helped these five anti-Communist movements continue their struggles to remove those five dictatorships but also has had other positive effects.

First, it gave the people caught inside these Communist dictatorships a greater sense of hope. The very existence of the armed anti-Communist resistance movements helped many victims of these dictatorships break through their sense of despair, submission, and passivity. The military resistance inspired moral, spiritual, and political resistance to the Communist regime, which prevented them from exercising total control over the people and their future.

President Reagan reminded us that Marxism-Leninism's war with its people becomes war with its neighbors. Indeed, these five new pro-Soviet regimes did cooperate with the Soviet Union in indirect aggression against peaceful neighboring countries. Therefore, these armed anti-Communist resistance movements served as a line of defense for the neighboring countries on all four continents by absorbing and deflecting resources the Communist regimes could otherwise have used for indirect aggression. In that sense these resistance movements have helped provide years of additional time for the neighboring countries to make political progress, develop their economies, and improve their capacity to deal with armed

365

subversion. In Central America, the Nicaraguan anti-Communist resistance in effect helped Honduras, El Salvador, and Guatemala to make transitions from right-wing authoritarian regimes to democracy. Further, the burden of supporting five allies against a total of more than 300,000 anti-Communist resistance fighters undoubtedly reduced the capacity of the Soviet Union to help additional pro-Soviet groups take power during the 1980s. As the analyst Alvin Bernstein concluded, the resistance movements, whether they ultimately win or lose, have already served "to keep the Soviets from being in a geostrategic position where they can prevent the United States from honoring its commitments in Europe, Asia and the Middle East."[80]

The constructive effects of the anti-Communist resistance movements have for the third time revealed a paradox in U.S. and Soviet relations. When the Soviet Union succeeds in its campaign of indirect aggression, as it did from 1945 to 1949 and from 1975 to 1979, the result is a crisis in relations with the United States and many of its allies. But when the pace of Soviet indirect aggression has been slowed, as in the 1980s, when no new pro-Soviet regimes were established, then a more stable U.S.–Soviet relationship can develop. As Jeane Kirkpatrick and Allan Gerson put it, the Reagan Doctrine "has in fact decreased rather than enhanced the prospects of war with our major adversary, the Soviet Union." They point out that the Reagan Doctrine is reactive: "It countenances counterintervention, not intervention."[81]

The anti-Communist resistance movements also demonstrated that, with external assistance, the peoples of newly conquered countries who had experienced Communist repression would fight year after year and inflict increasing casualties and military costs on the pro-Soviet regimes. The stamina of these movements may have forced Moscow and its allies to end or reduce sharply the use of a new technique of indirect aggression that began in 1975 with the Soviet deployment of Cuban troops in Angola.

In the struggles of these five anti-Communist movements, millions of people living in other Communist countries may have seen for the first time that newly established Communist dictatorships could be prevented from consolidating their power. Those people who themselves have been forced for years to submit to a Communist regime can best understand, respect, and be inspired by the courage of the anti-Communist resistance movements. The inability of the Soviet-backed Communist regimes to crush these five movements— or the nonviolent opposition of the Solidarity movement in Poland— may well have served as part of the inspiration for the gathering momentum of popular rebellion against the East European Communist regimes in 1989. Furthermore, the years of casualities inflicted on Soviet and allied troops and personnel (including East European Communists) by the anti-Communist resistance forces most likely were an important factor in the Soviet decision not to use force to control events in Eastern Europe in 1989. Perhaps if there had been no resistance in these five countries, the hardest-line Communist elements might have prevailed in Moscow and perhaps in Eastern Europe as well.

President Reagan understood that President Kennedy had been correct in calling upon the United States to help our friends win the "twilight struggles" that tyrannical regimes would cause—especially in the developing countries. President Reagan's commitment to help the anti-Communist resistance movements "not just fight and die for freedom but fight and win freedom" was a major step forward for the United States.

The challenge for the United States is to have a dual foreign policy toward the Soviet Union: on the one hand, acting prudently to encourage those seeking genuine democracy and improved living conditions while negotiating verifiable agreements of mutual interest and, on the other hand, maintaining deterrence through alliances and through sufficient military forces while helping friendly countries to defeat indirect aggression. The United States can still take the lead to help the armed anti-Communist resistance movements succeed in establishing independent non-Communist regimes in these five countries. This success for liberty would contribute immensely to the well-being of the peoples in those countries, to the prevention of future indirect aggression in vital regions of the world, to the peaceful evolution of the Soviet Union, and to the maintenance of stability and peace.

Notes

CHAPTER 1: INTRODUCTION

1. These include Guinea-Bissau, Mozambique, Vietnam, Cambodia, Laos, Angola, all in 1975; Ethiopia in 1977; South Yemen and Afghanistan in 1978; Grenada and Nicaragua in 1979.

2. See Frederic N. Smith, "The War in Lithuania and the Ukraine against Soviet Power," in Charles Moser, ed., *Combat on Communist Territory* (Washington, D.C.: Free Congress Research and Education Foundation, 1985), pp. 2–21.

3. Honduras, El Salvador, Guatemala, Brazil, Uruguay, Argentina, Bolivia, Peru, Grenada, the Philippines, Taiwan, and South Korea.

4. Address before a Joint Session of the Congress on the State of the Union, February 6, 1985, *Public Papers of the Presidents, Ronald Reagan, 1985,* bk. 1 (Washington, D.C.: GPO, 1988), p. 135.

5. Ibid.

6. Secretary of State George Shultz, "America and the Struggle for Freedom," speech of February 22, 1985, in *Department of State Bulletin,* April 1985, pp. 16–17.

7. Ibid., p. 18.

8. Ibid.

9. Ibid., pp. 17–18.

10. William J. Casey, "Collapse of the Marxist Model: America's New Calling," speech of January 9, 1985, published in *Scouting the Future: The Public Speeches of William J. Casey,* compiled by Herbert E. Meyer (Washington, D.C.: Regnery Gateway, 1989), p. 169.

11. Ibid., p. 171.

12. Ibid.

13. Charles Krauthammer, "The Reagan Doctrine," *Time,* April 1, 1985.

14. Alvin Bernstein, "Best Policy Available and How It Can Work," *Washington Times,* July 22, 1987. See also his longer discussion in *Policy Review* (Summer 1987).

15. Krauthammer, "The Reagan Doctrine," p. 182.

16. Casey, "Collapse of the Marxist Model."

17. Address to the 40th Session of the United Nations General Assembly in New York, New York, *Public Papers of the Presidents, Ronald Reagan, 1985,* bk. 2 (Washington, D.C.: GPO, 1988), p. 1288.

18. Constantine Menges, *Democratic Revolutionary Insurgency as an Alternative Strategy* (Santa Monica, Calif.: Rand Corporation, 1968), pp. 1–2.

19. Ibid.

20. Ibid., p. 10.

21. Ibid., pp. 10–11.

22. Constantine Menges, November 1980, manuscript in the author's possession.

23. For a fuller account, see Constantine C. Menges, *Inside the National Security Council: The True Story of the Making and Unmaking of Reagan's Foreign Policy* (New York: Simon & Schuster, 1988), chap. 1.

24. Casey, "Collapse of the Marxist Model," p. 170.

25. Casey, "The Lessons of World War II: Helping Occupied Nations Overthrow Totalitarian Regimes," speech of September 19, 1986, in *Scouting the Future*, p. 229.

26. Ibid.

27. These conversations and my other proposals for the second term, such as a much larger initiative to encourage peaceful transitions to democracy, are discussed in Menges, *Inside the National Security Council*, chap. 6.

28. The three presidential speechwriters were Anthony Dolan, Bentley Elliott, and Dana Rohrabacher, elected to Congress in 1988. The private citizen is Dr. Jack Wheeler, who has published insightful articles about the resistance movements based on his personal observations; many of these are cited later in this book.

29. Casey, "Collapse of the Marxist Model"; Address before a Joint Session of the Congress on the State of the Union, February 4, 1986, *Public Papers of the Presidents, Ronald Reagan, 1986,* bk. 1 (Washington, D.C.: GPO, 1988), p. 129.

30. See my discussion in *Inside the National Security Council,* chap. 9.

31. Ibid.

32. Address to the 40th Session of the United Nations General Assembly, p. 1288 (emphasis added). For a more complete discussion of this battle over the UN speech involving Casey, Shultz, NSC adviser McFarlane, the presidential speechwriters, and the author, see *Inside the National Security Council,* chap. 9.

33. Moser, ed., *Combat on Communist Territory,* cited in note 2 above.

34. Casey, "Collapse of the Marxist Model," p. 172.

35. *Scouting the Future,* p. 236.

36. Ibid.

37. "Creeping Imperialism: Soviet Strategy in the Middle East," speech of April 6, 1986, in *Scouting the Future,* p. 163.

38. Alexis de Tocqueville, *Democracy in America,* vol. 1 (New York: Knopf, 1960), pp. 234–35.

39. Ibid.

40. Richard Nixon, *1999: Victory Without War* (New York: Simon & Schuster, 1988), p. 64.

CHAPTER 2: THE SOVIET STRATEGY OF INDIRECT AGGRESSION

1. R. J. Rummel, "As Though a Nuclear War—The Death Toll of Absolutism," *International Journal on World Peace,* vol. 5, no. 3 (July–September 1988), p. 35. Rummel concludes that between 1918 and 1953 the Soviet government

killed 40 million of its own citizens, that the Chinese regime of Mao Tse-tung killed 45 million, and that the Hitler regime in Germany killed 17 million.

2. See Richard H. Shultz, Jr., *The Soviet Union and Revolutionary Warfare* (Stanford, Calif.: Hoover Institution Press, 1988), p. 16.

3. Jeane J. Kirkpatrick, ed., *The Strategy of Deception: A Study in World-Wide Communist Tactics* (New York: Farrar, Straus, 1963), p. xiii.

4. Ibid., p. xiv.

5. Ibid., p. xv.

6. Ibid., pp. xvii, xxiii.

7. Ibid., p. xxi.

8. Ibid., p. xviii.

9. See Thomas Hammond and Robert Farrell, eds., *The Anatomy of Communist Takeovers* (New Haven: Yale University Press, 1975).

10. Edward Jay Epstein, *Deception: The Invisible War between the KGB and the CIA* (New York: Simon & Schuster, 1989), pp. 246–53.

11. Shultz, *The Soviet Union and Revolutionary Warfare*, p. 17.

12. *New York Times*, May 26, 1989, p. A7.

13. Shultz, *The Soviet Union and Revolutionary Warfare*, pp. 4, 5.

14. Charles Burton Marshall, "The U.S. and the U.S.S.R. in the U.N.," in Kirkpatrick, *The Strategy of Deception*, pp. 432–33.

15. Shultz, *The Soviet Union and Revolutionary Warfare*, p. 19.

16. Ibid.

17. Ibid., p. 20.

18. Ibid.

19. Average for years 1982–1986. U.S. Arms Control and Disarmament Agency, *World Military Expenditures and Arms Transfers*, 1987, p. 127.

20. Shultz, *The Soviet Union and Revolutionary Warfare*, p. 21.

21. U.S. Department of State, "Cuba's Renewed Support for Violence in Latin America," Special Report no. 90, December 14, 1981, p. 3.

22. President John F. Kennedy, news conference of November 20, 1962, *Public Papers of the Presidents of the United States, 1962* (Washington, D.C.: GPO, 1963), p. 831.

23. State Department, "Cuba's Renewed Support," p. 3.

24. Ibid., p. 3.

25. See Constantine Menges, "Castro's Cuba: Thirty Years of Revolutionary Warfare," in Georges Fauriol, ed., *Cuba: The International Dimension* (New Brunswick, N.J.: Transaction Press, 1990); and Roger W. Fontaine, *Terrorism: The Cuban Connection* (New York: Crane Russak, 1988), p. 7.

26. Shultz, *The Soviet Union and Revolutionary Warfare*, p. 22.

27. Ibid., p. 23.

28. Ibid., p. 27.

29. See ibid., p. 23.

30. See Richard Nixon, *The Real War* (New York: Warner Books, 1980), p. 23.

31. *New York Times*, January 24, 1973.

32. See U.S. Department of Defense, *Prospects for Containment of Nicaragua's Communist Government*, May 1986.

33. See David Kopilow, *Castro, Israel, & the PLO* (Washington, D.C.: Cuban-American National Foundation, 1985).

34. L. H. Gann, "The Soviet Union and Sub-Saharan Africa, 1917–1974," in Dennis L. Bark, ed., *The Red Orchestra* (Stanford, Calif.: Hoover Institution Press, 1987), p. 21.

35. Shultz, *The Soviet Union and Revolutionary Warfare*, p. 29.

36. William J. Casey, "Regroup to Check the Soviet Thrust," *Wall Street Journal*, April 22, 1983.

37. See Samuel T. Francis, *The Soviet Strategy of Terror* (Washington, D.C.: Heritage Foundation, 1985), and Claire Sterling, *The Terror Network: The Secret War of International Terrorism* (New York: Holt, Rinehart, & Winston, 1981).

38. Michael A. Ledeen, "Intelligence, Training, and Support Components," in Uri Ra'anan et al., *Hydra of Carnage* (Lexington, Mass.: Lexington Books, 1986), pp. 155–62; Nixon, *The Real War*, p. 40.

39. *The Europa Yearbook, 1988*, pp. 2644–45. See also Paul Henze, *The Plot to Kill the Pope* (New York: Scribner, 1983); Claire Sterling, *The Time of the Assassins* (New York: Henry Holt, 1984).

40. Constantine Menges, "Central America and Its Enemies," *Commentary* (August 1981), pp. 32–38. See also Eusebio Mujal-Leon, *European Socialists and Central America* (Washington, D.C.: Center for Strategic and International Studies, 1989).

41. For an analysis of the consequences of four détente episodes during the postwar era, see Constantine C. Menges, "Detente's Dark History," *Wall Street Journal*, January 9, 1987, and Menges, "The Results of Previous U.S.-Soviet Efforts at Détente," Studies in International Policy Occasional Paper, American Enterprise Institute, Washington, D.C., May 1988.

42. Nixon, *The Real War*, p. 30.

43. William J. Casey, "The International Linkages—What Do We Know?" in Ra'anan et al., *Hydra of Carnage*, pp. 5–15.

44. Vladimir Bukovsky, "The Political Condition of the Soviet Union," in Henry S. Rowen and Charles Wolf, Jr., eds., *The Future of the Soviet Empire* (New York: St. Martin's Press, 1987), p. 21.

CHAPTER 3: AFGHANISTAN

1. A former Norwegian minister of defense in conversation with the author, 1985.

2. World Bank, *World Development Report*, Washington, D.C., 1980, p. 110.

3. Rosanne Klass, "The Great Game Revisited," in Rosanne Klass, ed., *Afghanistan: The Great Game Revisited* (New York: Freedom House, 1988).

4. Rosanne Klass, "A Summary Chronology of Afghan History" (appendix), in Klass, ed., *Afghanistan: The Great Game Revisited*, p. 378.

5. Ibid., p. 379.

6. Ibid. Refers to Khan Abdul Ghaffar Khan, who died in 1988. His son and successor, Khan Wali Khan, spends much time in Kabul and is reportedly a longtime Soviet agent.

7. Leon B. Poullada, "The Road to Crisis 1919–1980—American Failures, Afghan Errors, and Soviet Successes," in Klass, ed., *Afghanistan: The Great Game Revisited,* p. 39.

8. Klass, "Chronology of Afghan History," p. 381.

9. Poullada, "The Road to Crisis," p. 52.

10. Ibid.

11. Ibid., p. 53.

12. Ibid., p. 55.

13. Anthony Arnold and Rosanne Klass, "Afghanistan's Divided Communist Party," in Klass, ed., *Afghanistan: The Great Game Revisited,* p. 141.

14. Ibid., p. 142.

15. Ibid., p. 145.

16. Ibid., p. 146.

17. Ibid., p. 147.

18. Ibid. See also Michael Barry, "Afghanistan—Another Cambodia?" *Commentary* (August 1982).

19. See interview with Jean Ellenstein conducted by Drago Arsenijevic, *Tribune de Geneve,* November 3, 1983.

20. Klass, "Chronology of Afghan History," p. 386.

21. Ibid., p. 387.

22. Curiously, in February 1989 when the Soviets said they had withdrawn 100,000 troops, the State Department agreed that all were gone; as will be discussed later, there is evidence that some 30,000 Soviet military personnel may have remained or been secretly reinserted.

23. Adolph Dubs, deputy assistant secretary for Near Eastern and South Asian Affairs, testimony before the House Subcommittee on Asian and Pacific Affairs, March 16, 1978, *Department of State Bulletin,* May 1978.

24. U.S. Department of State, Post Report, Afghanistan, August 1979, p. 1.

25. Ibid., p. 2.

26. U.S. Department of State, *Afghanistan: Eight Years of Soviet Occupation,* Special Report no. 173, December 1987, pp. 19–20.

27. *Behind the Lines,* Humanitarian News Service, October 1987, vol. 6, no. 9.

28. State Department, *Afghanistan: Eight Years,* pp. 18–19.

29. Barnett R. Rubin, "Human Rights in Afghanistan," in Klass, ed., *Afghanistan: The Great Game Revisited.*

30. Richard Mackenzie, "A Brutal Force Batters a Country," *Insight,* December 5, 1988, pp. 9–10.

31. U.S. Department of State, *Afghan Resistance and Soviet Occupation,* Special Report no. 118, December 1984, p. 3.

32. Ibid., p. 7.

33. U.S. Department of State, *Chemical Warfare in Southeast Asia and Afghanistan: Report to the Congress from Secretary of State Alexander M. Haig, Jr.,* March 22, 1982, Special Report no. 98. See also U.S. Department of State, *Chemical Warfare in Southeast Asia and Afghanistan: An Update: Report from Secretary of State George P. Shultz, November 1982,* Special Report no. 104.

34. John Barron, "From Russia with Hate," *Reader's Digest*, November 1985. Also Claude Malhuret, "Report from Afghanistan," *Foreign Affairs* (Winter 1983–1984).

35. Rubin, "Human Rights in Afghanistan." The countries compared with Afghanistan include Mali (144 per 1,000 infant mortality), Burma (64), Mozambique (120), Madagascar (130), and Uganda (105). World Bank, *World Development Report*, Washington, D.C., 1988, p. 286.

36. James A. Phillips, "Updating U.S. Strategy for Helping Afghan Freedom Fighters," Heritage Foundation Backgrounder no. 552, December 22, 1986, p. 7.

37. State Department, *Afghanistan: Eight Years*.

38. Rubin, "Human Rights in Afghanistan."

39. John F. Shroder and Abdul Tawab Assifi, "Afghan Mineral Resources and Soviet Exploitation," in Klass, ed., *Afghanistan: The Great Game Revisited*.

40. Quoted in Klass, "The Great Game Revisited," p. 11.

41. Elie Krakowski, "Afghanistan and Soviet Global Interests," in Klass, ed., *Afghanistan: The Great Game Revisited*, p. 177.

42. U.S. Department of State, *Afghanistan: Seven Years of Soviet Occupation*, Special Report no. 155, December 1986, p. 10.

43. Cited in Phillips, "Updating U.S. Strategy," p. 5.

44. U.S. Department of State, *Afghan Resistance and Soviet Occupation*, p. 2; *Afghanistan: Six Years of Soviet Occupation*, Special Report no. 135, December 1985, p. 8; *Afghanistan: Eight Years*, p. 9.

45. State Department, *Afghanistan: Eight Years*, p. 12.

46. Nasir Shansab, "The Struggle for Afghanistan," in Charles Moser, ed., *Combat on Communist Territory* (Washington, D.C.: Free Congress Research and Education Foundation, 1985), p. 111.

47. Ibid., p. 113.

48. Ibid., p. 120.

49. Ibid., p. 123.

50. State Department, *Afghanistan: Eight Years*, p. 7.

51. Cited in Phillips, "Updating U.S. Strategy," p. 4.

52. Ibid., p. 5, and the *Washington Post*, May 19, 1987.

53. State Department, *Afghanistan: Eight Years*, p. 7.

54. Ibid., p. 8.

55. Abdul Rashid, "The Afghan Resistance," in Klass, ed., *Afghanistan: The Great Game Revisited*, p. 208.

56. Adapted from Klass, ed., *Afghanistan: The Great Game Revisited*, as is the ensuing discussion of the organizations and their leaders.

57. Klass, "The Great Game Revisited," p. 396.

58. Ibid. See also reports in the general press since 1980.

59. Ibid., p. 395. See also Edward Girardet, *Afghanistan—The Soviet War* (New York: St. Martin's Press, 1985), pp. 169–71; *New York Times*, July 18, 1989.

60. *Washington Post*, July 18, 1989; *Washington Times*, July 17, 1989.

61. Rashid, "The Afghan Resistance," p. 218.

62. Ibid., p. 219.

63. *Economist*, "Foreign Report" (London), November 13, 1986.

64. *Washington Post*, December 21, 1987. But one expert notes that most or all of it went to individual organizations, not to the alliance per se.

65. Ibid., January 24, 1988.

66. Personal communication, Rich Castrodale, State Department Special Working Group on Afghanistan (Bureau of International Organizations), April 1989.

67. State Department, *Afghanistan: Eight Years*.

68. U.S. Department of State, *Afghanistan: Soviet Occupation and Withdrawal*, Special Report no. 179, December 1988, p. 5.

69. Constantine Menges, *Military Aspects of International Relations in the Developing Areas* (Santa Monica, Calif.: Rand Corporation, 1966).

70. Krakowski, "Afghanistan and Soviet Global Interests," p. 180.

71. Ibid.

72. See Chong-Pin Lin, *China's Nuclear Weapons Strategy: Tradition within Evolution* (Lexington, Mass.: Lexington Books, 1988).

73. State Department, *Afghanistan: Eight Years*, p. 21.

74. "Armand Hammer Sees Brezhnev," *New York Times*, February 28, 1980.

75. Poullada, "The Road to Crisis, 1919–1980," p. 63.

76. *Washington Times*, November 17, 1987.

77. *Washington Post*, December 11, 1987.

78. Ibid., December 10, 1987.

79. Ibid., December 11, 1987.

80. Ibid., December 14, 1987.

81. See Senator Humphrey's statements in Constantine C. Menges, ed., "Afghanistan and the 1988 Agreement," Studies in International Policy Occasional Paper, American Enterprise Institute, Washington, D.C., May 1988; *New York Times*, February 11, 1988.

82. Senator Gordon Humphrey, "Fears of an Afghan Sell-out," *Washington Inquirer*, December 25, 1987.

83. I was personally involved in these efforts to provide information to President Reagan.

84. *Washington Post*, January 5, 1988.

85. Lally Weymouth, "Does Moscow Really Plan on Leaving Afghanistan?" *Washington Post*, February 21, 1988.

86. State Department, *Afghanistan: Eight Years*, p. 21.

87. Ibid., p. 20.

88. Lally Weymouth, "Moscow's 'Invisible War' of Terror Inside Pakistan," *Washington Post*, March 13, 1988.

89. Because of America's desire to prevent the proliferation of nuclear weapons, there is a general legislative provision barring any economic aid to countries thought to be developing such weapons. This prohibition can be waived, however, at the discretion of the Congress under the Symington amendment. In the case of Pakistan, however, that waiver had not been renewed.

90. Quoted in Weymouth, "Does Moscow Really Plan on Leaving Afghanistan?"

91. *Washington Post,* February 19, 1988.

92. See A. M. Rosenthal, "The Secret Treaty," *New York Times,* March 4, 1988.

93. *Washington Post,* March 31, 1988.

94. Weymouth, "Moscow's 'Invisible War.' "

95. *Washington Post,* April 11, 1988.

96. A. M. Rosenthal, "Saigon and Kabul," *New York Times,* April 12, 1988.

97. Senator Humphrey, "Fears of an Afghan Sell-out."

98. *New York Times,* February 26, 1988.

99. *Washington Post,* February 29, 1988.

100. The group of visitors, which included me, was led by Paul Weyrich.

101. *Department of State Bulletin,* June 1988, pp. 56–57.

102. See texts of agreements on Afghanistan, *Department of State Bulletin,* June 1988, p. 55. This U.S. statement is to be found *only* in the U.S. publication; it is *not* included in the texts of accords published by the United Nations and the USSR.

103. Selig S. Harrison, "Inside the Afghan Talks," *Foreign Policy,* no. 72 (Fall 1988), p. 58.

104. Ibid., p. 55.

105. Rosanne Klass, "Afghanistan: The Accords," *Foreign Affairs,* Summer 1988, p. 940, citing the testimony of Robert A. Peck before the House Subcommittee on Asian and Pacific Affairs, February 25, 1988.

106. Constantine C. Menges, "The Afghan Trap," *National Review,* April 1, 1988; Klass, "Afghanistan: The Accords"; Alan Keyes and Constantine C. Menges, "The Afghan Agreements: Victory or Blunder?" *Human Events,* July 16, 1988.

107. Quoted in Weymouth, "Does Moscow Really Plan on Leaving Afghanistan?"

108. U.S. Department of State, *Afghanistan: Soviet Occupation and Withdrawal,* p. 8.

109. A. M. Rosenthal, "The Story Goes On," *New York Times,* November 1, 1988.

110. State Department, *Afghanistan: Soviet Occupation and Withdrawal,* p. 10.

111. *Washington Post,* May 7, 1988.

112. Ibid., February 22, 1988.

113. Ibid.

114. Ibid., May 29, 1988.

115. Ibid., June 8, 1988.

116. Harrison, "Inside the Afghan Talks."

117. *Washington Times,* June 15, 1988.

118. Foreign Broadcast Information Service—*Report on the Soviet Union* (FBIS-SOV), June 28, 1988, pp. 32–34.

119. Ibid., July 1, 1988, p. 16.

120. Ibid., July 6, 1988, p. 34.

121. Ibid., July 20, 1988.

122. *New York Times,* August 16, 1988.

123. *Washington Post,* September 11, 1988.

124. See, for example, "No Sabotage Seen in Zia Crash," *New York Times*, September 11, 1988; "Malfunction Seen as Cause of Zia Crash," *New York Times*, October 14, 1988. But for the evidence of a Soviet-Kabul assassination, see John Barron, "Was President Zia Murdered?" *Reader's Digest*, August 1989, pp. 59–63; and Yossef Bodansky, "Who Killed President Zia—and How?" *Freedom at Issue* (March–April 1989), pp. 23–27.

125. Barron, "Was President Zia Murdered?"

126. Rowland Evans and Robert Novak, "State Dept. Sat on Evidence of Kremlin Role in Death of Pakistan Chief," *New York Post*, February 1, 1989.

127. Lally Weymouth, "If the Soviets Killed Zia, the State Dept. May Not Want to Know about It," *New York Post*, September 2, 1988.

128. *Washington Times*, June 14, 1989.

129. Quoted in the *New York Times*, June 25, 1989.

130. *Washington Post*, *New York Times*, November 5, 1988.

131. Representative Bill McCollum, "A Hollow Accord in Afghanistan," *Washington Times*, May 9, 1989.

132. Ibid.

133. See her comments in Menges, ed., "Afghanistan and the 1988 Agreement." During a February 1988 symposium at AEI, I had said: "In my judgment, accepting the Soviet proposal of February 8 would result in a false or defective settlement which [will see] the continuation of a Communist Afghanistan without the apparent presence of Soviet troops." Ibid., p. 35.

134. State Department, *Soviet Occupation and Withdrawal*, p. 7.

135. General Rabim Wardak, personal communication, July 27, 1989.

136. Resistance commander Abdul Haq, speaking at the Heritage Foundation, Washington, D.C., February 1989.

137. *New York Times*, February 9, 1989.

138. Ibid.

139. "Fractious Afghan Rebels Prepare for Council," *Washington Post*, February 8, 1989.

140. *New York Times*, February 9, 1989.

141. David Ottaway, "Kabul Forces Gaining Combat Edge," *Washington Post*, June 27, 1989.

142. *Washington Times*, June 8, 1988.

143. See, for example, "Food Shortages Reported in Kabul," *New York Times*, February 8, 1988, in which the chief UN relief official said that UN food supplies had to be moved to Kabul urgently, "because it was unclear whether aid could continue after all Soviet forces leave Afghanistan."

144. *New York Times*, February 8, 1989.

145. Harrison, "Inside the Afghan Talks," p. 58.

146. *Washington Times*, February 2, 1989.

147. Herbert Meyer, "Sleeping through a Quake," *Washington Times*, July 5, 1989.

148. *Washington Post*, June 27, 1989.

149. Address of Prime Minister Benazir Bhutto to a Joint Session of the Congress of the United States of America, Wednesday, June 7, 1989, text in my possession, pp. 7–10.

150. *New York Times*, June 8, 1989.
151. Ibid.
152. *Washington Times*, July 11, 1989.

CHAPTER 4: ANGOLA

1. Useful sources for the history of Portugal and its relations with Angola include James Duffy, *Portugal in Africa* (Cambridge, Mass.: Harvard University Press, 1962); David Abshire and Michael Samuels, eds., *Portuguese Africa—A Handbook* (New York: Praeger, 1970); Neil Bruce, *Portugal: The Last Empire* (North Pomfret, Vt.: David & Charles, Inc., 1975); and Arthur J. Klinghoffer, *The Angolan War: A Study in Soviet Policy in the Third World* (Boulder, Colo.: Westview Press, 1980).

2. Franz Borkenau, *The Communist International* (London: Faber & Faber, 1938), American edition entitled *World Communism*.

3. Alexander R. Alexiev and Nanette C. Brown, "UNITA of Angola: Profile of an Anti-Marxist Resistance Movement," Rand Working Draft 2745-USDP, October 1985, pp. 2, 3. See also Alexander R. Alexiev, "The Soviet Stake in Angola: Origins, Evolution, Prospects," in Dennis Bark, ed., *The Red Orchestra: The Case of Africa* (Stanford, Calif.: Hoover Institution Press, 1988), pp. 141–57. For an overview of the pre-MPLA history of Angola and the first stage of the war for Angola, see Lawrence W. Henderson, *Angola: Five Centuries of Conflict* (Ithaca, N.Y.: Cornell University Press, 1979); Gerald L. Bender, *Angola under the Portuguese: The Myth and the Reality* (Berkeley: University of California Press, 1978); and John Marcum, *The Angolan Revolution* (Cambridge: MIT Press, vol. 1, 1969, vol. 2, 1978).

4. Ibid., p. 3.

5. Writings about Savimbi include Fred Bridgland, *Jonas Savimbi: A Key to Africa* (Edinburgh: Mainstream, 1986); Williamson M. Evers, "Will the Real Jonas Savimbi Please Stand Up?" *Wall Street Journal*, February 11, 1986; and John Felton, "Savimbi: Selling Washington on Angola's War," *Congressional Quarterly Weekly Report*, vol. 44 (February 8, 1986), pp. 264–65.

6. Alexiev and Brown, "UNITA of Angola," p. 5.

7. Ibid., p. 5.

8. Speech of November 28, 1968, cited in *Angola: A Chronology of Major Political Developments, February 1961–January 1988* (Washington, D.C.: Angola Peace Fund, 1988), p. 10.

9. Bruce, *Portugal*, pp. 63–65.

10. Alexiev and Brown, "UNITA of Angola," p. 5.

11. Bruce, *Portugal*, p. 106.

12. *Chronology*, p. 12.

13. Ibid.

14. Congressional hearings on Angola cited in Alexiev and Brown, "UNITA of Angola," p. 8, n.15.

15. Alvor agreement, article 40, in *Alvor and Beyond: Political Trends and Legal Issues in Angola* (Angola Peace Fund, n.d.). See also Morgan Norval, *Red*

Star over Southern Africa (Washington, D.C.: Selous Foundation Press, 1988), pp. 204–11.

16. *Chronology*, p. 15.

17. Jiri Valenta, "The Soviet-Cuban Intervention in Angola, 1975," *Studies in Comparative Communism, An International Interdisciplinary Journal*, vol. 11, nos. 1 and 2 (Spring–Summer 1978), p. 1011.

18. *New York Times*, September 25, 1975.

19. Alexiev and Brown, "UNITA of Angola," p. 8.

20. *London Observer*, January 30, 1975.

21. Statement in a 1987 Canadian television documentary, "New Liberation Wars: Angola," cited in *Alvor and Beyond*, p. 14.

22. Quoted in Georgie Anne Geyer, *Washington Times*, July 15, 1988.

23. U.S. Department of Defense, *Prospects for Containment of Nicaragua's Communist Government*, May 1986, pp. 2–3. To provide perspective for negotiations in Central America, this report analyzes the facts of Communist performance in four war-termination agreements: Korea (1953), Indochina (1954), Laos (1962), and Vietnam (1973).

24. Congressional testimony of Secretary of State Henry Kissinger, January 29, 1976, in *Department of State Bulletin*, February 16, 1976.

25. *Chronology*, p. 16.

26. Alexiev and Brown, "UNITA of Angola," p. 9; *Alvor and Beyond*, pp. 15–16. See also Klinghoffer, *The Angolan War*.

27. Alexiev and Brown, "UNITA of Angola," p. 9. See also F. Stephen Larrabee, "Moscow and Angola," Radio Liberty Special Report RL 490/75, November 26, 1975.

28. Richard F. Staar, ed., *Yearbook on International Communist Affairs, 1976* (Stanford, Calif.: Hoover Institution Press, 1976), pp. 203, 208.

29. For further discussion of Soviet actions at this time see Chester A. Crocker, *Report on Angola* (Washington: Center for Strategic and International Studies, 1976); David Rees, "Soviet Strategic Penetration of Africa," *Conflict Studies*, no. 77 (London: Institute for the Study of Conflict, 1976); Walter Hahn and Alvin Cottrell, *Soviet Shadow over Africa*, Monograph on International Affairs, Center for Advanced International Studies, University of Miami, 1976; Christopher Stevens, *The Soviet Union and Black Africa* (New York: Holmes & Meier, 1976).

30. Statement to Commonwealth Club and World Affairs Council of Northern California, February 3, 1976, in *Department of State Bulletin*, February 23, 1976.

31. Ian Butterfield, "U.S. Policy toward Angola: Past Failures and Present Opportunities," Heritage Foundation Backgrounder no. 149, August 25, 1981, p. 15; U.S. Department of State, *Country Reports on Human Rights Practices for 1987*, Washington, D.C., 1988; Amnesty International, "Political Imprisonment in the People's Republic of Angola," Washington, D.C., March 1984.

32. State Department, *Country Reports on Human Rights Practices*.

33. Alexiev and Brown, "UNITA of Angola," p. 15.

34. Ibid., pp. 15, 16.

35. See U.S. Department of Defense, *Terrorist Group Profiles*, 1988, p. 129, stating that Angola and Zambia have given bases to the African National Congress. See also Juan Benemelis, "Castro, Subversion, and Terrorism in Africa" (Paper presented at the Institute for Soviet and East European Studies, Fourth International Conference, "Gorbachev's New Thinking and Soviet/Cuban Strategies in Angola and Namibia," Graduate School of International Studies, University of Miami, December 1988); and Rene Lemarchand, *American Policy in Southern Africa: The Stakes and the Stance* (Washington, D.C.: University Press of America, 1978).

36. Cited in Peter Vanneman, "The USSR and the Angolan Conflict" (Paper presented at the Institute for Soviet and East European Studies, Fourth International Conference, December 1988), p. 2.

37. Cited in David Shipler, "Soviet Denounces U.S. on Angola," *New York Times*, December 2, 1975.

38. *Angola: The Long Road to Freedom* (Washington, D.C.: Free Angola Information Society, 1988), p. 4.

39. Alexander R. Alexiev, "The Soviet Stake in Angola: Origins, Evolution, Prospects," in Bark, ed., *The Red Orchestra*, p. 151.

40. Jack Wheeler, "Fighting the Soviet Imperialists: UNITA in Angola," *Reason*, vol. 15 (April 1984), pp. 22–30.

41. Alexiev and Brown, "UNITA of Angola," p. 40.

42. Daniel W. Fisk, "Missing Opportunities in Angola & Mozambique: The Failure of Constructive Engagement," U.S. House of Representatives, Republican Study Committee, October 18, 1985, p. 3.

43. See Alexander Alexiev, *U.S. Policy in Angola: A Case of Nonconstructive Engagement*, Rand paper no. 7183 (Santa Monica, Calif.: Rand Corporation, 1986).

44. Vanneman, "The USSR and the Angolan Conflict," pp. 5–8.

45. Ibid., p. 8.

46. Jack Kemp, "The Reagan Doctrine in Angola: Advocating American Support for UNITA," *Africa Report*, vol. 31 (January–February 1986), pp. 12–14.

47. *Chronology*, p. 22.

48. Vanneman, "The USSR and the Angolan Conflict," pp. 9, 10.

49. Ibid., p. 11, and *Washington Post*, November 2, 1987.

50. Vanneman, "The USSR and the Angolan Conflict," p. 13. See also *Washington Post*, July 14, 1989.

51. Vanneman, "The USSR and the Angolan Conflict," p. 14.

52. William Pascoe, "In Southern Africa, the State Department Bets against the Reagan Doctrine," Heritage Foundation Backgrounder no. 633, February 12, 1988, p. 3.

53. Maldon Institute, "Strategic Implications of Angola's Military Buildup," *International Freedom Review*, vol. 2, no. 1 (Fall 1988), p. 27.

54. Ibid., p. 31.

55. Quoted in Vanneman, "The USSR and the Angolan Conflict," p. 16.

56. Ibid.

57. Maldon Institute, "Strategic Implications of Angola's Military Buildup," p. 34.

58. Vanneman, "The USSR and the Angolan Conflict," p. 19.

59. Michael Clough, ed., *Changing Realities in Southern Africa: Implications for American Policy* (Berkeley: Institute of International Studies, University of California, 1982), p. 220.

60. The largest tribe in Namibia is the Ovambo, with nearly 600,000 members; second is the Kavango, with 110,000. *The Europa Yearbook*, 1988, p. 1906.

61. Robert I. Rotberg, *Suffer the Future: Policy Choices in Southern Africa* (Cambridge, Mass.: Harvard University Press, 1980), p. 208.

62. Richard H. Shultz, Jr., "Conflict in Southern Africa: SWAPO and the USSR," in *The Soviet Union and Revolutionary Warfare* (Stanford, Calif.: Hoover Institution Press, 1988).

63. Vanneman, "The USSR and the Angolan Conflict," p. 14. See also Rotberg, *Suffer the Future*, p. 208, and Shultz, *The Soviet Union and Revolutionary Warfare*, chap. 5.

64. Henry W. Degenhardt, *Political Dissent* (Detroit: Gale Research Co., 1983), p. 294.

65. Reginald Green et al., eds., *Namibia: The Last Colony* (Harlow, Essex, England: Longman, 1981), pp. 185, 191.

66. Degenhardt, *Political Dissent*, p. 294.

67. Quoted in Clough, *Changing Realities in Southern Africa*, p. 220.

68. Quoted in *Red Locusts: Soviet Support for Terrorism in Southern Africa* (Alexandria, Va.: Western Goals, 1981), p. 37.

69. Quoted in Vanneman, "The USSR and the Angolan Conflict," pp. 14–15.

70. *Washington Times*, April 4, 1986.

71. Ibid., June 5, 1987.

72. *Amnesty International Annual Report 1987* (London: Amnesty International Publications, 1987), p. 83.

73. International Society for Human Rights, *Human Rights Violations in SWAPO Camps in Angola and Zambia* (London, 1988), p. 6.

74. "Namibia Prisoners Report Brutality," *New York Times*, July 5, 1989.

75. International Society for Human Rights, *Human Rights Violations*, pp. 26, 27.

76. Shultz, *The Soviet Union and Revolutionary Warfare*, chap. 5.

77. Alexiev and Brown, "UNITA of Angola," p. 45.

78. Quotations from ibid., pp. 46–47.

79. Ibid.

80. Edward P. Cain, "The Agony of Angola," in Charles Moser, ed., *Combat on Communist Territory* (Washington, D.C.: Free Congress Research and Education Foundation, 1985), p. 87.

81. Chester Crocker and William Lewis, "Missing Opportunities in Africa," *Foreign Policy*, no. 34 (Spring 1979).

82. Alexiev and Brown, "UNITA of Angola," and U.S. Congress, Sub-

committee on Africa, *United States Policy toward Southern Africa: Focus on Namibia, Angola and South Africa,* September 16, 1981.

83. Alexiev and Brown, "UNITA of Angola," pp. 51, 53.

84. Secretary of State George Shultz, "Southern Africa: Toward an American Consensus," April 16, 1985, Current Policy no. 685, U.S. Department of State, Bureau of Public Affairs.

85. President Reagan's State of the Union Address, February 6, 1985, *Department of State Bulletin,* April 1985, p. 9.

86. See Alexiev and Brown, "UNITA of Angola," p. 54.

87. Quoted in Constantine C. Menges, *Inside the National Security Council: The True Story of the Making and Unmaking of Reagan's Foreign Policy* (New York: Simon & Schuster, 1988), p. 241.

88. Ibid., pp. 241, 242, 249.

89. Keith Campbell, *The ANC: A Soviet Task Force?* (London: Institute for the Study of Terrorism, 1986), provides extensive documentation of the decades-long alliance between the South African Communist party and the ANC, pp. 54-57; see also Herbert Romerstein, *Soviet Support for International Terrorism* (Washington, D.C.: Foundation for Democratic Elections, 1981).

90. Constantine Menges, "Sanctions 1986," *National Interest,* Summer 1988.

91. Shultz, "Southern Africa: Toward an American Consensus," pp. 2-3.

92. Senator Dennis DeConcini, press release and letter, May 12, 1988.

93. "A Mission of Peace," Savimbi speech before the Angolan Task Force of the U.S. Congress, Monday, June 27, 1988.

94. On June 28, 1988, Dr. Savimbi spoke at the American Enterprise Institute in Washington, D.C. Before his speech, when he met privately with Representative Dan Burton (Republican, Indiana), Jeane Kirkpatrick, Alan Keyes, and me, these suggestions were made.

95. *Washington Post,* May 20, 1988, and *New York Times,* June 6, 1988.

96. *Reluctant Allies: A Case for Disengagement in Southern Africa* (Washington, D.C.: Angola Peace Fund, 1988), p. 30.

97. Letter from the "Stanton Group" to President Reagan, August 10, 1988; copy in my possession.

98. Letter from President Reagan to members of the Stanton Group, September 7, 1988; text in my possession.

99. Letter to President Ronald Reagan from Dr. Jonas Savimbi, September 1988; copy in my possession.

100. Quoted in Foreign Broadcast Information Service, Africa (FBIS-AFR), September 6, 1988, pp. 8-20.

101. *New York Times,* September 9, 1988.

102. *Washington Post,* September 30, 1988.

103. Transcript in my possession.

104. Ibid., p. 12.

105. Ibid., p. 16.

106. Quoted in Vanneman, "The USSR and the Angolan Conflict," p. 23.

107. *New York Times,* November 30, 1988. He also said this in a personal meeting with me on the same date.

108. *New York Times,* January 7, 1989.

109. Statement, December 13, 1988, *Department of State Bulletin,* February 1989, p. 10; *Washington Post* and *New York Times,* December 14, 1988.

110. Gerald J. Bender, "Namibia: Peace after Failure," *New York Times,* December 15, 1988.

111. Vernon V. Aspeturian, "Gorbachev's New Political Thinking and the Angolan Conflict" (Paper presented at the Institute for Soviet and East European Studies, Fourth International Conference, University of Miami, December 1988), p. 13.

112. Statement, December 22, 1988, *Department of State Bulletin,* February 1989, p. 11.

113. "Havana Uncertain of Pretoria's Willingness to Surrender Control," *Washington Times,* December 15, 1988; and FBIS-AFR, December 15, 1988, p. 37, and December 20, 1988, p. 13.

114. FBIS-AFR, December 27, 1988, p. 5.

115. *Wall Street Journal,* January 9, 1989.

116. *Washington Times,* January 6, 1989.

117. *New York Times,* October 5, 1988.

118. *New York Times,* May 26, 1988.

119. FBIS-AFR, September 26, 1988, p. 1.

120. *Windhoek Advertiser* (Namibia), March 14, 1989.

121. Letter from Secretary of State James A. Baker III to Senator Ernest F. Hollings, received June 12, 1989; and "It Will Only Heat Up the War," *New York Times,* June 10, 1989. An accompanying article, Constantine C. Menges, "The Only Brake on Communism," proposed more aid and warned of a 1989 MPLA offensive against UNITA, which began in December 1989.

122. Letter to me from Jardo Muekalia, UNITA chief representative in the United States, June 21, 1989; *New York Times,* June 23, 1989.

123. *Washington Times,* June 29, 1989; and *Washington Post,* July 10, 1989.

124. *New York Times,* June 30, 1989.

125. *Washington Post,* July 1, 1989.

126. *Washington Times,* June 30, 1989.

127. *Angola News Briefs,* vol. 2, no. 1, June 15–30, 1989.

128. *Washington Times,* February 2, 1989.

129. FBIS-AFR, December 23, 1988, pp. 1–4; Secretary of State Shultz replied that those remarks were inappropriate.

130. U.S. Congress, Senate Select Committee on Intelligence, "Soviet Presence in the U.N. Secretariat," 1985. See also Charles M. Lichenstein, "Soviet Espionage: Using the UN against the U.S.," Heritage Foundation, September 9, 1985, which documents the problem of Soviet manipulation of UN institutions.

CHAPTER 5: MOZAMBIQUE

1. For a general overview, see Thomas H. Henriksen, *Mozambique: A Short History* (London: Rex Collings, 1978); and Harold D. Nelson, ed., *Mozambique:*

A Country Study (Washington, D.C.: American University Foreign Area Studies, 1985).

2. Thomas H. Henriksen, "The People's Republic of Mozambique," in Dennis L. Bark, ed., *The Red Orchestra: The Case of Africa* (Stanford, Calif.: Hoover Institution Press, 1988), p. 164.

3. Henriksen, "The People's Republic of Mozambique," p. 162. See also David Ottaway and Marina Ottaway, *Afrocommunism* (Holmes & Meier, 1981), and Eduardo Mondlane, *The Struggle for Mozambique* (Penguin, 1969).

4. Edward P. Cain, "Mozambique's Hidden War," in Charles Moser, ed., *Combat on Communist Territory* (Washington, D.C.: Free Congress Research and Education Foundation, 1985), p. 38.

5. Henriksen, "The People's Republic of Mozambique," p. 162. See also Barry Munslow, *Mozambique: The Revolution and Its Origins* (London and New York: Longman, 1983).

6. Henriksen, "The People's Republic of Mozambique," p. 162.

7. Ibid., p. 165. See also Clifford A. Kiracofe, "The Communist Takeover of Mozambique: An Overview," *Journal of Social, Political, and Economic Studies*, vol. 7 (Spring–Summer 1982), pp. 115–28.

8. Henriksen, "The People's Republic of Mozambique," p. 164.

9. Ibid., p. 165.

10. *New York Times*, April 27, 1974.

11. U.S. Department of State, *Department of State Bulletin*, July 21, 1975.

12. State Department, *Department of State Bulletin*, October 6 and October 13, 1975. For examples of the conventional celebratory view of Frelimo's victory, see "Mozambique: Free at Last," *Africa Today*, July-September 1975, and Julian Burgess, "New Mozambique: The Era of Construction Begins," *African Development*, vol. 9 (June 1975), pp. 17–18.

13. U.S. Department of State, *Country Reports on Human Rights Practices for 1986*, 1987, p. 211 (citing Amnesty International).

14. Machel said in 1986 that he would incarcerate another 200,000 persons. Foreign Broadcast Information Service—Africa (FBIS-AFR), May 5, 1986.

15. Undated Renamo communiqué in my possession.

16. This includes 1.3 million in South Africa (South African Ministry of Transportion estimate) and 300,000 along the Malawi border (Frelimo estimate reported by the *Washington Post*, May 12, 1986). This does not include the 230,000 Portuguese who fled.

17. U.S. Department of State, *Country Reports on Human Rights Practices for 1987*, 1988, p. 202; Frelimo estimate is 1 million, as reported in the *Washington Times*.

18. Congressional Research Service, *The Soviet Union in the Third World*, Washington, D.C., 1985, p. 241. The *Frontline Fellowship Prayer and Praise Newsletter* of January-February 1986 puts the estimate at 200,000 for 1983–1986.

19. From Gillian Gunn, "Mozambique After Machel," in Helen Kitchen, ed., *Angola, Mozambique, and the West* (Washington, D.C.: Center for Strategic and International Studies, 1987), pp. 117–96.

20. See, for example, Kenneth Adelman, "Afrocommunism: Angola, Mozambique," *Freedom At Issue*, March-April 1978, pp. 12–16.

21. Henriksen, "The People's Republic of Mozambique," p. 168. See also Roger Mann, "Mozambique's Stalled Revolution: From Colony to Police State," *New Leader*, vol. 59 (August 16, 1976), pp. 5–6.

22. Cain, "Mozambique's Hidden War," p. 43.

23. Quoted by Luis Serapiao, *African Concord*, January 16, 1986.

24. "Report on the Use of Torture in the People's Republic of Mozambique," Amnesty International, April 1985; Renamo communiqué, April 1986. See also the annual human rights reports of the U.S. Department of State and of Amnesty International.

25. Cain, "Mozambique's Hidden War," p. 42. See also Barbara Barnes, "Education for Socialism in Mozambique," *Comparative Education Review*, vol. 26 (October 1982), pp. 406–19.

26. Quoted in Cain, "Mozambique's Hidden War," p. 40.

27. Henriksen, "The People's Republic of Mozambique," p. 167.

28. Ibid.

29. Cain, "Mozambique's Hidden War," p. 43.

30. Michael Cecil, unpublished manuscript, July 1988, pp. 12–13.

31. Cain, "Mozambique's Hidden War," p. 41.

32. U.S. Arms Control and Disarmament Agency, *World Military Expenditures and Arms Transfers, 1987,* (Washington, D.C., 1988), pp. 112, 127.

33. Cain, "Mozambique's Hidden War," p. 40.

34. Keith Campbell, *The ANC: A Soviet Task Force?* (London: Institute for the Study of Terrorism, 1986).

35. Henriksen, "The People's Republic of Mozambique," p. 173.

36. Assistant Secretary of State Chester Crocker, "U.S. Policy toward Mozambique," in U.S. Department of State, *Department of State Bulletin*, September 1987, p. 21.

37. Cain, "Mozambique's Hidden War," p. 46.

38. Ibid., p. 47.

39. Ibid., p. 47; Henriksen, "The People's Republic of Mozambique," p. 173.

40. Cain, "Mozambique's Hidden War," pp. 62–63 for 1980–1984; 1986 estimate from the *Washington Times*, December 15, 1986.

41. "Mozambique National Resistance Program," c. 1987, manuscript in my possession.

42. *Washington Times*, December 15, 1987. See also Jack Wheeler, "From Rovuma to Maputo: Mozambique's Guerrilla War," *Reason*, vol. 17 (December 1985), pp. 31–38.

43. *Washington Times*, December 15, 1987.

44. Cecil, unpublished manuscript, p. 4.

45. Ibid., p. 5.

46. Ibid.

47. Ibid., p. 6.

48. *New York Times*, July 31, 1988.

49. Quoted in the *Washington Post*, August 1, 1988.

50. William Pascoe, "The Controversial State Department Report on Mozambique," Heritage Foundation Backgrounder Update no. 75, May 4, 1988, p. 2.

51. Providing an example of this practice by another pro-Soviet regime, defectors from the Sandinista secret police testified that the Nicaraguan Communist government had set up units to impersonate anti-Communist guerrillas. See U.S. Department of State, *Inside the Sandinista Regime: A Special Investigator's Perspective*, Department of State Publication no. 9466, February 1986.

52. Western observers began noting Frelimo pragmatism in economic matters in 1976. See Tony Hodges, "Mozambique: Machel Wants Production, Not Ideology," *African Development* (London), vol. 10 (December 1976), pp. 1236–37. See also Robin Knight, "Mozambique's Marxism—With a Grain of Salt," *U.S. News & World Report*, July 14, 1980, pp. 39–40.

53. Henriksen, "The People's Republic of Mozambique," p. 169.

54. Gunn, "Mozambique After Machel," p. 126.

55. Cain, "Mozambique's Hidden War," p. 51.

56. Gillian Gunn, "Cuba and Mozambique," Center for Strategic and International Studies, Africa Notes no. 80, December 28, 1987, p. 5.

57. Crocker, "U.S. Policy toward Mozambique."

58. Gunn, "Mozambique After Machel," p. 131.

59. *New York Times*, July 31, 1988.

60. Secretary of State George Shultz, "Southern Africa: Toward an American Consensus," U.S. Department of State, Current Policy no. 685, April 16, 1985.

61. See Crocker, "U.S. Policy toward Mozambique."

62. Ibid.

63. Henriksen, "The People's Republic of Mozambique," pp. 175–76.

64. Ibid.

65. See Crocker, "U.S. Policy toward Mozambique."

66. Quoted in Gunn, "Mozambique After Machel," p. 121.

67. Ibid., p. 122.

68. Henriksen, "The People's Republic of Mozambique," p. 171. See also Michael Radu, "Mozambique: Non-Alignment or a New Dependence?" *Current History*, vol. 83 (March 1984), pp. 101–4.

69. See Crocker, "U.S. Policy toward Mozambique."

70. See ibid.

71. Quoted in Gunn, "Mozambique after Machel," p. 122.

72. Crocker, "U.S. Policy toward Mozambique."

CHAPTER 6: CAMBODIA

1. U.S. Department of State, *Background Notes, Cambodia*, April 1987. For an overview of contemporary Cambodia, see David P. Chandler, *A History of Cambodia* (Boulder, Colo.: Westview Press, 1982), and Ben Kiernan and Chanthou Boua, eds., *Peasants and Politics in Kampuchea, 1942–1981* (London: Zed Press, 1982).

2. See Robert F. Turner, *Vietnamese Communism: Its Origins and Development* (Stanford, Calif.: Hoover Institution Press, 1975), chap. 2, pp. 15–28; see also "Kampuchea: Torture and Political Imprisonment in the People's

Republic of Kampuchea (Cambodia)," Amnesty International, London, June 1987, p. 14.

3. See Turner, *Vietnamese Communism*, pp. 42, 43.

4. Quoted in ibid., p. 80.

5. "Kampuchea: Torture and Political Imprisonment," p. 15.

6. Joseph Zasloff and MacAlister Brown, *Communism in Indochina* (Lexington, Mass.: Heath, 1975).

7. Turner, *Vietnamese Communism*, p. 44.

8. Quoted in ibid.

9. Quoted in ibid., pp. 141–42.

10. U.S. Department of Defense, *Prospects for Containment of Nicaragua's Communist Government*, May 1986. This report includes an analysis of Communist violations of four previous war termination agreements, including those in Laos and Vietnam.

11. Within months of the Communist takeover of South Vietnam in 1975, there were 350,000 South Vietnamese in concentration camps. Warren H. Carroll, *70 Years of the Communist Revolution* (Manassas, Va.: Trinity Communications, 1989), p. 474. Partly as a result of repression, partly because of economic deprivation due to the failure of collectivization and other Communist policies in South Vietnam, nearly 500,000 South Vietnamese fled from South Vietnam in 1977, 1978, and 1979. Nguyen Van Cahn, *Vietnam under Communism: 1975–82* (Stanford, Calif.: Hoover Institution Press,1983), p. 136.

12. Kenneth J. Conboy, "What Hanoi Must Do to Merit U.S. Help," Heritage Foundation Executive Memorandum no. 206, June 22, 1988.

13. See *Wall Street Journal*, July 22, 1988.

14. See U.S. Department of State, *Chemical Warfare in Southeast Asia and Afghanistan*, Special Report no. 98, March 22, 1982, and *Chemical Warfare in Southeast Asia and Afghanistan: An Update*, Special Report no. 104, November 1982.

15. Al Santoli, "How the Soviets Use Chemical Warfare," *Parade Magazine*, June 26, 1983, p. 6, and personal communication, August 18, 1989.

16. Lawyers' Committee for Human Rights, *Refuge Denied* (New York: LCHR, 1988), p. 3. See also Al Santoli, "Little Girl in the Yellow Rain," *Reader's Digest*, April 1984, p. 77.

17. U.S. Department of State, *Country Reports on Human Rights Practices for 1979*, p. 483.

18. Among the descriptions of the Khmer Rouge regime are John Barron, *Murder of a Gentle Land: The Untold Story of Communist Genocide in Cambodia* (New York: Reader's Digest Press, 1977); David P. Chandler and Ben Kiernan, *Revolution and Its Aftermath in Kampuchea: Eight Essays* (New Haven, Conn.: Yale University Press, 1983); Francois Ponchaud, *Cambodia: Year Zero* (New York: Holt, Rinehart, 1978); Elizabeth Becker, *When the War Is Over: The Voices of Cambodia's Revolution and Its People* (New York: Simon & Schuster, 1986).

19. "Kampuchea: Torture and Political Imprisonment," p. 15.

20. R. J. Rummel, "As Though a Nuclear War—The Death Toll of Absolutism," *International Journal on World Peace*, vol. 5 (July–September 1988), pp. 33–35. Rummel estimates that the Hitler regime killed 17 million, the

Soviet regime from 1918 to 1953, 39 million; the Communist regime of Mao, 45 million; and the Khmer Rouge, 2 million. Per ten thousand inhabitants this tragic toll becomes USSR, 2,323 per 10,000; China, 672; Khmer Rouge, 2,667.

21. Arnold R. Isaacs, *Without Honor: Defeat in Vietnam and Cambodia* (Baltimore: Johns Hopkins University Press, 1983), p. 25, cited in Carroll, *70 Years*, p. 468.

22. Carroll, *70 Years*, pp. 465–66.

23. Haing Ngor, *A Cambodian Odyssey* (New York: Macmillan, 1987), pp. 82–85.

24. Carroll, *70 Years*, p. 467.

25. Ngor, *A Cambodian Odyssey*, p. 71.

26. Ibid., p. 259.

27. State Department, *Background Notes: Cambodia*, 1987, p. 7.

28. Ngor, *A Cambodian Odyssey*, pp. 406–7.

29. Ibid., p. 403.

30. See Ben Kiernan, *How Pol Pot Came to Power: A History of Communism in Kampuchea, 1930–1975* (London: Verso, 1985).

31. Ngor, *A Cambodian Odyssey*, p. 403.

32. Ibid., p. 406.

33. Al Santoli, "Cambodia: Freedom's Frontline in Southeast Asia," in Charles Moser, ed., *Combat on Communist Territory* (Washington, D.C.: Free Congress Research and Educational Foundation, 1985), p. 131.

34. For estimated Soviet aid from 1978 to 1986, see U.S. Department of Defense, *Soviet Military Power*, 1987, p. 137. See also "Blocking Soviet Gains in Asia," Heritage Foundation Backgrounder, Washington, D.C., March 29, 1988.

35. Santoli, "Freedom's Frontline," p. 130.

36. Quoted in ibid., p. 130.

37. Ngor, *A Cambodian Odyssey*, p. 405.

38. U.S. Department of State, *Country Reports on Human Rights Practices for 1983*, p. 798.

39. "Kampuchea: Torture and Political Imprisonment," p. 5. In a report of March 19, 1989, Amnesty International said "thousands of political prisoners" have been held by the PRK regime. The report listed some two hundred names but claimed many more people have been imprisoned whose names are unknown. Torture and executions were cited as "widespread." Cited by Santoli, personal communication, August 18, 1989.

40. Quoted in Santoli, "Freedom's Frontline," p. 137.

41. *The Europa Year Book, 1988* (London: Europa Publications, 1988), p. 1583.

42. U.S. Arms Control and Disarmament Agency, *World Military Expenditures and Arms Transfers, 1987*, pp. 52, 94, 128.

43. Ngor, *A Cambodian Odyssey*, pp. 290–91.

44. Ibid., p. 343.

45. State Department, *Background Notes: Cambodia*, 1987, p. 8.

46. See Santoli, "Freedom's Frontline," p. 131.

47. Ibid., pp. 137–40. See also Joo-Jock Lim, ed., *Armed Communist Movements in Southeast Asia* (New York: St. Martin's Press, 1984).

48. Esmeralda Luciolli, *Le mur de bambou* (Paris, 1987).

49. Santoli, personal communication, August 18, 1989.

50. Santoli, "Freedom's Frontline," p. 132.

51. State Department, *Background Notes: Cambodia*, 1984.

52. Ibid., p. 147.

53. Santoli, personal communication, August 18, 1989.

54. For an overview of the anti-Communist resistance, see also Jack Wheeler, "Fighting the Soviet Imperialists: The Khmer in Cambodia," *Reason*, February 1985, pp. 24–33.

55. In "Cambodians Test Hanoi for Signs of Withdrawal," *New York Times*, May 22, 1988, Barbara Crossette describes the KPNLF as having only "a few thousand . . . because of the attacks and rifts in the organization."

56. *Washington Post*, March 16, 1989.

57. Santoli, "Freedom's Frontline," p. 132. See also Norodom Sihanouk Varman, *War and Hope: The Case for Cambodia* (New York: Pantheon, 1980).

58. Santoli, "Freedom's Frontline," p. 132.

59. Ibid., p. 133.

60. Ibid., p. 145.

61. Ibid., p. 134.

62. Ibid., p. 133.

63. Ibid., p. 134.

64. Ibid., p. 136.

65. *Washington Post*, July 26, 1989.

66. Don Oberdorfer, "Sihanouk's Cambodian Forces Asking U.S. for Arms Aid," *Washington Post*, March 16, 1989.

67. Steven Erlanger, "The Return of the Khmer Rouge," *New York Times Magazine*, March 5, 1989, p. 27; governance described by State Department, *Background Notes: Cambodia*, 1987, p. 9.

68. Erlanger, "The Return of the Khmer Rouge," p. 27.

69. Santoli, "Freedom's Frontline," p. 133.

70. State Department, *Background Notes: Cambodia*, 1987, p. 9.

71. Santoli, "Freedom's Frontline," p. 145.

72. Erlanger, "The Return of Khmer Rouge," p. 51.

73. Ibid., p. 27.

74. Ibid., p. 51.

75. Ngor, *A Cambodian Odyssey*, p. 230.

76. See Erlanger, "The Return of the Khmer Rouge," p. 51.

77. *Washington Post*, November 29, 1988.

78. This is the consensus Western view; in April 1989 one report quoted the foreign minister of Vietnam, Nguyen Co Thach, as saying: "Inside Cambodia, the Khmer Rouge don't control a single village." *New York Times*, April 11, 1989.

79. Santoli, personal communication, August 18, 1989.

80. *New Republic*, April 3, 1989.

81. Kenneth J. Conboy, "Cracks Appear in the US-Thai Relationship,"

Heritage Foundation Backgrounder no. 75, March 8, 1988, p. 3. For analysis of Chinese and Vietnamese foreign policy on Cambodia, see Kent Bolton, "Sino-Khmer Relations: An Appraisal of China's Foreign Policy Imperatives," *Journal of International and Area Studies*, Fall 1986, pp. 65–89; and Pao-Min Chang, "Kampuchea in Chinese and Vietnamese Policies: The Root of the Conflict," *Studies in Comparative Communism*, Autumn 1983, pp. 203–21.

82. Santoli, "Freedom's Frontline," p. 149.

83. For the Thai perspective, see Sukhumbhand Paribatra, "Strategic Implications of the Indochina Conflict: Thai Perspectives," *Asian Affairs*, Fall 1984, pp. 28–46.

84. For the perspective from Southeast Asia, see Kishore Mahbubani, "The Kampuchean Problem: A Southeast Asian Perception," *Foreign Affairs* (Winter 1983–1984), pp. 407–25.

85. State Department, *Background Notes: Cambodia*, 1987, p. 11. In what follows, see also pp. 8 and 11.

86. This figure is extrapolated from the 1985 total relief budget of $35 million, of which the United States contributed $12 million.

87. Two analyses that provide views of U.S. policy since 1979 are Justus M. van der Kroef, "The United States and Cambodia: The Limits of Compromise and Intervention," *Contemporary Southeast Asia*, vol. 7 (March 1986), pp. 251–67; and Bernard K. Gordon, "The Third Indo-China Conflict," *Foreign Affairs*, vol. 65 (Fall 1986), pp. 66–85.

88. Statement at Geneva Conference on Kampuchea Relief, May 26, 1980, in *Department of State Bulletin*, July 1980, p. 23.

89. Testimony before the House Subcommittee on Asian and Pacific Affairs, July 15, 1981, in *Department of State Bulletin*, October 1981, pp. 35–37.

90. Statement of Assistant Secretary for East Asian and Pacific Affairs John Holdridge before the House Subcommittee on Asian and Pacific Affairs, September 15, 1982, in *Department of State Bulletin*, November 1983, pp. 31–34, 35.

91. Statement of September 11, 1984, in *Department of State Bulletin*, November 1984, p. 53. Wolfowitz subsequently served as U.S. ambassador to Indonesia and in 1989 was appointed under secretary of defense for policy by President Bush. The under secretary of defense for policy plays a significant role in shaping U.S. policy toward Cambodia.

92. Address to Far East–America Council/Asia Society, New York City, January 29, 1985, in *Department of State Bulletin*, April 1985, p. 34.

93. Remarks to a news conference in Kuala Lumpur, Malaysia, July 10, 1985, in *Department of State Bulletin*, September 1985, p. 23.

94. MacAlister Brown, "The U.S. Congress Speaks on Kampuchea," *Asian Affairs*, vol. 13 (Summer 1986), pp. 1–9.

95. *Department of State Bulletin*, July 1986, p. 59.

96. Data for FY 1985–1987 are from State Department, *Background Notes, Cambodia*, 1987, p. 11; for FYs 1989 and 1990, from the testimony of David F. Lambertson, deputy assistant secretary for East Asian and Pacific Affairs, before the House Subcommittee on Asian and Pacific Affairs, March 1, 1989, pp. 6–7.

97. Lambertson testimony, pp. 2–11.

98. See *Los Angeles Times*, June 21, 1989.

99. "Baker Determined to Arm Cambodia Groups," *Washington Times*, July 10, 1989.

100. *New York Times*, July 22, 1989.

101. See, for example, Joseph Douglas, *Why the Soviet Union Violates Arms Control Agreements* (Elmsford, N.Y.: Pergamon-Brassey's, 1988).

102. *New York Times*, December 3 and December 4, 1987.

103. Address by Charles H. Twining, director of the Office of Vietnam, Laos, and Cambodia Affairs, U.S. Department of State, September 29, 1988, in *Department of State Bulletin*, December 1988, pp. 31–33.

104. *Washington Post*, July 1, 1988.

105. Lambertson testimony, p. 12.

106. Twining address, in *Department of State Bulletin*; Lambertson testimony.

107. Lambertson testimony.

108. Foreign Broadcast Information Service, *East Asia Survey* (FBIS-EAS), January 23, 1989, p. 45.

109. Another example was the report that "Khmer Rouge guerrillas have moved several thousand Cambodian refugees from a UN-supported camp in Thailand across the border into Cambodia where they will face food shortages, poor medical care, and possible military attacks . . . because [the guerrillas] feared losing control over a population base." *Washington Post*, January 26, 1990.

110. *Washington Post*, February 10, 1989.

111. FBIS-EAS, December 30, 1988, p. 42; January 9, 1989, pp. 38, 76; January 12, 1989.

112. FBIS-EAS, January 12, 1989.

113. Ibid., January 9, 1989; Statement by PRK foreign minister (later prime minister) Hun Sen, FBIS-EAS, January 6, 1989, p. 47.

114. Quoted in Lally Weymouth, "Cambodia's Hun Sen Is No Savior," *Washington Post*, April 16, 1989.

115. *New York Times*, July 23, 1989; Santoli, personal communication, August 18, 1989.

116. *New Republic*, April 3, 1989, p. 8.

117. Al Santoli, "Designing a U.S. Policy toward Cambodia," Center for Security Policy, Washington, D.C., May 12, 1989.

118. Lambertson testimony, p. 2.

119. Santoli, "Designing a U.S. Policy."

120. Lambertson testimony, pp. 2, 4.

121. *Washington Post*, April 23, 1989.

122. Ibid., April 26, 1989.

123. Ibid., February 20, 1989.

124. "U.S. Warned on Aid to Sihanouk Force," *New York Times*, April 28, 1989.

125. FBIS-EAS, January 9, 1989.

126. "A New U.S. Policy toward Cambodia: A Commitment to a Demo-

cratic Process," Center for Security Policy, Washington, D.C., June 12, 1989, p. 2.

127. See text at note 142 below.

128. Cord Meyer, "Challenges and Opportunities," *Washington Times*, January 20, 1989.

129. Richard D. Fisher, Jr., "Blocking Soviet Gains in Asia with a Reinvigorated Reagan Doctrine," Heritage Foundation, Asian Studies Center Backgrounder no. 76, March 25, 1988, p. 9.

130. Al Santoli, "US–Vietnam Diplomacy: Cambodia Betrayed," *Freedom Fighter*, vol. 4, no. 8 (February 1989), p. 5. In what follows, see ibid.

131. *Washington Times*, May 11, 1989.

132. Santoli, "Designing a U.S. Policy," p. 3.

133. Ambassador Sisowath Sirirath, "Cambodia: Arm Sihanouk," *Washington Post*, May 14, 1989.

134. Ambassadors Mohd Suni bin Haji Idris of Brunei, Abdul Rachman Ramly of Indonesia, Albert S. Talalla of Malaysia, Emmanuel Pelaez of the Philippines, Tommy T.B. Koh of Singapore, and Vitthya Vejjajva of Thailand, "To Help Him Negotiate," *Washington Post*, May 14, 1989.

135. *Los Angeles Times*, June 21, 1989, p. 12.

136. See Lally Weymouth, "What Gorbachev Will Tell Deng," *Washington Post*, May 14, 1989.

137. Richard Fisher, "Crafting a U.S. Response to Gorbachev's 'Peace' Initiatives in Asia," Heritage Foundation, Washington, D.C., July 24, 1989, p. 7.

138. Lally Weymouth, "Cambodia's Hun Sen Is No Savior."

139. *Washington Times*, July 25, 1989.

140. *Washington Post*, July 25, 1989.

141. Ibid.

142. Ibid.

143. Aspen Institute, *Recommendations for the New Administration on United States Policy toward Indochina* (Washington, D.C.: AI, 1988), p. v.

144. Chang Song, "The Facts of Life," manuscript dated May 12, 1989, pp. 1–2.

145. "A New U.S. Policy toward Cambodia," p. 6. These excellent recommendations were written by Al Santoli.

CHAPTER 7: NICARAGUA

1. Quoted in J. Lloyd Mecham, *A Survey of United States–Latin American Relations* (Boston: Houghton Mifflin, 1965), p. 67.

2. Ibid., p. 335. See also Bernard Diederich, *Somoza and the Legacy of U.S. Involvement in Central America* (New York: Dutton, 1981).

3. Mecham, *United States–Latin American Relations*, pp. 114–25.

4. Timothy Ashby, *The Bear in the Back Yard: Moscow's Caribbean Strategy* (Lexington, Mass.: Lexington Books, 1987), p. 3. In what follows, see also ibid., pp. 6–8.

5. See Mecham, *United States–Latin American Relations*, pp. 157–77. In what follows, see ibid., pp. 166, 175, and 182.

6. Ibid., p. 173. In what follows, see ibid., pp. 176 and 311.

7. Ibid., pp. 214–15. See also Ronald M. Schneider, *Communism in Guatemala, 1944–1954* (New York: Praeger, 1959); J. D. Martz, *Communist Infiltration in Guatemala* (New York: Vintage Press, 1956). There is a literature disputing these and other accounts of Communist infiltration of the Arbenz government, including Stephen Schlesinger and Stephen Kinzer, *Bitter Fruit* (New York: Anchor Books, 1983), and Richard H. Immerman, *The CIA in Guatemala: The Foreign Policy of Intervention* (Austin: University of Texas Press, 1982). My reading of the evidence leads me to accept the analysis of Mecham, Schneider, and Martz as essentially correct. In what follows, see Mecham, pp. 215–17.

8. Mecham, *United States–Latin American Relations*, p. 218.

9. Ibid.

10. Hugh Thomas, *Cuba: The Pursuit of Freedom* (New York: Harper & Row, 1971).

11. Ashby, *Bear in the Back Yard*, p. 22.

12. Nearly two years before Castro took power in Cuba, Alice Leone Moats ("The Strange Past of Fidel Castro," *National Review*, August 24, 1957) had warned that even if the guerrilla chief was not a Communist, he was "playing the Communist game."

13. Armando Valladares, *Against All Hope* (New York: Knopf, 1986), p. 5.

14. Warren H. Carroll, *70 Years of the Communist Revolution* (Manassas, Va.: Trinity Communications, 1989), p. 371.

15. Ashby, *Bear in the Back Yard*, p. 26.

16. Ibid., p. 25.

17. Ibid., p. 27. See also Leon Goure, "Soviet-Cuban Military Relations," in Irving Louis Horowitz, ed., *Cuban Communism* (New Brunswick, Conn.: Transaction Books, 1987).

18. Ashby, *Bear in the Back Yard*, p. 31.

19. Goure, "Soviet–Cuban Military Relations," p. 624. See also Jaime Suchlicki, ed., *The Cuban Military under Castro* (Miami, Fla.: University of Miami Press, 1989).

20. Goure, "Soviet–Cuban Military Relations," p. 624.

21. Ashby, *Bear in the Back Yard*, pp. 50–51.

22. U.S. Department of Defense and U.S. Department of State, *The Challenge to Democracy in Latin America*, 1986, pp. 8–10.

23. Raymond Garthoff, *Reflections on the Cuban Missile Crisis*, 2d rev. ed. (Washington, D.C.: Brookings Institution, 1989), pp. 35–36.

24. Defense Department, State Department, *The Challenge to Democracy*, second printing, October 1986.

25. For an overview, see Mark Falcoff, "Cuba's Strategy in Exporting Revolution," in Howard Wiarda and Mark Falcoff, eds., *The Communist Challenge in the Caribbean and Central America* (Washington, D.C.: American Enterprise Institute, 1987), pp. 13–51.

26. Quoted in Ashby, *Bear in the Back Yard*, p. 28.

27. President Ronald Reagan, remarks at the Western Hemisphere Legislative Leaders Forum, January 24, 1985, *Public Papers of the Presidents—Ronald Reagan*, vol. 1 (Washington, D.C.: GPO, 1985), pp. 66–68. See also John Norton Moore, *The Secret War in Central America: Sandinista Assault on World Order* (Frederick, Md.: University Publications of America, 1987).

28. David J. Kopilow, *Castro, Israel, and the PLO* (Washington, D.C.: Cuban-American National Foundation, 1984); U.S. Department of State, *The Sandinistas and Middle Eastern Radicals*, August 1985; U.S. Department of State, *Libyan Activities in the Western Hemisphere*, August 1986.

29. Antonio J. Ybarra-Rojas, "The Cuban-Nicaraguan Connection," in Horowitz, ed., *Cuban Communism*, p. 62.

30. Kopilow, *Castro, Israel, and the PLO*, p. 32.

31. Carlos A. Montaner, *Secret Report on the Cuban Revolution* (New York: Transaction Books, 1981), pp. 29–34.

32. Falcoff, "Cuba's Strategy in Exporting Revolution," p. 144.

33. Robert A. Packenham, "Cuba and the USSR since 1959: What Kind of Dependency?" in Horowitz, ed., *Cuban Communism*, p. 116.

34. U.S. Department of State, *Cuba's Renewed Support for Violence in Latin America*, Special Report no. 90, December 14, 1981, p. 4.

35. Ibid.

36. Montaner, *Secret Report*, p. 33.

37. U.S. Department of State, *Nicaraguan Biographies: A Resource Book*, Special Report no. 174, January 1988, p. 4. See also Douglas W. Payne, *The Democratic Mask: The Consolidation of the Sandinista Revolution* (New York: Freedom House, 1985).

38. State Department, *Nicaraguan Biographies*, p. 4. See also Thomas W. Walker, *Nicaragua: The Land of Sandino*, 2d ed. (Boulder, Colo.: Westview Press, 1986), and David Nolan, *The Ideology of the Sandinistas and the Nicaraguan Revolution* (Coral Gables, Fla.: University of Miami Institute of Inter-American Studies, 1984).

39. State Department, *Cuba's Renewed Support for Violence*, p. 6.

40. State Department, *Nicaraguan Biographies*, p. 4.

41. See, for example, Shirley Christian, *Nicaragua: Revolution in the Family* (New York: Random House, 1985).

42. State Department, *Cuba's Renewed Support for Violence*, p. 6.

43. Ibid.

44. Ibid.

45. Christian, *Nicaragua: Revolution*, and Mark Klugmann, "Carter's Unfulfilled Deal," *Washington Times*, January 26, 1988.

46. Organization of American States, *Seventeenth Meeting of Consultation of Ministers of Foreign Affairs*, Resolution 2, Document 40/79, Washington, D.C., June 23, 1979.

47. See Paul Hollander, *Political Hospitality and Tourism: Cuba and Nicaragua* (Washington, D.C.: Cuban-American National Foundation, 1986).

48. Jiri Valenta and Virginia Valenta, "Soviet Strategy and Policies in the Caribbean Basin," in Howard J. Wiarda, ed., *Rift and Revolution: The Central American Imbroglio* (Washington, D.C.: American Enterprise Institute, 1984), p. 229.

49. U.S. Department of State, "Revolution beyond Our Borders": *Sandinista Intervention in Central America,* Special Report no. 132, September 1985, p. 37.

50. "The Seventy-two Hour Document," September 1979, in Robert S. Leiken and Barry Rubin, eds., *The Central America Crisis Reader* (New York: Summit Books, 1987).

51. Foreign Broadcast Information Service, *Report on Latin America* (FBIS-LAT), July 21, 1981.

52. U.S. government data. See also James R. Whelan and Patricia B. Bozell, *Catastrophe in the Caribbean* (Ottawa, Ill.: Jameson Books, 1984).

53. See Roy Prosterman and Mary Temple, "Land Reform in El Salvador," *Free Trade Union News,* AFL-CIO, June 1980.

54. U.S. Department of State and U.S. Department of Defense, *Background Paper: Central America,* May 27, 1983, p. 6.

55. State Department, Defense Department, *Background Paper,* May 1983.

56. "Nicaraguan Aggression against Costa Rica, Honduras, 1979 to Present," June 26, 1985, U.S. government unclassified chronology for public information, manuscript in my possession.

57. U.S. Department of State, *Communist Armed Interference in El Salvador,* February 14, 1981.

58. State Department, Defense Department, *Background Paper,* May 1983, p. 11.

59. Ibid., p. 13.

60. Secretary of State George Shultz, "Nicaragua: Will Democracy Prevail?" U.S. Department of State, Current Policy Bulletin no. 797, February 27, 1986.

61. State Department, *Nicaraguan Biographies,* p. 9.

62. Excerpts from the Sandinista plan of September 1979 which the United States designated "The Seventy-two Hour Document," in Leiken and Rubin, eds., *The Central American Crisis Reader,* pp. 218–26.

63. State Department, *Nicaraguan Biographies,* pp. 4, 17.

64. AFL-CIO, *Persecution of Nicaraguan Trade Unions;* U.S. Department of State, *Human Rights in Nicaragua under the Sandinistas: From Revolution to Repression,* Publication 9467, December 1986; "Nicaraguan Repression of Labor Unions," *White House Digest,* August 24, 1983.

65. "Persecution of the Jewish Community in Nicaragua," *White House Digest,* 1983.

66. Humberto Belli, *Breaking Faith: The Sandinista Revolution and Its Impact on Freedom and Christian Faith in Nicaragua* (Garden City, Mich.: Puebla Institute, 1985), pp. 6, 9.

67. Foreign Broadcast Information Service-Latin America, July 21, 1982, p. 13.

68. See the gripping account of the struggle against Sandinista censorship by the editor who waged it for many years, Jaime Chamorro Cardenal, *La Prensa: The Republic of Paper* (New York: Freedom House, 1988).

69. U.S. Department of State, *Nicaragua's Interior Ministry: Instrument of Political Consolidation,* August 1987, p. 5ff. By the end of 1979 the State

Department estimated that there had been 400 secret executions and that the Sandinistas already were holding about 7,000 prisoners (including some common criminals). The Department estimated that in 1980 there were more than 5,000 political prisoners. U.S. Department of State, *Country Reports on Human Rights Practices for 1980*, p. 489.

70. U.S. Department of State, *Country Reports on Human Rights Practices for 1987*, p. 553. Adolfo Calero, a political leader of the resistance, estimated 7,000 political prisoners in conversation with me, July 17, 1989.

71. Quoted in Defense Department and State Department, *The Challenge to Democracy*, p. 25.

72. State Department, *Nicaraguan Biographies*, p. 6.

73. Richard E. Burr, "Central America's Hidden Refugees," *American Spectator*, October 1987; Puebla Institute, *Fleeing Their Homeland*, Garden City, Mich., April 1987.

74. See Hollander, *Political Hospitality and Tourism*; Paul Hollander, "The Newest Political Pilgrims," *Commentary*, vol. 80, no. 2, (August 1985); Robert S. Leiken, "Nicaragua's Untold Stories," *New Republic*, October 8, 1984.

75. U.S. Department of State, *Comandante Bayardo Arce's Secret Speech before the Nicaraguan Socialist Party*, March 1985, p. 7.

76. The presidential candidate, Arturo J. Cruz, describes the election process in *Nicaragua's Continuing Struggle* (New York: Freedom House, 1988). Shirley Christian, in *Nicaragua: Revolution*, p. 299ff., provides further information on the means used to rig the outcome of the 1984 election.

77. A UN study "concluded the electoral rules put forward by Nicaragua are essentially democratic." *Washington Post*, July 22, 1989.

78. *Department of State Bulletin*, June 1989, pp. 1–3. In 1989 a private bipartisan commission chaired by Ambassador Curtin Winsor held hearings and published criteria for a fair and free election in Nicaragua. World Freedom Foundation, *The Bipartisan Commission on Free and Fair Elections in Nicaragua—A Blueprint*, Washington, D.C., 1989.

79. American Institute for Free Labor Development, *The Nicaraguan Elections, a Pre-election Perspective*, Washington, D.C., February 21, 1990, pp. 3–4. See also Center for Security Policy, *This Is No "Free and Fair Election" in Nicaragua*, Washington, D.C., February 20, 1990, pp. 1–5.

80. David W. Jones, "Chamorro Triumphs," *Washington Times*, February 27, 1990, p. 1.

81. William Branigan and Julia Preston, "President Indicates Sandinistas May Try to Keep Control of Army," *Washington Post*, February 28, 1990, p. 1.

82. Foreign Broadcast Information Service-Asia, June 12, 1980, p. D-17.

83. "Nicaragua and the World," *Christianity and Crisis*, May 12, 1980, p. 141.

84. Quoted in *Est et Ouest*, Paris, August 25, 1981.

85. Quoted in "Cuban, Nicaraguan, Soviet Bloc and Other International Support for the Extreme Leftists Forces in Central America—A Compendium of Evidence," February 9, 1983, p. 32. Manuscript in my possession.

86. Defense Department, State Department, *The Challenge to Democracy*, 1986, p. 20; 1989 estimates are from U.S. government sources.

87. On the basis of U.S. government data published by the *Washington Times* on May 17, 1989, Soviet-bloc military deliveries to Nicaragua totaled $330 million in 1985; $600 million in 1986; $540 million in 1987; $507 million in 1988; and $85 million in the first quarter of 1989.

88. See Jiri Valenta and Virginia Valenta, "Sandinistas in Power," *Problems of Communism*, vol. 34, September-October 1985, pp. 1–28; and Richard L. Millett, "Nicaragua's Frustrated Revolution," *Current History*, vol. 85 (January 1986), pp. 5–8.

89. State Department, *Nicaraguan Biographies*, p. 5.

90. See, for example, Bernard Nietschmann, "The Unreported War against the Sandinistas: 6,000 Indian Guerrillas Are Fighting for Their Land," *Policy Review*, Summer 1984, pp. 32–39.

91. State Department, *Nicaraguan Biographies*, p. 91.

92. Defense Department and State Department, *The Challenge to Democracy*, pp. 41, 42. See also U.S. Department of State, *Inside the Sandinista Regime: A Special Investigator's Perspective*, Publication 9466, February 1986. The author is Alvaro Baldizon, who left the Nicaraguan secret police and subsequently died under questionable circumstances in Los Angeles. Baldizon described the propaganda operations of the Sandinistas in a press conference at the Heritage Foundation, Washington, D.C., March 14, 1986. See also Curtin Winsor, Jr., *The Washington Battle for Central America: The Unmet Challenge of the "Red Chorus"* (Washington, D.C.: Washington Institute for Values in Public Policy, 1987).

93. See Moore, *The Secret War*, for the detailed legal reasoning.

94. See Max Singer, "Can the Contras Win?" *National Review*, February 13, 1987, pp. 30–34; and Constantine Menges, "Central America's Future: Communism or Democracy," *World Affairs* (Summer, 1988).

95. Aid from other countries was estimated at about $27 million in 1984–1985, according to U.S. Senate Select Committee on Secret Military Assistance to Iran and the Nicaraguan Opposition, U.S. House of Representatives Select Committee to Investigate Covert Arms Transactions with Iran, *Report of the Congressional Committees Investigating the Iran-Contra Affair*, Washington, D.C., November 1987. This included the estimated $3.8 million unauthorized diversion from the 1986 military sales to Iran, which triggered the Iran-contra investigations and prosecutions of 1986–1990.

96. For different perspectives on the resistance see Jack Wheeler, "Fighting the Soviet Imperialists: The Contras in Nicaragua; An Inside Look at Nicaragua's Anti-Marxist Rebels—Who They Are and Why They Are Fighting," *Reason*, vol. 16 (June-July 1984), pp. 28–36; Christopher Dickey, *With the Contras: A Reporter in the Wilds of Nicaragua* (New York: Simon & Schuster, 1985); Dieter Eich and Carlos Rincon, *The Contras: Interviews with Anti-Sandinistas* (San Francisco: Synthesis Publications, 1985); and Michael Radu, "The Origins and Evolution of the Nicaraguan Insurgencies, 1979–1985," *Orbis*, vol. 29, Winter 1986, pp. 821–40.

97. See the Tower Commission report. For my analysis of the Iran-contra issue, see my *Inside the National Security Council* (New York: Simon & Schuster, 1988).

98. *National Policy Watch*, vol. 4, no. 2 (March-April 1987).

99. *Diario Las Americas*, July 3 and July 21, 1987.

100. George Gedda, AP dispatch, June 15, 1987. See also William A. Depalo, Jr., "The Military Situation in Nicaragua," *Military Review*, vol. 66 (August 1986), pp. 28–41; and James P. Wootten, "Contra Prospects: The Military Situation in Nicaragua and Honduras," *Congressional Research Service Review*, vol. 8 (March 1987), pp. 10–12.

101. *Los Angeles Times*, July 8, 1987.

102. *Washington Times*, October 15, 1987.

103. *Diario Las Americas*, December 12, 1987.

104. Comments to me by two resistance leaders, spring 1988.

105. *Washington Times*, January 6, 1989.

106. President Reagan, "Central America: Defending Our Vital Interests," address before a joint session of Congress, April 27, 1983, State Department, Current Policy Bulletin no. 482.

107. *New York Times*, December 5, 1981.

108. The Declaration of San Jose is reproduced in Leiken and Rubin, *Central America Crisis Reader*, pp. 636–37.

109. 1978 U.S. economic aid: $10.7 million to Guatemala, $11.0 million to El Salvador, $14.0 million to Nicaragua, $17.1 million to Honduras, and $9.0 million to Costa Rica. "U.S. Overseas Loans and Grants, Vol. II—Latin America and the Caribbean," FY 1946–FY 1986, Agency for International Development, PPC/PB/RPA.

110. Quoted in Constantine C. Menges, "Mexico Hanging in the Balance," *Washington Times*, March 9, 1988.

111. *Report of the National Bipartisan Commission on Central America*, Washington, D.C., January 1984, p. 93.

112. U.S. Department of State, *Central America Democracy, Peace and Development Initiative*, March 1984.

113. President Reagan, "U.S. Interests in Central America," speech delivered to the nation, May 9, 1984, U.S. Department of State, Current Policy Bulletin no. 576.

114. Nina M. Serafino, "U.S. Assistance to Nicaraguan Guerrillas: Issues for the Congress," Congressional Research Service, no. IB84139, updated March 1, 1988, p. 11.

115. "Contra Aid Reportedly Hurt Anti-Drug Effort in Early 80s," *Washington Times*, April 14, 1989.

116. See, for example, Susan Kaufman Purcell, "Demystifying Contadora," in Mark Falcoff and Robert Royal, eds., *The Continuing Crisis* (Washington, D.C.: Ethics and Public Policy Center, 1987). For a chronological summary of the Contadora process through mid-1987 and the texts of important related documents, see U.S. Department of State, *Negotiations in Central America: A Chronology 1981–1987*, Publication 9551, May 1987.

117. See my *Inside the National Security Council*, chaps. 3–8.

118. As told to me by Rep. Jack Kemp. See Constantine C. Menges, "What Next on Arias?" *Washington Times*, November 9, 1987.

119. Enrique Bermudez, "The Contras' Valley Forge," *Policy Review*, Summer 1988, p. 62.

120. Quoted in Douglas W. Payne, "How the Sandinistas Turned the Tide: A Chronicle of the 'Peace Process,' " *Strategic Review*, Fall 1987, p. 11.
121. See ibid., p. 22.
122. *Miami Herald*, December 2, 1987; *Washington Post*, January 7, 1988.
123. *Washington Post*, January 17, 1989.
124. *New York Times*, May 25, 1988.
125. President Reagan, "Aid to the Nicaraguan Democratic Resistance," *Department of State Bulletin*, August 1988, p. 78.
126. *Washington Post*, August 4, 1989.
127. Bermudez, "The Contras' Valley Forge," p. 62.

CHAPTER 8: COMPARATIVE ANALYSIS AND ALTERNATIVE FUTURES

1. U.S. Department of Defense, *Soviet Military Power*, Washington, D.C., 1989, p. 2 of the preface by Secretary of Defense Richard Cheney; and his speech of October 16, 1989, *New York Times*, October 17, 1989.
2. Secretary of State James A. Baker III, "Points of Mutual Advantage: Perestroika and American Foreign Policy," speech of October 16, 1989, of Department of State text, p. 3.
3. President George Bush, speech to the nation, as quoted in the *New York Times*, November 23, 1989.
4. Baker, "Points of Mutual Advantage."
5. As stated, for example, by Paul Wolfowitz, Under Secretary of Defense, in a speech on regional conflicts, November 2, 1989, Department of Defense text, p. 8; and in his article, "Glasnost in Order on Regional Conflicts," *Wall Street Journal*, November 7, 1989.
6. Testimony of Robert A. Peck, Deputy Assistant Secretary of State, before the U.S. Senate Subcommittee on Asian and Pacific Affairs, May 18, 1988, p. 5.
7. *New York Times*, October 10, 1989.
8. *Washington Times*, August 8, 1989; Foreign Broadcast Information Service, *Near East Survey* (FBIS-NES), 89-15i, August 8, 1989, p. 46.
9. David Ottaway, "CIA Removes Afghan Rebel Aid Director," *Washington Post*, September 2, 1989.
10. "Stalemate in Afghanistan, Democracy in Pakistan," a report to the Senate Committee on Foreign Relations, by Senator Claiborne Pell, October 1, 1989.
11. Robert Pear, "US Says Soviet Troops Still in Afghanistan," *New York Times*, October 10, 1989.
12. Lally Weymouth, "Pakistan Imperiled Prime Minister," *Washington Post*, October 8, 1989.
13. Pear, "Still in Afghanistan."
14. Paul Lewis, "Soviets Said to Double Cambodia Aid," *New York Times*, October 6, 1989.
15. See the discussion and analysis in Center for Security Policy, *Giving Peace a Chance in Cambodia: A Primer for U.S. Policy*, Washington, D.C., February 27, 1990.

16. White House statement as quoted in the *New York Times*, October 6, 1989.

17. Ibid.

18. Statement by Jeremias Chitunda, vice-president of UNITA, at a meeting at the American Enterprise Institute, Washington, D.C., February 2, 1990, attended by me and Ambassador Jeane Kirkpatrick. See also James Morrison, "Senate Raps Moscow for Angolan Offensive," *Washington Times*, February 2, 1990, for bipartisan criticism by Senators Robert Dole (R-Kan.), Dennis DeConcini (D-Ariz.), and Steve Symms (R-Idaho) of the Soviet-aided MPLA military attack on UNITA since December 1989. No U.S. military supplies were delivered from February to November 1989.

19. Karl Maier, "War Ravaged Town Mirrors Mozambique's Problems," *Washington Post*, October 23, 1989.

20. Ibid.

21. See "Bush Wants Mozambique off Marxist List," *Washington Times*, October 23, 1989. Shortly thereafter, Mozambique was removed from the list of Marxist-Leninist countries.

22. Maier, "War Ravaged Town."

23. *New York Times*, August 8, 1989.

24. See my article, "Contras at the Point of No Return," *Washington Times*, July 28, 1989.

25. Jaime Daremblum, "Soviets Move In to Fill Policy Vacuum in Central America," *Wall Street Journal*, October 20, 1989.

26. Wolfowitz, "Glasnost in Order," and Lawrence Tracy, "Will Shipboard Summit Consider Garden Party's 'Unwanted Animals'?" *Officer*, December 1989, pp. 1–4.

27. "Shevardnadze Plan Would Trim US Role in Central America," *Washington Post*, October 6, 1989.

28. Ibid.

29. Daremblum, "Soviets Move In"; *Washington Post*, "Shevardnadze Plan."

30. See *Washington Post*, October 14, 1989; John Goshko, "UN Chief Repudiates Contra Remark," *Washington Post*, October 17, 1989.

31. See, for example, Wilson Ring, "Honduras Says It Seized Arms Bound for Salvadoran Rebels," *Washington Post*, October 20, 1989.

32. Secretary of State James Baker, speech to the OAS, November 13, 1989, Department of State Press Release no. 227, November 15, 1989.

33. Mark A. Uhlig, "Sandinistas Warn They Want Control of the Military," *New York Times*, March 6, 1990, p. A10.

34. Haing Ngor, *A Cambodian Odyssey* (New York: Macmillan, 1987), p. 404.

35. William J. Casey, *Scouting the Future: The Public Speeches of William J. Casey*, compiled by Herbert E. Meyer (Washington, D.C.: Regnery Gateway, 1989), p. 163.

36. U.S. Department of Defense, *The Containment of Communist Nicaragua*, Washington, D.C., May 1986, pp. 1–6.

37. Peter Vanneman, "The Soviet Union and Angola," in Owen Kahn, ed., *Disengagement from Southwest Africa* (New Brunswick, N.J.: Transaction Books, 1990), p. 21.

38. In 1985, CIA Director Casey publicly estimated Soviet expenditures in these countries at $8 billion annually (see Casey, *Scouting the Future*, p. 172); and in 1990 Secretary of State James Baker estimated $15 billion spent annually, including about $5 billion for Cuba (see Thomas Friedman, "Baker Braves the Gauntlet in the Moscow Parliament," *New York Times*, February 11, 1990, p. 20).

39. Andre Ryerson, "The Munich Men: How Chamberlain and Roosevelt Invited World War II," *Policy Review*, Summer 1988, p. 14.

40. For a more complete discussion of this internal conflict of the Reagan years, see my *Inside the National Security Council* (New York: Simon & Schuster, 1988), chaps. 3–5.

41. See ibid., chap. 9.

42. See ibid., pp. 243–46. See also my "The Diplomacy of Defeat," *Policy Review* (Summer 1988).

43. For an overview of congressional actions, see Maureen Taft-Morales and Mark P. Sullivan, *Congress and U.S. Policy toward Central America and Panama in 1988*, Congressional Research Service, Library of Congress, Washington, D.C., September 25, 1989.

44. Defense Department, *The Containment of Communist Nicaragua*, pp. 1–6.

45. Darenblum, "Soviets Move In."

46. Jeane Kirkpatrick, *Legitimacy and Force*, vol. 1 (New Brunswick, N.J.: Transaction Books, 1988), p. 438.

47. Robert Pear, "FBI Allowed to Investigate Crash That Killed Zia," *New York Times*, June 25, 1989; Rowland Evans and Robert Novak, "State Dept. Sat on Evidence of Kremlin Role in Death of Pakistan Chief," *New York Post*, February 1, 1989.

48. Robert Morris, *Our Globe under Siege* (Mantoloking, N.J.: J & W Enterprises, 1987), p. 33.

49. Joseph D. Douglass, *Why the Soviets Violate Arms Control Treaties* (Elmsford, N.Y.: Pergamon-Brassey's, 1988), cites the reports of defectors on this major strategic decision.

50. James Phillips, "Planning for a Post-Khomeni Iran," Heritage Foundation Backgrounder, December 27, 1987, p. 9.

51. Raymond Zontag and James Beddie, *Nazi-Soviet Relations, 1939–41: Documents from the Archives of the German Foreign Office*, U.S. Department of State, Washington, D.C., 1948, p. 259.

52. George Lenkowsky, *Soviet Gains in the Middle East* (Washington, D.C.: American Enterprise Institute, 1972), p. 44.

53. James Phillips, "Responding to the Soviet Challenge in the Persian Gulf," Heritage Foundation Backgrounder no. 731, October 20, 1989, pp. 7–8.

54. Constantine Menges, "The Turning Point," *New Republic*, December 15, 1979.

55. James Phillips, "Moscow Stalks the Persian Gulf," Heritage Foundation Backgrounder no. 333, February 27, 1984, p. 12. See also Robert Moss, "What Russia Wants," *New Republic*, January 19, 1980.

56. Phillips, "Moscow Stalks the Persian Gulf," p. 11, citing *Time*, October 25, 1982, p. 49.

57. Ibid., p. 11.

58. Ibid., citing Robert Moss, "Reaching for Oil: The Soviets' Bold Middle East Strategy," *Saturday Review*, April 12, 1980, p. 21.

59. Aryh Yodfat, "Moscow and the Persian Gulf States," *Soviet Analyst*, February 9, 1983, p. 4, as cited in Phillips, "Moscow Stalks the Persian Gulf," p. 13.

60. Morris, *Our Globe under Siege*, p. 76.

61. FBIS, *Daily Report, South Asia*, January 28, 1982, p. c–1.

62. Peter Younghusband, "Namibia's Five Days of Elections May Give SWAPO Ticket to Rule," *Washington Times*, November 6, 1989.

63. Quoted in "U.S. Criticizes Soviet Role in Battling Angolan Rebels," *Washington Times*, January 9, 1990.

64. Howard Phillips, transcript of his November 1989 conversation with Peter Hampton who was arrested by Frelimo and saw Soviet-made helicopters and bombers on Mozambique airfields.

65. See, for example, U.S. Department of State, *Communist Influence in South Africa*, report to Congress, Washington, D.C., 1987, which concludes: "The South African Communist Party . . . has exercised considerable influence through its alliance with the African National Congress" (p. 1). See also David Roberts, Jr., "The ANC in Its Own Words," *Commentary*, July 1988; and Michael Radur, "The African National Congress: Cadres and Credo," *Problems of Communism*, July–August 1987.

66. Vanneman, "The Soviet Union and Angola," p. 1.

67. Paul Johnson, "The Race for South Africa," *Commentary*, September 1985.

68. Morris, *Our Globe under Siege*, p. 13.

69. As cited in Richard Nixon, *The Real War* (New York: Warner Books, 1980), p. 23.

70. National Bipartisan Commission on Central America, *Report to the President*, January 1984, p. 93.

71. Personal communication, ambassador of El Salvador to the United States, December 7, 1989.

72. Strobe Talbott, *Time*, August 8, 1983, p. 79, as quoted in James R. Whelan and Patricia B. Bozell, *Catastrophe in the Caribbean* (Ottawa, Ill.: Jameson Books, 1984), p. 94. See also my article, "Mexico: The Iran Next Door?" *San Diego Union*, August 5, 1979, in which I analyzed the strengths and vulnerabilities of the Mexican political-economic system and suggested that if Communist regimes were in all of Central America, there would be a grave risk of a Communist takeover in Mexico.

73. Computed as follows: Announced costs for settling 100,000 Cuban refugees in 1980 were $500 million for six months, or roughly $1 billion per 100,000 refugees per year, which equals $10 billion per 1 million refugees for one year resettlement, assumed to be the amount of time needed for successful adaptation. For 10 million to 20 million refugees, the cost estimate would be $100 billion to $200 billion.

74. National Bipartisan Commission, *Report to the President*, p. 93.

75. Charles Waterman, "Resistance Movements in the Soviet Empire," in Henry S. Rowen and Charles Wolf, Jr., eds., *The Future of the Soviet Empire* (New York: St. Martin's Press, 1987), p. 180.

76. Richard Pipes, "The Russians Are Still Coming," *New York Times*, October 9, 1989, p. 22.

77. Vladimir Bukovsky, quoted in Charles Wolf, "The Costs and Benefits of the Soviet Empire," in Rowen and Wolf, eds., *The Future of the Soviet Empire*, p. 127.

78. Waterman, "Resistance Movements," p. 177.

79. Under Secretary of State Michael Armacost, "Regional Issues and U.S.-Soviet Relations," speech of June 22, 1988, published by the U.S. Department of State as Current Policy Bulletin no. 1089, Washington, D.C., June 1988, p. 2.

80. Alvin Bernstein, "Insurgents against Moscow," *Policy Review*, Summer 1987.

81. Allan Gerson and Jeane Kirkpatrick, "The Reagan Doctrine: Human Rights and International Law," in *Right v. Might, International Law and the Use of Force* (New York: Council on Foreign Relations, 1989), pp. 14, 17.

An Illustrative Bibliography

CHAPTER 1: INTRODUCTION

Books

Abshire, David M. *Preventing World War III.* New York: Harper & Row, 1988.
Casey, William J. *Scouting the Future: The Public Speeches of William J. Casey.* Compiled by Herbert E. Meyer. Washington, D.C.: Regnery Gateway, 1989.
Mager, N. H., and Jacques Katel. *Conquest without War.* New York: Simon & Schuster, 1961.
Moser, Charles, ed. *Combat on Communist Territory.* Washington, D.C.: Free Congress Research and Educational Foundation, 1985.
Nitze, Paul H. *From Hiroshima to Glasnost: At the Center of Decision—A Memoir.* New York: Grove Weidenfeld, 1989.
Nixon, Richard. *The Real War.* New York: Warner Books, 1980.
Wolf, Charles, Jr., and Katharine Watkins Webb. *Developing Cooperative Forces in the Third World.* Lexington, Mass.: Lexington Books, 1987.

Articles

Bernstein, Alvin. "Insurgents against Moscow." *Policy Review,* Summer 1987.
Bode, William R. "The Reagan Doctrine." *Strategic Review,* Winter 1986.
Krauthammer, Charles. "The Poverty of Realism." *New Republic,* February 17, 1986.
———. "The Reagan Doctrine." *Time,* April 1, 1985.
Ledeen, Michael. "Fighting Back." *Commentary,* August 1985.
Menges, Constantine. "Democratic Revolutionary Insurgence as an Alternative." Santa Monica, Calif.: Rand Corporation, 1968.
Rosenfeld, Stephen S. "The Guns of July." *Foreign Affairs,* Spring 1986.
Tucker, Robert W. "Intervention and the Reagan Doctrine." New York: Council on Religion and International Affairs, 1985.

CHAPTER 2: THE SOVIET STRATEGY OF INDIRECT AGGRESSION

Books

Barnett, Frank, Hugh Tovar, and Richard Shultz, eds. *Special Operations in U.S. Strategy.* Washington, D.C.: National Defense University Press, 1984.

Barron, John. *KGB Today*. New York: Reader's Digest Press, 1983.
Blechman, Barry, and Stephen Kaplan, eds. *Force without War*. Washington, D.C.: Brookings Institution, 1978.
Borkenau, Franz. *World Communism*. Ann Arbor: University of Michigan Press, 1962.
Carr, E. H. *The Twilight of Comintern, 1930–1935*. New York: Pantheon, 1983.
Cline, Ray, and Yonah Alexander. *Terrorism: The Soviet Connection*. New York: Crane Russak, 1984.
Fontaine, Roger W. *Terrorism: The Cuban Connection*. New York: Crane Russak, 1988.
Francis, Samuel T. *The Soviet Strategy of Terror*. Washington, D.C.: Heritage Foundation, 1985.
Godson, Roy. *Intelligence Requirements for the 1980s*. Lexington, Mass.: Heath, 1986.
———. *Labor in the Soviet Global Strategy*. New York: National Strategy Information Center, 1984.
Goren, Roberta. *The Soviet Union and Terrorism*. London: Allen & Unwin, 1984.
Hammond, Thomas, and Robert Farrell, eds. *The Anatomy of Communist Takeovers*. New Haven: Yale University Press, 1975.
Hazan, Baruch. *Soviet Impregnational Propaganda*. Ann Arbor, Mich.: Ardis, 1982.
Hosmer, Stephen, and George Tanham. *Countering Covert Aggression*. Santa Monica, Calif.: Rand Corporation, 1986.
Hosmer, Stephen, and Thomas Wolfe. *Soviet Policy and Practice toward Third World Conflicts*. Lexington, Mass.: Lexington Books, 1983.
Hough, Jerry. *The Struggle for the Third World*. Washington, D.C.: Brookings Institution, 1986.
Huyn, Hans Graf. *Die Doppelfalle—Das Risiko Gorbatschow*. Munich: Universitas-Verlag, 1989.
Johnson, Chalmers. *Revolutionary Change*. Boston: Little, Brown, 1966.
Kaplan, Stephen S., ed. *Diplomacy of Power: Soviet Armed Forces as a Political Instrument*. Washington, D.C.: Brookings Institution, 1981.
Kirkpatrick, Jeane J., ed. *The Strategy of Deception: A Study in World-Wide Communist Tactics*. New York: Farrar, Straus, 1963.
Laqueur, Walter, ed. *The Patterns of Soviet Conduct in the Third World*. New York: Praeger, 1983.
Livingstone, Neil, and Terrell Arnold, eds. *Fighting Back: Winning the War against Terrorism*. Lexington, Mass.: Lexington Books, 1985.
MacFarlane, S. Neil. *Superpower Rivalry and Third World Radicalism: The Idea of National Liberation*. Baltimore, Md.: Johns Hopkins University Press, 1985.
Nollau, Gunther. *International Communism and World Revolution, History and Methods*. London: Hollis & Carter, 1961.
Ponomarev, Boris. *Lenin and the World Revolutionary Process*. Moscow: Progress Publishers, 1980.
Porter, Bruce D. *The U.S.S.R. in Third World Conflicts: Soviet Arms and Diplomacy in Local Wars, 1945–1980*. Cambridge, Eng.: Cambridge University Press, 1984.

Ra'anan, Uri, Robert L. Pfaltzgraff, Jr., Richard Shultz, Igor Lukes, and Ernst Halperin, eds. *Hydra of Carnage: International Linkages of Terrorism. The Witnesses Speak.* Lexington, Mass.: Lexington Books, 1986.

Schultz, Richard, and Roy Godson. *Dezinformatsia: Active Measures in Soviet Strategy.* New York: Pergamon-Brassey, 1984.

Shultz, Richard H., Jr. *The Soviet Union and Revolutionary Warfare.* Stanford, Calif.: Hoover Institution Press, 1988.

Sterling, Claire. *The Terror Network.* New York: Holt, Rinehart & Winston, 1981.

Ulam, Adam. *Expansion and Coexistence: Soviet Foreign Policy 1917–1973.* New York: Praeger, 1974.

U.S. Congress. *The Soviet Union in the Third World, 1980–85: An Imperial Burden or Political Asset?* Committee on Foreign Affairs, U.S. House of Representatives. Washington, D.C.: Government Printing Office, 1985.

Articles

Becker, Abraham S. "The Soviet Union and the Third World: The Economic Dimension." *Soviet Economy,* July–September 1986.

Bukovsky, Vladimir. "The Political Condition of the Soviet Union." In Henry S. Rowen and Charles Wolf, Jr., eds., *The Future of the Soviet Empire.* New York: St. Martin's Press, 1987.

Gann, L. H. "The Soviet Union and Sub-Saharan Africa, 1917–1974." In Dennis L. Bark, ed., *The Red Orchestra: The Case of Africa.* Stanford, Calif.: Hoover Institution Press, 1988.

Hagerty, Randy, and Roger E. Kanet. "U.S. and Soviet Involvement in the Third World." *Harvard International Review,* January–February 1986.

Ledeen, Michael A. "Intelligence, Training, and Support Components." In Uri Ra'anan et al., *Hydra of Carnage.* Lexington, Mass.: Lexington Books, 1986.

Menges, Constantine. "Castro's Cuba: Thirty Years of Revolutionary Warfare." In Georges Fauriol, ed., *Cuba: The International Dimension.* New Brunswick, N.J.: Transaction Books, 1990.

Rummel, R. J. "As Though a Nuclear War—The Death Toll of Absolutism." *International Journal on World Peace,* July–September 1988.

Chapter 3: Afghanistan

Books

Bradsher, Henry. *Afghanistan and the Soviet Union.* Durham, N.C.: Duke University Press, 1985.

Girardet, Edward. *Afghanistan—The Soviet War.* New York: St. Martin's Press, 1985.

Klass, Rosanne, ed. *Afghanistan: The Great Game Revisited.* New York: Freedom House, 1988.

Articles

Barron, John. "From Russia with Hate." *Reader's Digest,* November 1985.

————. "Was President Zia Murdered?" *Reader's Digest,* August 1989.

Barry, Michael. "Afghanistan—Another Cambodia?" *Commentary*, August 1982.
Harrison, Selig S. "Inside the Afghan Talks." *Foreign Policy*, Fall 1988.
Keyes, Alan, and Constantine Menges. "The Afghan Agreements: Victory or Blunder." *Human Events*, July 16, 1988.
Klass, Rosanne. "Afghanistan: The Accords." *Foreign Affairs*, Summer 1988.
Krakowski, Eli. "Red Star over Afghanistan." *Global Affairs*, Spring 1990.
McCollum, Bill. "A Hollow Accord in Afghanistan." *Washington Times*, May 9, 1989.
Menges, Constantine C. "The Afghan Trap." *National Review*, April 1, 1988.
———, ed. *Afghanistan and the 1988 Agreements*. AEI Working Papers. Washington, D.C.: American Enterprise Institute, 1988.
Phillips, James A. "Updating U.S. Strategy for Helping Afghan Freedom Fighters." Heritage Foundation Backgrounder no. 552, December 22, 1986.
Rosenthal, A. M. "The Secret Treaty." *New York Times*, March 4, 1988.
U.S. Department of State. "Chemical Warfare in Southeast Asia and Afghanistan: Report to the Congress from Secretary of State Alexander M. Haig, Jr., March 22, 1982." Special Report no. 98.
Weymouth, Lally. "Moscow's 'Invisible War' of Terror inside Pakistan." *Washington Post*, March 13, 1988.

CHAPTER 4: ANGOLA

Books

Adelman, Kenneth. *African Realities*. New York: Crane Russak, 1980.
Bank, Dennis, ed. *The Red Orchestra—The Case of Africa*. Stanford, Calif.: Hoover Institution Press, 1988.
Bridgland, Fred. *Jonas Savimbi: A Key to Africa*. Edinburgh: Mainstream, 1986.
Hahn, Walter, and Alvin Cottrell. *Soviet Shadow over Africa*. Coral Gables, Fla.: University of Miami Advanced International Studies Institute, 1976.
Henderson, Lawrence W. *Angola: Five Centuries of Conflict*. Ithaca, N.Y.: Cornell University Press, 1979.
Klinghoffer, Arthur J. *The Angolan War: A Study in Soviet Policy in the Third World*. Boulder, Colo.: Westview Press, 1980.
LeoGrande, William, et al. *Cuba in Africa*. Pittsburgh, Pa.: University of Pittsburgh Press, 1980.

Articles

Alexiev, Alexander R. "The Soviet Stake in Angola: Origins, Evolution, Prospects." In Dennis L. Bark, ed. *The Red Orchestra: The Case of Africa*. Stanford, Calif.: Hoover Institution Press, 1988.
Crocker, Chester. "Southern Africa: Eight Years Later." *Foreign Affairs*, Fall 1989.

Crocker, Chester, and William Lewis. "Missing Opportunities in Africa." *Foreign Policy*, Spring 1979.

Valenta, Jiri. "The Soviet-Cuban Intervention in Angola, 1975." *Studies in Comparative Communism, An International Interdisciplinary Journal*, Spring–Summer 1978.

Wheeler, Jack. "Fighting the Soviet Imperialists: UNITA in Angola." *Reason*, April 1984.

CHAPTER 5: MOZAMBIQUE

Books

Abshire, David, and Michael Samuels, eds. *Portuguese Africa—A Handbook*. New York: Praeger, 1970.

Campbell, Keith. *The ANC: A Soviet Task Force?* London: Institute for the Study of Terrorism, 1986.

Duffy, James. *Portugal in Africa*. Cambridge, Mass.: Harvard University Press, 1962.

Henricksen, Thomas H. *Mozambique: A Short History*. London: Rex Collings, 1978.

———. *Revolution and Counter-Revolution: Mozambique's War of Independence, 1964–1974*. Westport, Conn.: Greenwood, 1983.

Kitchen, Helen, ed. *Angola, Mozambique, and the West*. Washington, D.C.: Center for Strategic and International Studies, 1987.

Munslow, Barry. *Mozambique: The Revolution and Its Origins*. London and New York: Longman, 1983.

Nelson, Harold D., ed. *Mozambique: A Country Study*. Washington, D.C.: American University Foreign Area Studies, 1985.

Saul, John, ed. *Mozambique: A Difficult Road to Socialism*. New York: Monthly Review Press, 1985.

Seiler, John, ed. *Southern Africa since the Portuguese Coup*. Boulder, Colo.: Westview Press, 1980.

Serapiao, Luis B. *Mozambique in the Twentieth Century: From Colonialism to Independence*. Washington, D.C.: University Press of America, 1979.

Zartman, William I. *Ripe for Revolutuion: Conflict and Intervention in Africa*. New York: Council on Foreign Relations, 1985.

Articles

Clough, Michael. "American Policy Options." *Africa Report*, November-December 1982.

Henriksen, Keith. "The People's Republic of Mozambique." In *The Red Orchestra—The Case of Africa*, ed. Dennis Bank. Stanford, Calif.: Hoover Institution Press, 1988.

"Marxists Dye the Red Flag Blue in Southern Africa." *Economist*, March 29, 1980.

Ottaway, Marina. "African Marxist Regimes and U.S. Policy: Ideology and Interest." *SAIS Review*, Summer–Fall, 1986.

Wright, Robin. "Mozambique Prepares for Independence." *New Leader*, June 23, 1975.

CHAPTER 6: CAMBODIA

Books

Barron, John. *Murder of a Gentle Land: The Untold Story of Communist Genocide in Cambodia.* New York: Reader's Digest Press, 1977.
Becker, Elizabeth. *When the War Is Over: The Voices of Cambodia's Revolution and Its People.* New York: Simon & Schuster, 1986.
Chandler, David P. *A History of Cambodia.* Boulder, Colo.: Westview Press, 1982.
Elliott, David W. P. *The Third Indochina Conflict.* Boulder, Colo.: Westview Press, 1981.
Fall, Bernard. *The Two Vietnams.* New York: Praeger, 1967.
Isaacs, Arnold R. *Without Honor: Defeat in Vietnam and Cambodia.* Baltimore, Md.: John Hopkins University Press, 1983.
Kiernan, Ben, and Chanthou Boua, eds. *Peasants and Politics in Kampuchea, 1942–1981.* London: Zed Press, 1982.
Ngor, Haing. *A Cambodian Odyssey.* New York: Macmillan, 1987.
Ponchaud, Francois. *Cambodia: Year Zero.* New York: Holt, Rinehart, 1978.
Schanberg, Sydney. *The Death and Life of Dith Pran.* New York: Penguin, 1985.
Shaplen, Robert. *Bitter Victory: A Veteran Correspondent's Dramatic Account of His Return to Vietnam and Cambodia Ten Years after the End of the War.* New York: Harper & Row, 1986.
Shawcross, William. *The Quality of Mercy: Cambodia, Holocaust, and Modern Conscience; With a Report from Ethiopia.* New York: Simon & Schuster, 1985.
Turner, Robert F. *Vietnamese Communism: Its Origins and Development.* Stanford, Calif.: Hoover Institution Press, 1975.
Zasloff, Joseph, and MacAlister Brown. *Communism in Indochina.* Lexington, Mass.: Heath, 1975.

Articles

Back, William. "A Chance in Cambodia." *Foreign Policy*, Spring 1986.
Becker, Elizabeth. "Stalemate in Cambodia." *Current History*, April 1987.
Santoli, Al. "Endless Insurgency: Cambodia." *Washington Quarterly*, Spring 1985.
Schiefer, H. B. "The Possible Use of Chemical Warfare Agents in Southeast Asia." *Conflict Quarterly*, Winter 1983.
U.S. Department of State. "Chemical Warfare in Southeast Asia and Afghanistan." Special Report no. 98, March 1982. Also, "Chemical Warfare in Southeast Asia and Afghanistan: An Update." Special Report no. 104, November 1982.
Van der Kroef, Justus M. "The Kampuchean Conflict: Edging toward Compromise?" *Asian Affairs*, Spring 1985.

CHAPTER 7: NICARAGUA

Books

Ashby, Timothy. *The Bear in the Back Yard: Moscow's Caribbean Strategy.* Lexington, Mass.: Lexington Books, 1987.

Belli, Humberto. *Breaking Faith: The Sandinista Revolution and Its Impact on Freedom and Christian Faith in Nicaragua*. Westchester, Ill.: Crossway, 1985.

Carroll, Warren H. *70 Years of the Communist Revolution*. Manassas, Va.: Trinity Communications, 1989.

Christian, Shirley. *Nicaragua: Revolution in the Family*. New York: Random House, 1985.

Diederich, Bernard. *Somoza and the Legacy of U.S. Involvement in Central America*. New York: Dutton, 1981.

Falcoff, Mark, and Robert Royal, eds. *The Continuing Crisis: U.S. Policy in Central America and the Caribbean*. Washington, D.C.: Ethics and Public Policy Center, 1987.

Falcoff, Mark, and Robert Royal, eds. *Crisis and Opportunity*. Washington, D.C.: Ethics and Public Policy Center, 1984.

Falk, Pamela. *Cuban Foreign Policy*. Lexington, Mass.: Lexington Books, 1985.

Goure, Leon, and Morris Rothenberg. *Soviet Penetration of Latin America*. Coral Gables, Fla.: University of Miami Press, 1975.

Hollander, Paul. *Political Hospitality and Tourism: Cuba and Nicaragua*. Washington, D.C.: Cuban-American National Foundation, 1986.

Horowitz, Irving Louis, ed. *Cuban Communism*. New Brunswick, N.J.: Transaction Books, 1987.

Kopilow, David J. *Castro, Israel, and the PLO*. Washington, D.C.: Cuban-American National Foundation, 1984.

Ledeen, Michael. *Central America: The Future of the Democratic Revolution*. Washington, D.C.: Gulf and Caribbean Foundation, 1984.

Leiken, Robert, and Barry Rubin. *The Central American Crisis Reader*. New York: Summit Books, 1987.

McMichael, R. Daniel, and John D. Paulus, eds. *Western Hemisphere Stability*. Pittsburgh, Pa.: World Affairs Council, 1984.

Mecham, J. Lloyd. *A Survey of United States–Latin American Relations*. Boston: Houghton Mifflin, 1965.

Muravchik, Joshua. *Nicaragua's Slow March to Communism*. Washington, D.C.: Cuban-American National Foundation, 1986.

Nolan, David. *FSLN*. Coral Gables, Fla.: University of Miami Institute of Inter-American Studies, 1984.

Suchlicki, Jaime. *Cuba—From Columbus to Castro*. Elmsford, N.Y.: Pergamon-Brassey, 1986.

Thomas, Hugh. *Cuba: The Pursuit of Freedom*. New York: Harper & Row, 1971.

Walker, Thomas W., ed. *Nicaragua: The First Five Years*. New York: Praeger, 1985.

Wesson, Robert. *Communism in Central America and the Caribbean*. Stanford, Calif.: Hoover Institution Press, 1982.

Whelan, James R., and Patricia B. Bozell. *Catastrophe in the Caribbean*. Ottawa, Ill.: Jameson Books, 1984.

Wiarda, Howard J., ed. *Rift and Revolution: The Central American Imbroglio*. Washington, D.C.: American Enterprise Institute, 1984.

Winsor, Curtin, Jr. *The Washington Battle for Central America: The Unmet*

Challenge of the "Red Chorus." Washington, D.C.: Washington Institute for Values in Public Policy, 1987.

Articles

Bermudez, Enrique. "The Contras' Valley Forge." *Policy Review*, Summer 1988.
Fauriol, Georges A. "Latin America." *Foreign Affairs: America and the World—1989/90*, 1990.
Fein, Bruce, and Albert Blaustein. "Nicaragua's Constitution: Echos of Mein Kampf." *Freedom at Issue*, March–April 1987.
Krauss, Clifford. "Revolution in Central America?" *Foreign Affairs*, Summer 1987.
Leiken, Robert S. "Fantasies and Fact: The Soviet Union and Nicaragua." *Current History*, October 1984.
Liska, George. "The Reagan Doctrine: Monroe and Dulles Reincarnate?" *SAIS Review*, Summer–Fall 1986.
McColm, R. Bruce. "Nicaragua: Facing the Issue." *Freedom at Issue*, November–December 1986.
Menges, Constantine C. "Central America and Its Enemies." *Commentary*, August 1981.
———. "Central America's Future—Communism or Democracy." *Global Affairs*, Summer, 1987.
Millett, Richard L. "Nicaragua's Frustrated Revolution." *Current History*, January 1986.
Moore, John Norton. "The Secret War in Central America and the Future of World Order." *American Journal of International Law*, January 1986.
Payne, Douglas W. "How the Sandinistas Turned the Tide: A Chronicle of the 'Peace Process.' " *Strategic Review*, Fall 1987.
———. "The 'Mantos' of Sandinista Deception." *Strategic Review*, Spring 1985.
———. "Sandinistas Bid 'Farewell to the West.' " *Freedom at Issue*, November–December 1985.
Prosterman, Roy, and Mary Temple. "Land Reform in El Salvador." *Free Trade Union News*, June 1980.
Ronfeldt, David F. "Rethinking the Monroe Doctrine." *Orbis*, Winter 1985.
Sanchez, Nestor D. "Revolutionary Change and the Nicaraguan People." *Strategic Review*, Summer 1984.
Singer, Max. "Can the Contras Win?" *National Review*, February 13, 1987.
Valenta, Jiri. "The USSR, Cuba, and the Crisis in Central America." *Orbis*, Fall 1981.
Valenta, Jiri, and Virginia Valenta. "Sandinistas in Power." *Problems of Communism*, September–October 1985.

CHAPTER 8: COMPARATIVE ANALYSIS AND ALTERNATIVE FUTURES

Books

Levine, Herbert. *World Politics Debated*. New York: McGraw-Hill, 1989.
Rowen, Henry S., and Charles Wolf, Jr. *The Future of the Soviet Empire*. New York: St. Martin's Press, 1987.

Staar, Richard F., ed. *Public Diplomacy: USA versus USSR*. Stanford, Calif.: Hoover Institution Press, 1986.

Wolf, Charles, K. C. Yeh, Edmund Brunner, Aaron Gurwitz, and Marilee Lawrence. *The Costs of the Soviet Empire*. Santa Monica, Calif.: Rand Corporation, 1983.

Articles

Barrows, Walter L. "Superpower Statecraft in the Third World." *Harvard International Review*, January–February 1986.

Fukuyama, Francis. "Gorbachev and the Third World." *Foreign Affairs*, Spring 1986.

Nacht, Michael. "Internal Change and Regime Stability." *Adelphia Papers*, no. 167, Summer 1981.

Simes, Dimitri. "Gorbachev: A New Foreign Policy." *Foreign Affairs*, Winter 1987.

Solarz, Stephen J. "When to Intervene." *Foreign Policy*, Summer 1986.

Winsor, Curtin. "From Reagan Doctrine to Detente: An American Tragedy." *Global Affairs*, Winter 1988.

Index

Khmer Rouge regime, 188–92
Khmer Rouge resistance group, 185,
 195, 196, 201–4, 315
meetings and negotiations, 210–16,
 364
payment for Soviet supplies, 328
PRK strategy and subversion, 30,
 313, 314, 317, 325
resistance movements and goals,
 194–202, 315
resistance problems, 317
resistance support, 316, 365
Soviet support, 181, 193, 205–6,
 210–13, 216, 217, 220, 303, 304
U.S. policy, 2, 200, 202, 206–10, 213,
 215, 216, 218–22, 240, 330, 332,
 334
Vietnam invasion of, 65, 181, 188,
 192–94
Canada, 220, 230
Carballo, Bismarck, 259
Caribbean Basin Initiative, 282
Carrión Cruz, Luis, 310
Carter, Jimmy, 262–63, 338
Carter administration, 33
 Afghanistan policy, 2, 45, 365
 Angola policy, 116, 123, 126–27
 Cambodia policy, 200
 Central America policy, 247
 Cuba relations, 29, 239
 Nicaragua policy, 242, 244–45, 255,
  264, 269, 287, 329–30, 357
 Soviet relations, 301
Carter Doctrine, 5
Carter Presidential Center, 262
Casey, William J., 3–4, 6–10, 29, 33, 129,
 320, 329–31, 363
Castro, Fidel, 120, 232. See also Cuba
Castro, Raul, 234, 351
Catholic church, 258–60, 270
Catholic Standard (Washington, D.C.), 259
Cecil, Michael, 160, 164–66
Center for Security Policy, 222
Central America
 political background, 227–33
 Soviet subversion, 230, 298–99
 See also specific countries
Central Asia, 1, 16
Central Intelligence Agency (CIA), 6, 39–
 40, 270, 275, 276, 334
Cerezo, Marcos Vinicio, 252, 285
Chamberlain, Neville, 329
Cham ethnic group, 181
Chamorro, Adolfo, 276
Chamorro, Diego, 228
Chamorro, Pedro Joaquin, 242, 260

Chamorro, Violeta Barrios de, 260, 263,
 300, 355
Chea Sim, 215
Chemical weapons use, 48, 188, 351
Chernenko, Konstantin, 33
Chhea Chut, 198
Child mortality rates, 113
Chile, 26, 239, 254, 335
China, People's Republic of
 Afghanistan position, 63, 65–66, 96
 Afghan resistance support, 62, 79,
  96, 217, 316
 Cambodia/Vietnam conflict, 181,
  192–93, 200–202, 211–13, 216, 217,
  220, 306
 Indian territory claimed by, 64
 internal policies, 185, 190, 205–6
 Mozambique assistance, 154
 Pakistan relations, 64
 political background, 16, 18, 22
 Soviet relations, 63–64, 96
Chissano, Joaquim, 157, 170–72, 175
Chitunda, Jeremias, 139, 306, 307
Christian Democratic party (El Salvador),
 248
Christian Democratic party (Nicaragua),
 258, 262
Christopher, Warren, 207
Cisneros, Henry, 283
Clark, Dick, 111, 126
Clark amendment, 111, 119, 126–29
Coalition Government of Democratic
 Kampuchea (CGDK), 201, 208, 213,
 220, 306
Cohen, Herman, 147
Collins, Peter, 275
Colombia, 232, 238, 254, 287
Combat on Communist Territory (Moser,
 ed.), 9
Combined Friends of the Islamic Revolu-
 tion, 58
Comintern (Communist International),
 14, 16–18, 21, 230
Committees for the Defense of the Revo-
 lution, 235, 257
Communist party of Afghanistan. See
 People's Democratic party of Afghani-
 stan
Communist party of Costa Rica, 254
Communist party of Cuba, 230. See also
 Cuba
Communist party of El Salvador, 230,
 248
Communist party of Guatemala, 230,
 232–33, 249, 252
Communist party of Honduras, 253

About the Author

CONSTANTINE C. MENGES, a resident scholar at the American Enterprise Institute from 1987 to 1990, was a special assistant to the president for national security affairs from 1983 to 1986. He has also been deputy assistant secretary of education, a national intelligence officer for Latin America at the CIA, a staff member of the Hudson Institute and the Rand Corporation, and a professor at the University of Wisconsin. His articles have appeared in *Commentary*, the *New Republic*, the *Wall Street Journal*, the *New York Times*, and elsewhere. His book about his experiences with the Reagan administration, *Inside the National Security Council*, was published in 1988. Mr. Menges received his undergraduate degree and a doctorate in political science from Columbia University.

A NOTE ON THE BOOK

*This book was edited by Andrea Posner, Dana Lane, and Ann Petty of
the publications staff of the American Enterprise Institute.
The index was prepared by Patricia Ruggiero, and the figures were drawn by
Hördur Karlsson.
The text was set in Palatino, a typeface designed by the twentieth-century
Swiss designer Hermann Zapf. Coghill Composition Company,
of Richmond, Virginia, set the type, and Edwards Brothers Incorporated,
of Ann Arbor, Michigan, printed and bound the book,
using permanent acid-free paper.*

The AEI PRESS is the publisher for the American Enterprise Institute for
Public Policy Research, 1150 17th Street, N.W., Washington, D.C. 20036:
Christopher C. DeMuth, publisher; Edward Styles, director; *Dana Lane*, editor;
Ann Petty, editor; *Cheryl Weissman*, editor; *Susan Moran*, editorial assistant
(rights and permissions). Books published by the AEI PRESS are distributed
by arrangement with the University Press of America, 4720 Boston Way,
Lanham, Md. 20706.